D1551791

Bury St. Edmunds
and the Urban Crisis:
1290-1539

Bury St. Edmunds
and the Urban Crisis:
1290-1539

———

ROBERT S. GOTTFRIED

PRINCETON UNIVERSITY PRESS
PRINCETON, NEW JERSEY

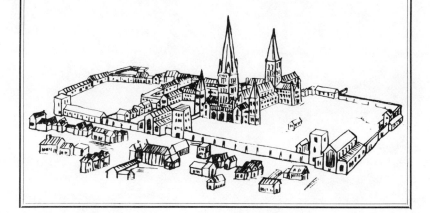

Library of Congress Cataloging in Publication Data will be
found on the last printed page of this book

Publication of this book has been aided by a grant from publications program
of the National Endowment for the Humanities

This book has been composed in Linotron Baskerville

Clothbound editions of Princeton University Press Books
are printed on acid-free paper, and binding materials are
chosen for strength and durability

Printed in the United States of America by Princeton
University Press, Princeton, New Jersey

For Esther L. and William A. Gottfried

Acknowledgments

I owe many debts. Librarians and archivists were, without exception, courteous and informative. I would like to thank those who helped me at: Rutgers University Libraries; the Graduate Library of the University of Michigan; the Regenstein Library of the University of Chicago; the British Library of the British Museum; the Wellcome Historical Medical Library; the Public Record Office, London; the Institute of Historical Research, London; the University Library, Cambridge University; and the county record offices in Norwich, Ipswich, and especially Bury St. Edmunds. Kenneth Hall and Margaret Statham of the Bury office deserve special mention.

I have received generous financial aid from the National Endowment for the Humanities and the Rutgers University Research Council. David Pramer and C. F. Main of the Rutgers Research Council were always very supportive and enthusiastic. Financial support allowed me to travel to archive offices and afforded the luxury of research assistants, computer keypunchers, and proofreaders. Among them were Claire Griffin, Sarah Hunt, Patricia Lanni, Monica Murphy, Pari Stave, Joann Verrier, and Michael Wilbur. John Beck and Jim Bernard drew my maps. Thanks are due also to the editors and staff of Princeton University Press. In particular, I would like to thank R. Miriam Brokaw, Joanna Hitchcock, and Ann Spahr.

Many scholars graciously read all or parts of this book in manuscript form. They include Rudolph Bell, the late E. M. Carus-Wilson, Paul Clemens, John Gillis, William Gottfried, Gerald Grob, David Herlihy, Richard Kaeuper, Richard Kohn, Maurice Lee, Jr., Elizabeth McLachlan, John Mundy, Richard Sayers, Roger Schofield, Daniel Scott Smith, Trian Stoianovich, Joseph Strayer, Sylvia Thrupp, and Donald Weinstein. I must single out two of these scholars. Richard Sayers, the distinguished economic historian, gave me a marvelous tour of Bury during the beautiful summer of 1976. He showed me and told me things about the town that I could not have learned from anyone else. My colleague Maurice Lee read through what must have seemed like innumerable choppy and convoluted drafts of the manuscript and never once complained, at least directly to me. In retrospect, it seems that those parts of the book which read smoothly ought to be credited to him. Without the aid of these people and others there would have been many more errors than the ones which remain.

Table of Contents

Acknowledgments   vii
List of Tables and Graphs   xi
List of Maps   xiii
List of Abbreviations   xv
Introduction   xvii

Chapter One: THE PHYSICAL SETTING   14
  THE GREATER URBAN REGION   14
  THE TOWN IN 1295   23
  TOPOGRAPHICAL CHANGES IN THE FOURTEENTH AND
    FIFTEENTH CENTURIES   34
  THE TOWN IN THE SIXTEENTH CENTURY   39

Chapter Two: THE DEMOGRAPHIC BASIS FOR
        CHANGE   46

Chapter Three: THE ECONOMIC BASIS FOR CHANGE   73
  THE ECONOMIC ROLE OF THE ABBEY   73
  THE MARKETPLACE AND TRADE   84
  WOOL AND CLOTH   94
  GUILDS, OCCUPATIONS AND THE NON-TEXTILE INDUSTRIES 107
  THE WEALTH OF THE TOWN AND THE TOWNSMEN   116

Chapter Four: THE BURGHAL ÉLITE AND THE
        FOUNDATIONS OF BOROUGH POWER   131
  CIVIC OFFICE AND PROMINENT ALDERMEN   131
  THE GREAT BURGESSES   143
  THE GREAT FAMILIES; THE EXAMPLES OF THE BARETS AND
    THE DRURYS   153

Chapter Five: THE EXTENT AND DIVISION OF
        BURGHAL CORPORATE POWER   167
  THE PRIVILEGES AND POWER OF ST. EDMUNDS ABBEY   167

THE CONTROL OF THE GAOL   172
FRATERNITIES, CHARITY AND SOCIAL SECURITY   180
THE MEDICAL COMMUNITY   192
EDUCATION   207

Chapter Six: THE POLITICAL IMPLICATIONS; THE
             RISINGS OF THE BURGESSES   215

Chapter Seven: THE DISSOLUTION OF THE ABBEY
               AND THE TRANSFER OF POWER   237

Conclusions: BURY ST. EDMUNDS, THE URBAN
             CRISIS, AND LATE MEDIEVAL SOCIETY   246

Appendix A: THE SOURCES   255

Appendix B: THE LATE MEDIEVAL ABBOTS AND
            ALDERMEN   269

Appendix C: THE TOWN RENTALS   272

Appendix D: PLACE-NAME SURNAMES OF BURY ST.
            EDMUNDS' INHABITANTS   278

Appendix E: LANDHOLDING AND INHERITANCE   284

Appendix F: STATISTICAL INFORMATION ON THE
            BURGHAL ÉLITE   288

Bibliography   291

Index   307

List of Tables and Graphs

Table 1.1	The Lay Subsidy of 1523-1524 by Ward	40
Table 2.1	Estimates of Bury St. Edmunds' Population	54
Table 2.2	Male Replacement Ratios	56
Table 2.3	Female Replacement Ratios	57
Graph 2.1	Testamentary Mortality, 1390 to 1530	58
Graph 2.2	Marriage and Fertility Rates	60
Table 2.4	Marriage and Remarriage Ratios	62
Table 2.5	Seasonal Mortality	66
Table 2.6	Migration Trends from Place Name Evidence	69
Table 3.1	*Hadgoval* Stallage Rents in the Great Market, Fourteenth Century	88
Table 3.2	Testamentary Evidence for Debts	89
Table 3.3	English Exports in Cloth and Raw Wool	97
Table 3.4	Occupational Breakdown of Stour Valley Villages, 1522	100
Table 3.5	Occupations by Frequency	111
Table 3.6	Frequency by Social Class	113
Table 3.7	Occupation Classification	117
Table 3.8	Leading Occupations of Three Midland Towns in the Early Sixteenth Century	120
Table 3.9	Percentage of Traders in Three Midlands Towns	120
Table 3.10	The Welsh Wars Subsidy of 1282; Ranking of London and the Leading East Anglian Towns	121
Table 3.11	The Lay Subsidy of 1327; The Ranking of the Suffolk Towns	121
Table 3.12	The Lay Subsidy of 1334; The Ten Leading Towns in England	122
Table 3.13	The Lay Subsidy of 1334; The Ranking of the Leading East Anglian Towns	122
Table 3.14	The Poll Tax of 1377; The Ranking of the East Anglian Towns	123

Table 3.15   The Lay Subsidy of 1523/24; The Fifteen
              Leading Towns in England   125
Table 3.16   The Wealth of Individuals in Bury St.
              Edmunds   126
Table 3.17   The Wealth of Individuals in East Anglia,
              1430-1480   128
Table 4.1   Genealogy of the Baret Family   155
Table 4.2   Genealogy of the Drury Family   160
Table 5.1   Pious Bequests from the Testamentary   183
              Evidence, 1440-1530   189
Table 5.2   Parish Guilds in Bury St. Edmunds, 1389
Table 5.3   Guild Tally from Testamentary Bequests,   191
              1440-1530   269
Table B.1   Late Medieval Abbots   269
Table B.2   Late Medieval Aldermen   272
Table C.1   The 1295 Rental
Table C.2   The St. Peter's Hospital Supplement to the   273
              1295 Rental
Table C.3   Late 14th Century Sacrist's Rental of Thomas   273
              Rudham   274
Table C.4   The Sacrist's *Hadgoval* Rental, 1433   275
Table C.5   The Bury *Relevia*, 1353-1539   276
Table C.6   The Dissolution Rentals, 1539 and 1553
Table D.1   Place-Name Surnames of Bury St. Edmunds'   278
              Inhabitants; Archdeaconry of Sudbury
Table D.2   Place-Name Surnames of Bury St. Edmunds'   279
              Inhabitants; Archdeaconry of Suffolk
Table D.3   Place-Name Surnames of Bury St. Edmunds'   280
              Inhabitants; Archdeaconry of Norwich
Table D.4   Place-Name Surnames of Bury St. Edmunds'   281
              Inhabitants; Archdeaconry of Norfolk
Table D.5   Place-Name Surnames of Bury St. Edmunds'   281
              Inhabitants; Others (Domestic)
Table D.6   Place-Name Surnames of Bury St. Edmunds'   283
              Inhabitants; Others (Foreign)
Table E.1   Inheritance Patterns from the Testamentary   286
              Evidence, 1354-1530
Table E.2   Land Descriptions from the Testamentary   287
              Evidence, 1354-1530
Table F.1   Demographic and Social Characteristics of the 290
              Burghal Élite

List of Maps

Map 1   The Major Towns of Late Medieval England   4
Map 2   The Banleuca of Bury St. Edmunds   16-17
Map 3   The Greater Urban Region of Bury St.
         Edmunds   21
Map 4   The Town of Bury St. Edmunds   27
Map 5   Bury St. Edmunds' Wards; 13th Century
         Tenement Density   28
Map 6   Bury St. Edmunds' Wards; 14th Century
         Tenement Density   35
Map 7   Bury St. Edmunds' Wards; 15th Century
         Tenement Density   37
Map 8   Bury St. Edmunds' Wards; *Relevia* Density,
         14th-16th Centuries   39
Map 9   Bury St. Edmunds' Wards; 16th Century
         Tenement Density   42
Map 10   The Liberty of St. Edmund   76

List of Abbreviations

Arnold	Thomas Arnold, ed., *Memorials of St. Edmunds Abbey*, 3 vols. (London: Kraus Reprints, 1965).
Bacon	The Bacon Collection, Regenstein Library, The University of Chicago.
B.M.	The British Library, The British Museum, London.
C.C.R.	Calendar of Close Rolls, 1272-1513.
C.F.R.	Calendar of Fine Rolls, 1272-1501.
C. of I.	Calendar of Inquisitions, 1307-1399.
C.P.R.	Calendar of Patent Rolls, 1272-1513.
C.U.L.	Cambridge University Library, Cambridge, England.
Dugdale	William Dugdale, *Monasticon Anglicanum* (London: James Bohn, 1846).
Ec.H.R.	*Economic History Review*
Jocelin	Jocelin of Brakelond, *The Chronicle*, ed. H. E. Butler (New York: Oxford University Press, 1949).
Lobel, *The Borough*	M. D. Lobel, *The Borough of Bury St. Edmunds* (Oxford: The Clarendon Press, 1935).
P.C.B.S.E.	Peculiar Court of Bury St. Edmunds Wills, Bury St. Edmunds and West Suffolk County Record Office, Bury St. Edmunds, England.
P.C.C.	Prerogative Court of Canterbury Wills, The Public Record Office, London.
P.R.O.	The Public Record Office, London.
P.S.I.	*Proceedings of the Suffolk Institute of Archeology*
Tymms	Samuel Tymms, *Wills and Inventories from the*

Registers of the Commissary of Bury St. Edmunds and the Archdeaconry of Sudbury (London: Camden Society, xlix, 1850).

V.C.H.   *Victoria County History of England: Suffolk*

Bury St. Edmunds
and the Urban Crisis:
1290-1539

Introduction

In 1433, with the war in France growing in cost and intensity and the rivalries among the leading English lords becoming ever more acrimonious, the advisers of the English boy-king Henry VI decided to take him from London to eastern England. One of the stops on his tour was the West Suffolk town of Bury St. Edmunds. Bury had been a favorite town for several English monarchs, including Canute, Edward the Confessor, Henry III, and his son, Edward I. In time, the pious Henry VI would become a personal friend of the abbot of St. Edmunds, William Curteys, with whom he would stay during several extended visits. But in 1433 no king had come to town for over a century, and both the monks of the abbey and the burgesses and commons from the borough were determined to make a strong, positive impression.

A flurry of activity preceded the royal visitation.[1] The abbey complex, sacked and burned several times during the civil disturbances of the fourteenth century, had finally been restored. St. Mary's Church, one of the two parish churches in the borough,[2] had its bells polished and newly plumbed. Bury's major municipal buildings, the alderman's Guildhall, where the burgesses met to decide Bury's civic policies, and the abbot's Tollhouse, where rents due to the abbey, were paid to its bailiffs, were repaired and cleaned. The principal hostels and inns along the Brentgoval and the Mustowe—Moyses Hall, The Saracen's Head, The Hart, The Woodhouse, Colet's House, and others—were made ready for the influx of retainers, courtiers, favor seekers, and just the curious who invariably accompanied the appearance of a king. Merchants and craftsmen, with their open stalls arrayed along Cooks' Row, Hatter Street, and Goldsmiths' Row prepared their wares. Such a royal visit meant more than simply prestige for Bury's ecclesiastical

---

[1] A full account of the 1433 visit is provided by Dugdale, iii, pp. 113 ff.

[2] Some authorities count a third parish, represented by the abbey church of St. Edmund, within the abbey complex.

Map 1: THE MAJOR TOWNS OF LATE MEDIEVAL ENGLAND.

and secular leaders; it also meant a great deal of new business for shopkeepers at all levels.

Although some members of the king's entourage appeared as early as mid-autumn, Henry VI did not arrive until December. Coming from the west along the Holeway from Cambridge, the royal party, stretching a mile in length, must have been impressed at its first glimpse of the town. Standing on a slope, surrounded on three sides by water, with a skyline of steeples formed by the abbey church, the parish churches of St. Mary and St. James, the Tollhouse, the Guildhall, and Moyses Hall, Bury St. Edmunds presented an impressive and perhaps inspirational sight for travellers coming east from the marsh and fenlands.

The king was met at New Market Heath by the civic leaders, the alderman and his burgesses. Dressed in scarlet, they were followed by five hundred of the town's commons, perhaps half its adult males, outfitted in red liveries by the Alderman's Guild. From the heath the procession moved toward town, crossing the Linnet River at newly rebuilt Stanwerp Bridge, and entering the borough walls through South Gate. Once inside, the pageant was joined by Abbot Curteys, the bishop of Norwich, and officers of St. Edmunds Abbey, and proceded up Southgate Street to the abbey church, acclaimed the entire way by townsfolk lining both sides of the road. At St. Edmunds, Abbot Curteys sprinkled Henry with holy water and pressed a cross to his lips. Then, accompanied by lute-playing musicians, the procession entered the abbey church to celebrate a mass. Here, the communal affair took a new turn. The townsmen, alderman and burgesses included, were locked out of St. Edmunds, while the abbot and his monks and the king and his lords sang a private mass.

In many ways, this procession of Henry VI was symbolic of the history of late medieval Bury St. Edmunds. It was a rich town, well-favored by economic and geographic circumstances, growing and prospering at a time when many provincial centers were entering a period of acute economic decline.[3] But, as it prospered economically, late medieval Bury was undergoing a fundamental cultural and political crisis. The basic underpinnings of its traditional social and governmental institutions and the people who controlled them—the abbot and his ecclesiastical and lay appointees—were being challenged by the borough's mercantile and industrial factions. Long excluded from the inner circles of political power, the merchants began to demand political authority commensurate with

[3] A fine summary article of the historiography of late medieval English towns is Charles Phythian-Adams, "Urban Decay in Late Medieval England," in Philip Abrams and Wrigley, E. A., eds., *Towns in Societies* (Cambridge: Cambridge University Press, 1978). Also see: R. B. Dobson, "Urban Decline in Late Medieval England," *Transactions of the Royal Historical Society*, 5th series, 27, 1977; and S. H. Rigby, "Urban Decline in the Later Middle Ages," *Urban History Yearbook*, 1979.

their economic strength. Bury was not unique in the general outline of its constitutional woes. Many of the borough, market, and provincial towns of late-medieval England underwent institutional and governmental crises. But, in its particulars, Bury's crisis was unusual. Because its economy was expanding rapidly instead of contracting, the burghal community was not reacting simply out of frustration, as did its counterparts in Coventry and other towns.[4] And in Bury the problem was compounded by the presence of the Abbey of St. Edmunds, one of the richest and most powerful Benedictine houses in England. Conservative and influential, with most of its wealth spread throughout West Suffolk, St. Edmunds would resist the demands of the aldermen and burgesses until its dissolution. The result was a bitter struggle which encompassed virtually every aspect of the history of late medieval Bury.

Many scholars have been aware of the broad implications of Bury's crisis, and have written extensively about them. But most analysis has focused on administrative developments. The goals of this book include supplementing these administrative arguments by examining the social and economic aspects of the emergence of the secular community. In the introduction to her study on the government of the borough, Mary D. Lobel concluded with an apology for her lack of attention to such things: "Evidence for the economic and social life of the borough is almost entirely lacking, and these aspects of town life have been omitted of necessity. . . ."[5]

Little new documentation has been unearthed in the forty plus years since Lobel's book was published, but it is now possible to investigate the social and economic history of late medieval Bury in far more detail than she had imagined.[6] This is primarily the result of the perfection and introduction into historical research

[4] See Charles Phythian-Adams, *Desolation of a City; Coventry and the Urban Crisis of the Late Middle Ages* (Cambridge: Cambridge University Press, 1979).

[5] Lobel, *The Borough*, p. xi.

[6] D. D. Knowles, in the first volume of his monumental *Religious Orders in England* (Cambridge: Cambridge University Press, 1950), p. 311, makes an interesting comment: "No adequate account of Bury exists, although it has been the subject of a number of articles and studies. *The Memorials of St. Edmunds*, rich as they are, by no means exhaust the materials with which the historian of the house would have to deal." As the final sentence obviously indicates, Knowles's primary concern was the abbey.

of new tools and techniques of analysis and catalogue, and, indeed, an entirely new approach to the study of history. Using much of the same documentation that Dugdale, Yates, Goodwin, Lobel, and others have, but applying these new tools and techniques, I will try to reconstruct the social and economic life of Bury St. Edmunds from the late thirteenth to the mid-sixteenth centuries, as it affected the rise of the town.[7]

Bury's continuing economic success, its colorful political history, and the presence within the borough walls of one of England's largest and most influential monasteries are sufficient reason to justify such a study. But there is at least one more factor which makes medieval Bury interesting. Its influence stretched well beyond the borough walls, and, indeed, beyond the four crosses which delineated the banleuca, or suburban limits. It acted as a greater urban region in the sense in which the term is used to describe industrial metropolitan cities. Bury served not only as the market center for a region extending twenty to twenty-five miles from the abbey gates, but also as a cultural, educational, medical, religious, and social magnet for all of West Suffolk. This in itself is not unique. Clark and Slack have identified several dozen regional centers in pre-industrial England, and East Anglia *per se* can be divided into at least four major market centers, each of which was surrounded by smaller, more local, village markets.[8] But Bury was somewhat special, even among the four East Anglia market towns. The influence, resources, and patronage of the abbey added considerable weight to the town's medical, cultural, and educational attractions. And for the final hundred years of the later middle ages Bury's marketplace was of special prominence because it served as a principal outlet for the woolen cloth produced in the Stour River Valley, one of the major industrial areas in England during the fifteenth and sixteenth centuries.[9] Bury had a significant cloth industry within the borough, and served as a market for the finished textiles

[7] Dugdale, iii; A. Goodwin, *The Abbey of St. Edmundsbury* (Oxford: Basil Blackwell, 1931); Lobel, *The Borough*; and Richard Yates, *The History and Antiquities of the Abbey of Bury St. Edmunds* (London: J. B. Nichols and Son, 1843).

[8] Peter Clark and Paul Slack, *English Towns in Transition, 1500-1700* (Oxford: Oxford University Press, 1976), pp. 17-32, 46-61.

[9] A study covering Sudbury and its relationship to the area is John Patten, "Village and Town: An Occupational Study," *Agricultural History Review*, 20, 1972.

from Lavenham, Long Melford, and other cloth villages which were located within its urban region. Consequently, its Great Market attracted not only local folk, but merchants from London, Norwich, King's Lynn, Great Yarmouth, and aliens from the Low Countries, Germany, and northern Italy, all in pursuit of cloth made from perhaps the finest fleece in western Europe.

Bury St. Edmunds must also be viewed in a national context. Much of the groundwork for late medieval urban studies was laid in the nineteenth century by scholars like William Denton and the Greens.[10] They believed that demographic and economic contraction led to a decline in most aspects of fourteenth- and fifteenth-century urban life, and caused considerable social and political tensions. Despite some questioning and modification, this concept of decline survived into the twentieth century, and was synthesized by M. M. Postan.[11] Using empirical methods, Postan built a general model of late-medieval economic stagnation and decay. Towns were more or less peripheral to his argument, which stressed the overwhelming importance of the rural economy, but he did comment on urban life:

> With the exception of London, which continued to grow; of Bristol, which benefited from the resilience of the western and southern trades, and the possibility of Southampton, which occupied a special position by virtue of its connection with Italian imports and its function as one of the outposts of the London region, the bulk of English trading centers, whether the ancient county towns or the old seaports, suffered a decline.[12]

Despite this general image, virtually all experts have pointed to some exceptions. Postan conceded that towns in regions dominated by the new cloth industry, one of which was East Anglia, might

[10] W. Denton, *England in the Fifteenth Century* (London: George Bell and Sons, 1888), pp. 127-131; J. R. Green, *A History of the English Peoples* (New York, Harper, 1874), pp. 482-576; Mrs. J. R. Green, *English Towns in the Fifteenth Century*, 2 vols. (London: Macmillan, 1894), especially i, pp. 1-43.

[11] An attempt at modification is C. J. Kingsford, *Prejudice and Promise in Fifteenth Century England* (Oxford: Oxford University Press, 1925), pp. 1-21, 107-145. The Postan works can be found in his *Medieval Agriculture and General Problems* (Cambridge: Cambridge University Press, 1973), especially in the chapters "The Fifteenth Century," pp. 41-48; and "Some Agrarian Evidence of Declining Population in the Later Middle Ages," pp. 186-213.

[12] Postan, "The Fifteenth Century," p. 44.

have grown both in prosperity and numbers. This perspective has been pressed by many local historians, but was perhaps best expressed by E. M. Carus-Wilson.[13] Carus-Wilson stressed the distinctions rather than the similarities between provincial towns, the difficulty of generalization on the basis of limited evidence, and the importance of local research. It was only through the latter that the successful, relatively prosperous late medieval towns like Newcastle and Salisbury could be distinguished from the fading ones, like Lincoln and York.[14] Her position has been bolstered by the work of A. R. Bridbury.[15] Like Postan, Bridbury was concerned with a broad interpretation of late medieval society and economy, and inevitably turned to towns. He too stressed their individuality and focused on their peculiarities, and like Carus-Wilson pointed out the new-found prosperity of the cloth towns and their hinterlands. Bridbury relied heavily in his interpretation on lay subsidies and freemen's rolls, sources which have come under heavy criticism, but his argument remains forceful and compelling.[16]

In recent years the debate over the condition of late-medieval towns has swung back toward decline. Two surveys, by Colin Platt and Susan Reynolds, bemoan inadequate source materials, but then go on to follow the basics of the Postan argument.[17] Platt, who shows a keener interest in the topographical rather than the social and economic aspects of urban life, emphasizes the small size of most English towns, especially when measured by continental standards. He sees great expansion for London in the fourteenth and fifteenth centuries, usually at the expense of provincial centers.[18] Reynolds believes that the later medieval urban decline was the

[13] E. M. Carus-Wilson, *The Expansion of Exeter at the Close of the Middle Ages* (Exeter: The University of Exeter, 1963), especially pp. 3-10. Also, see her "The First Half-Century of the Borough of Stratford-upon-Avon," *Economic History Review*, 2nd series, xviii, 1965, pp. 46-63.

[14] Carus-Wilson, *The Expansion of Exeter*, pp. 3-5.

[15] A. R. Bridbury, *Economic Growth: England in the Later Middle Ages*, 2nd ed. (New York: Barnes and Noble, 1975).

[16] R. B. Dobson, "Admissions to the Freedom of the city of York in the later middle ages," *Economic History Review*, 2nd series, xxv, 1973, pp. 1-21.

[17] Colin Platt, *The English Medieval Town* (London: Secker and Warburg, 1976); Susan Reynolds, *An Introduction to the History of English Medieval Towns* (Oxford: Clarendon Press, 1977).

[18] Platt, *The English Medieval Town*, pp. 75-95.

result of more than just a fall in population and fluctuations in the wool and cloth trade. Competition for ever-shrinking segments of the towns' resources produced social and political tensions that in some cases ended in the emergence of élite oligarchies.[19]

The most significant work done on late medieval urban life in the last few years is that of R. B. Dobson and Charles Phythian-Adams.[20] Like Platt and Reynolds, they generally agree with the Postan theory of declining town life. Dobson cites the increasing reluctance of burgesses in the fifteenth and early sixteenth centuries to hold civic office, and stresses what he calls an "urban malaise," especially in the larger provincial centers.[21] Phythian-Adams, an expert on Coventry, believes that the urban decline was not general to the entire period 1270 to 1530, but rather was concentrated primarily from 1420 to 1530. One of the most dramatic aspects of this theory of decline was a marked population drop and "hence a shrinking of demand."[22] York's population, for example, fell from 12,000 to 8,000 from the fifteenth to the early sixteenth century, while Coventry went from 10,000 folk in 1400 to 7,500 in 1500, to 6,000 by 1523. Further, claims Phythian-Adams, since England's overall population had begun to rise by the sixteenth century this decline is even more significant.

The views of Charles Phythian-Adams are very much in the mainstream of current late medieval urban studies. The consensus holds that, with the exception of London, a few select provincial marketing and exporting centers, and perhaps some towns in the cloth-producing regions of Oxfordshire, Yorkshire, and East Anglia, English towns experienced a steady and marked decline. One of my goals is to try to place Bury St. Edmunds in this broader urban spectrum.

The dates selected for this study, the 1290s to 1539, were chosen for a variety of reasons. The earlier date marks what many authorities consider the beginning of the later middle ages, the last part of the reign of Edward I, and the apogee of medieval economic development. Although the latter date is generally considered to be "Tudor" rather than late medieval, it is the obvious and ideal

[19] Reynolds, *An Introduction*, pp. 160-187.
[20] As cited above, note 3.
[21] Dobson, "Urban Decline," pp. 20-22.
[22] Phythian-Adams, "Urban Decay," pp. 183-185.

date to terminate a study of a monastic town—the final date of Dissolution. The period 1290 to 1539 was also selected because of its cohesive and comparatively abundant and accessible source materials. Bury is a fine example of G. R. Elton's comment that the number and quality of records, especially governmental records, improve dramatically from the late thirteenth century.[23] The key sources are land rentals, deeds, probated wills and letters of admonition, sacrists' and other abbey officers' registers, guild records and regulations, gaol delivery rolls, royal close, fine and patent rolls, chronicles and narrative sources, manorial records from the estates of the abbey, a smattering of independent trade and industrial data, a great deal of physical and archeological remains, and an assortment of miscellaneous evidence from scattered sources.[24] To the modernist, this may not seem overwhelming, and, indeed, there are a number of key questions about which one can only speculate. But, for the medievalist, especially the social and economic specialist, the information is unusually full, and in some instances even allows for statistical analysis. Finally, the period 1290 to 1539 encompasses the entire spectrum of town-abbey relations. Late in the thirteenth century St. Edmunds Abbey stood at the peak of its powers, and, while the borough was prosperous, the burgesses were entirely subservient to the abbot and his officers. By the 1530s, even before its formal dissolution, the abbey was crumbling, a shell of its former self, while the secular town was stronger than ever.

Drawing on the available sources, I will discuss different aspects of Bury's social and economic history in relation to the emergence of the burghal community. Chapter 1 provides a physical and topographical background, stressing the changing patterns of settlement from the thirteenth through the sixteenth centuries. Chapter 2 picks up the theme of change and transition, concentrating on Bury's demographic history. Long-term population movements were a direct factor in the progress of the town's economy, the subject of Chapter 3. Before the burgesses could realistically raise their political ambitions, they needed a secure economic base. In many respects, the economic development of late medieval West Suffolk was the single most important factor in the emergence of

[23] G. R. Elton, *England, 1200-1640* (Ithaca, N.Y.: Cornell University Press, 1969).

[24] Full discussion of all sources used in the text is in Appendix A.

the commune. Chapter 3 charts the rise of Bury St. Edmunds' cloth industry from a cottage, regional marketing level to that of a center of national and even international importance.

Economic fruition engendered a strong, closely knit patriciate that dominated the commune's social and political affairs. Chapter 4 analyzes the key civic offices and the individuals who held them, how they initially reached positions of power, and whether they were able to maintain them and pass them on to their progeny. Chapter 5 tells of the struggle between abbey and town officials for control over the key social, cultural, and governmental institutions in the borough. It outlines the extent of abbey wealth, power, and privilege, and focuses on the various institutions—social fraternities and vehicles of charity, gaols and courts, the six hospitals, and the almshouses and schools—in which much of the power and landed endowment of the borough was vested. All of these elements—topographical, economic, social, institutional, and corporate—caused considerable political tensions. Chapter 6 deals with the political upheaval that they combined to produce. Finally, Chapter 7 accounts for the last years of the abbey, focusing on why it was toppled with such ease by the agents of Henry VIII in 1539.

There is a major omission from this study; it concentrates on the town rather than on the Benedictine abbey. There is extensive information on late medieval St. Edmunds, and it is possible to write an exhaustive monograph on its economic fortunes.[25] It may even be possible to write a manorial-economic study of the abbey's estates, as Finberg, DuBoulay, and Miller have done for other great ecclesiastical houses.[26] But, while the financial fortunes and corporate, governmental powers of the abbey were essential in the rise of the commune and have been included, its general political, social, and economic history is not. My perspective is that of the borough,

[25] Much of the evidence from the Bacon collection in the Regenstein Library, The University of Chicago, which centers on the West Suffolk estates of the abbey, has already been studied, especially by Richard Smith of the Cambridge Group for the History of Population and Social Structure.

[26] H.P.R. Finberg, *Tavistock Abbey: A Study in the Social and Economic History of Devon* (Newton Abbot, Devon, David Charles, 1969, 2nd ed.); F.R.H. DuBoulay, *The Lordship of Canterbury* (London: Thomas Nelson, 1966); Edward Miller, *The Abbey and Bishopric of Ely* (Cambridge: Cambridge University Press, 1951).

its suburbs and its market region, and St. Edmunds will be studied only as it directly affected the life of the town.

This book is in no sense a general, comprehensive socio-economic history of late medieval Bury St. Edmunds. Available sources do not allow for such, and any broader study would have to incorporate a thorough analysis of dozens of court rolls from surrounding West Suffolk rural estates. Rather, its intention is to try to explain the rise and prosperity of one important provincial town in an era when many provincial towns were stagnating or crumbling and falling into obscurity.

Chapter One

THE PHYSICAL SETTING

THE GREATER URBAN REGION

Recent research has considerably widened our conceptions of the medieval town and what constituted an urban or metropolitan area. No longer is it equated solely with legal burgage tenure or the municipal-constitutional designation, "borough."[1] Carus-Wilson, Hilton, Thrupp, and others have shown that borough walls did not define or restrict a city.[2] Such was clearly the case with Bury St. Edmunds in the later middle ages. Bury obtained borough status by the eleventh century, but its influence extended far beyond its crumbling town walls, and even beyond the banleuca which delineated the special jurisdiction of the abbot. This is evident to twentieth-century historians, and was clear to Bury's medieval denizens. In order to understand the late-medieval town, its role as the hub

[1] Among the best books that define the legal limits of medieval English towns are: James Tait, *The Medieval English Borough* (Manchester: The University of Manchester Press, 1936); and May McKisack, *The Parliamentary Representation of the English Boroughs During the Middle Ages* (Oxford: Oxford University Press, 1932). A current bibliography of medieval urban studies can be found in Susan Reynolds, *An Introduction to the History of English Medieval Towns* (Oxford: Clarendon Press, 1977).

[2] Among their many works, see: E. M. Carus-Wilson, *Medieval Merchant Venturers* (London: Methuen, 1954); Carus-Wilson, "Stratford-Upon-Avon in the Later Middle Ages," *Ec.H.R.*, 2nd series, 18, 1965; Carus-Wilson, *The Expansion of Exeter at the Close of the Middle Ages* (Exeter: University of Exeter Press, 1963); R. H. Hilton, "The Small Town as Part of Peasant Society," in his *The Peasantry in Later Medieval England* (Oxford: Clarendon Press, 1975); S. L. Thrupp, "Social Control in the Medieval Town," in Raymond Grew and Nicholas Steneck, eds., *Society and History: Essays by Sylvia Thrupp* (Ann Arbor, Mich.: University of Michigan Press, 1977).

of a larger urban network covering virtually all of West Suffolk must first be examined.[3]

One of the major reasons for Bury's development was geographic. It was situated on a small rise, about twenty-six miles northwest of Ipswich, thirty-six miles southwest of Norwich, thirty-seven miles southeast of King's Lynn, twenty-eight miles north of Colchester, and twenty-eight miles east of Cambridge—in effect, so located as to create its own regional hinterland without impinging upon those of the neighboring provincial centers. Contemporaries thought this physical setting was ideal. In his 1530 trip through East Anglia, John Leland, the keeper of the king's libraries, was lavish in his praise: "The sun does not shine on a town more prettily situated, so delicately does it hang on a gentle slope, with a gentle stream flowing on its east side."[4] Leland's gentle slope notwithstanding, Bury, like most of East Anglia, was on relatively low, wet ground, surrounded by waterways. The most important of these was the River Lark, Leland's gentle stream, running northwest into the Ouse, and then the Wash and the North Sea. The Lark was narrow and shallow. Deep-draught vessels could not ordinarily navigate upstream, but barges could, and poled by men or pulled by mules and oxen they played an important role in

[3] This idea of urban regions has been popular among geographers and sociologists since the 1930s. Among other things, see W. Christaller, *Central Places in Southern Germany* (Englewood, N.J.: Prentice Hall, 1966); and Emrys Jones, *Towns and Cities* (Oxford: Oxford University Press, 1966). An attempt to divide medieval Europe into urban regions can be found in J. C. Russell, *Medieval Regions and their Cities* (Bloomington, Ind.: University of Indiana Press, 1972). Also, see Gerald Breese, ed., *The City in Newly Developed Countries* (Englewood Cliffs, N.J.: Prentice Hall, 1969); G. Sjoberg, *The Preindustrial City: Past and Present* (New York, The Free Press, 1960). The Hundred of Babergh, in southwestern Suffolk, has been nicely analyzed by John Patten, "Village and Town: An Occupational Study," *Agricultural History*, 20, 1972.

[4] John Leland, *Itinerary in England: In or About the Years, 1535-1543*, ed., Lucy Toulmin-Smith (London: George Bell and Sons, 1908). Leland's praise is especially noteworthy in that most of his commentary on provincial towns was pejorative. A good seventeenth-century description of Bury is in R. Reyce, "The Breviary of Suffolk," B.M. Ms. Harl. 3873; and B.M. Mss. Add. 1915, 5828 and 8200. It has been transcribed and edited by Francis Hervey, *Suffolk in the Seventeenth Century* (Oxford: Oxford University Press, 1902). A good collective description of Bury's topography can be found in *The Archaeological Journal*, cviii, 1951.

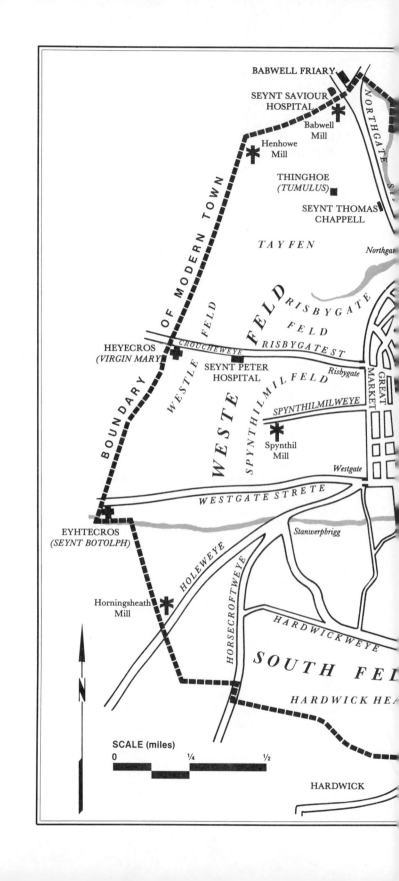

BABWELL FRIARY

SEYNT SAVIOUR
HOSPITAL

Babwell
Mill

Henhowe
Mill

NORTHGATE

THINGHOE
(TUMULUS)

SEYNT THOMAS
CHAPPELL

TAY FEN

Northga

OF MODERN TOWN

WESTLE FELD

*RISBYGATE
FELD*

RISBYGATE ST

HEYECROS
(VIRGIN MARY)

CROUCHEWEYE

SEYNT PETER
HOSPITAL

SPYNTHILMIL FELD

Risbygate

*GREAT
MARKET*

WESTE FELD

SPYNTHILMILWEYE

SPYNTHIL

Spynthil
Mill

BOUNDARY

Westgate

WESTGATE STRETE

EYHTECROS
(SEYNT BOTOLPH)

Stanwerpbrigg

HOLEWEYE

HORSECROFTWEYE

Horningsheath
Mill

HARDWICKWEYE

SOUTH FEL

HARDWICK HEA

N

SCALE (miles)

0   ¼   ½

HARDWICK

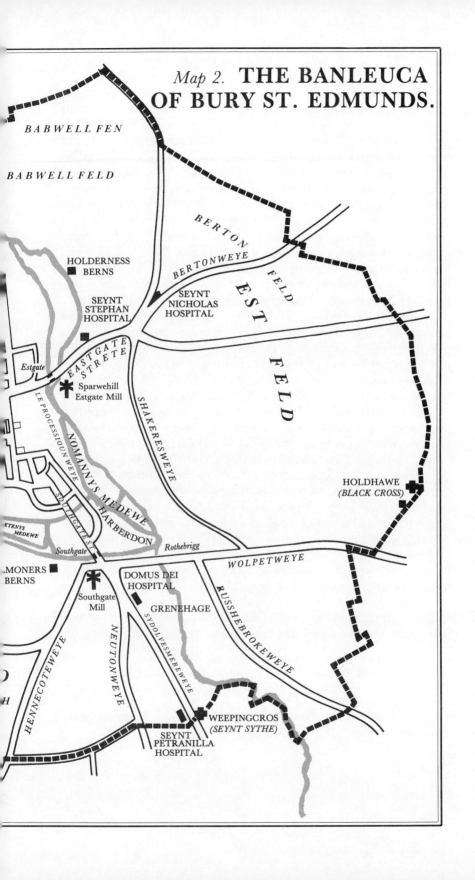

Map 2. **THE BANLEUCA OF BURY ST. EDMUNDS.**

BABWELL FEN

BABWELL FELD

BERTON

HOLDERNESS
BERNS

BERTONWEYE

SEYNT
NICHOLAS
HOSPITAL

FELD

SEYNT
STEPHAN
HOSPITAL

EST

Estgate

*EASTGATE
STRETE*

Sparwehill
Estgate Mill

LE PROCESSIOUN WEYE

SHAKERESWEYE

FELD

NOMANNYS MEDEWE

SOUTHGATES

HARBERDON

*TENYS
MEDEWE*

Southgate

Rothebrigg

WOLPETWEYE

HOLDHAWE
(*BLACK CROSS*)

MONERS
BERNS

*Southgate
Mill*

DOMUS DEI
HOSPITAL

GRENEHAGE

RUSSHEBROKEWEYE

HENNECOTEWEYE

NEUTONWEYE

SYDOLVESMEREWEYE

WEEPINGCROS
(*SEYNT SYTHE*)

SEYNT
PETRANILLA
HOSPITAL

Bury's economic life. To the south was the River Linnet, smaller and of more limited economic use than the Lark. Both streams provided much of the town's drinking water, power for its fulling machines and mills, and a system of waste disposal. The Lark and the Linnet were crucial to the fishing industry which flourished through the fourteenth century, and provided a network of local transportation. Directly north was Babwell Fen, another important source of drinking water, and northwest was Tayfen, well stocked with fish. The only area surrounding the borough which was high and dry was directly west, which in turn meant that all contiguous expansion could come only in that direction. This was to be an important factor in the topographical evolution of the greater urban region. Water provided part of Bury's physical milieu, the borough on its slope, water glistening around most of its girth.

Beyond the borough walls lay the banleuca, or banlieu, in the later middle ages a concept of fairly recent origin (Map 2).[5] This was the special jurisdiction of the abbot of St. Edmunds. It included the town proper and all the land abutting on its walls and ditches, and was contained within the four crosses situated on the roads and in the fields surrounding the borough (Map 2). Although much of the banleuca without the walls was rural, it was clearly regarded as an extension and integral part of the greater town—*suburbium*, or suburban, as contemporaries called it. When the borough walls began to disintegrate in the twelfth and thirteenth centuries and large numbers of people moved to built-up tenements on Risbygate Street and Eastgate Street Without, the distinction became blurred to the point of insignificance. Many buildings crucial to the town lay in the suburbs, including all its major mills and the six hospitals which made late medieval Bury an important medical center.

The western boundary of Bury's banleuca was marked by the cross of St. Botolph, standing at Eldo, or Eldhawe, or Eythecross, as it was alternatively called (Map 2). Redstone believed that the cross had been built on an old haugh, or Anglo-Saxon burial ground, which helps to explain its rather unusual place name.[6] On the south, the boundary was the cross of St. Sythe, also called the

[5] For an account of medieval banleucas, see M. D. Lobel, "The Ecclesiastical Banleuca in England," in F. M. Powicke, ed., *Oxford Essays in Medieval History* (Oxford: Oxford University Press, 1934). Also, see Lobel, *The Borough*, pp. 5-22.

[6] V. B. Redstone, "St. Edmunds Bury and the Town Rental of 1295," *P.S.I.*, xiii, 1909.

Weeping Cross, on the Sydolvesmereweye, the major road in and out of the borough. As St. Sythe was a thirteenth century Italian figure, it has been suggested that the cross was erected during the early part of the reign of Edward I.[7] This may be so, but the name Weeping Cross, like Eldhawe, suggests pre-Norman roots. Because of its location, and because it stood next to the very popular Hospital of St. Petranilla, an institution primarily for lepers, St. Sythe was the object of considerable pious charity, and was probably the best maintained of the four banleuca crosses. In time, a chapel was erected at its base, with a resident chaplain who received a salary of four pence a week. The eastern border of the banleuca was marked by the Black Cross, standing amidst East Field, at Holdhaw. It too had a chapel, and by 1295 was sufficiently well endowed to support a resident priest with an annual wage of eight shillings, eight pence. The fourth market stood to the northwest, beyond the Great Market, along the Crouchweye at Heyecross. It was dedicated to the Virgin Mary, a favorite Suffolk patroness.[8]

Buildings and activities burgeoned in the suburbs from the thirteenth century onward. Babwell Friary stood outside the banleuca in the village of the same name; the village developed from a sleepy little hamlet to a bustling place offering a wide variety of goods and services. There were additional suburban clusterings of tenements around the town mills. These mills, of which more will be said, were six in number: Spinthil, Eastgate, Southgate, Horningsheath, Henhaw, and Babwell.[9] Other settled parts of the suburbs included the rows of tenements and messuages lining all the major roads which led to town. Some, such as the Tayfen, were heavily settled; the Doomsday survey lists dozens of tenements on it, and, while this marked a medieval high point, it remained continuously inhabited throughout the later middle ages, with its denizens remitting to the abbey's pittancer and cellarer.[10] But, these developments aside, open fields predominated, along with extensive meadows and woodlands, and it is possible that the initial purpose of this

[7] *Ibid.*, pp. 6-7.

[8] There was no official cross directly north of the borough, but the far northern boundary was delineated by Babwell Priory, which may have served as a *de facto* fifth marker.

[9] See below, pp. 73-84.

[10] This can be seen from the pittancers' rentals, the best of which is B.M. Harl. Ms. 27, f.5; and the cellarers' rentals, the best of which is C.U.L. Ms. Gg 4, 4.

outer fringe of the banleuca was to provide some contiguous land
on which the abbot might hunt, and from which the larger abbey
community could collect a substantial portion of its foodstuffs.
Much of what the monks ate, as opposed to what they grew to sell,
appears to have come from it.

Together, the borough and the suburbs—the banleuca—constituted the legal and political boundaries of greater Bury St. Edmunds. But the social and economic borders of the urban region
stretched well beyond the four crosses, through virtually all of West
Suffolk and the archdeaconry of Sudbury. A major goal of this
study is to show that Bury served as the marketing, skilled industrial, cultural, religious, and medical center for this hinterland;
indeed, Bury St. Edmunds fits well into the pattern of urban rank-
size relationships developed by geographers.[11] But there was another geographic subdivision which was more immediate to the
town than West Suffolk and was for all intents and purposes part
of the borough and suburbs. Seventeen rural parishes surrounded
the banleuca.[12] The economic and governmental life of their inhabitants was completely controlled by the abbey, and the villagers
depended on the town for all but their most basic goods and needs.
All the parishes were within five miles of the abbey gates (Map 3),
easy daily walking distance, and some of their inhabitants probably
took part- or full-time work within the borough. This relationship
was reciprocal. Land deeds from the fourteenth and fifteenth centuries show that some merchants who owned shops in Bury lived
in the villages. Each village had its own parish church, which meant
that part of its socio-religious life would be local, but more complex
needs could be satisfied only in town.

It may well have been that this great urban region extended
farther still, yet another five miles, to include a rough circle of
villages about ten miles from the abbey gates (Map 3). We must be
less confident about lumping this outer zone in with the proposed
"greater" town, in part because distances made daily journeys in

[11] Harold Mayer and C. F. Kohn, eds., *Readings in Urban Geography* (Chicago: University of Chicago Press, 1959).

[12] The parishes were: Risby, Hargrave, Chevington, Ickworth, Little Saxham, Great Saxham, Westley, Fornham All Saints, Fornham St. Martin,
Fornham St. Genevieve, Hengrave, Horningsheath (Horringer), Nowton,
Great Barton, Hardwicke, Timworth, and Culford. The deeds used come
from the West Suffolk Record Office, Bury St. Edmunds, Hengrave Register, 1, 449.

Map 3.
THE GREATER URBAN REGION OF BURY ST. EDMUNDS.

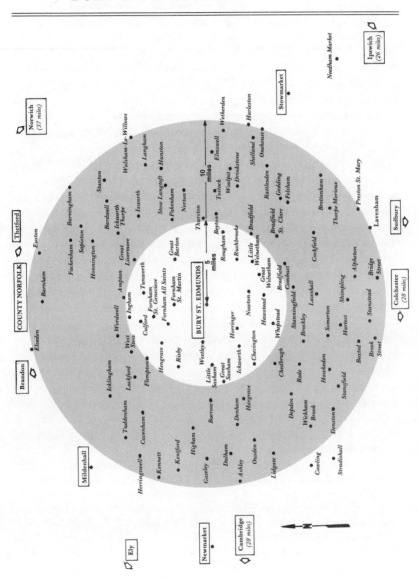

and out of the borough more difficult. But these "second-circle" villages clearly depended on Bury socially, economically, and culturally. At one time or another, most had important Bury figures living in them, and were reliant on the tri-weekly fairs in the Risbygate Great Market. Further, the borough and ten-mile villages formed part of an even larger West Suffolk market system, which included Newmarket, Stow Market, Thetford (at one time the metropolis of western East Anglia), Haverhill, and Sudbury.[13] These lesser market towns each had their own five-mile spheres, capable of providing basic goods and services, but they depended upon Bury St. Edmunds for more sophisticated needs.

Bury's central function, then, was owing partly to the presence of the monastic community, and partly to its location in the center of a larger region which itself served as the crossroads between the heart of England and the towns of the Low Countries.[14] All of this made it an important and prosperous regional market from at least the twelfth century onward, competing with Ipswich, Ely, Cambridge, and King's Lynn for the role of the second town of East Anglia in the thirteenth and fourteenth centuries. In the fifteenth century, however, this changed. The English cloth industry began to boom. Suddenly, because of major technological innovations, much of the industrial production of woolen cloth came from the small Suffolk villages in the southern perimeter of the larger Bury St. Edmunds' urban region. Villages like Woolpit, Rattlesden, Thorpe Morieux, Boxstead, Icklingham, Stansted, and Lavenham were all part of "greater" Bury; and if this ten-mile perimeter is extended just a few miles farther, other major textile areas like

[13] For a similar attempt to do so see: Patten, "Village and Town"; and Carus-Wilson, "Stratford-Upon-Avon."

[14] This strong connection has been cited by many historians for many aspects of social and economic life. E. M. Carus-Wilson, *Medieval Merchant Venturers*, contains articles of relevance, as do the many studies of the woolen cloth trade, such as Eileen Power, *The Medieval Wool Trade* (Oxford: Oxford University Press, 1941); and T. H. Lloyd, *The English Wool Trade in the Middle Ages* (Cambridge: Cambridge University Press, 1977). From the Netherlandish perspective, see: Herman van der Wee, *The Growth of the Antwerp Market*, 3 vols. (The Hague: Mouton, 1963). Also, see S. L. Thrupp's work on aliens, especially "A Survey of the Alien Population in 1440," *Speculum*, 32, 1957; and "Aliens in and Around London in the Fifteenth Century," in A. Hollaender and W. Kellaway, eds., *Studies in London History* (London: Hodder and Stoughton, 1969).

Mildenhall and Long Melford can be included. These villages were the industrial centers, and Bury was their marketplace. From 1450 to the late sixteenth century, when London and continental merchants came to procure Suffolk textiles, many came to the Risbygate market. By the end of the fifteenth century, the greater urban region of Bury St. Edmunds was one of the principal cloth-producing and marketing regions in England.

THE TOWN IN 1295

One of the many legacies of St. Edmunds Abbey is a superb series of topographical surveys that describe settlement patterns in the banleuca. The earliest and most complete of these comes from 1295 and lists the holdings of a dozen monastic officers, including the sacrist, the cellarer, the almoner, the infirmarer, the warder of the chapel of St. Mary, the prior, the hosteler, the subcellarer, the pittancer, the chamberlain, and the wardens of the hospitals of St. Peter, *Domus Dei*, St. Nicholas, and St. Petranilla.[15] The rental, detailed in full in Appendix C, depicts a bustling and prosperous town. Its center was organized around a grid plan, one of England's few pre-Norman towns to be so laid out, with two squares, one near Risbygate, serving as the major marketplace, and the other west of the abbey, serving almost as a grand promenade. This design took inspiration from an old merchant adage of two squares, one for God and one for commerce.[16] The streets were comparatively wide and spacious, perhaps the result of having been built along the furlongs of ploughlands, and the surveys show a so-

[15] B.M. Harl. Mss. 743, 4626. The rental has been edited and printed by Redstone, "St. Edmunds Bury." In addition to being discussed in Appendix A, it is transcribed in Appendix C.

[16] Like Bury St. Edmunds, Coventry had only two parishes; reflective of its greater population, however, Coventry had ten wards. For town plans, see Lawrence Butler, "Evolution of Towns: Planted Towns after 1066," in M. W. Barley, ed., *The Plans and Topography of Medieval Towns in England and Wales* (London: C.C.B.A. Research Report No. 14, 1976). Perhaps its town plan was the reason that Bury was so favored by medieval monarchs. Edward I visited at least fifteen times and kept a permanent residence in the abbey complex. Other studies of town planning include J. T. Smith, "A Note on the Origin of the Town Plan of Bury St. Edmunds," *The Archaeological Journal*, cviii, 1951, for Bury; and M. L. Beresford, *New Towns of the Middle Ages* (New York: Praeger Press, 1967), in general.

phisticated and complex road system of nine major highway networks leading right up to the borough walls (Map 2).

Bertonway went to the east, past St. Nicholas Hospital to Pakenham, and ultimately north to Norwich. It had a series of trunk roads which led through Berton and East Fields, all converging at St. Nicholas, then passing through to East Gate, on to Eastgate Street and *Le Mustow*. Settlement began below Sparrow Hill and Eastgate Mill; these were low-rent tenements inhabited by folk too poor to live in the borough. There were two major approaches from the west. The first system came from the southwest, the other due west. The former was itself a complex network of several smaller roads. One part passed Eythecross, one of the major markers of the banleuca, and was an extension of the road to New Market and Cambridge. The other was further divided. One wing, the Holeway, connected Bury with Haverhill. It passed Horningheath Mill and met the Horsecroftway coming north from the industrial villages of the Stour Valley, and crossing the Linnet at Stanwerp Bridge. Together, the Holeway and the Horsecroftway then passed through West Gate, meeting the road from Eythecross as both entered through the town walls. The other western approaches to Bury were farther north, terminating at Risby Gate. This system was usually referred to as the Crouchway, and was one of the most important routes in later medieval East Anglia. It passed Heyecross, went through West Field by St. Peter's Hospital, through Risby Gate, and into the Great Market. Despite its late development, Risbygate Street was already one of Bury's major thoroughfares in 1295. It lay on the one dry area directly abutting the town walls, and by the mid-fourteenth century was one of the major streets in the borough.[17]

The final western approach to Bury St. Edmunds was the Spinthilmillway. It was primarily a trunk road, leading through Spinthilmill and West Fields, to Spinthil Mill itself. It ended at the southwest corner of the Great Market, emptying into Cooks' Row, and is of special interest because according to the borough murage

[17] Many of the tenements were held by the cellarer, and this image of Risbygate Street might not be complete. In 1295 the street had seven tenements and five granges, two of which had gardens. In many ways its development was like that of the London ward, Farringdon Without. For comparison, see C. L. Kingsford, "London in the Fifteenth Century," in his *Prejudice and Promise in Fifteenth Century England* (Oxford: Oxford University Press, 1925). For the cellarers' rentals, see C.U.L. Ms. Gg 4 4.

records it ended at the stone walls of the town. Indeed, this may well be the best statement on borough defenses in the later middle ages—a road which passed through what should have been solid wall, rather than a gate. Two major murages were granted early in the fourteenth century, but the necessary repairs were never completed.[18] Spinthilmillway was more narrow than the other roads cutting through the suburbs, and may well have been impassable for larger carts.

The most heavily used approaches to Bury were those running north and south, the town being on the major route between London and Norwich, the latter ranking for much of the later middle ages as the second city of the kingdom. Some of these roads terminated in East Gate, and eventually snaked their way to Norwich, but the most direct route was via Northgate Street. It passed through the borough at North Gate, by St. Saviour's Hospital and St. Thomas' Chapel, on the high ground between Tay and Babwell fens. Perhaps the marshy lands above the abbey were the reason that Northgate Street was the only road leading due north, for it was difficult to build and expensive to maintain, and in a chronic state of disrepair. Beyond Babwell Friary, Northgate forked in two directions, one going to Thetford and then to Norwich, the other to Mildenhall, and eventually to Ely and King's Lynn. As King's Lynn was the port most frequented by Bury merchants, the road was of major importance.

Five roads converged on Southgate Street at its bridge over the Linnet. Hennecoteway led to the southwest; it moved through South Field and Hardwick Heath, and went to Haverhill. East of Hennecoteway were Newtonway and Sydolvesmerway, the latter passed the Weeping Cross and seems to have been the most heavily travelled of all the banleuca's trunk roads. Two other roads, Rushbrookeway and Woolpitway, ran into South Gate from the southeast. Both led to the villages after which they were named—and were in turn called the Buryway—and then to Stow Market and Needham Market, and finally to Ipswich, the center of the East Suffolk urban region. Despite geographic problems of terrain, Bury could be reached in some fashion from every direction, and,

[18] C.P.R., Edward I, 1304, p. 227; C.P.R., Edward III, 1330, p. 526. Also, see H. L. Turner, *Town Defenses in England and Wales* (London: John Baker, 1971); and S. E. West, "Evacuation of the Town Defenses at Tayfen Road, Bury St. Edmunds," *P.S.I.*, xxxii, 1973.

by the standards of contemporary travel, had an excellent road
system, a necessity for an urban marketing center. The roads were
connected by what today might be called a "ring-road" network.
From the Southgate roads, Shakersway moved north to the con-
fluence of Bertonway and the Eastgate system, bisecting Norman
Meadow and East Field. The Southgate and Westgate roads were
in turn connected to Hardwickway, cutting through the wastes of
Hardwick Heath and South Field, with the almoner's barns on the
north. All were crucial to Bury's economic role as the distribution
center of West Suffolk.

Most of the 1295 rental concerns the area contained within the
town walls (Map 4). Bury was divided into five wards, one for each
gate (Map 5). Eastgate Ward was the smallest and poorest; it was
also most directly under the thumb of the abbot and the sacrist,
with wardship of the gates and tolls collections entirely in their
control. This was the result of geographic proximity to the abbey
complex, and probably explains the late medieval exodus of many
residents to the streets immediately outside the gate, where rents
were cheaper. Its major streets were Eastgate Street and *Le Mustow*.
Le Mustow was the first site of the town mootcourt; as the name
suggests, it was the stow, or place where the moothall stood. In the
eleventh and twelfth centuries, it was called Frenchman's Street,
perhaps a reflection of a Norman presence.[19] In 1065, Edward the
Confessor established a royal mint on it, with the mint remaining
active through the fourteenth century.[20] But, most important, *Le
Mustow*, along with the Horse Market in Southgate Ward, was home
to most of the banleuca's blacksmiths. A number of shops are mentioned in the 1295 survey, in various wills, and in the 1539 report
to the royal court of Augmentations.[21]

Southgate Ward was the oldest and, in the late thirteenth century,
richest ward in the borough. It was densely settled, and was industrial in addition to being residential. At its southern tip, between
the walls and the Linnet, were heavy concentrations of fullers' and
lavenders' mills, using the water necessary for production. There
were also open spaces at the southern extreme, including pasture

[19] Redstone, "St. Edmunds Bury," p. 7.
[20] Dugdale, iii, pp. 100-101. As late as 1314, Roger Rede, the mint's
moneyer, certified that he had coined £22,480 of bullion.
[21] L. J. Redstone, "First Ministers' Accounts of the Possessions of the
Abbey of St. Edmunds," *Suffolk Institute of Archaeology and Natural History*,
xiii, 3, 1909.

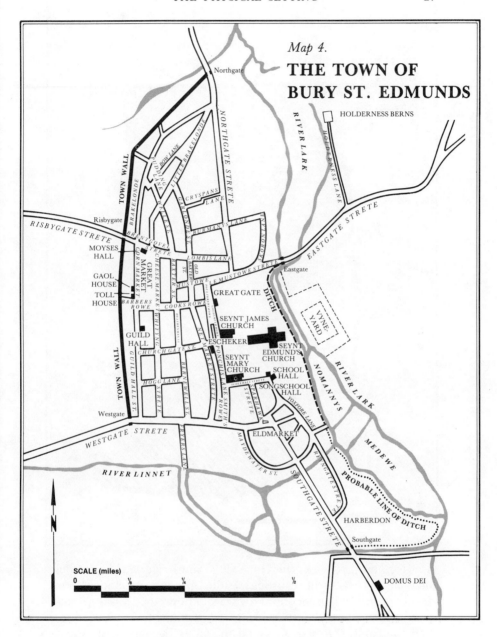

Map 4.

THE TOWN OF
BURY ST. EDMUNDS

HOLDERNESS BERNS

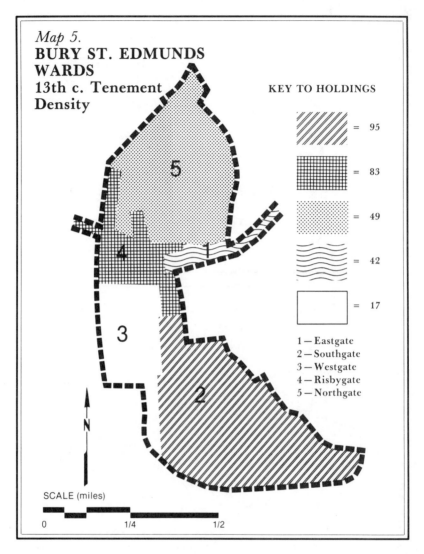

Map 5.
BURY ST. EDMUNDS WARDS
13th c. Tenement Density

KEY TO HOLDINGS

= 95

= 83

= 49

= 42

= 17

1 — Eastgate
2 — Southgate
3 — Westgate
4 — Risbygate
5 — Northgate

SCALE (miles)

0   1/4   1/2

and legume patches in the Haberdon. Southgate Ward was commercial, as well, and because it was the original Anglo-Saxon *burh* from which the late medieval town would develop, it was the one ward which came closest to being self-contained. At its northern end was Smiths' Row, also called the Churchgoval, or St. Mary's Goval. Running south were Ponch's Lane, alternatively known and famous as Goldsmiths' Row, and Schoolhall Street, initially named not for its two institutions of learning but after a famous local family.[22]

At the heart of Southgate Ward was the Horse or Old Market. Originally the Horse Market was the major, indeed the only, market in the borough. In the thirteenth century it was superseded by the Great Market, but it continued to have some shops which carried goods for local consumption. Running through the market was Southgate Street, Southgate Ward's major thoroughfare. From the earliest survey until Dissolution it was among the most heavily settled, widest, and most spacious avenues in Bury St. Edmunds. Many of its tenements had gardens or attached meadows, and the majority of the secular and ecclesiastical processions entering the town were channeled through it, en route to the abbey.[23] Other populous streets included Reyngate, Maydewater, and Yoxfore Lane, all running off Southgate Street. But the most exclusive road was the Sparhawk, between the Horse Market and Schoolhall Street. In 1295 its residents included a half dozen gentlemen, and its residences Coveshall, one of the largest mansions in Bury.

Westgate Ward was the least-developed part of late thirteenth century Bury. Its streets followed a well-laid grid plan, but had few tenants or even tenements. Much of it was held by the cellarer, whose full list of renters did not appear in the 1295 survey. But even acknowledging some degree of tenancy underenumeration it appears as a comparatively uninhabited corner of the borough at a time of optimum population density. Indeed, its principal attraction in the thirteenth century seems to have been the high quality of its arable; as there were areas in the suburbs with tenements, so parts of the borough proper contained farm land. Westgate Ward even had a small farm, Maydewater Manor, entirely within its jurisdiction, one of the few parts of town not held directly of the abbey.[24] Along with the far reaches of Southgate and Northgate Wards, Westgate provided open spaces within the borough boundaries.

[22] See below, p. 211.

[23] Dugdale, iii, pp. 113-114. There are records of royal visitations in the thirteenth and fourteenth centuries. Both times Southgate Street was cleaned and decorated, and lined with lute players, and Bury's secular and religious leaders gathered to greet the royal party. Southgate Street was known as the royal processional, the traditional route of the king.

[24] Redstone, "St. Edmunds Bury," p. 17; Lobel, *The Borough*, p. 17; C.C.R., Edward III, 1335, pp. 385-386.

The most densely settled part and commercial center of Bury was Risbygate Ward. It included the Great Market, which developed from the twelfth century onward and overtook the Horse Market as the major business district. Like Westgate Ward, it was built along a grid plan, and, while it did not quite match the popular conception of narrow and crooked urban lanes, it was clearly cluttered and congested, with smaller and more tightly packed tenements, messuages, and alleys than any other ward. The Great Market was a collection of smaller markets which formed rows of stalls within it. On its north side was the Brentgoval, with many of Bury's inns and hostels. To the west was the Corn Market, the source of meat and dairy goods. On the south were Barbers' and Cooks' Rows, the latter lined with cook shops, or small restaurants. The Great Market was at its busiest on the three weekly market days, usually Monday, Wednesday, and Saturday, when peasants from throughout West Suffolk brought in their produce, but most of its goods and services were available at all times.

Many of Bury's finest and most famous buildings overlooked the Great Market. On the west side was the Tollhouse. It was a large stone building used by the bailiffs to conduct town-abbey business and serving as the collection center for rents and tithings. Its bell tower was one of the finest in the borough, and formed a prominent part of Bury's skyline. A second notable structure was the borough gaol, next to the Tollhouse, directly facing the Corn Market.[25] A third was the old Guildhall, where the alderman, burgesses, and the Alderman's Guild conducted municipal business.[26] In the fourteenth century, town and abbey officials quarreled over just who was responsible for its upkeep; they were unable to agree, and it was neglected by both parties and fell into ruin. Consequently, the burgesses built a new Guildhall around the turn of the fifteenth

[25] The location of the gaol has been the subject of considerable debate. Some authorities claim that it was located on Gildhall Street, and others in the ground floor of Moyses Hall, but the best evidence suggests a site next to the Tollhouse. See: Redstone, "St. Edmunds Bury"; Lobel, *The Borough*; Lobel, "The Gaol of Bury St. Edmunds," *P.S.I.*, xxi, 3, 1933; and Ralph Pugh, *Imprisonment in Medieval England* (Cambridge: Cambridge University Press, 1968).

[26] Lobel and Redstone, as cited above, note 25, are the principal authorities. Also, see Margaret Statham, "The Guildhall of Bury St. Edmunds," *P.S.I.*, xxxi, 1967-70; and H.J.M. Maltby, "The Town Hall and the Guildhall," *The Archaeological Journal*, cviii, 1951.

century, and placed it on Gildhall Street, as far from the abbey as possible.[27]

The greatest building on the Great Market and in all of Bury St. Edmunds outside of the abbey complex was Moyses Hall, along the Brentgoval. Moyses Hall has been the subject of controversy. Some scholars, relying in part on its name, claim that it was initially a synagogue, built in the eleventh century. There was a Jewish community in high medieval Bury, and Moyses Hall is Norman in architectural style. Further, the Jewish community was quite prosperous, with several of its members serving the abbey as financiers. In the course of the twelfth century, however, they were accused of the ritual murder of a small boy named Robert, ultimately beatified, and in 1197 the entire community was expelled by Abbot Samson. But it is unlikely that a Jew ever lived there, and almost certain that the house never served as a synagogue. Bury's Jewry centered around Hatter Street, at one point called Heathenman's Street, a few blocks south from Moyses Hall.[28] Given the unfriendly environment in the town, a synagogue probably would not have been built outside the ghetto. Further, no synagogue would be constructed so that its east side, the side with the altar facing Jerusalem, would overlook Hog Hill, where much of the town's slaughtering was done. Finally, Moyses was a common East Anglian Christian surname. Since much of the speculation about Jewish ownership is predicated on name and location, the origins of

[27] C.C.R., Richard II, 1389. The Guildhall was of great symbolic value to the town, and a constant source of friction between the abbot and the alderman. The townsmen felt that, though they might build it, it was the abbey's obligation to maintain the fabric, as was generally the custom on all buildings on which rent was paid. The abbot disagreed; if the alderman was going to hold forth therein, it was the duty of his guild to repair it. It is likely that the construction of the new Guildhall on Gildhall Street was the result of the deterioration of the old in the late fourteenth century, when things had become so bad that the abbot found it necessary to secure a royal writ to support his side of the dispute. For further information, see below, pp. 186-187.

[28] Redstone, "St. Edmunds Bury," pp. 9-11, writes about this, as does Colin Platt, *The English Medieval Town* (London: Seeker and Warburg, 1976), p. 58. Also of use are: A. R. Edwardson, *Moyses Hall Museum* (Bury St. Edmunds: pamphlet, n.d.); Margaret E. Wood, "Moyses Hall: A Description of the Building"; and H.J.M. Maltby, "Moyses Hall: A History of the Building and the Museum Collections," both in *The Archaeological Journal*, cviii, 1951.

Moyses Hall probably lie elsewhere. Strong evidence suggests that it was built by a wealthy late eleventh-early twelfth century merchant of either Norman or other continental connections.[29] The name Moyses may not even have come from the original owner, but from a later tenant, perhaps Robert Mose, a prominent butcher active in thirteenth-century civic affairs.

Moyses Hall had both private and public functions. For much of the later middle ages it was held by the Kings, one of Bury's most illustrious families: they lived on the upper floors and leased out the rest.[30] It was used as a tavern and inn, and probably served as a customs house whenever the Tollhouse was being repaired.[31] Indeed, as Bury's grandest secular structure—a double facade with barn and gardens backing all the way to Pudding Lane—it could at one point or another have been used for just about any public occasion. It was expensive to maintain, even for wealthy mercers like the Kings, and rentals and communal functions would have helped defray high costs.[32] Moyses Hall was one of many opulent mansions in the borough, and part of Leland's favorable impression of sixteenth-century Bury must have been due to buildings like it, Paddock's Pole on Smiths' Row, the Boat on Southgate Street, the Pickerel on the Net Market, the Styewell at Risbygate, and several other famous houses scattered throughout the town.[33]

[29] Very little has been written about Bury's Jewish community. See Redstone, "St. Edmunds Bury"; and Jocelin.

[30] See below, pp. 145-147.

[31] Arnold, ii, pp. 349-350.

[32] See above, note 28.

[33] We have considerable information on the structure and architecture of Moyses Hall. It consisted of twin facades designed in Norman-Romanesque style, built primarily from famous, durable Norfolk flint. The will of Richard King describes it in great detail. Upon entrance through a large wooden door on the right side of the right facade was the Great Hall. It had a beamed, vaulted ceiling, and was the principal room in the house, occupying the entire floor. The first floor consisted of main chambers, guest chambers, a butlery, kitchen, bakehouse, and brewery. The second floor had rooms for family, servants, and storage; like all the great buildings in town, it had a steeple that formed part of Bury's skyline, and a clock tower, probably dating from the fifteenth century. It was an impressive building, and only select structures in the abbey complex rivaled it in the eyes of contemporaries. Among the other grand houses in the borough were: The George; The Hart; *Le Kynge*; The Woodhouse; The Cutler; The Barettys; Colet's House; Salterway; Swatens; The Saracen's Head,

The Great Market, with its fine townhouses and bustling trade stalls, was the heart of Risbygate Ward, but by no means its only important feature. Running due north was the Long Brakelond, an elegant street facing the northwest defenses of the borough. Extending west, through Risby Gate and into the suburbs was Risbygate Street, destined in the fifteenth century to become one of the most populous places in the entire banleuca. In the eastern part of the ward was a concentration of streets and lanes named for crafts still primarily settled on them in the thirteenth century. This area, stretching all the way to the Mustow, was industrial, as the Great Market was commercial. Lombs' Lane continued from the Brentgoval to Northgate Street. Directly south, the Mustow was crowded with breweries, taverns, and inns. Baxter Street ran north-south, as did the Net or Meat Market and Poulterers' Row; and south of them was Cooks' Row, also called High or Churchgate Street, running from the Great Market to the great gates of the abbey complex. Like Southgate Street, Cooks' Row was often used by both ecclesiastical and municipal authorities as a processional for important occasions.

Northgate Ward, the fifth of the borough, covered the most territory. Like Westgate, it was comparatively open and unsettled, had arable land which was actively and directly exploited, and may well have been used for hunting as late as the twelfth century.[34] Parts of the Long Brakelond and the Little Brakelond were in Northgate Ward, but its principal artery was Northgate Street. All these thoroughfares were sparsely settled in the thirteenth century, but the tenements were large and spacious and often had attached gardens, and many of the wealthiest and most influential burgesses lived there.[35] Bow and Skorun Lanes had no full-time inhabitants, but their tenements and meadows were in sufficient demand to

which for long periods of time was an inn; The Mayhews; and The Cotton Lane.

[34] Dugdale, *Monasticon*, iii, p. 102. Also, M. R. James, *On the Abbey of St. Edmunds Bury* (Cambridge: Deighton Bell, 1895).

[35] We have detailed plans of one of these houses. It had a large Great Hall, with two solars, two garderobes or counting rooms (indicating perhaps that it belonged at one point to a prominent merchant), a serving hall, and a kitchen. It also had a series of outhouses, including a brewery and a poultery. In an age when two rooms was considered adequate even for middling folk, the luxury of Bury's finest houses is one of the best indications of the prosperity of its great merchants.

carry the highest rents in the banleuca. Northgate was a mixture of large prestigious houses and productive farms. In 1295 it, like Westgate Ward, seemed to be a potential area for future borough growth.

Late-thirteenth-century Bury St. Edmunds was a busy, prosperous market center, approaching its medieval peak. The business center was in the northwest, as far as possible from the abbey complex, and contained most of the victuallers, clothiers, and craftsmen. There were two other commercial areas. One was a series of luxury shops across Goldsmiths' Row from the abbey, and the other in the Horse Market, still active in local victualling and livestock trades. Surrounding these commercial areas in Risbygate and Southgate Wards were the major industrial and residential parts of town. In effect, the richest and busiest parts of thirteenth-century Bury lay on a diagonal axis of relatively high ground, stretching from Risby Gate to the Southgate Street bridge over the Linnet.

TOPOGRAPHICAL CHANGES IN THE FOURTEENTH AND FIFTEENTH CENTURIES

The 1295 rental provides the fullest picture of late medieval Bury. Although nothing like it survives for the rest of the middle ages, there are a number of sacrists' rentals which give a more limited but still serviceable picture of the borough in the fourteenth and fifteenth centuries. The first of these is the rental of Thomas Rudham, sacrist late in the fourteenth century; as depicted in Map 6, it shows some significant changes.[36] Southgate Street was the most populous in town, followed by Goldsmiths' Row. But newer areas had developed along the borough's west walls, especially on Gildhall Street. Eastgate Street, Linendrapers' Row, *Le Mustow*, Whiting Street, Barbers' and Cooks' Row, the Mustow, the Long Brakelond, and Risbygate and Northgate Streets were also well settled. In essence, while the Risby Gate - Southgate Street axis remained heavily settled, most of the new growth was in Westgate Ward. Further, there was extensive external settlement along the approaches into

[36] The rental can be found in C.U.L. Ms. Ff 2 33. It is described in detail in Appendix A, and transcribed in Appendix C. Maps 5 through 9 are based on computer maps constructed by the computer graphics program SYMAP.

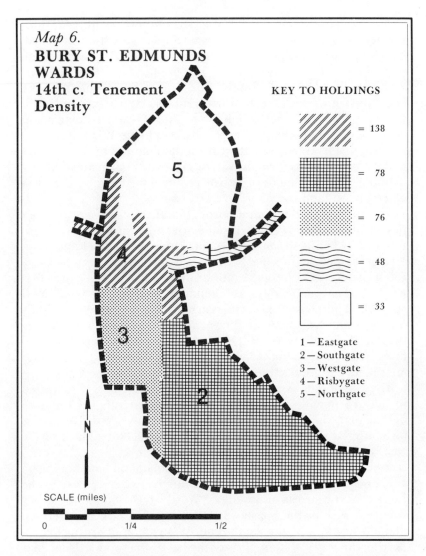

Map 6.
**BURY ST. EDMUNDS
WARDS**
14th c. Tenement
Density

KEY TO HOLDINGS

= 138

= 78

= 76

= 48

= 33

1 — Eastgate
2 — Southgate
3 — Westgate
4 — Risbygate
5 — Northgate

N

SCALE (miles)

0   1/4   1/2

town, just outside the borough gates. Because population had contracted rather than expanded from the late thirteenth century, the Rudham rental suggests a major geographic-demographic shift to newer, previously undeveloped properties. In part, this was a natural move to higher and newer lands in the west; in part, it was a flight from the high rent districts in well-established parts of the borough to cheaper areas on the periphery and outside the town walls. In relative terms, the old Anglo-Saxon *burh*, Southgate Ward was declining. Southgate and Reyngate Streets were still well settled, but had proportionally fewer tenants in relation to overall borough population in the 1380s than they had in the 1290s. The Old Market, Schoolhall Lane, and Smiths' Row, once prime properties, were beginning to decay. The Rudham rental is clearly incomplete; if more rentals from other major abbey officials survived they might alter the declining image of expensive Southgate Ward. But those few fragments which are extant from the holdings of the almoner and the pittancer confirm the sacrist's record.[37] In a pattern similar to those of many modern urban centers, the original core was emptying out and the periphery growing.

The process of peripheral borough and suburban growth continued, albeit at a slower pace, in the fifteenth century. The sacrist's rental of 1433 lists all *hadgoval* tenants, those persons holding property developed before the Norman Conquest. In effect, *hadgoval* was a pre-Norman burgage rent of one half penny per measure, per half year, per holding. By definition and because many merchants had purchased exemptions, it tends to underestimate slightly Westgate and Northgate holdings and to undercount substantially those in Risbygate Ward. But the *hadgoval* listings are accompanied by a partial, non-*hadgoval* rental, and if the inherent shortcomings are noted, the 1433 survey can be of considerable use.[38]

The rental data is presented by ward in Map 7, and reprinted in full in Appendix C. Southgate Ward, apparently beginning to decline in the fourteenth century, appears rejuvenated. Tenements on Southgate and Reyngate Streets and even the Horse Market were well settled, despite continuing high rents. Even here, however, there is a *caveat*; the houses in greatest demand on both Southgate and Reyngate Streets were on the southern extreme, close to the Linnet. Those streets in Southgate Ward which abutted the abbey complex, such as the Sparhawk and Schoolhall Street, suffered a marked decline. At the same time, Westgate and Northgate, especially the northwestern parts of the latter, the two wards farthest from the abbey and generally offering the lowest rents, registered

[37] For the pittancers' rentals, the best corrobative source, see B.M. Harl. Ms. 27.

[38] The rental can be found in B.M. Harl. Ms. 58, f. 22. It is described in detail in Appendix A, and transcribed in Appendix C. For more information on the nature of *hadgoval* rentals, see Lobel, *The Borough*, pp. 7-8, 54-55.

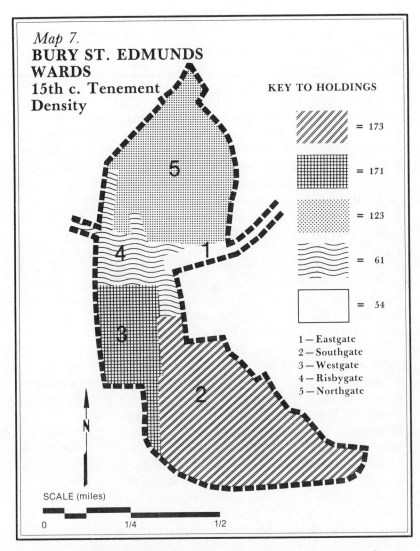

Map 7.
**BURY ST. EDMUNDS
WARDS**
15th c. Tenement
Density

KEY TO HOLDINGS

= 173

= 171

= 123

= 61

= 54

1 — Eastgate
2 — Southgate
3 — Westgate
4 — Risbygate
5 — Northgate

N

SCALE (miles)

0   1/4   1/2

the largest gains. Gildhall Street continued to be one of the fastest
growing parts of Bury, and probably would show even greater
growth if the Westgate returns for 1433 were complete. By contrast,
Eastgate Ward, small, compact, and literally under the shadow of
the abbey, registered fewer tenants than any part of the town. Its
only real expansion came on those parts of Eastgate Street without
the town walls. It is not possible to make definitive statements for

a one-hundred-year period on the basis of a single, incomplete rental, the very nature of which makes an accurate assessment of one ward, Risbygate, impossible. But the 1433 survey does indicate that the decline of Bury's central core was continuing apace.

This conception is reinforced by another topographical survey, the *relevia*, dating from 1353 to the 1539 Dissolution, and presented by ward in Map 8.[39] As with the sacrist's rental of 1433, it is not comprehensive for the entire borough. But if it is assumed that people on a given street died in numbers proportional to those who survived on the said streets, an index emerges showing changes through time. Westgate Ward had the largest number of *relevia* payers, followed by Southgate Ward. Both had their largest number of turnovers in the last seventy years of the *relevia*, when Bury's population was expanding. Northgate and Eastgate Wards had far less activity, while the returns for Risbygate are incomplete, since *relevia* is essentially a report of *hadgoval* tenants. Bearing this in mind, we seem to find that Bury's most active real estate lay near the borough's borders. A street-by-street analysis confirms this. Early in the survey, the largest number of fines appear for tenements around the Horse Market; toward the end, they occur on Gildhall, Churchgate, and Whiting Streets, and even around the Great Market (Appendix C). But most telling is the striking absence of *relevia* turnovers in the central part of the town, immediately to the west of the abbey complex. One of the great mysteries of the *relevia* and, indeed, of all the rentals, is the absence of rent-paying tenants from these streets, especially the Master Andrew and Cooks' Row. Perhaps this is the result of special privileges for tenants, or holdership of rights by unnamed external parties. But, as no records survive from any sources which mention large numbers of inhabitants in this segment of the borough, it is most likely that the central core of Bury St. Edmunds, the heart of the high medieval town, was largely unsettled in the later middle ages.[40]

[39] The rental is B.M. Harl. 58, f. 48. It is discussed in detail in Appendix A, and is transcribed in full in Appendix C.

[40] Surprisingly little has been written about this seemingly deserted part of town. Lobel, *The Borough*; A. Goodwin, *The Abbey of St. Edmundsbury* (Oxford: Basil Blackwell, 1931); Richard Yates, *The History and Antiquities of the Abbey of Bury St. Edmunds* (London: J. B. Nichols and Son, 1843); and other authorities do not discuss it.

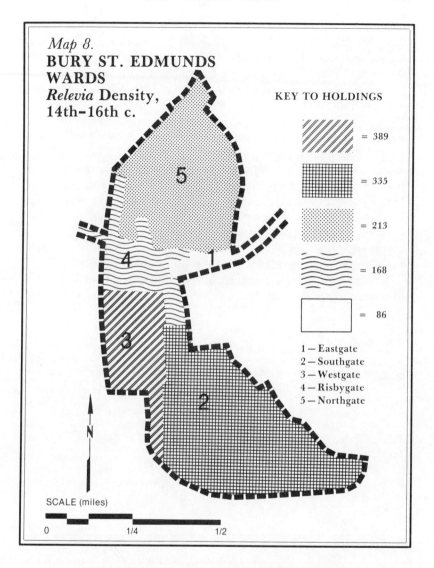

Map 8.
BURY ST. EDMUNDS WARDS
Relevia Density, 14th–16th c.

KEY TO HOLDINGS

= 389

= 335

= 213

= 168

= 86

1 — Eastgate
2 — Southgate
3 — Westgate
4 — Risbygate
5 — Northgate

SCALE (miles)

0   1/4   1/2

THE TOWN IN THE SIXTEENTH CENTURY

The final topographical pictures of Bury St. Edmunds come on the eve of Dissolution. There are two records: the 1523/24 Lay Subsidy and its anticipation; and the 1539 and 1553 borough rentals. The lay subsidy is of topographical interest because it gives a ward-by-ward assessment of wealth, with its most prosperous residents getting a tax discount if they paid their premiums early.[41] This provides information on the geographical distribution of the richest folk in town on the eve of the Reformation.[42] The data are presented in Table 1.1, and confirm the earlier assessment of the slow, rather graceful decline of Southgate Ward. It still had mansions and prominent residents, but by the 1520s had fallen well behind Risbygate in total wealth, and was passed by Westgate in the total assessment, if not in the anticipation. The occupations of those paying the anticipation suggest a reason for this demise. Southgate Ward had but a single representative from the "new money," the textile industries, which had propelled Bury to high ranking in the larger national subsidy. Most of the great wealth in the ward came from what might be described as "old money," that is, income derived primarily from property. Among Southgate's richest residents were one gentleman, three yeomen, and a bellfounder, bell-founding being a profitable business in an abbey town.[43]

Westgate Ward stood second in the total assessment and third in the anticipation, with its wealthiest denizens living on Gildhall

TABLE 1.1: THE LAY SUBSIDY OF 1523-1524 BY WARD

	Southgate	Westgate	Risbygate	Westgate	Eastgate
A. *Entire Sample*					
Total assessed	140	141	175	99	94
Total assessed over £10	15	12	12	8	8
Total collected	£38,3/4	£35,19/4	£63,4/6	£18,3/0	£13,18/6
B. *The Anticipation*					
Total paying	8	7	17	4	4
Total collected	£18	£20	£27,14/	10 marks	£11,13/4

[41] S.H.A. Hervey, *Suffolk in 1524: Being the Return for a Subsidy Granted in 1523, Suffolk Green Books*, x (Woodbridge, Suffolk: George Booth, 1910). For additional information, see below, Appendix A.

[42] The subsidy is used to assess the town's wealth below, pp. 124-125.

[43] The bellfounder, Thomas Chirche, was one of the wealthiest men in town. Given the connection suggested by Carlo Cipolla in his *Guns, Sails and Empires* (New York, Minerva Press, 1965), between bells and cannon founding, he may well have been a royal gunmaker.

Street. The ward had seven persons assessed over the £40 tax maximum, six of whom were merchants, as befitted a ward of rather "late" prosperity. Northgate and Eastgate Wards remained the poorest in town, despite the modest gains made by the former early in the fifteenth century. In Northgate Ward, four men were singled out in the anticipation, and reflected its continuing bucolic character. Two were gentlemen, one of whom, Thomas Eden, was assessed at £400, making him the wealthiest individual in Bury. Another was a yeoman, and the fourth the only merchant, a tanner engaged in the sale of finished leather goods. Eastgate Ward also had four residents wealthy enough to make the anticipation, all of whom drew the bulk of their income from landed sources.

The inhabitants of Risbygate Ward had the largest lay subsidy assessment and the highest number of individual participants. In a sense, this symbolizes the transition from Old to Great Market, and landed wealth to commerce and industry. The bulk of the ward's prosperity rested in the sale and production of textiles, with nine of the seventeen respondents of the anticipation being so characterized. Of the nine, four were mercers, all among the richest figures in Bury, four were drapers, and one a coverlet weaver. Beds and bedclothing were increasingly popular in the late fifteenth and sixteenth centuries, and it is not surprising that this newest entrepreneur should live alongside the Great Market. Of the rest of Risbygate's élite, three were widows drawing their incomes from property investments and one was a surgeon. The latter, Thomas Stacy, was assessed at £80, a level often attained by university-trained physicians but quite rare for provincial surgeons, who were ordinarily considered to be mere craftsmen, associating with barbers and occasionally even butchers.[44]

The final topographical records for Bury St. Edmunds are the 1539 and 1553 rentals.[45] After the Dissolution, Henry VIII granted what remained of the abbey's property and rentals to John Eyer, a gentleman, and his heirs. Fourteen years later this was sold to Sir John Holt, a prominent burgess. Through these combined records

[44] For discussion, see below, pp. 192-207. It has been suggested that the practice of medicine was "professionalized" in the late middle ages. See Vern L. Bullough, *The Development of Medicine as a Profession* (Basel: S. Karger, 1966); and Margaret Pelling and Charles Webster, "Medical Practitioners," in Charles Webster, ed., *Health, Medicine and Mortality in the Sixteenth Century* (Cambridge: Cambridge University Press, 1979).

[45] B.M. Harl. Ms. 58, f. 124. Also, see below, Appendix A.

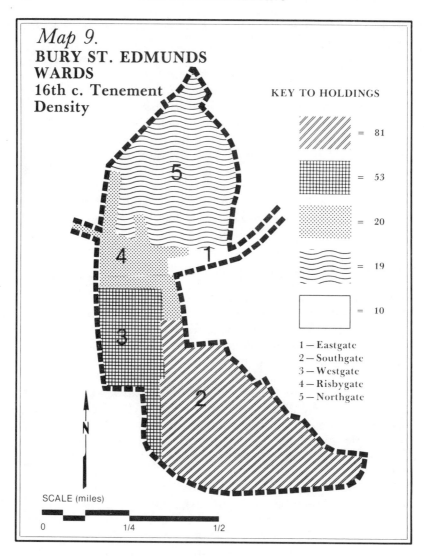

Map 9.
BURY ST. EDMUNDS
WARDS
16th c. Tenement
Density

KEY TO HOLDINGS

= 81

= 53

= 20

= 19

= 10

1 — Eastgate
2 — Southgate
3 — Westgate
4 — Risbygate
5 — Northgate

N

SCALE (miles)

0   1/4   1/2

comes the last picture of the late medieval borough's patterns of settlement.

The aggregate results are presented by ward in Map 9. In its last decades, the abbey lost control over most of the borough and suburbs. At a time when Bury's population was regaining its thirteenth-century peak, the number of holdings accountable in one form or another to St. Edmunds had declined to its lowest level since 1295.

This may well have been a reflection of the financial decline of the abbey from the mid 1520s, which forced it to sell its endowment outright in order to make ends meet. Most of the major streets show rent-paying tenants and tenements in proportions equal to those of earlier rentals, but at much diminished levels. Southgate and Westgate were the most densely settled wards and Eastgate the least so. Southgate and Reyngate Streets and the Horse Market in Southgate Ward, the Great Market and Risbygate Street in Risbygate Ward, Gildhall, Westgate, and Whiting Streets in Westgate Ward, along with the Long Brakelond and Eastgate Streets, had the largest numbers of rent-paying tenants. But all appear in far smaller figures than they did in earlier rentals, and it is likely that prosperous townsfolk, anxious to enter the ranks of landed *rentiers*, were buying up leases on tenements as quickly as the abbey offered them for sale.[46]

There is another image from these final rentals: considerable parts of the borough were in decay. As Bury expanded to the periphery of the old borough walls and beyond, and as newer properties were developed, older areas in the town, especially in Eastgate, the far eastern part of Risbygate and the northern tip of Southgate Wards, fell into ruin. The inner city began to rot as people moved to the outskirts of the borough and suburbs. The 1539 statement of the royal Court of Arrears lists dozens of properties, mostly in the town center, in so poor a condition that they could not be rented.[47] Special allowances had to be made for other abbey holdings, lest these properties too fall into complete disuse. The abbey tried to repair as much as it could, but being short of funds was able to do very little except sell tenements at whatever price could be gained.

Dilapidations were also of concern to the burgesses. It was one thing for unrented abbey property to deteriorate, but quite another for major municipal buildings or possessions held directly or even owned by townsmen to do the same. From the mid-fifteenth century onwards, concerted efforts were made by municipal authorities to

[46] See below, pp. 137-143 ff. Charles Phythian-Adams, *Desolation of a City; Coventry and the Urban Crisis of the Late Middle Ages* (Cambridge: Cambridge University Press, 1979), pp. 191-192, notes a similar movement of population from Coventry's central core to its outskirts. The reasons in Coventry, however, are very different.

[47] L. J. Redstone, "First Ministers' Account," p. 10, among many references.

channel charitable funds and activity into the repair of the town's fabrice. By and large, the civic aspects of this drive were successful. In 1467, for example, John Baret, one of Bury's greatest figures, declared in his will that: "Risbygate, the most ruinous of the town, be fixed with freston, brick, and arched and embattled with the image of Our Lady. If brick be no good, use calcyon [perhaps limestone] and mortar."[48] Risby Gate may have been the most ruinous, but it was not alone; from 1450 until well into the sixteenth century there were dozens of private bequests to repair all the borough gates. Efforts to improve Bury's road system met with similar success. Here was something dear to the hearts of the rich merchant benefactors; good transportation was essential for commerce. Between 1470 and 1520 money was provided to fix every road leading from Bury to the surrounding market towns, and, in 1511, a single prominent draper, John Parfay, provided sufficient cash to pave the entire road from South Gate to Ipswich.[49] Considerable attention was paid to the streets within the borough, and, in 1511, a good year for general road repair, all bridges spanning the Linnet were fixed and a civic road repair fund was established.[50]

Civic pride and private benevolence were also directed to the major buildings in town. The Tollhouse, the Guildhall, Moyses Hall, Paddock's Pole, the parish churches of St. James and St. Mary, were all repaired and embellished after 1450. The parish churches in particular proved to be favorite objects of pious charity. Both were completely restyled in the fifteenth and sixteenth centuries, with St. Mary's getting a clock and a belltower, the latter being used to sound vespers.[51] In addition to these donations, considerable expense and attention was focused on the repair of privately held property. Conversely, there were practically no bequests to repair parts of the abbey complex other than the church of St. Edmunds, and little evidence of abbey expenditure to fix municipal buildings,

---

[48] Baret's wills are reprinted in Tymms, pp. 15-43.

[49] Tymms, pp. 108-113.

[50] P.C.B.S.E., Mason, for the year 1512, provides a nice sampling.

[51] The most interesting bequest was that of John Parfay, whose will is cited above, in note 49. A wealthy draper, Parfay left funds so that the bells in St. James's tower would be rung every evening at vespers. One night, while outside the borough walls, Parfay lost his way in dense fog, and was able to stumble home by following the sounds of the bells, ringing curfew. As Parfay loved St. James's bells, so John Baret loved its clock. He provided a large endowment to ensure that it would be repaired whenever necessary.

including the Tollhouse or the parish churches. Perhaps more important, there is virtually no record of the abbey's allotting funds to fix its own house, or repair uninhabited or run-down properties in the borough. In all, it appears that, with the abbey's increasing financial difficulties, urban blight spread through the older and less desirable parts of town. This in turn reinforces our perspective of the topographical evolution of late medieval Bury St. Edmunds. Settlement began to branch out from the original Anglo-Saxon center in the thirteenth century to the northwest, and in the fourteenth century to the west, to the highest, driest part of the borough. There, rents were lower and tenements farther from the prying eyes and grasping tax reach of the abbey tax assessors. In the fifteenth and sixteenth centuries, parts of Southgate Ward were revived, but the focal points of the town had clearly moved to its corners. The periphery was flourishing, while areas near St. Edmunds were floundering. From the fourteenth century onward, the physical focal points of Bury moved away from the abbey—a major aspect of the rise of the secular community.

Chapter Two

————

THE DEMOGRAPHIC BASIS
FOR CHANGE

From the late 1930s, scholars have emphasized the importance of population movements and levels in influencing broader social and economic developments in pre-industrial England.[1] This was clearly the case in late medieval Bury St. Edmunds. Demographic changes in the fourteenth and fifteenth centuries contributed to major economic changes, which in turn helped to upset the existing social and political balance. Falling population, among other things, could mean diminished rent levels for *rentiers* like St. Edmunds Abbey, while rising population could spur domestic demand and provide a larger base of skilled industrial workers. Indeed, in many respects population movements proved to be the major catalyst in the rise of the secular community. In order to comprehend fully the scope and nuances of the transfer of power from abbey to town, it is essential to understand in detail the mechanics of population movements and their general implications.

Relatively good sources survive from which population can be studied.[2] They include: the 1377 Poll Tax; the 1522 military muster

---

[1] The historiography is extensive. The latest and in many ways best study is John Hatcher, *Plague, Population and the English Economy, 1348-1530* (London: Macmillan, 1977). Pages 81-91 list an annotated bibliography. A good case in microcosm is Charles Phythian-Adams, *Desolation of a City: Coventry and the Urban Crisis of the Late Middle Ages* (Cambridge: Cambridge University Press, 1979). A more extensive study of Bury's population is Robert S. Gottfried, "Bury St. Edmunds and the Populations of Late Medieval English Towns," *The Journal of British Studies*, Autumn, 1980.

[2] For details on the sources used in this chapter, see Appendix A. For

roll; abbey mortality lists from the Black Death; and probate and other testamentary records.[3] From them, town population can be estimated in the fourteenth and early sixteenth centuries, and trends extrapolated for the period in between. The 1377 Poll Tax purported to list all men and women over age 12, and assess them at a rate of 4 pence per head. This tax apparently took most folk by surprise; while the rate must have been oppressive for a family with three or four children of age, experts agree that it was paid by virtually all of those on whom it was imposed. Unfortunately, since the individual returns from Suffolk are lost, the tax assessors' aggregate statistics must be used.[4] Dividing the total sum paid by 4 pence yields a population of 2,445 persons, in theory all Bury's teenage and adult men and women. If the individual returns survived, definitive statements could be made about gender ratios; since they do not, further extrapolation is necessary. Twentieth-century ratios stand at 105 at birth, that is, 105 males to 100 females; gradually approach parity during adolescence; and then begin to

details of the method, see Robert S. Gottfried, *Epidemic Disease in Fifteenth Century England* (New Brunswick, N.J., Rutgers University Press, 1978); Leicester: Leicester University Press and Gottfried, "Population, Plague and the Sweating Sickness: Demographic Movements in Late Fifteenth Century England," *Journal of British Studies*, Fall 1977.

[3] For details on the Poll Tax, see: M. L. Beresford, *Lay Subsidies and Poll Taxes* (Canterbury, Phillimores, 1963); J. C. Russell, *British Medieval Population* (Albuquerque, N.M.; University of New Mexico Press, 1948); Charles Creighton, *A History of Epidemics in Britain*, i (Cambridge: Cambridge University Press, 1894); Charles Oman, *The Great Revolt of 1381* (New York: Haskell House Reprints, 1968, 2nd ed.); and several studies in H. C. Darby, ed., *New Historical Geography of England* (Cambridge: Cambridge University Press, 1973). For the muster roll, see below, Appendix A. The muster manuscript, B.M. Stowe Ms. 570, f. 165, has been transcribed by Edgar Powell, "The Muster Rolls of the Territorials in Tudor Times," *P.S.I.*, xv, 1918; and Edgar Powell, same title and journal, slightly changed, xvi, 1918. For details about abbey mortality, see Carson Ritchie, "The Black Death at St. Edmunds Abbey," *P.S.I.*, xxviii, 1956. Also of interest is the use of the Canterbury Cathedral Priory obituary list in Hatcher, *Plague, Population*, pp. 17-18 and 29-30. A complete list of the will registers can be found below, pp. 291-292.

[4] Oman, *The Great Revolt*, pp. 159-161; Beresford, *Lay Subsidies*, pp. 21-22.

shift heavily in favor of females through time. Most scholars believe that exorbitant maternal mortality, perhaps as high as 20 percent, would have altered this in pre-industrial societies, giving a predominance of males until average age of female menopause, sometime in the late thirties or early forties. After age 50, greater male mortality resulted first in parity and thereafter in female dominated gender ratios. Using the 1377 individual returns from those regions in which they survive allows more precision. In rural areas, the ratios favored males, with aggregate figures close to the 105 found at birth. Urban ratios, however, were more varied. For London, they were 107, for Oxford 111, for Rochester 110; for two eastern towns rather like Bury, Kingston-upon-Hull and Colchester, they were 93 and 95. The closest of these to Bury St. Edmunds in function and location was Colchester, and since it had 2,995 taxpayers in 1377, its gender ratios will be taken as those most approximate to Bury.[5] Accordingly, a Poll Tax population of 2,445 adults yields 1,138 men and 1,307 women.

From this base, it is possible to estimate the proportion of population under age 12, male and female. As with the consideration of gender ratios, most of this must be extrapolated, beginning with the assumption that pre-pubescent sex ratios were about 105. In contemporary societies which are not fully industrialized, the proportion of those under 12 is often extremely high, ranging in some cases to 50 percent and even more of total population, a result of a very high birth rate, well into the 40s/1,000.[6] For late medieval England, however, a rate of even 40/1,000 is too great. Fertility was probably at a pre-industrial low for at least a century after the Black Death—perhaps as low as the mid 20s/1000.[7] Hence, percentages of children from modern "Third World" populations cannot be applied. A potential source of information is the Coale-Demeny model life tables. In some circumstances they allow for total reconstruction of population from selected fragments of demo-

[5] All of the above data have been taken from Russell, *British Medieval Population*, pp. 161-201.

[6] There are many accounts. See E. A. Wrigley, *Population and History* (New York: McGraw-Hill, 1969), pp. 161-201.

[7] *Ibid.* Also, see Louis Chevalier, "Towards a History of Population," in D. V. Glass and D.E.C. Eversley, eds., *Population in History* (London: Edward Arnold, 1965), pp. 339-353.

graphic data.[8] But for late medieval England they too present serious problems. The tables are based on stable or stationary
populations, a condition which never existed in late medieval Suffolk. Further, all the data are taken from figures derived after 1870,
and Hollingsworth has shown how these sources differ from those
from 1500 to 1700, to say nothing of even earlier populations.[9]
None of the Coale-Demeny tables, north, south, east, or west, can
be said to describe accurately later medieval England. It is possible
to extrapolate life tables with birth rates in the mid 30s/1,000 and
death rates in the high 30s/1,000, the best estimates for the fourteenth and fifteenth centuries, but to do so requires considerable
manipulation.[10] In effect, modelling attempts for medieval Bury

[8] A. J. Coale and Demeny, Paul, *Regional Model Life Tables and Stable
Populations* (Princeton: Princeton University Press, 1966).

[9] T. H. Hollingsworth, *Historical Demography* (Ithaca, N.Y.: Cornell University Press, 1969), pp. 339-353.

[10] Despite the reservations expressed in the text, extensive attempts at
modelling based on the Coale-Demeny tables were made. In efforts to find
the portion of the male population under age 12, data were taken from
those North and South tables, which had death rates in the mid to high
30s, and birth rates in the high 20s to mid 30s. The North tables that were
used included: mortality level 5, R = -5, R = -10; mortality level 4, G.R.R. = 2,
G.R.R. = 2.25; mortality level 5, G.R.R. = 1.75, G.R.R. = 2.00. The South
tables, which seemed most appropriate for demographic conditions in late
medieval Bury, included: mortality level 3, R = -5, R = -10; mortality level
4, R = -5; mortality level 2, G.R.R. = 2.50; mortality level 3, G.R.R. = 2.00,
G.R.R. = 2.25; mortality level 4, G.R.R. = 2.00, G.R.R. = 2.25, mortality
level 5, G.R.R. = 2.00. The proportions of males under age 14 ranged from
24.46 percent to 32.26 percent; and the portions of males over age 60
from 7.22 percent to 12.25 percent. The best set of data appears to come
from the South tables, mortality level 4, G.R.R. = 2.00. It provides a
birth rate of 30.4, a death rate of 36.9, a growth rate of -6.5, average age
of 31.7, life expectancy of 32.9, proportion of males over age 60 of 11.81
percent, and the proportion of males under age 14 at 26.49 percent. All
but the very last figure seem to fit to some degree with the most informed
estimates of fifteenth-century demographic conditions, but there are too
many problems with the Coale-Demeny figures to allow for their general
application. In addition to the objections discussed above, I have taken as
the starting points not bits of hard data but rather subjective estimates as
to probable birth and death rates. The major difficulty in using the Coale-
Demeny life tables seems to rest with the birthrates, which are too low in
many of the tables in which the deathrates are about right, and with infant

St. Edmunds are sufficiently subjective to be no more convincing than traditional methods of estimating medieval population levels and differentials.

J. C. Russell has proposed a denominator which helps to calculate Bury's total population in the late fourteenth century. He believed that 33 percent of the population was under age 12, providing an overall figure of 3,668.[11] Given contemporary information about birth rates in industrializing nations and the dismally low evidence of replacement ratios to be presented, Russell's suppositions for numbers of children seem reasonable. It is likely, however, that his estimates of total population are too low. First, immigration into Bury must have been a crucial factor in influencing overall demographic levels. Many recent immigrants to Bury probably did not have sufficient movable wealth to be included; this segment of the population might conservatively be placed at about 5 percent.[12] Second and even more important is the question of under-enumeration in the tax rolls. Despite the strong convictions of many scholars that the Poll Tax was comprehensive, some segments of town population must have evaded the count, or simply been too

mortality levels, which are probably also too low, because of the mitigating effects of modern medical techniques, even in the poorest nineteenth and twentieth century societies. All of this, coupled with the dramatic fluctuations in pre-industrial mortality caused by disease and famine, plus the general rule that an urban area defeats the entire assumption of a closed population, has convinced me not to rely too heavily on the Coale-Demeny models.

[11] Russell, *British Medieval Population*, pp. 142, 284. Russell's figures have been the subject of considerable controversy; Postan, Titow, and others suggest that Russell makes early errors of under-enumeration and then carries them through in his final calculations. I have reworked Russell's first set of data, and generally agree with his results; I have not carried his figures beyond my initial calculations. The Postan-Titow position is summed up in J. Z. Titow, *English Rural Society* (London: George Allen, 1969), pp. 65-99. Others attempting Poll Tax estimates include: Oman, *The Great Revolt*, pp. 158-166; Creighton, *History of Epidemics*, i, pp. 200-201; and M. D. Lobel, "A Detailed Account of the 1327 Rising at Bury St. Edmunds and the Subsequent Trial," *P.S.I.*, xxl, 3, 1933, in which she misleadingly accepts the 1377 Poll Tax as complete for the entire town population.

[12] Phythian-Adams, *Desolation of a City*, p. 235, believes that Coventry had minimal immigration in the late fifteenth and sixteenth centuries.

poor to pay anything; 10 percent is a minimal figure.[13] Hence, Russell's estimates can be padded by a modest 15 percent, giving an overall population of 4,219. Since this figure is a gross estimate, it might well be rounded off to 4,200.[14]

If one builds further on unstable foundations, the 1377 estimates can be extended back into the early fourteenth century. The 4,200 figure, whatever the degree of its accuracy, was reduced from the 1340s by the Black Death, the *pestis secunda* of 1361-1362, and subsequent plague epidemics in 1369 and 1374. If pre-plague population can be estimated, it will provide some conception of Bury St. Edmunds at a demographic peak. Useful here is a mortality record from the abbey during the Black Death. On 19 January, 1351, Pope Clement VI granted Abbot William de Bernham permission to ordain as priests ten monks under age 25.[15] The bull states that this was the result of high mortality and the resulting shortage of monks due to plague. In 1260, St. Edmunds had 80 monks and 21 chaplains. In 1381, after several epidemics, this had fallen to 47 monks. According to the report, 40 were killed by the Black Death alone, making morbidity about 50 percent. This is an enormous rate, and, although it confirms the older estimates made by Jessop, considerable caution must be used before applying it to the larger town population.[16] Could half the inhabitants of Bury have succumbed to the Black Death alone? Perhaps; corroborating evidence survives from the abbot's rural estates, indicating that the death rate on certain surrounding manors reached 60 percent.[17] Further, topographical and archeological evidence, some of which was presented in Chapter 1, show that large numbers of tenements in the central core of Bury were deserted and in ruin by the early fifteenth century.[18] As was the case with town population for 1377, a cautious estimate is probably best for 1347. If the monastic figures

---

[13] The 10 percent is a "traditional" figure. See the articles in Darby, ed., *New Historical Geography.*

[14] All of the estimates have been taken very conservatively. They are crude and subject to scrutiny, but such errors as do exist are probably on the low side.

[15] Carson Ritchie, "The Black Death," pp. 50-53.

[16] A. J. Jessop, "The Black Death in East Anglia," in his *The Coming of the Friars* (London: T. F. Unwin, 1889, pp. 166-261.)

[17] Bacon, 21.

[18] See above, pp. 44-45. Also, see Phythian-Adams, *Desolation of a City,* pp. 191-193.

of 1381, which include recruitment, are applied with their proportional losses to town figures for 1377, which include supplemental migration, the 1347 population comes to about 7,150, which means a population loss of over 40 percent in a period of three decades. This figure, while taken rather conservatively—or heroically, as some might argue—is still far higher than any other estimate of Bury's pre-plague population.

There is no evidence from which total town population can be estimated with any degree of precision for the next 150 years, until the 1522 military muster. Within the franchise of Bury St. Edmunds, a total of 6,476 men were presented, with 2,900 said to be able, and 543 ultimately selected for service. The discrepancy between the 6,476 and those considered able provides some assurance as to the completeness of the male sample, but there are still major problems. The first and most difficult concerns geographic delineation; what was meant by franchise? In some circumstances, franchise was tantamount to liberty; if this were so the 1,522 military muster would have covered most of West Suffolk, as shown in Map 10.[19] But, given the description of the muster, which discusses separately men from other West Suffolk hundreds like Babergh and Cosford, this was probably not the case for the Bury franchise early in the sixteenth century.[20] Bury's franchise was clearly more than the borough, and probably more than the banleuca, Thingoe and Thedwastrey Hundreds, but no clear, concise contemporary explanations or definitions of it survive. The only alternative is to use the work of constitutional authorities such as Redstone, Cam, Lobel, and others, and proportions of will makers in the borough and its surrounding parishes to try to get a more precise definition. On this basis, borough population will be calculated at 25 percent of the franchise total of 6,476, yielding a sample of 1,619 males between 16 and 60 in the borough proper.[21] The portion of men over

[19] For example, see: S.F.C. Milson, ed., Pollock and Maitland, *The History of English Law*, i (Cambridge: Cambridge University Press, 1968), pp. 571-584, 642-667; and T.F.T. Plucknett, ed., Taswell-Langmead's *English Constitutional History*, 11th ed. (London: Sweet and Maxwell, 1960), pp. 20-21.

[20] B.M. Stowe Ms. 570, f. 165.

[21] For this crucial point in the text, fundamental to the entire sixteenth-century method of calculation, my system is rather haphazard. The following literary and narrative accounts have been used: Lobel, *The Borough*; L. J. Redstone, "The Liberty of St. Edmunds," *P.S.I.*, xv, 1914; Helen Cam,

60 can be calculated in rough fashion from the model life tables; they add approximately 9 percent and bring the total to 1,765.[22] But if the 1,619 men are accepted as accurate, two additional familiar problems remain: what was the gender ratio, and, more important, what proportion of the population was under age 16?

Gender ratios are a greater obstacle in 1522 than they were for the 1370s. No individual returns survived for the later period, as they had for the earlier. And the issue of the under-16s remains as before. Should model life tables be used, and, if so, which ones; or is it best to rely on more traditional "informed" scholarly estimates. The problems have been partially worked out by Cornwall in his analysis of the population of Rutland from the 1522 muster and the 1523-1524 Lay Subsidy.[23] After extensive argument, he settled on a sex ratio of 100, under-enumeration at 10 percent, and an under-16 population of 40 percent. I will follow suit. If one adheres to the assumption of 1,619 adult males in Bury, the 1522 borough population works out to be 5,438. This figure, like that for 1347, is far higher than any previous scholarly estimate; because of the tenuous nature of the franchise-borough ratio estimates, it must be treated with considerable caution.[24] But, however impre-

Liberties and Communities in Medieval England, (New York: Barnes and Noble, 1963); Helen M. Jewell, *English Local Administration* (New York: Barnes and Noble, 1972); and H. E. Butler, ed., *The Chronicle of Jocelin of Brakelond* (New York: Oxford University Press, 1949), specifically pp. xxiv-xxvi. A comparative survey was also made from wills registered in the Peculiar Court of Bury St. Edmunds, and wills registered in the Archdeaconry Court of Sudbury, perhaps an area somewhat smaller than the "franchise" in question. The archdeaconry wills stand in relation to the borough wills at a ratio of about 5 to 1. From the narrative sources, especially L. Redstone, I have somewhat subjectively decided that the borough represented about 30 percent of the total franchise population. The final figure of 25 percent is a compromise between the testamentary and the literary figures. The shortcomings of such a procedure, especially in a study that has pretence towards empirical method, are obvious, but no other, more satisfactory procedure was worked out. If the estimate of 25 percent is incorrect, it will apply, of course, only to the 1520s' population estimate.

[22] See above, note 10.

[23] Julian Cornwall, "English Country Towns in the 1520s," *Ec.H.R.*, 2nd series, xv, 1962, pp. 54-69; and his "English Population in the Early Sixteenth Century," *Ec.H.R.*, 2nd series, xxiii, 1970, pp. 32-44.

[24] Peter Clark and Paul Slack, *English Towns in Transition, 1500-1700,*

TABLE 2.1: ESTIMATES OF BURY ST. EDMUNDS' POPULATION

Year	Gross Population Estimates	% Change from 1347
1347	7,150	—
1377	4,200	−41.3
1522	5,438	−30.0

cise the gross figure may be, there is a clear upward trend which represents a considerable demographic resurgence from the post-plague nadir.

Gross population cannot even be estimated with certainty for any other points in the later middle ages, but, by using the mortality, nuptiality, replacement ratio, and migration data from the testamentary records, supplemented by evidence from the abbot's manors, secular trends of demographic movements can be established. Initial data come from the 1340s and 1350s, from the rural estates of the abbey. Manorial evidence does not yield total population and applies primarily to the surrounding villages rather than to Bury itself, but through entrance fines and the amount of arable cultivated in given seasons, certain trends emerge. In Redgrave, traditionally one of the abbot's most profitable manors, cultivated acreage dropped from 320 in 1340 to 240 by 1349.[25] Further, this is just the tip of the iceberg; it is likely that peasants who survived the first onslaughts of plague took advantage of depopulation to enlarge their patrimonies. Average holding size illustrates this. Before 1348 it was falling dramatically, while after the Black Death it increased.[26] The Redgrave records from 1349 show a general

(Oxford: Oxford University Press, 1976), p. 83, estimates a 1520 population of 3,550. Their sources and methods are not discussed. More detailed is the analysis of J.H.C. Patten, "Population Distribution in Norfolk and Suffolk During the Sixteenth and Seventeenth Centuries," *The Institute of British Geographers*, lxv. 1975, p. 49. He too picks 3,550, and it may be that Clark and Slack have used his data. Phythian-Adams, *Desolation of a City*, pp. 12-14, places Bury's 1520 population at 4,000 to 5,000, and ranks it among England's ten most populous provincial towns. He uses tax data that I have found to be unreliable.

[25] Bacon, 240.
[26] *Ibid.*, 21.

shortage of tenants on arable land, a condition which was to be endemic for the next 130 years, and a crude estimate of demographic losses from court rolls in 1342, 1345, 1347-1349, and 1351 indicates a fall in tenants of close to 60 percent.[27] In all, the manorial data suggest that the population of Bury St. Edmunds peaked sometime late in the thirteenth or early in the fourteenth century, probably dipped during the famines of the 1310s and 1330s, but came back in the 1340s to reach levels close to the highs of a generation earlier.

Evidence from the abbey's manors shows a fall in population from the mid-1350s into the mid-fifteenth century. Data from Redgrave Manor indicate a continued withdrawal from cultivation of the lord's demesne in 1369, 1390 and 1420, with a small respite in the 1430s, followed again by retrenchment and decline in the 1440s and 1450s. Records of abandoned property survive from 1413, 1418, 1423, and 1431—records which have counterparts within Bury St. Edmunds itself.[28] None of these results is definitive; there are many agrarian economic explanations, including enclosure and changes in husbandry patterns. But corroborative evidence is replete with references to continual plague epidemics right down to 1479-1480, and the overall impression from the manorial documents is of late-fourteenth and early-fifteenth-century population decline.

The rural Bacon evidence can help to establish long-term trends, but to get information from within the borough itself it is necessary to turn to the wills. There are several ways in which they can be exploited. At first glance, it seems plausible simply to count raw totals of probates from 1354 to 1530, and make generalizations from them or their logarithmic graphs (Graph 2.1). But because the wills represent only a portion of the adult population, a better strategy is to turn to the various ratio measures of mortality, fertility, and nuptiality, which rely on the completeness of each individual will rather than on their completeness for the entire population. Some sense of secular trends comes from parent-child replacement ratios, indirect evidence for net replacement ratios.[29]

[27] *Ibid.*, 32, 39, 351, 369, 380.
[28] See above, pp. 34-38.
[29] An interesting method of figuring replacement ratios is Phythian-Adams, *Desolation of a City*, p. 231. My purpose is to figure trends, and not present absolute numbers.

TABLE 2.2: MALE REPLACEMENT RATIOS

	n	% Will R.R.	% Distribution of Progeny				
			0	1	2	3	4+
A. *Entire Sample/All Males*							
1354-1530	2,116	47	68.0	20.3	9.2	2.2	.4
1354-1400	354	42	69.2	21.8	7.0	1.7	.3
1401-1440	373	45	70.8	17.8	8.8	2.0	.6
1441-1450	142	46	67.6	21.1	9.2	2.1	—
1451-1460	104	46	65.6	25.6	6.7	2.2	—
1461-1470	131	37	74.8	15.3	7.5	2.3	—
1471-1480	229	43	69.9	19.7	7.9	2.6	—
1481-1490	49	64	69.7	15.2	3.0	9.1	3.0
1491-1500	149	50	67.3	19.0	10.2	2.7	.7
1501-1510	198	64	59.3	20.6	16.6	3.5	—
1511-1520	149	58	65.8	17.4	12.1	2.7	1.3
1521-1530	238	47	62.9	28.9	6.9	—	.7
B. *Males/Male Progeny*							
1354-1530	1,713	48	67.3	21.3	8.9	1.9	.6
1354-1400	293	45	67.5	22.7	7.5	2.0	—
1401-1440	297	45	70.5	18.3	8.6	1.8	.4
1441-1450	118	48	66.9	20.3	10.2	2.5	—
1451-1460	82	44	64.8	28.2	5.6	1.4	—
1461-1470	106	38	74.8	15.1	8.5	1.9	—
1471-1480	192	44	65.8	20.8	7.8	2.6	—
1481-1490	39	69	65.4	19.2	3.8	7.7	3.8
1491-1500	110	56	65.1	19.3	11.0	3.7	.9
1501-1510	155	58	59.6	23.7	16.0	.6	—
1511-1520	117	57	65.0	18.8	12.0	2.6	1.7
1521-1530	204	44	64.4	28.9	5.9	.7	—
C. *Females/Male Progeny*							
1354-1530	403	46	70.8	16.6	8.7	3.7	.3
1354-1400	61	27	78.0	16.9	5.1	—	—
1401-1440	76	44	71.4	8.7	2.9	—	—
1441-1480	122	39	74.7	14.5	7.2	3.6	—
1481-1520	130	63	65.0	15.7	12.0	6.4	.7

TABLE 2.3: FEMALE REPLACEMENT RATIOS

	n	% Will R.R.	Testators with no Daughter
A. *Entire Sample/All Females*			
1354-1530	2,116	36	76.4
			79.8
1354-1400	354	29	79.8
1401-1440	373	27	80.5
1441-1450	142	32	80.3
1451-1460	104	30	82.2
1461-1470	131	35	74.0
1470-1480	229	38	75.1
1481-1490	49	52	78.8
1491-1500	149	35	77.6
1501-1510	198	58	63.3
1511-1520	149	43	73.7
1521-1530	238	47	73.0
B. *Males/Female Progeny*			
1354-1530	1,713	35	76.8
1354-1400	293	29	79.3
1401-1440	297	23	82.1
1441-1450	118	27	83.1
1451-1460	82	32	81.7
1461-1470	106	37	74.5
1471-1480	192	36	77.1
1481-1490	39	54	76.9
1491-1500	110	36	76.1
1501-1510	155	58	62.2
1511-1520	117	41	74.4
1521-1530	204	42	74.8
C. *Females/Female Progeny*			
1354-1530	403	43	73.7
1354-1400	61	31	81.4
1401-1440	76	41	73.9
1441-1480	122	39	71.1
1480-1520	130	54	71.4

Graph 2.1
Graphed Testamentary Mortality, 1390-1530

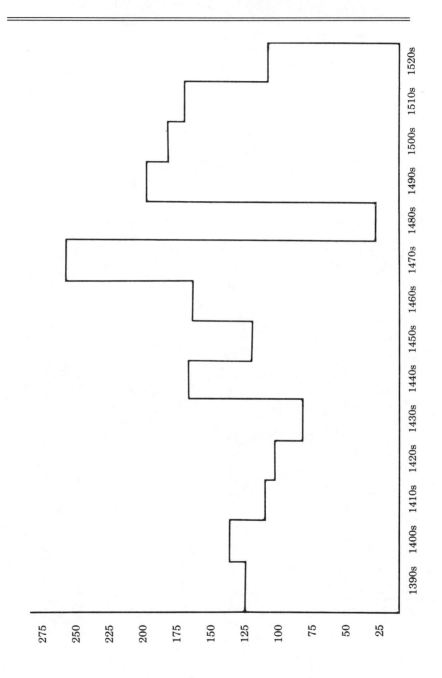

Data for male testators, presented in Table 2.2, show strikingly low figures. From 1354 to 1530, the proportion of all male testators to all sons listed in the wills was a meager 47 percent. If this measure is accurate for generations measured at or about the same age, it means that less than half the adult males in Bury St. Edmunds produced aggregate numbers of sons to follow them. The female ratios, presented in Table 2.3, are even lower, a paltry 37 percent. Much of the latter is the result of under-enumeration, but, in the best of circumstances, given the gender ratios described above, female replacement figures could not have been much higher than those for males. When selected segments from any of the samples are surveyed, the replacement ratios rise; gentlemen and wealthy merchants, for example, have ratios slightly over 60 percent. But even these figures are far below the replacement level, and their lowness is corroborated by outside, non-testamentary evidence taken from manorial evidence.[30] In the period 1384 to 1387, court rolls from Thorney Manor indicate that over half the population died without either male or female heirs.[31] This pattern was repeated in the fifteenth century from 1414 to 1422, and is made more noteworthy by the fact that rural ratios were ordinarily higher than their urban counterparts.[32] Replacement ratios were suffi-

[30] Some assessment on fertility differentials can be made from the indirect evidence of replacement ratios when surveying diverse sexual, occupational, and socio-economic sub-groups within the sample. For all the groups, the most striking feature is their low level. For example, the ratio for all male testators to all male progeny was: for gentry, 60; for drapers, grocers, and mercers, 61; for textile workers, 56; for blacksmiths and bakers, 60; for small shopkeepers, 56. The ratio for all male testators to all female progeny was: for gentry, 50; for drapers, grocers, and mercers, 47; for textile workers, 45; for blacksmiths and bakers, 38; for small shopkeepers, 42. In decennial runs for these and other groups, the highest replacement ratio figures were 82 percent for males and 61 percent for females. The distribution of sons was consistently low, and numbers of families with two or more sons was never higher than 20 percent. The merchants of Bury St. Edmunds, the social, economic and political élite of their community, suffered from the same problems of biological attrition as did the lesser folk, and their peers in London. See S. L. Thrupp, *The Merchant Class of Medieval London* (Chicago: University of Chicago Press, 1948), pp. 191-206; and Phythian-Adams, *Desolation of a City*, pp. 221-237, for comparative figures. Phythian-Adam's data are strikingly low.

[31] Bacon, 27, 29.

[32] Gottfried, *Epidemic Disease*, pp. 187-204.

Graph 2.2: MARRIAGE AND FERTILITY RATES.

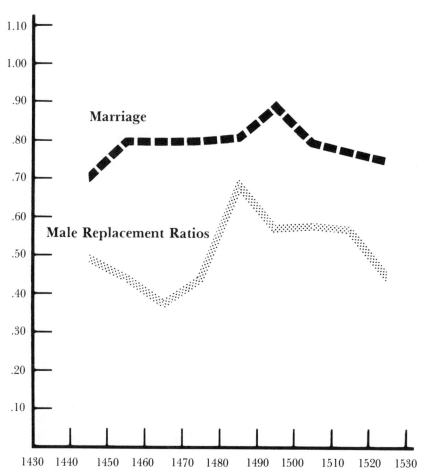

ciently depressed, whatever the death rates might have been, to make migration essential in bolstering Bury's overall population levels.

Despite their low levels—perhaps artificially so—a sense of long-term demographic trends can be gained from the replacement ratios. Graph 2.2 shows them, along with the proportion of the population ever married, and indicates a significant secular trend. From the mid-1460s replacement ratios began a steady ascent, which became rather marked in the 1480s, and continued at a relatively high level through the first two decades of the sixteenth century. The scope of this upturn is quite modest; at its peak, only two-thirds of the testamentary sample produced male offspring, and even in the most élite samples the ratios did not reach the unity replacement mark of 100, or even 85. Modal numbers of sons never approached 1, and only in the 1520s did the numbers of families with no male heirs fall under 60 percent. Multiple-son households also remained low, a tiny segment of the larger testamentary sample. But the upward trend toward the end of the fifteenth century is notable, even for a "secondary" demographic factor like fertility. Further, it is clear from the nuptiality ratios, presented in Table 2.4, that the proportions of the population which married did not vary significantly with the replacement ratios. As Graph 2.2 indicates, marital rates remained stable through most of the period 1440 to 1530, with the single, exceptional shortlived increase in the 1490s coming over a decade after the peaking of male replacement ratios.[33] And, while it can only be approximated, age of first marriage for females also seemed to have remained steady throughout the period.[34] Hence, if falling mortality levels can be established

[33] *Ibid.*, pp. 175-183, provides more information on the relationship between marriage and fertility in fifteenth-century East Anglia. Marriage was clearly the accepted social norm for craftsmen, wage workers, and merchants alike. Two *banna matrimonalia* survive in the will registers, and show the simplicity and ease of the process. Full texts of the *banna* can be found in P.C.B.S.E., Hawlee, ff. 166 and 167. Also, see Michael Sheehan, "The Formation and Stability of Medieval Marriage," *Journal of Medieval Studies*, 33, 1971.

[34] This is done by dividing the testamentary sample into three crude groups. One group, with grandchildren or children of age, was considered to be over 50. A second sample, with children under age, was taken as being between 25 and 50, and a third group, with parents alive at the time of probate, was considered to be under age 25. This latter group, which constituted less than 5 percent of the entire testamentary population, was then surveyed for marriage to see if the results would fit with the findings of John Hajnal, "European Marriage Patterns in Perspective," in Glass and Eversley, eds., *Population in History*. Hajnal found a "modern West European" pattern of first marriage for females coming after age 25, and this was clearly the case with the Bury sample, where 94 percent of the women were not married. The method I have employed is, of course, highly tentative, and differs considerably with the age groupings presented in other studies; nevertheless, it is useful as a corroborative measure. See Gottfried, *Epidemic Disease*, pp. 175-183; and Hervé Lè Bras, "Parents, grandparents, Bisäieux," *Population*, p. 28, 1973.

TABLE 2.4: MARRIAGE AND REMARRIAGE RATIOS

	n	*Mean*	Number of Times Married			
			0	*1*	*2*	*3+*
A. *Entire Sample*						
1354-1530	2,116	77	25.4	72.4	2.0	.1
1354-1400	354	69	33.1	66.4	.3	.3
1401-1440	373	79	22.9	75.4	1.4	.3
1441-1450	142	68	33.1	66.2	.7	—
1451-1460	104	82	18.9	80.0	1.1	—
1461-1470	131	81	20.6	77.9	1.5	—
1471-1480	229	81	24.9	69.9	4.4	.9
1481-1490	49	76	24.2	75.8	—	—
1491-1500	149	89	15.6	79.6	4.8	—
1501-1510	198	80	21.6	76.4	2.0	—
1511-1520	149	79	23.5	74.5	2.0	—
1521-1530	238	76	28.3	67.3	4.4	—
B. *Males Only*						
1354-1530	1,713	77	24.6	73.7	1.5	.2
1354-1400	293	74	28.5	70.8	.3	.3
1401-1440	297	80	20.8	78.1	1.1	—
1441-1450	118	70	30.5	69.5	—	—
1451-1460	82	80	22.5	76.1	1.4	—
1461-1470	106	81	20.8	77.4	1.9	—
1471-1480	192	80	26.0	68.8	4.2	1.0
1481-1490	39	81	19.2	80.8	—	—
1491-1500	110	87	16.5	79.8	3.7	—
1501-1510	155	80	23.7	75.6	.6	—
1511-1520	117	77	23.1	76.9	—	—
1521-1530	204	74	29.6	66.7	3.7	—
C. *Females Only*						
1354-1530	403	76	28.7	66.8	4.2	.3
1354-1400	61	42	57.6	42.4	—	—
1401-1440	76	77	30.4	65.2	2.9	1.4
1441-1480	122	86	16.9	80.7	2.4	—
1481-1520	130	89	19.3	72.9	7.9	—

for some point late in the fifteenth or early in the sixteenth century, the 1522 estimate of partial demographic recovery can be substantiated, and the date of the projected population upturn identified more precisely.

Mortality has traditionally been seen as the demographic pacesetter in pre-industrial Europe, and later medieval East Anglia was no exception. If anything, it played an even larger role than is usually recognized, and, within the stricture of mortality, the key element seems to have been epidemic disease, particularly plague. In a frequency unmatched in English history, the kingdom was devastated by infectious diseases and other often related climatic disasters between 1348 and 1479-1480.[35] From 1348 to 1351, the Black Death raged. In 1353 there was a harvest failure, and, although its effect must surely have been mitigated by the depopulation of the plague, it added to the general misery. From 1361-1362, the *pestis secunda* devastated East Anglia, followed in 1369 by the *pestis tertia*. These in turn were succeeded by yet another plague epidemic in 1374-1375. This pattern was then established in a cycle in which plague struck about once every five to ten years, until the 1410s and the 1420s, when it was joined by cycles of dysentery and influenza. At the same time, plague became even more frequent. From 1430 to 1480 it recurred in cycles of about once every four years. Many of these epidemics were rather localized, even within the relatively confined environs of East Anglia, but the overall effect was calamitous, with decennial mortality rates probably running well into the 40s/1,000.

Epidemic disease continued to be of major importance in Bury St. Edmunds and West Suffolk after 1480, but plague's effect on mortality was lessened considerably because of what was probably an etiological-ecological change in insect and rodent vectors.[36] The epidemic of 1479-1480 proved to be the worst in the borough since the *pestis secunda* of 1361-1362, killing perhaps 15 percent of the adult population. In the ashes of this major demographic blow,

[35] See the table in Gottfried, *Epidemic Disease*, pp. 47-50; and Creighton, *History of Epidemics*, i, pp. 177-233.

[36] *Ibid.* The relationship between disease, climate, and social change is well summed up in: J.-N. Biraben, *Les Hommes et la Peste*, 2 vols. (The Hague: Mouton, 1975); J. D. Chambers, *Population, Economy and Society in Preindustrial England* (Oxford: Oxford University Press, 1972); and E. LeRoy Ladurie, "Un Concept: L'Unification Microbienne du Monde (XIVe–XVIIe Siècles)," *Schweizerische Zeitschrift für Geschichte*, 1973.

however, plague appears to have shifted to a longer frequency cycle. Minor epidemics flared in other parts of England from 1485 to 1487, but Bury did not suffer another major mortality crisis until the plague epidemic of 1499-1500, followed by yet another in 1509, and a third in 1530. Hence, following a fifty-year period of continual epidemics came a half century of comparative respite. A new infectious disease, the Sweating Sickness, appeared four times from 1485 to 1528, but, while it received considerable attention in the narrative and medical records, its demographic impact was minimal, and actually less significant than the earlier influenza epidemics of the 1420s.[37] Another new disease, syphilis, made its English debut late in the fifteenth century, but, like the Sweating Sickness, had little real effect on mortality differentials.[38] Of greater consequence was the coming of typhus, to be of major importance in the later sixteenth century. It first struck Bury St. Edmunds in 1522, but this initial onslaught made relatively small inroads, especially when compared with its impact a generation later.[39] Overall, plague was the most important disease affecting Bury's mortality rates, and its dimunition from the 1480s meant that a major cause of high death rates had been removed at the same time that fertility rates seem to have been on the upswing.[40]

Some of the empirical effects of epidemic disease can be seen through the testamentary evidence. Although wills do not give precise dates or actual causes of death, they do provide several helpful clues. Probate generally took place within three weeks of death, and major infectious diseases tended to be seasonal in occurrence. For complex biological and environmental reasons, plague struck East Anglia in autumn, dysentery in late summer and early autumn, influenza and typhus in winter, and smallpox in early spring.[41] Smallpox was primarily a childhood disease, and

---

[37] Gottfried, "Population, Plague and the Sweating Sickness," pp. 12-37.

[38] Creighton, *History of Epidemics*, i, pp. 429-438.

[39] *Ibid.*, pp. 374-383. Also, see Andrew Appleby, "Disease or Famine? Mortality in Cumberland and Westmoreland, 1580-1640," *Ec.H.R.*, 2nd series, 1973, pp. 403-461, for a comparison.

[40] A new, rather interesting approach to the topic is in Hatcher, *Plague, Population*, pp. 63-67.

[41] Gottfried, *Epidemic Disease*, pp. 84-154. Also of interest are: J.J.T. Bailey, *Mathematical Theory of Epidemics* (London: Hafner, 1959); and Hollingsworth, *Historical Demography*, pp. 355-374.

reached epidemic proportions only in 1463, so that spring mortality before the 1520s usually reflected the absence of major killing diseases. This in turn provides an interesting contrast with autumn dominant mortality patterns, which were usually indicative of plague. Hence, a clustering of mortality patterns on a seasonal basis can provide a quantitative measure of the impact of this crucial demographic variable.

Data on seasonal mortality are presented in Table 2.5, reflecting the clustering of the raw figures presented in Graph 2.1. Before 1436, seasonal figures are rather sporadic, but still useful. In 1361 mortality during the spring quarter was nine times higher than that of the next mortality peak in the entire fourteenth century, showing the highly virulent pneumonic strain of the *pestis secunda*. Autumnal dominance, indicative of bubonic plague, can be seen throughout the course of the sample, particularly from the 1420s to 1480. There were major mortality crises in: spring, 1427, probably influenza, with mortality spilling over from the winter quarter; autumn, 1441, probably bubonic plague; summer, 1441, dysentery; autumn, 1452, bubonic plague; autumn, 1471, bubonic plague; and autumn, 1479, plague. The numbers assessed on a quarterly basis are at times rather small and their standard deviations rather high, but corroborated as all are by multiple literary references the case for the primary role of epidemic disease in determining late medieval Bury's mortality patterns can be presented rather strongly.[42]

Further support for the crucial role of infectious disease comes from the seasonal distributions of mortality, presented in Table 2.5. Total mortality for the sample was dominant in autumn, again reflective of bubonic plague. This pattern prevailed for virtually every time frame and occupational group surveyed until the early sixteenth century. The 1480s sample, which is heavily skewed toward autumn, is incomplete, and those from the 1490s and 1500s show the effects of the last major plague outbreaks in 1499-1500 and 1509-1510. But, except for select seasons in the 1500s, from the mid 1480s onward the autumnal trends apparent before 1479-1480 begin to shift toward spring, suggestive of the postulated

[42] The 1440s appear initially to be exceptional, but on closer inspection the winter dominant patterns reflect a series of influenza epidemics and pneumonic, as well as bubonic plague. Similarly, the spring patterns in the 1460s can in part be explained not by an absence of plague but rather by the impact of the pox of 1462-1463.

TABLE 2.5: SEASONAL MORTALITY

	n	Modal Season	Distribution*			
			W	Sp	Su	A
A. *Entire Sample*						
1354-1530	2,116	A	20.9	24.3	22.5	26.1
1354-1400	354	A	15.7	20.2	17.1	22.3
1401-1440	373	A	19.0	24.1	24.4	32.3
1441-1450	142	W	32.4	18.3	25.4	23.9
1451-1460	104	A	16.7	22.2	21.1	40.0
1461-1470	131	Sp	22.1	33.6	25.2	19.1
1471-1480	229	A	24.5	23.1	21.0	31.4
1481-1490	49	A	15.2	33.3	12.1	34.2
1491-1500	149	A	26.5	21.8	23.8	27.2
1501-1510	198	A	22.1	18.1	24.6	33.7
1511-1520	149	Sp	16.8	39.6	20.1	22.1
1521-1530	238	Sp	20.1	27.0	26.5	26.0
B. *Males Only*						
1354-1530	1,713	A	20.5	23.9	23.2	26.1
1354-1400	293	A	15.3	19.7	17.3	22.2
1401-1440	297	A	18.6	21.9	24.6	33.0
1441-1450	118	W	34.7	16.9	27.1	21.2
1451-1460	82	A	14.1	21.1	21.1	43.7
1461-1470	106	Sp	21.7	36.8	27.4	14.2
1471-1480	192	A	24.5	22.4	21.9	31.2
1481-1490	39	Sp	19.2	17.3	25.0	36.5
1491-1500	110	A	25.7	22.9	22.9	27.5
1501-1510	155	A	19.2	17.3	25.0	36.5
1511-1520	117	Sp	16.2	41.9	17.1	23.9
1521-1530	204	Sp	20.0	28.9	26.7	23.7
C. *Females Only*						
1354-1530	403	A	22.9	25.8	18.9	25.9
1354-1400	61	A	18.6	22.0	13.6	22.4
1401-1440	76	Sp	21.7	31.9	17.9	27.0
1441-1480	122	A	24.1	24.1	18.1	33.7
1481-1520	130	Sp	21.8	32.1	15.6	29.1

* The balance of the distribution percentage, adding up to 100 percent, is unclassifiable because of insufficient data.

lengthening of intervals in plague cycles. These decades and the more general autumnal patterns of the rest of the sample contrast with the mortality clusterings of the 1510s and 1520s. During these later decades there are no surviving references to important spring-dominant diseases, and indeed, few references to any epidemics of major importance, all indicative of the absence of infectious disease as the major mortality factor.

If the postulated high mortality and low fertility levels presented for late medieval Bury are valid, and the town relied exclusively on its own natural reproductive capacities, population levels would have shrunk by well over 75 percent. They did not; even if there were a significant population fall from 1348 through the late fifteenth century, a borough base of 2,500 to 3,000 persons must always have been maintained.[43] Further, a population rise has been projected for the early sixteenth century, and if this was in part due to a fall in death rates and a slight rise in marital fertility, neither was sufficient to explain the full extent of the increase. A possible explanation is migration. Migration has been recognized as a crucial factor in maintaining pre-industrial urban populations, and it must have been essential in Bury St. Edmunds.[44]

Some evidence comes from the estates of the abbey. Court and account rolls show what a powerful attraction the town held in the fourteenth and fifteenth centuries. Several entries indicate that, whatever fears urban centers may have held for the peasantry, their attractions proved far greater. There are a number of records from the Bacon collection which show a steady stream of rural denizens moving to Bury.[45] Unfortunately, these rural records can offer only a subjective view; more precise information is provided by wills and place-name evidence. Wills are useful because some

[43] Phythian-Adams, *Desolation of a City*, suggests that Coventry may have lost almost three-quarters of its population early in the sixteenth century. Clark and Slack, *English Towns in Transition*, make similar allusions for a number of provincial towns.

[44] General discussion of medieval migration can be found in J. C. Russell, "Population in Europe, 500-1500," in Carlo Cipolla, ed., *The Fontana Economic History of Europe: The Middle Ages* (London: Collins, 1972). For England, see J. A. Raftis, *Tenure and Mobility* (Toronto: Pontifical Institute of Mediaeval Studies, 1964). Phythian-Adams, *Desolation of a City*, p. 235, finds minimal immigration into Coventry. Bury, with its booming markets and industry, was more attractive.

[45] For example, Bacon, 127, 129.

testators give not only parish of burial, but also parish of birth. There are shortcomings. At best, the wills provide only a one-way measure, the flow of migrants into town. More serious are problems with the source itself; even if the relative completeness of the male testamentary population is accepted, what proportion of will makers who were not born in Bury St. Edmunds bothered to list a parish of birth? Whatever the extent, it was certainly not 100 percent. The first shortcoming is mitigated by evidence from rural estates. Data from the Bacon records indicate that the flow was almost entirely into the town, and, except for a few wealthy merchants, rarely out to the countryside.[46] But the second problem remains, and cannot be circumvented. The testamentary evidence for mobility is almost certainly incomplete, and it can only be hoped that the data available are representative geographically, if not proportionally.

From 1364 to 1460, about 10 percent of all will makers listed a birth place other than the three Bury St. Edmunds parishes. This is obviously too low to be accurate, but even within the established constraints the evidence shows important trends. From 1460, close to the suggested time of a demographic upturn, levels of will-making immigrants picked up to over 15 percent of the total population. Small as this may seem, it is significant; coupled with the higher replacement ratios and the changing seasonal patterns of mortality, it is another piece in the puzzle of Bury's population movements. The testamentary evidence also provides geographic information on the migrants. The results are not surprising. Over half the immigrants came from neighboring West Suffolk villages—in effect, people moving from the periphery to the center of their greater urban region. The bulk of the rest came from Norfolk and East Suffolk, with a few more from Cambridgeshire and Essex.[47]

Another source exists: Eckwall, McKinley, and most recently McClure have demonstrated how place-name analysis can yield

[46] Further research into the archival records of Bury St. Edmunds shows that few families remained in trade for more than three generations; they either died out in the male line, or made enough money to pass into the ranks of the landed gentry. The two most influential families in late medieval Bury, the Drurys and Barets, both had their starts in the draperies. For further information, see below, pp. 153-156.

[47] The precise percentages are: West Suffolk, 53.4 percent; Norfolk, 23.1 percent; East Suffolk, 13.3 percent; Cambridgeshire and Essex, 8.9 percent; and others, 1.3 percent.

information on percentages and places of migration.[48] There are problems with this method, the most obvious being the geographic validity of place-name surnames by the fourteenth, fifteenth, and sixteenth centuries. But it is an interesting idea, and the results, presented in Table 2.6 and Appendix D, show some fascinating trends. They confirm the testamentary evidence on proportions and even geography of the migrants. The largest numbers came from the archdeaconry of Sudbury, the western half of Suffolk. Of

TABLE 2.6: MIGRATION TRENDS FROM PLACE NAME EVIDENCE

Region	n	% Total Pop.	% Sample Pop.	Distribution 1354-1440	1441-1530
Sudbury Archd.	121	5.9	38.1	82	39
Suffolk Archd.	55	2.6	17.3	39	16
Norwich Archd.	49	2.4	15.4	32	17
Norfolk Archd.	37	1.8	11.6	27	10
East Anglia Total	262	12.8	82.4	180	82
Other-Domestic	52	2.5	16.4	28	24
Other-Foreign	4	—	1.2	2	2
TOTALS	318	15.6	100.0	210	108

the others, who represented 15 percent of the larger testamentary population, most came from the other East Anglian archdeaconries. About 2.6 percent of the total and 16 percent of the place-name population were from the archdeaconry of Norwich, basically the central part of county Norfolk, and 3.7 percent and 10 percent from the archdeaconry of Norfolk, primarily the eastern and western parts of county Norfolk, the least densely populated segments of the region. These constituted the bulk of the immigrants; the rest came from Cambridgeshire, Essex, and Lincolnshire. In general, the Bury St. Edmunds patterns conform with those found by

[48] Eilert Ekwall, *Studies in the Population of Medieval London* (Stockholm: Almquist and Wiksell, 1956); R. A. McKinley, *Norfolk, and Suffolk Surnames in the Middle Ages* (London: Phillimores, 1975); Peter McClure, "Patterns of Migration in the Late Middle Ages; The Evidence of English Place Name Surnames," *Ec.H.R.*, 2nd series, xxxii, pp. 167-182.

McClure for the early fourteenth century in Leicester, Nottingham, and York. About 60 percent of the immigrants came from a radius of 20 miles or less, about 18 percent from a radius of between 21 and 40 miles, and about 8 percent from between 41 and 60 miles.[49]

Unlike their geographic distribution, the chronological evidence of immigrants from their place names differs from the testamentary evidence. The place-name migrants fell by about one-half from the mid-fifteenth century onward, and, if these figures are accurate, they may well reflect diminishing numbers of folk coming into Bury. This, however, is unlikely. Rather, it is more probable that place-name surnames began to change from the mid-fifteenth century, at the very latest, much as occupational names had changed about a century earlier. Other evidence shows that surnames based on Christian names and descriptive terms were becoming more popular, while those derived from occupations and place names, if not yet completely antiquated, at least ceased to describe accurately their bearers.[50] Occupational surnames rarely described the crafts of their possessor in the fifteenth century, and it is likely that place names, valid earlier, were no longer representative of geographic origin. The chronological trends of place-name migration probably represent social rather than demographic change.

In sum, testamentary data and other demographic evidence provide some sense of the secular trends of Bury's population from 1340 to 1530. Population reached a fourteenth-century peak and was then decimated by the Black Death; mortality may well have ranged between 40 percent and 50 percent of the town's population. From 1351 to at least the mid-fifteenth century and perhaps until the 1480s, it continued to decline. If accurate generalizations can be made from replacement-ratio evidence, the decline bottomed out in the 1440s and stood at perhaps less than half of the pre-1348 levels. From 1440 to 1480, mortality continued to run at

[49] McClure, "Patterns of Migration." The figures for 1 to 20 miles, 21 to 40 miles, and 41 to 60 miles for Leicester, Nottingham, York, and London are, respectively: 69.5 percent, 12.2 percent, 8.2 percent; 55.7 percent, 18.6 percent, 10.4 percent; 68.9 percent, 20.7 percent, 3.0 percent; 21.1 percent, 26.5 percent, and 18.2 percent. London, obviously had patterns of migration far different from the provincial towns.

[50] A. H. Smith, "English Place Name Elements," *English Place Name Society*, xxvi, 1956; Eilert Ekwall, *A Dictionary of English Place Names* (Oxford: Oxford University Press, 1939); and McKinley, *Norfolk and Suffolk Surnames*.

a high pace, but there was a slight upswing in replacement ratios; if overall population did not rise, the pace of population decline must have slowed, perhaps to stagnation. But from 1480, plague cycles lengthened, replacement ratios rose, and at least one source shows an upward trend in levels of immigration. If any particular factor must be singled out as the most important in this renewed demographic growth, it was probably the decline in mortality rates from 1480 to 1520. By the early sixteenth century, the population of Bury St. Edmunds was rising rather steadily, and by Dissolution may well have reached pre-plague levels.

The demographic data are of great intrinsic interest, but need to be placed in the larger context of the rise of the secular commune. What was their role in the changes that occurred in late medieval Bury St. Edmunds? It was complex and of the utmost importance, and will be referred to continuously throughout the rest of this book. Briefly, the massive demographic contractions of the late fourteenth and first two-thirds of the fifteenth centuries—the key time period in the emergence of the secular community—were instrumental in the new economic conditions which allowed the burghal leaders to build their independent commercial and industrial bases. By 1450, declining population had produced crippling conditions for large landholders like the Abbey of St. Edmunds. Wages soared and food prices tumbled. Those entirely dependent on landed income who failed to find new, more profitable means of extracting wealth from their property suffered enormous financial setbacks. It was difficult to find tenants, except on long leases at low rents, and to make ends meet the abbey found it increasingly necessary to sell off parcels of its endowment. In the negative sense, declining population contributed to the rise of the town by seriously damaging the financial base of the abbey.

At the same time, depopulation had a generally positive effect for many townsmen. Most made their livings from non-landed sources, and, as standards of living rose after the Black Death, many craftsmen and merchants dramatically increased their retail sales. If depopulation in the fourteenth and fifteenth centuries did not usher in a boom in the town, it hurt the burgesses far less than it did the monks of the abbey. Most important, the demographic upswing late in the fifteenth and early in the sixteenth centuries came at the same time and was probably connected with the fruition of the Suffolk textile industry. Rising population would first mean larger domestic demand, and, later, workers for a wider national and international market. All of this will be discussed in some detail below. But if economic power were the instrument which the burgesses of Bury St. Edmunds used to gain autonomy from their monastic overlords, demographic movements were in part responsible for the economic changes.

Chapter Three

THE ECONOMIC BASIS
FOR CHANGE

THE ECONOMIC ROLE OF THE ABBEY

Of the important aspects of the history of late medieval Bury St. Edmunds, those which have been least investigated are economic activities. There are platitudes about the prosperity of the cloth industry in south Suffolk, and casual allusions to Bury's place in it, but most attention has been focused on the industrial villages such as Lavenham and Long Melford.[1] There are good explanations for these concentrations. Evidence of economic activity in the borough and throughout West Suffolk is spotty and at times virtually nonexistent. Many questions, in particular statistical queries about trade and industry, cannot be answered. But through the use of a wide variety of sources, including guild records, tax accounts, commercial contracts, land deeds and rentals, and wills, a general picture of the region's economic life can be pieced together.

While the town was still a market community named Boedricsworth, the abbey of St. Edmunds was already one of the largest and most prosperous Benedictine houses in England.[2] My principal

---

[1] A good example is Nigel Heard, *Wool: East Anglia's Golden Fleece* (Lavenham, Suffolk: T. Dalton, 1970). Such attitudes have also affected basic touring books and professional historical surveys. See: John Burke, *Suffolk* (London: B. T. Batsford, 1971); and Bernard E. Dorman, *Norfolk* (London: B. T. Batsford, 1972); and the parts dealing with the economy in May McKisack, *The Fourteenth Century, 1307-1399* (Oxford: The Clarendon Press, 1959); and E. F. Jacob, *The Fifteenth Century, 1399-1485* (Oxford: The Clarendon Press, 1961). It is also often true of older textbooks on economic history. See, for example, M. W. Thomas, *A Survey of English Economic History* (London: Blackie and Son, 1957).

[2] This point is stressed by Charles Cox, in "The Abbey of St. Edmunds and its Customary," in V. B. Redstone, ed., *Memorials of Old Suffolk* (Lon-

interests center on the town rather than on the abbey, but, in order
to understand the emergence of the former, it is essential to discuss
the basis of the latter's wealth, and its economic functions in the
larger secular community.[3] St. Edmunds' major economic role was
indirect. Its prosperity stemmed not from trade or industry, but
rather its vast landed endowment and the profits of land ownership.
With the exception of the Crown, it was probably the largest single
landholder in West Suffolk. Aside from a few tenements and pas-
tures, the abbey held all property in the borough and in the suburbs.
Others might rent, trade, or sell land, bequeath, divide, or alienate
it, but in some way, at some point in time, the abbey reaped a profit

---

don: Bemrose and Sons, 1908). He ranks St. Edmunds Abbey fifth in
England, basing his ratings on the 1535 *Valor Ecclesiasticus*. On p. 94, Cox
presents the following table:

Abbey	Assessment in £
Westminster	3,977
Glastonbury	3,508
St. Albans	2,510
Canterbury (CC)	2,489
ST. EDMUNDSBURY	2,336
Reading	2,116
York	2,085
Abingdon	2,002

The best accounts of the abbey proper can be found in: A. Goodwin, *The
Abbey of St. Edmundsbury* (Oxford: Basil Blackwell, 1936), particularly pp.
65-81; Dugdale, *Monasticon*, iii; and Richard Yates, *The History and Antiquities of the Abbey of Bury St. Edmunds* (J. B. Nichols and Son, 1843). Useful
for a comparative perspective is D. D. Knowles, *The Religious Orders in
England*, 2 vols. (Cambridge: Cambridge University Press, 1950-1955).

   [3] In discussing St. Edmunds, we are faced not with a dearth but rather
a glut of documents, if such a term can ever be used to describe late
medieval evidence. Indeed, sufficient records survive to allow for a rural
economic history of the abbey's estates, as others have done for Gloucester,
Ramsey, Tavistock, Crowley, Ely, and other houses. See, for example:
H.P.R. Finberg, *Tavistock Abbey: A Study in the Social and Economic History
of Devon* (Cambridge: Cambridge University Press, 1951); J. A. Raftis, *The
Estates of Ramsey Abbey* (Toronto: The Pontifical Institute, 1957); Edward
Miller, *The Abbey and Bishopric of Ely* (Cambridge: Cambridge University
Press, 1951); and F.R.H. DuBoulay, *The Lordship of Canterbury* (London:
Thomas Nelson, 1966). I shall not attempt to do this, just as I have also
avoided studying the abbey's administrative structure, but will restrict
myself to the abbey's social and economic impact on the town.

on all property dealings in the banleuca. Ultimately, there was no question as to whether rent was due on banleuca property, but rather its extent and the means of collection.[4] Further, this ownership extended beyond the borders of the banleuca to the sac and soc of the liberty, a large rural tract of eight and one-half hundreds over which the abbot had been given extensive economic, jurisprudential and governmental authority (Map 10).[5] The abbey originally obtained the liberty through royal gift, and then supplemented it with pious charity, bequests in mortmain, and open purchase. By the late thirteenth century, the estates were scattered throughout eastern England, from Yorkshire to Kent. These vast holdings, in the borough of Bury St. Edmunds and its suburbs, West Suffolk, East Anglia, and the rest of the kingdom, formed the heart of abbey income and influence.[6]

[4] Details on jurisdictional issues can be found in: V. B. Redstone, "St. Edmund's Bury Rentals, 1295," P.S.I., xiii, 2, 1908, pp. 1-19; Lobel, The Borough, pp. 5-22; Lobel, "The Ecclesiastical Banleuca in England," in F. M. Powicke, ed., Oxford Essays in Medieval History (Oxford: Clarendon Press, 1934); Godwin, The Abbey, pp. 39-61; and Helen Cam, Liberties and Communities in Medieval England (New York: Barnes and Noble, 1963). For contemporary attempts to define the problems, see: C.P.R., Edward I, 1304, p. 284; C.C.R., Richard II, 1390, p. 268; C.P.R., Richard II, 1391, p. 441.

[5] This map has been taken from H. E. Butler, ed., The Chronicle of Jocelin of Brakelond (New York: Oxford University Press, 1949).

[6] Three major sets of records exist that describe the rural holdings of the abbey. They are: Bacon; The Hengrave Lists and Calendars, The West Suffolk County Record Office, Bury St. Edmunds; and The Abbey Holdings, The West Suffolk County Record Office, Bury St. Edmunds. Further, there are a number of additional records that list holdings, including: B.M. Additional Ms. 10108; B.M. Additional Ms. 14849; B.M. Harl. Ms. 1005; B.M. Harl. Ms. 4626; B.M. Harl. Ms. 645. The list of abbey lands was enormous. First, of course, there was the banleuca, the town, and the suburbs. Next, there were extensive rural manors, including complete estates at Fornham St. Martin, Fornham St. Genevieve, Fornham All Saints, Ingham, Risby, Chevington, Soham, Saxham, Hargrave, Culford, Monk's Soham, and Wrotham, all in West Suffolk. Further, these were all complete, self-contained manors. There were also pieces of lands, arable, meadows, woodlands, and the like in Nowton, Horringer, Whepstead, Elmswell, Redgrave, Culford, Hargrave, Barton Magna, and Hawstead, to name a few from which records survive. These lands formed the core of St. Edmund's estates in West Suffolk, but by no means all of it, and they represent

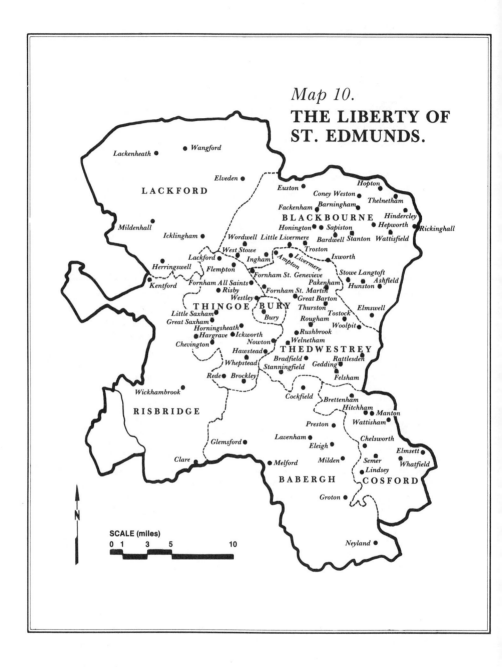

Map 10.
**THE LIBERTY OF
ST. EDMUNDS.**

Lackenheath •   • Wangford

LACKFORD

Elveden •

Hopton •

Euston •   Coney Weston •   Thelnetham •

Fackenham •   Barningham •

BLACKBOURNE   Hindercley •

Honington •   Sapiston •   Hepworth •   Rickinghall

Mildenhall •   Icklingham •   Wordwell • Little Livermere   Bardwell Stanton Wattisfield

West Stowe •   Troston •

Herringswell •   Lackford •   Ingham •   Ampton   Livermere   Ixworth

Flempton •   Fornham St. Genevieve   Stowe Langtoft

Kentford •   Fornham All Saints •   Pakenham   Ashfield

Risby •   Hunston •

Westley •   Fornham St. Martin

THINGOE   BURY   Great Barton •

Little Saxham •   Thurston •   Elmswell •

Great Saxham •   Bury •   Tostock •

Horningsheath •   Rougham •   Woolpit •

Hargrave •   Ickworth •   Rushbrook •

Chevington •   Nowton •   Welnetham •

Hawstead •   **THEDWESTREY**

Bradfield •   Rattlesden •

Whepstead •   Stanningfield   Gedding •

Rede •   Brockley •   Felsham •

Wickhambrook •   Cockfield •   Brettenham •

Hitcham •   Manton •

RISBRIDGE   Preston •   Wattisham •

Lavenham •   Chelsworth •

Glemsford •   Eleigh •   Elmsett •

Clare •   Milden •   Semer •   Whatfield

Melford •   Lindsey •

BABERGH   **COSFORD**

Groton •

N

SCALE (miles)
0 1   3   5   10

Neyland •

St. Edmunds was a dynamic part of the West Suffolk land market. Although primarily a *rentier* for most of the later middle ages, it was never completely passive in exploiting its estates.[7] The abbot and his chief agent in rural matters, the cellarer, constantly purchased parcels to add to those parts of the demesne which were actively cultivated, and sold off other pieces thought to be expendable or less valuable.[8] Local deeds are filled with such records, and court rolls show St. Edmunds entering into arrangements with the most influential and powerful of the townsfolk, such as Richard Charman, John Nottingham, John Baret, John Smith, the Drurys and the de Veres.[9] But the abbot dealt with anyone who had cash or something else to trade, from the humblest peasant to corporate boroughs. In the late fourteenth and fifteenth centuries, for example, he was involved in a series of East Suffolk transactions with the borough of Beccles, and at several junctures took the town to court over disputed points of ownership.[10] As late as the 1460s, just a few years before abbey officials began an irrevocable trend of selling their endowment—a trend which lasted through the 1530s— Abbot John Bohun was playing Lancastrian against Yorkist in order to increase St. Edmunds' estates.[11]

The profits from land holdership were enormous. It is not possible to calculate total abbey wealth until Dissolution, but major sources, patterns, and trends of income can be charted. First among the sources was rent. In one form or another, from customhold to

properties held by the abbey continuously for the 250 years being covered. Additional West Suffolk lands were held for shorter periods, and there were certainly lands for which records have been lost. Beyond West Suffolk, the abbot had property in East Suffolk, Norfolk, Essex, Cambridgeshire, Bedfordshire, Huntingdonshire, Lincolnshire, Northamptonshire, London, and Middlesex.

[7] This view is held by most economic historians. For two interesting perspectives, see: the works of M. M. Postan listed in the bibliography; and A. R. Bridbury, *Economic Growth: England in the Later Middle Ages* (London: George Allen and Unwin, 1962).

[8] For examples, see the Hengrave Collection, particularly: 2/12; 2/26; 2/27; 2/168; 2/221; 2/225; 2/244; 2/245; 2/261; 2/269; 2/274; 2/285; 2/286; 2/287; 2/293; 2/542; 2/545; 2/550; 2/559; 2/560; 2/625.

[9] *Ibid.* Also, see: C.C.R., Edward III, 1339, p. 224; C.C.R., Richard II, 1386, p. 36; C.P.R., Henry VI, 1444, p. 282; *ibid.*, 1449, p. 112.

[10] C.C.R., Richard II, 1386, p. 36; C.C.R., Henry VI, 1449, p. 112.

[11] C.P.R., Henry VI, 1459, p. 571.

copyhold, from *hadgoval* ground rents to leasing fees for suburban arable, virtually all property holders in the urban region of West Suffolk paid some recompense to St. Edmunds. This was constant and immutable, and usually engendered little opposition. Rent was a widely accepted obligation, and, even during the fiercest of the fourteenth-century riots, the rebel leaders refrained from abrogating tenant rental obligations. Although it can not be stated definitively, it is likely that rent was the single largest and most consistent source of abbey income throughout the later middle ages.[12]

Ownership of property provided for many other sources of wealth. Privileges granted to St. Edmunds before the economic fruition of the town in the fifteenth century gave the monks control over all marketplaces in the banleuca. Not only did the abbey collect ground rents on market properties, but it also took a second share on any wealth gained through commerce or industry. Further, there were the profits of government. The abbot's control over the sac and soc of the liberty, of which Bury was part and parcel, provided extensive administrative and jurisprudential privileges. Such powers were initially conferred in the mid-eleventh century by Edward the Confessor, and were reaffirmed by every king down through Henry VIII. Reaffirmation was expensive, costing up to £300 per royal reign, but was well worth it.[13] Governmental profits from the liberty included fees from manorial and borough courts and gaols, probate and registration of wills, fines, executed and returned writs, and virtually every aspect of local government. After rents from the arable and market tolls, such fees probably formed the largest part of abbey income.

The profits of land extended beyond rent and governmental services. Although St. Edmunds was primarily a *rentier*, parts of its patrimony were directly exploited, and some agrarian ventures proved highly profitable. In the land-extensive rural economy of the late fourteenth and fifteenth centuries, animal husbandry was among the most lucrative. Before the mid-fifteenth century, cattle

[12] See the various rentals, as discussed above, Chapter 2. Also, see: C.P.R., Edward I, 1300, p. 520; C.P.R., Edward III, 1330, p. 527; C.P.R., Henry VI, 1459, p. 571. Also, C.P.R., Edward III, 1350, p. 482; *ibid.*, 1349, p. 401; C.P.R., Richard II, 1392, p. 145; *ibid.*, 1396, p. 679.

[13] For details about the process, see: Helen M. Jewell, *English Local Administration* (Newton Abbot: David Charles, 1972); and S. B. Chrimes, *An Introduction to the Administrative History of England* (Oxford: Oxford University Press, 1952).

were kept throughout the suburbs, with the abbey supplying beef to the Net Market stalls, and hides for Bury's leather workers. From the 1440s, sheep proved more valuable, and select sheepfolds throughout the banleuca were among the most profitable of the abbey's farms. The cellarers' rentals indicate that even in the four-teenth century, before the maturation of the south Suffolk textile industry, several thousand sheep were kept in the suburban pas-tures. While no numerical evidence survives from the fifteenth century, it is likely that the size of the flocks grew along with the increased demand for wool.[14] Thirteenth-century data from the Hundred of Blackbourne gave some indication of the extent of animal husbandry. In 1292, an area in which only 1,350 taxpayers were assessed above six shillings, eight pence, contained 14,041 sheep, 1,452 horses and oxen, 4,298 cows and calves, and 1,842 pigs. All of this did not belong to the abbot, and much of the hundred lands were leased out, rather than exploited directly.[15] But remembering in turn that Blackbourne represented only a small fraction of St. Edmunds' total endowment, we get a real sense of the value of livestock.

Land ownership produced other sources of wealth. Among the most important were profits from agricultural and industrial mills. In many rural estates, tenants had no milling rights whatsoever. This was not the case in the West Suffolk liberty. Peasants could operate hand mills for personal consumption, a valuable ancient right which tenants of other monastic enclaves, such as St. Albans, were denied.[16] In the late twelfth century, this was confirmed by Abbot Samson, and it cut into overall abbey milling profits.[17] Still, losses on such singular modes of production could not have been too great, and all major grain and industrial mills remained within

[14] Lobel, *The Borough*, pp. 20-21. Further information is provided in the cellarers' rentals, especially C.U.L. Ms. Ff 2 29; and C.U.L. Ms. Gg 4 4. There was a "Shepe Market" somewhere in the borough in 1539, perhaps in the Old Market, listed in L. J. Redstone, "First Ministers' Account of the Possessions of the Abbey of St. Edmund," *Suffolk Institute of Archeology and Natural History*, xiii, 3, 1909, p. 21.

[15] M. M. Postan, "Village Livestock in the Thirteenth Century," *Ec.H.R.*, 2nd series, xv, 1962. Further information can be found in D. L. Farmer, "Some Livestock Price Movements in Thirteenth Century England," *Ec.H.R.*, 2nd series, xxii, 1969.

[16] Lobel, *The Borough*, p. 27; Jocelin, p. 132; Dugdale, iii, pp. 116-117.

[17] Jocelin, p. 132.

the abbot's prerogatives. As Bury became more central to English cloth production, profits from the industrial mills rose considerably. These mills were often farmed out *en masse* for flat rates over extended time periods, especially after 1470, or were leased for a fixed share of the final profits. But, in some way, all large-scale milling operations contributed to the abbey's coffers.[18]

Other sources of income included control over the West Suffolk waterways which flowed through the liberty, and were of great importance to the economic wellbeing of Bury St. Edmunds. The abbot held all rights to the Lark, the Linnet and Tayfen, and drew income from whatever profits they might produce.[19] These included water power for the mills, with the abbey taking a second share above and beyond its leasing income. There were tolls from barges carrying goods, and a share of the fish taken. Tayfen and the Lark above Rothbridge were among the most profitable inland fisheries in East Anglia, and in the fourteenth century proved to be a major money-maker for the cellarer. Indeed, so lucrative was fishing that the abbey invested in fishing ponds outside its liberty, in Soham Mere, along the East Suffolk coast.[20]

Long-standing proprietary rights produced more tolls and taxes. In addition to a tithing from ordinary commercial transactions, the abbot reaped tolls from the triweekly local markets and the annual trade fairs. Such tolls were fixed by the fourteenth century, and, although the proportional share collected by the abbey was eventually reduced by inflation, they remained relatively profitable until late in the fifteenth century. Fees such as stallage formed a significant part of abbey revenue, and, while select individuals or crafts might win exemptions, these were gained only after the payment of large sums of cash.[21] The importance of these dwindling tolls to the merchant community will be assessed below, but they cannot be discounted entirely as income producers. As late as 1404, the Alderman's Guild lost an appeal in a royal court to be relieved completely of weekly market obligations. Until 1539, some portion of the profits of trade in and around the borough went to St. Edmunds.[22]

[18] Lobel, *The Borough*, pp. 27-28; Dugdale, iii, pp. 116-117.
[19] C.U.L. Ms. Gg 4 4.
[20] C.U.L. Ms. Ee 3 60.
[21] B. M. Harl. Ms. 645.
[22] C.P.R., Henry IV, 1404, p. 466. Also, see C.P.R., Edward III, 1331, p. 147.

The abbey also had a series of lesser sources of revenue. It held the monopoly on tournaments throughout the banleuca and liberty. If the local gentry wished to display their martial prowess, they were able to do so only at the profit of St. Edmunds.[23] All manure in Bury's streets belonged to the cellarer. He in turn leased the franchise out at considerable profit to interested farmers.[24] All chalk and white clay, essential materials for building, belonged to the abbey; again, while rights to both were often leased out, they were done through the sale of costly licenses.[25] All royal bequests of murage and pannage went to the abbey.[26] It had control over the assize of bread, custody of unclaimed holdings, the profits of probate court, a slew of local fines, and custody of the lands and rents of all wards and orphans.[27] Supplementing all of this was a continuous flow of funds from pilgrims coming to abbey shrines, and a very high level of pious charity. The latter often included land, even after Edward I's 1279 Statute of Mortmain. In 1300, for example, two chaplains connected to the abbey applied for license of mortmain for the produce of demesnes from twenty-seven different towns.[28] In 1323, the hospital of *Domus Dei*, whose property was controlled by the sacrist, asked for license to accept a large tract of woodlands in West Suffolk, and, in 1392, for fifty-four acres and four messuages of prime arable.[29] The abbey itself continually sued for license, and for the year 1328 alone its requests filled two pages of the Calendar of Patent Rolls.[30] Such bequests began to diminish during the last quarter of the fifteenth century, but never dried up completely. Even in times of utmost crisis, such as the Black Death, abbey officials found the opportunity to submit requests for license in mortmain to accept more property.[31]

The abbey's role transcended that of great landholder, *rentier*, and wealthy consumer in the marketplace. It supervised a royal

[23] C.P.R., Edward II, 1313, p. 5.
[24] Lobel, *The Borough*, pp. 24-25.
[25] *Ibid.* Also, see C.P.R., Edward III, 1331, p. 147.
[26] *Ibid.* Also, C.P.R., Edward I, 1304, p. 227; *ibid.*, p. 267.
[27] C.P.R., Edward I, 1304, p. 283.
[28] C.P.R., Edward I, 1300, p. 520.
[29] C.P.R., Edward II, 1323, p. 287; C.P.R., Richard II, 1392, p. 145.
[30] C.P.R., Edward III, 1328, pp. 370-371.
[31] C.P.R., Edward III, 1349, p. 401; *ibid.*, 1350, p. 482; C.P.R., Henry VI, 1459, p. 571.

mint on *Le Mustow*.[32] The mint was of obvious financial importance
to the town as well as to St. Edmunds, especially in the twelfth and
thirteenth centuries, when it was operating at peak production, and
this fact helps to account for the presence of Bury's large and
prosperous community of goldsmiths. Records which detail the
extent of the mint's operation do not survive, but the abbey considered it one of its most valuable assets. The mint was mentioned
as early as the reign of Edward the Martyr late in the tenth century,
and, though its operations stopped around the time of the Norman
Conquest, it was back in business by 1105.[33] The abbot and his
agents supervised the entire coining process, and jealously guarded
their perquisite. When it was threatened, the abbot was quick to
the defense, and always ready to point an accusing finger elsewhere.
Several times in the twelfth century, St. Edmunds was charged with
supplementing its minting-profits income by clipping coins. The
abbey moneyers in turn accused the local Jewish community, although no records survive which link them at any time with the
minting process.[34] The Jews were expelled from Bury late in the
century by Abbot Samson, and, when similar accusations of tampering were alleged one hundred years later, the goldsmiths were
selected as the scapegoats. Indeed, in 1278, they were rounded up
along with several prominent burgesses, accused of debasement,
and sent to London for trial.[35] But, while the abbots and their
deputies may well have supplemented their regular income with
coin clipping and shaving, ordinary profits were usually high
enough. In 1329 agents acting for Abbot Richard de Draughton
succeeded in getting royal grants to continue the abbey's monopoly
of coinage and the assay of gold.[36] The monopoly was well employed. Eleven years later, the royal treasurer and barons of the
exchequer were ordered to deliver to Abbot William de Bernham
a new stamp "for the making of money." So often had the old plates
been used that they were reputedly too worn out to be retooled,

[32] C.P.R., Edward III, 1329, p. 411; *ibid.*, 1340, p. 363; *ibid.*, 1344, p. 31;
C.U.L. Ms. Ff 2 33, f.122.

[33] Lobel, *The Borough*, pp. 3, 11; Godwin, *The Abbey*, p. 9.

[34] Lobel, *The Borough*, p. 53. Also, Antonia Grandson, ed., *The Chronicle
of Bury St. Edmunds*, 1212-1301 (London: Thomas Nelson, 1964), xxii;
Jocelin, pp. 45-46.

[35] Grandson, *The Chronicle*, pp. 75-83.

[36] C.P.R., Edward III, 1329, p. 411.

and were discarded.[37] As with many of its other long-standing prerogatives, St. Edmunds managed to hold onto its minting rights until the sixteenth century.

Some sense of total abbey revenues can be had from the income of various abbey officials. The 1291 *Taxatio Ecclesiastica*, a papal assessment of the wealth of the parishes, bishoprics, and monastic houses in England, valued the income of some of St. Edmunds' officers. The cellarer, drawing wealth primarily from the suburbs and rural environs, reported £360 *per annum*. The sacrist, drawing from the borough, took in £134, the chamberlain £69, the almoner £11, and the pittancer £11.[38] This, of course, was just what these officials decided to report, and probably represents only a share of their overall income. A similar record survives from late in the fourteenth century. In 1373 Abbot de Brinkley called on all his officers to contribute to the upkeep of their fellow monks in Gloucester Hall, the Benedictine college at Oxford.[39] This provides another good comparative measure of wealth, at a time when a skilled worker might take in less than 7 pence per day. The treasurer contributed 60 shillings, the cellarer and sacrist 50 each, the chamberlain, hosteler, almoner, and shrine keeper 10 each. Such contributions could not have represented more than a tiny fraction of total income, and imply that abbey officials were at least as wealthy as the great burgesses of the borough. It is not surprising that the son of so prominent a figure as John Baret II would decide on a career in the Benedictine abbey. In time, he became treasurer, and may have shared in greater riches than his clothier father.[40]

Briefly, then, St. Edmunds, particularly in reference to the banleuca, was a rich, powerful institution, with at least 80 monks and 200 servants in its thirteenth-fourteenth century heyday, and perhaps two-thirds those numbers through the late fourteenth, fifteenth, and early sixteenth centuries. Because of its large income

[37] C.C.R., Edward III, 1340, p. 363. Also, *ibid.*, 1344, p. 114.

[38] *V.C.H.*, ii, pp. 56-72; Dugdale, iii, pp. 116-117.

[39] Yates, *History and Antiquities*, pp. 195-207. The best source for medieval wage and price information is E. H. Phelps-Brown and S. V. Hopkins, "Seven Centuries of Building Wages," *Economica*, xxii, 1955; and their "Seven Centuries of the Prices of Consumables, Compared with Builders' Wages Rates," *Economica*, xxiii, 1956. Worth consulting is the wage-price discussion in John Hatcher, *Plague, Population and the English Economy*, 1348-1530 (London: Macmillan, 1977), pp. 47-54.

[40] For a full discussion of the Baret family, see below, pp. 153-159.

and ready supply of cash, and the fact that it was a lavish patron, the abbey was a major consumer in Bury's marketplaces. Many of the town's specialist industries and crafts existed solely because of it. St. Edmunds also used its liquid capital to carve for itself an important role in local and West Suffolk money markets, a theme pursued in some detail below. But these positive roles were over-shadowed by more negative ones. The abbey was a large and pri-marily passive landlord. It did little to improve its rural holdings, and drained a great deal of capital in rents, services, and assorted banalities and miscellaneous tenant obligations; much of this capital went outside the borough, for such things as maintenance of the abbot's London townhouse. And, although its economic role was largely a passive one, St. Edmunds ultimately proved to be a re-tardant to the growth of the secular aspects of the borough's econ-omy, particularly commercial and industrial expansion. Through its well-established ancient prerogatives, the abbey took a sizeable portion of just about everyone's profits, and, while contemporaries recognized its economic contributions, they generally regarded it as a hindrance to continued economic development. When profit margins were low, abbey financial demands might represent the difference between solvency and bankruptcy. The economic history of late medieval Bury St. Edmunds, so crucial in the course of political and constitutional independence, is much the story of the struggle of the merchant community to free itself from or at least minimize its fiscal obligations.

THE MARKETPLACE AND TRADE

The initial economic importance of the commune stemmed from its role as the market center of prosperous West Suffolk. Although this market function was aided by the presence of the monastic community, its inception actually predated the foundation of St. Edmunds. Commercial activity centered around the borough's two marketplaces, the Great Market in Risbygate Ward, and the Horse or Old Market in Southgate Ward, along with a smaller area of Goldsmiths' Row, due west of the abbey complex. The latter con-sisted primarily of small specialty shops catering to abbey officers, and by the eleventh century activity in the Old Market was generally restricted to neighborhood victuallers and livestock. This meant that most local and virtually all regional, national, and international commerce centered on the Great Market. The earliest description of it comes from Jocelin of Brakelond, late in the twelfth century.[41] Jocelin repeatedly emphasizes a single, overriding point: market rights were firmly and jealously regarded as a crucial proprietary privilege by the abbot. Both denizen and alien merchants resented this control, and throughout the middle ages tried to extricate themselves from tolls and obligations. In the late twelfth century, London merchants told Abbot Samson that they should be relieved of all fees in the Great Market, part of a larger privilege they enjoyed throughout England.[42] But income from the abbot's share of trade profits was so high that Samson went to court to protect his rights. The abbot wanted a portion of all goods traded in his town; the Londoners claimed that privileges granted by Henry II exempted them from tolls in England, including Bury. Samson countered by saying that the market was within his liberty of eight-and-one-half hundreds, beyond the jurisdiction of even the Plantagenet kings, and that exemptions could come only from him. This, he retorted, was a privilege that extended back before the Conquest, was granted to St. Edmunds by Edward the Confessor, and could not be overturned by subsequent monarchs. The wily abbot then declared that, while he was not against the Londoners, tradition bound him; however he might personally be inclined, he could not make them free of obligations since it would violate the trust bestowed upon him. The Londoners were equally adamant about defending what they regarded as their just due, and organized a boycott of goods traded in the Great Market. The boycott lasted for two years, hurt both parties, and ultimately produced a compromise. The London men would pay the tolls for appearance's sake, and then get much of them back in direct cash rebates. Samson felt this "disguise of liberty" was essential in protecting abbatial market rights, lest native Bury merchants get similar ideas and attempt to win their own exemptions.

The confrontation with the Bury townsfolk that Samson feared came a decade later, in 1198. Borough merchants were embarking on the long period of commercial and industrial development that would blossom in the sixteenth century, and, as the market began to prosper, many of the local burgesses felt that the portion of their profits tithed by the abbey was too large. Ironically, this sentiment was shared by many of the monks of St. Edmunds, for the bulk of

[41] Jocelin, pp. 66-77.
[42] *Ibid.*, pp. 75-77. Also, see Lobel, *The Borough*, pp. 140-145.

the tolls went not to the abbey as such but to the abbot, the sacrist, the cellarer, the prior, and a few other key officials.[43] The rest of the 70 or so monks were left with £40 to divide among themselves. Hence, Samson found his market policy subject to criticism from two sides. The burgesses acted first. Following the example of the Londoners, they argued that, while the abbey's prerogatives were indeed ancient, they were no longer in step with current economic conditions, and therefore should be abrogated. They also claimed that if the abbey's privileges were ancient, they should apply only to those tenements held before the Conquest. New ones—that is to say, most of the stalls in the Great Market—should be quit. Finally, they argued that anyone who held municipal property for one year and one day without paying rent should forever be exempt from taxation. With consummate timing, the burgesses struck while Samson was in Germany on a royal diplomatic mission. They offered the monks, who, it will be recalled, made little from the tolls, sizable cash recompense to agree to the new proposals. The monks did, and when Samson returned he was confronted with a *fait accompli*; he too was offered a lump sum in cash, along with a set rather than a proportional share of marketplace income. With little alternative, he accepted.[44] Hence, while Bury merchants still had to pay fees after 1200, they were always fixed. As inflation took its toll in a 300-year period, the burden of payment to the abbey diminished considerably. Further, this confrontation initiated a period in which there were continual challenges to St. Edmunds' market privileges. In 1380, for example, Alice of Hilborough set up a stall in her house, and argued that since she already paid *hadgoval* the stall did not come under marketplace jurisdiction.[45] Fearing the spread of similar claims, the abbot sued her and won. But such successes were becoming less and less common. By the fifteenth century, abbey interference in borough trade was minimal, a crucial factor in the economic rise of the town.

Bury's markets were primarily regional, but because of the importance of West Suffolk and the built-in presence of a large monastic consumer, they offered a wide range of goods and services. Borough merchants were not as well organized as their London, Norwich, Bristol, or York counterparts. There were no local staples

[43] *Ibid.*, pp. 78-81.
[44] *Ibid.*
[45] C.U.L. Mss. Ff 2 33; Ee 3 60.

or adventurer groups, and the general composition of the marketplaces was left to the control of basic commodity or craft organizations. This in turn was watched over by the Alderman's Guild.[46] Composed of the leading merchants and craftsmen in Bury, the Alderman's Guild leased property around 1200 in the Great Market and constructed the stone Tollhouse.[47] There, the borough's bailiffs supervised the volume and quality of goods traded, and collected their tolls. And there too the burgesses held their meetings, until the construction of their guildhall late in the fourteenth century.[48] Beyond this very general system of controls, the only rules that applied to market organization were those of supply and demand.

Several sources provide information on the merchandise and physical setup of the Great Market. The earliest, the 1295 rental, lists the merchants and craftsmen who used it on a daily basis.[49] A principal feature was the Corn Market. Located throughout the thirteenth century at various points within the main market square, it was a focus of the regional grain trade. Stalls in the Corn Market did business seven days a week, but were busiest on the three market days, Monday, Wednesday and Friday, when peasants journeyed in from the surrounding villages. Although primarily concerned with local commodity items, the triweekly markets sometimes attracted merchants from beyond the greater urban region. In addition to the Corn Market, the Great Market contained Ironmongers' and Skinners' Rows, long series of stalls that carried finished and scrap leather, and iron and hardware. Along the perimeters stood the Cheese Market, Poulterers' Row, and the Net or Meat Market. There, most of the regional alimentary marketing was done, although livestock trade in the thirteenth century still centered in the Horse Market. Indeed, of all the major merchants in Bury, only the goldsmiths had their shops more than a few yards away. Around the Risbygate Market were additional food, cloth, and clothing shops, and most of the basic crafts. Services too could be had; most of Bury's tailor, butcher, cook and barber shops ringed the market square, or ran down adjacent avenues like Cooks' Row

[46] For details of the organization of the alderman's or merchant's guild, see below, pp. 129-136.

[47] Redstone, *St. Edmund's Bury*, pp. 9-11.

[48] M. P. Statham, "The Guildhall of Bury St. Edmunds," *P.S.I.*, xxxi, 1967-1970.

[49] Redstone, "St. Edmund's Bury."

or Hatter Street, the latter a haberdashery and garment center of the West Suffolk urban region.

The Great Market continued to prosper in the fourteenth and fifteenth centuries. A list of stallage fees, probably from the late fourteenth century, provides a comparative perspective.[50] The list is incomplete, but shows a portion of those merchants paying *hadgoval* rents, classifying them by numbers of stalls and levels of rent. The data are presented in Table 3.1. Thirty-seven stalls were operated by bakers; 22 by fishmongers, 16 by shoemakers, 7 by cappers, 9 by cattle dealers, indicating that by 1400 at least some of the livestock trade of the Horse Market and *Le Mustow* had moved to the Great Market; 31 for alien meat sellers, suggesting that local meat salesmen had won or bought *hadgoval* exemptions; 21 by blacksmiths, suggesting that the servicing of livestock had in part moved from *Le Mustow*; and 19 by drapers and skinners, an odd combination and rather smaller concentration than might be expected; along with a conglomerate assortment of lesser dealers. There were more developments in the fifteenth century. By 1433, the Corn Market had become more permanent, being centered in the middle of the Great Market.[51] We need only reiterate the obvious: among all of its social, governmental, ecclesiastical, and medical functions, Bury St. Edmunds was first and foremost one of the major regional markets in later medieval England.

TABLE 3.1: *HADGOVAL* STALLAGE RENTS IN THE GREAT MARKET, FOURTEENTH CENTURY

Stalls	Numbers Paying
Bakers	37
Scoppis mercanari	37
Meat sellers (alien)	31
Corvisers and Cappers	23 (16 and 7)
Fishmongers	22
Blacksmiths	21
Drapers and Skinners	19
Cattle dealers	9

[50] B. M. Harl. Ms. 58.
[51] B. M. Harl. Ms. 645.

Another service was available in Bury's marketplaces. By late medieval standards it was a financial center. The presence of provincial money markets has long been postulated by scholars, and evidence from the abbot's estates indicates that it was practiced at the manorial level.[52] Money markets probably existed in most English towns, and foreign merchants and financiers were active throughout the kingdom. In Bury, the abbey was an important patron of the great Italian banking house of Bardi, and the Italians probably offered their services to the burgesses.[53] There were also indigenous money-lenders, including virtually every major merchant in the borough; indeed, it will be suggested that one of the distinguishing features of Bury's mercantile élite was their role as financiers.[54] The best quantitative evidence for such activities comes from the testamentary records, data from which are presented in Table 3.2.

Over twenty percent of the will-makers owed debts, and this may well be just scratching the surface, since mention of debts listed in the opening "formula" part of the testaments, often unreliable, was not counted toward the overall total. Table 3.2. lists only those debtors and creditors who went into details about the extent of their activities, stating size and something about how the debts were

TABLE 3.2: TESTAMENTARY EVIDENCE FOR DEBTS

Description	Frequency	% Total Sample (2116)	Mean Group Bequest to High Altar
No debts	1646	77.8	13 pence
Lenders	55	2.6	20 shillings
Debtors	438	20.7	3 shillings
Lenders and debtors	27	1.3	18 shillings

[52] Bacon, 17. Information of further possibilities can be found in Hengrave, 2/320; and *ibid.*, 2/328. See also: C.P.R., Henry IV, 1411, p. 257; C.C.R., Edward II, 1325, p. 491; C.C.R., Henry VI, 1439, p. 314; C.C.R., Edward IV, 1478, p. 127, to name a few.

[53] C.U.L. Ms. Mm 4 19, f.61.

[54] See below, pp. 135-143.

to be discharged. Aside from the comparatively large proportion of testators involved in Bury's money markets, the data yield few surprises. Mean wealth for debtors was about 3 shillings, or category C, the middling income level, as will be presented in the "individual wealth" breakdown in Table 3.16.[55] Many borrowers appear to have negotiated loans for investment purposes as well as to keep body and soul together. Will-makers who were exclusively lenders, rather predictably, were among the richest men in the community, having an average bequest to the high altar of the parish church of their burial of 20 shillings. Those who both lent and borrowed were also quite well heeled, with a mean wealth measurement of 18 shillings. It was the great and prosperous merchants of Bury who had available capital and were able to build on their initial investments.

There may have been one additional major money-lender in town, the abbey of St. Edmunds. There is no hard evidence to substantiate this assertion. But the abbey had become a major *rentier* by the fifteenth century, and by the standards of the townsfolk had a great deal of liquid, readily available capital. St. Edmunds collected tolls and engaged in a number of commercial ventures, and was often quick to capitalize on easy ways of turning a profit. It is perhaps a small step beyond this to think of the abbot, or more probably his surrogates the bailiffs, making money available in return for a fee. Whatever the ultimate composition of Bury St. Edmunds' creditors, they existed, probably flourished by the late fourteenth century, and offered an important service in the town marketplaces.

The major focus of Bury's trade was regional, but town markets did have a wider attraction. As early as the thirteenth century, its annual trade fair, one of the largest in England, was drawing merchants from Ypres and Bruges. So zealous were these Flemings that edicts had to be passed to prevent them from monopolizing commerce in leather and velvet goods.[56] Bury was well situated for overseas trade, despite its inland location. The fens cut it off from much of the rest of England, while its rivers and roads connected it with ports along the East Anglian coast. Consequently, Bury merchants, like those from King's Lynn, Norwich, Great Yarmouth,

[55] For details on the formulation of wealth, see below, pp. 124-130.

[56] Lobel, *The Borough*, pp. 65-66, 119, 144; *C. Charter Rolls*, 5, 1406, p. 431. For details, see Arnold, i, p. 304; and Godwin, p. 16.

and Ipswich, directed much of their trade to a Channel commercial sphere that included eastern England, the Low Countries, and northwestern France. London merchants were aware of this connection, and banded together with Bury men a number of times for continental ventures. In the 1440s, for example, several Burians entered into a venture with some London skinners and grocers; among them was William Bass, one of the richest men in the borough.[57]

Early records of Bury merchants trading outside of England usually show them participating in the fashion of William Bass in joint ventures with their more sophisticated and better organized counterparts from London, Norwich, and Ipswich.[58] Before 1350, the Bury men were invariably junior partners. But from the late fourteenth century onward, they began trading on their own. Most expeditions were directed toward markets in Brabant and Flanders, and the problem arose of finding a port with direct sea access. There were merchants from other eastern towns with whom they had to compete, especially denizens of the ports along the Wash, the Channel, and the North Sea. Potential points of embarkation included East Suffolk coastal towns like Ipswich, the older borough of Dunwich, Felixstowe, and Southwold, and surviving evidence indicates that Bury merchants sailed from all of these places at various times.[59] In the fourteenth century, for example, the Bury vintner John Asty exported considerable amounts of woolen cloth from Ipswich and several surrounding villages. But these East Suffolk ports were not the most widely used.[60] Perhaps there were bitter incidents stemming from the rivalry between the largest towns in East and West Suffolk, or tariffs and other restrictions on alien merchants. More likely, Bury merchants seldom used East Suffolk ports because the bulk of their trade was directed to the northern reaches of the Channel trading area. These destinations—Brabant, Picardy, Holland and Flanders—were most easily reached through county Norfolk ports, especially King's Lynn and Great

[57] C.C.R., Henry VI, 1449, p. 135.
[58] For details of the organization of these and other groups, see E. M. Carus-Wilson, *Medieval Merchant Venturers* (London: Methuen, 1954).
[59] C.P.R., Henry VI, 1443, p. 199; C.C.R., Henry VI, 1449, p. 168.
[60] C.P.R., Edward III, 1364, p. 17.

Yarmouth.[61] King's Lynn was the most favored. It stood on the Wash, at the headwaters of the River Ouse, into which the Lark and the Linnet flowed, and proved a convenient *entrepôt* for heavy goods, such as raw wool and hides. The lack of quantifiable evidence makes definitive statements impossible, but it is likely that by 1450 about half of all of Bury's exports were shipped through Lynn.[62]

Raw wool and finished cloth were the most frequently exported goods, and Iberia, the Celtic parts of the British Isles, and Scandinavia the major destinations after the Netherlands.[63] The Iberians were primarily interested in raw wool, while the Scots and Irish wanted finished cloth and, to a lesser extent, foodstuffs.[64] In 1310 a Suffolk expedition led by the Bury merchant John de Lynn was given a royal safe-conduct by the kings of England and Scotland to carry cloth and grain to Edinburgh.[65] Lynn and his colleagues appear to have been successful, and as a result were awarded the monopoly to trade corn throughout the Scottish east coast. In 1445 Richard Bossohow, a mercer, was the principal provisioner of the Earl of Shrewsbury and his army on their Irish campaign. Bossohow made connections with Irish merchants and became a major carrier of grain across the Celtic Sea for the next twenty years.[66] Commerce with Ireland and Scotland was not a one-way path. The Scots merchant Thomas Thomson traded extensively in East Anglia during the mid-fifteenth century, concentrating on West Suffolk and using the port facilities of King's Lynn. He went to Bury's

[61] C.P.R., Edward II, 1310, p. 215; C.P.R., Edward III, 1363, p. 364; C.P.R., Henry V, 1415, p. 332; C.P.R., Henry VI, 1436, p. 57. Also, see E. M. Carus-Wilson, "The Medieval Trade of the Ports of the Wash," *Medieval Archaeology*, pp. vi-vii, 1962-1963. Some Bury merchants were actually freemen of King's Lynn. See the *Calendar of the Freemen of Lynn, 1292-1836* (Norwich: Norwich and Norfolk Archaeology Society, 1913), p. 29.

[62] Indeed, the inland town of Bury St. Edmunds was sufficiently water-oriented so that in 1379 the royal council saw fit to authorize the burgesses, along with their comrades from Thetford, another inland town, to build a ship to be incorporated into the royal navy. See C.C.R., Richard II, 1378, p. 43; and *ibid.*, 1379, p. 181.

[63] Among these references, see: C.F.R., Edward I, 1290, p. 286; C.C.R., Edward II, 1311, p. 358; C.P.R., Henry VI, 1436, pp. 548-581; *ibid.*, 1454, p. 160.

[64] C.P.R., Henry VI, 1452, p. 26.

[65] C.P.R., Edward II, 1310, p. 215.

[66] C.P.R., Henry VI, 1445, p. 432.

Risbygate Market several times, and in 1480 decided to settle permanently in the town.[67]

Scotsmen were not the only foreigners attracted to Bury St. Edmunds. There was a steady flow of merchants from the Low Countries. As early as 1294, Dutchmen trading throughout eastern England and using the ports of Blakeney and Great Yarmouth decided to make Bury their home base.[68] Alien registries, taken periodically in the later middle ages at royal instigation, provide further evidence. The 1436 mandate, permitting aliens to reside in England, listed six resident foreigners in Bury St. Edmunds, four merchants, a weaver, and a tailor.[69] They were two Dutchmen, two Brabanters, and two Germans from "lydyk," perhaps Lübeck. And while they usually restricted their activities to London, southern and western ports, a few Italians found their way to the Bury markets. The role of the Lombards and Florentines as financiers has been discussed; several of them also traded in wool and cloth.

Bury merchants generally maintained good relations with the people and officials in the lands in which they traded, an essential condition for continuing business ties. There were, however, a few exceptions. Petitions survive from Suffolk merchants to their kings, seeking justice for alleged grievances. This happened several times in the Low Countries from the thirteenth through the sixteenth century, but the most noteworthy of such incidents occurred in the fourteenth century, and involved a Scandinavian venture.[70] In 1361 a group of East Anglian merchants, including James Marham of Bury, set sail from Great Yarmouth for Norway with a cargo of woolen cloth, assessed by the aulnagers at around 2000 marks. At Coft the Englishmen were caught in a storm and their ship went down. The survivors of the wreck sought a license for salvage, won the cooperation of the local Norwegian townsfolk, and managed to save much of their cargo. But in the process of the salvage agents of King Magnus of Norway learned of the affair and laid claim to a share of the goods, citing the crown's right to a portion of the "produce of the sea." The East Anglians claimed that this violated a long-standing trade agreement, but their pleas were turned down. They returned to England and appealed to King Edward III for

[67] C.P.R., Edward IV, 1480, p. 217.
[68] C.P.R., Edward I, 1294, p. 111.
[69] C.P.R., Henry VI, 1436, pp. 548-581.
[70] C.C.R., Edward III, 1361, pp. 348-349.

help.[71] It is a testament to the extent and importance of late medieval commerce that the merchants would be inclined to appeal to their king for support in such circumstances. Edward did intercede in their behalf, and, while there is no record of how the affair was finally resolved, trade relations between the East Anglians and the Norwegians soon resumed, suggesting a settlement of some kind. In effect, then, while the most important concentrations of Bury merchants were local and regional, some traders, in pursuit of the very high profits that only international trade could produce, ventured out into distant markets. Further, they did so in growing numbers from the late fourteenth century onward.

WOOL AND CLOTH

As important to the economic well-being of Bury St. Edmunds as its role as a regional market center was its position in the production of textiles.[72] Bury was a major component in the south Suffolk cloth industry, which flourished in the Stour River Valley in the fifteenth and sixteenth centuries. Records of "cottage"-level cloth production in Suffolk survive from the Roman settlement, and the product was noted for its excellence throughout northern Europe as early as the eighth century.[73] But, before 1400, the region was most famous for its raw wool. In part this was a reflection of the relative lack of industrial development in England when compared with Flanders and Brabant, and in part a reflection of climate. British weather produced sheep with thick, luxurious fleece. Sheep were easy to keep, especially on large estates, and many landlords turned exclusively to their husbandry. English middlemen or for-

[71] The dispute takes added interest through the formal overtones of the letter that Edward sent to Magnus, and because of the analogies that the king of England draws between his subjects and those of Norway.

[72] There are many studies of the textile trade in England and on the continent. Perhaps the best starting points are: Eileen Power, *The Wool Trade in Medieval England* (Oxford: Oxford University Press, 1941); T. C. Lloyd, *The English Wool Trade in the Middle Ages* (Cambridge: Cambridge University Press, 1976); E. M. Carus-Wilson, "The Woollen Trade in the Middle Ages," in M. M. Postan, ed., *The Cambridge Economic History of Europe*, ii (Cambridge: Cambridge University Press, 1952).

[73] A summary of the textile process can be found in Gerald A. J. Hodgett, *A Social and Economic History of Medieval Europe* (London: Methuen, 1972), pp. 137-139.

eign procurers would go to rural sheepfolds, buy wool, process it, and at times have it made into yarn. It was then sold to alien merchants, who in turn shipped it to continental cloth producers. Organized English industry first appeared late in the tenth century. It was small in scale, directed almost entirely to local markets, and generally restricted to small and middling-sized towns, like Lincoln, Beverley, and Boston, and could not compete with its Netherland-ish rivals. Overall, eastern England's role in western Europe's textile industry remained primarily as a supplier of raw materials rather than as a producer of finished goods. This pattern would continue until the fifteenth century, but from the 1190s a series of changes occurred which would in time foster a dynamic, indigenous cloth industry, able to utilize the kingdom's natural advantages and enable it to compete in European markets.

These changes have been well documented and described, and can be discussed briefly.[74] The first, dating from the 1190s and early 1200s, was technological, the development of a water-driven fulling machine. After the cloth was woven, it was given to fullers. Fulling prepared the cloth for the last stages of the production process, dyeing and finishing. Traditionally, it was the most obnoxious stage, performed by men treading on cloth covered by fuller's earth, in troughs filled with urine. It was designed to clean further the cloth, removing more oil and dirt, first spreading and then shrinking the bolts. The procedure was long, arduous, inefficient, and expensive. When it was completed, the cloth had to be hung and stretched between tenterhooks, to be formed into the desired shape and size.

The new fulling machine changed all of this.[75] The action of human feet was replaced by bicycle-like pedals. The new machine was heavy and cumbersome, and difficult to maneuver. It was also expensive, and, most significantly, although it fulled far more efficiently and rapidly than the old method, had to be powered by running water, with a revolving drum linked to a waterwheel. Ultimately, it was this switch to waterpower that made for the most significant changes in the cloth industry. With running water essential, most of the slow, stagnant streams next to established me-

---

[74] E. M. Carus-Wilson, "An Industrial Revolution of the Thirteenth Century," in *Medieval Merchant Venturers*.

[75] *Ibid.* Also, see her "English Cloth Industry in the 12th and 13th Centuries," in *Medieval Merchant Venturers*.

dieval towns proved inadequate. Further, restrictive policies of some craft guilds in the older towns slowed down production and added to costs. When in the thirteenth century entrepreneurs chose to relocate the cloth industry, many elected not to set up in towns but in rural areas, where power and labor were cheaper and more readily available. One of the major new centers was in the Cotswolds, in Oxfordshire. Another was in the Stour Valley, the northern part of which fell within the southern perimeter of Bury's market area.

The new fulling machine provided the English cloth industry with the potential it needed to lower costs and to expand production, but English merchants still had to capture a market long dominated by Flemish and north Italian cloth. This was to prove a long and arduous process that would not come to fruition until the late fifteenth-early sixteenth centuries, and was started with a political push, the tax levies on wool and cloth. The events by which England's kings placed a sizable excise on their most sought-after export, raw wool, are well known even to the proverbial English schoolboy.[76] As Edward III pursued a more aggressive and adventurous foreign policy, his need for capital rose to the point where he taxed wool to one-third of its aulnage value. Because cloth was considered of minor importance as late as the fourteenth century, its excise was left at less than 2 percent of total value. This marked a true beginning; it did not take long for enterprising merchants to see where the highest potential profits lay. Coupled with the new fulling machine and the best supplies of raw wool in western Europe, the English cloth industry began to come into its own late in the fourteenth century. In the course of the fifteenth century, the English wool monopoly, controlled by the Merchants of the Staple and centered in Calais, steadily lost ground to the new, dynamic Merchant Adventurers.[77] Increased demand for Suffolk cloth, especially in the lands around the Baltic Sea and north German hinterlands, meant increased production and good times for Stour Valley producers and exporters (Table 3.3).[78]

Bury's role in the wool-cloth cycle was both commercial and in-

[76] Others might wish to consult Power, *The Wool Trade*.

[77] E. M. Carus-Wilson, "The Rise of the Merchant Adventurers"; and her "Development of the Merchant Adventurers Organization in London," both in *Medieval Merchant Venturers*.

[78] Lobel, *The Borough*, p. 159. The data in the table are from Bridbury, *Economic Growth*, p. 32.

TABLE 3.3: ENGLISH EXPORTS IN CLOTH AND RAW WOOL*

Years	Cloth	Wool
1281-1290		26,856
1301-1310		34,493
1311-1320		30,686
1321-1330		25,268
1331-1340		29,569
1341-1350		22,013
1351-1360	1,267	32,655
1361-1370	3,024	28,302
1371-1380	3,432	23,241
1381-1390	5,521	17,988
1391-1400	8,967	17,679
1401-1410	7,651	13,922
1411-1420	6,364	13,487
1421-1430	9,309	13,696
1431-1440	10,051	7,377
1441-1450	11,803	9,398
1451-1460	8,445	8,058
1461-1470	7,667	8,237
1471-1480	10,125	9,299
1481-1490	12,230	8,858
1491-1500	13,891	8,149
1501-1510	18,700	7,562
1511-1520	20,388	7,634
1521-1530	20,305	4,990
1531-1540	23,424	3,481

* Sacks of wool and raw wool equivalent for cloth.

dustrial. As with the marketing of other goods, its merchants were less well organized than those from London and from many of the larger provincial towns, and were primarily oriented towards regional sales. Denizens who traded in wider markets tended to be "rugged individualists" who struck out on their own, or banded together with merchants from other towns. But, mostly, alien merchants came to the Risbygate Market. Several times in the fourteenth and fifteenth centuries, trade fairs organized around wool and cloth products were held on the feast of St. Matthew, in late

September. By the 1420s these fairs had become annual events, and by the 1450s were sufficiently important so that Bury merchants, in return for concessions in their fair, were exempted by the Crown of all tolls in fairs throughout the rest of England.[79] Raw wool remained a valuable commodity even after 1400. It was the subject of an infamous corruption scandal involving royal officials in the 1360s, and a century later was still profitable enough to form the principal part of the trading activities of two of Bury's wealthiest merchants, John Baret II and John Smith.[80] But, as important as it was, wool could be purchased in many market towns throughout England, and if it had been the sole attraction of Bury's markets, London merchants would not have ventured out in great numbers. High-quality finished woolen cloth, however, was different. It was available in very few places, and as its value rose in the late fourteenth century, more and more local merchants began to market it. By 1400 cloth was the most valuable commodity traded in the Risbygate Market.

Several Bury men made fortunes in the merceries. A prominent example was John Clever. He won the right to the farm of the cloth subsidy throughout all of East Anglia, one of the most lucrative franchises in the kingdom.[81] Clever was given control over the local aulnage, the royal tax assessed on all cloth designated for export, initially at six pence on scarlets and five for all other colors. For this profitable privilege, Clever paid the king's agents a lump

[79] C.P.R., Edward III, 1364, p. 22; C.P.R., Henry IV, 1404, p. 466. Also, *C. Charter Rolls*, 5, 1406, p. 43.

[80] C.P.R., Edward III, 1363, p. 362, 364. We have details from a trading scheme of one of Bury's leading merchants, Robert de Eriswell, on the eve of Edward III's initial campaign. Later, he was involved in the infamous 1360s corruption case with a royal official named John Spor. Spor, ". . . a mere woolwyndere . . . skilled at clening and preparing woll for sale . . ." decided not only to prepare Eriswell's wool, but also to market it on the side for his own aggrandizement. Secretly, Spor disposed of more than seven sacks of wool worth over 50 shillings each, plus assorted smaller packets, until he was discovered and arrested. When apprehended, he pleaded that he had found the wool on a wrecked ship off the Norfolk coastal town of Wells-on-the-Sea. But his claims for spoils went for naught; the wool was too valuable, and on Eriswell's insistence, he was brought to Westminster for trial in the Treasury Court, and his wool and profits confiscated. For details on the lives of Smith and Baret, see below, pp. 141-143 and 154-158.

[81] C.C.R., Edward III, 1363, p. 302.

sum of £20; in turn, he must have reaped profits of several hundred percent. Both Clever and the Crown seem to have been happy with the arrangement, for, at the end of the initial tenure in 1369, the franchise was renewed for three more years at the same terms, initiating a long period in which Bury merchants held the cloth farm.[82]

There are many other examples that show the importance of the cloth industry to Bury St. Edmunds' economy. Late in the 1390s, two Bury mercers succeeded in gaining control over cloth exports from the East Suffolk port of Orwell.[83] While exports from Orwell were never so great as those from King's Lynn and Great Yarmouth, they did add new dimensions and directions to the cloth industry. So valuable had the cloth trade become that Richard II found it necessary to order Bury's bailiffs to proclaim that no finished cloth could be exported without the official aulnage seal—a good indication that unofficial export was occurring on a fairly regular basis.[84]

Some of the cloth Bury merchants sold was produced within the banleuca, but most of it came from the textile villages along the Stour. Ultimately, the town's most important role in the late medieval textile industry was as a principal regional market for these villages. Foremost among them was Lavenham, sufficiently prosperous to rank fourteenth in wealth among English towns in the 1524 Lay Subsidy.[85] Its development from a rather ordinary market village was due to the new conditions of textile production engendered by the water powered fulling machine; it had cheap labor, running water, a ready supply of wool, and a very active and dynamic group of entrepreneurs, such as the three generations of Thomas Springs. Much of the production in Lavenham and the other Stour Valley towns was self-contained, or farmed out within a five-mile radius. Raw wool was brought in from neighboring sheepfolds, and all the industrial processes were performed in or around the towns. This is illustrated by the data in Table 3.4. Taken from the 1522 military muster roll, they show major cloth villages

[82] C.C.R., Edward III, 1369, p. 89; *ibid.*, 1372, p. 423.
[83] C.C.R., Richard II, 1397, p. 119.
[84] *Ibid.* Also, C.C.R., Richard II, 1378, p. 140.
[85] Barbara McClenaghan, *The Springs of Lavenham and the Suffolk Cloth Trade of the XV and XVI Centuries* (Ipswich, W. E. Harrison, 1924).

TABLE 3.4: OCCUPATIONAL BREAKDOWN OF STOUR VALLEY
VILLAGES, 1522

Village	Total	Clothmakers	Weavers	Dyers	Fullers	Sherman
Lavenham	57	34	15	3	3	2
Glemsford	29	20	5	—	4	—
Neyland	35	14	8	—	4	9
Boxford	60	11	37	4	2	6
Long Melford	28	8	6	3	9	2
Sudbury	27	8	11	1	5	2
Stoke-Neyland	9	5	4	—	—	—
Waldingfeld *Mag.*	12	4	6	1	—	1
Waldingfeld *Par.*	9	3	3	—	2	1
Edwardstone	7	3	4	—	—	—
Groton	14	3	8	—	1	2
Brent Eleigh	4	2	1	—	—	1
Cavendish	2	2	—	—	—	—
Monks Eleigh	3	1	—	1	1	—
Stanstead	4	1	—	—	3	—
Conerd *Magna*	2	1	1	—	—	—
Conerd *Parva*	1	—	1	—	—	—
Bures	7	—	—	—	6	1
Acton	1	—	—	—	1	—
	311	120	110	13	41	27

and the craftsmen who worked in them.[86] There was a local, highly
developed, completely interwoven pattern whereby one town might
have a high concentration of weavers, another of dyers, and a third
of fullers. Bury's role in this system, despite the presence of some
important Lavenham mercers and drapers like the Springs, was as
a marketing center. A large portion of south Suffolk cloth found
its way to the Great Market in Risbygate Ward.

Bury St. Edmunds was not the sole market for Stour Valley cloth.
It had to compete with Ipswich and Colchester, both of which had
far better port facilities, and the peripatetic drapers and mercers

[86] Edgar Powell, "Muster Rolls of the Territorials in Tudor Times,"
P.S.I., xv, 1915.

of London. Because it was inland, Bury men were placed at considerable disadvantage, and had to work hard to overcome the problems of transporting bulk goods overland. But the merchants managed, and even prospered. They went to Lavenham and brought cloth back to the Great Market. Topographical records show that the "Buryweye," the road between the two towns, was the most heavily travelled in West Suffolk. Evidence indicates that the Springs of Lavenham started out in Bury St. Edmunds late in the fourteenth century, and continued to trade in the Risbygate Market on a regular basis well into the sixteenth century.[87] They were involved in land deals in and around the banleuca, and, appropriately enough, Thomas Spring II left provisions in his 1486 will to repair many roads around Lavenham, but "especially those leading Buryweye."[88] The strength of the Lavenham-Bury connection is further illustrated in bequests in other wills from Lavenham testators; Bury, its markets and its roads, are mentioned over twice as frequently as those from Ipswich and Colchester combined.[89] In 1530, Richard Trype, another prominent Lavenham clothier, left money for road repair, exclusively designed for the mending of the "highweye at the town . . . [leading] . . . burywarde."[90] Roads from Lavenham led in many directions, but the most important went north to the Great Market of Bury St. Edmunds.

While Bury's principal role in the textile industry was as a market, it did have some indigenous cloth production. Indeed, next to Lavenham, Colchester, and perhaps Long Melford, it was probably the leading cloth producer in western East Anglia. Characteristic of the Bury industry was the clustering of its more mobile craftsmen—weavers, dyers, shermen, combers, carders, and the like— around the sources of running water to which the fullers were more or less tied. The banleuca had good sources of running water, several mills, and enough fullers to make them the fifth most frequently encountered occupation in the testamentary records. Most lived in Eastgate and Southgate Wards, close to the shops and

[87] McClenaghan, *The Springs*, Chapter 2. The book has no page numbers.
[88] *Ibid.*
[89] I have found references to Bury-Lavenham road repairs in thirty-three wills, and references to Ipswich and Colchester in sixteen. Although wills from the Peculiar Court of Bury St. Edmunds and the archdeaconries of Suffolk and Sudbury have been searched, those from Essex have not.
[90] P.C.C., Thower, i, as cited in McClenaghan, *The Springs*, Chapter 2.

factories in which they worked. The occupational breakdown of
the testamentary population will be discussed shortly; suffice it to
note here that six of the seven most frequently encountered occupations were connected with textiles, and two of these were directly associated with production.[91]

Sources discussing Bury's textile production are rare, but one
survives that allows detailed analysis: the 1477 collection of the
bylaws of the weavers' and linendrapers' guild.[92] The weavers were
the most numerous of all Bury craftsmen in the later middle ages,
and their period of greatest prosperity came from the late fourteenth century onwards. It has been alleged that formal guild organization was often a feature of decline, an attempt to monopolize
when no longer competitive.[93] This does not apply to the Bury
weavers, who were sufficiently powerful to incorporate under their
auspices all local woolmen and linen-drapers. In a real sense, formal
incorporation meant a coming of age. Before the fifteenth century,
cloth production had usually been conducted at the cottage level,
with craftsmen selling their finished wares among themselves. But,
in the fifteenth century, as the cloth industry became increasingly
capitalistic in organization, great entrepreneurs threatened to dominate all levels of the industry. Many of the textile crafts were faced
with a loss of independence, due to an inability to buy essential raw
materials and to sell their finished goods. Such was the fate of
Bury's shermen, carders, and combers, but the most powerful
craftsmen, the dyers and especially the weavers, were able to resist.
The weavers' response to such things as the burgesses' ordinance in
1447 restricting the sale of cloth in Bury on specific days and only
in the wool hall was to organize and incorporate. The 1477 bylaws,
sanctioned by Edward IV, were the culmination of a series of regulations describing what the weavers perceived to be their ancient
prerogatives.

The ordinances show a vigorous and thriving craft that employed
not only local males but local women and children, and men from
outside the banleuca. One of the major concerns of the guild leaders
was parttimers—persons tempted by potentially high profits or

[91] See below, pp. 107-121.

[92] The entire document is reprinted in Arnold, iii, pp. 358-370.

[93] A fine discussion of the implications of medieval incorporation can be
found in Phillipe Dolinger, *The Hansa* (Palo Alto, Cal.: Stanford University
Press, 1970), Parts II and III.

wages into weaving a bit on the side, outside formal guild strictures. The bylaws attempted to restrict such activities, but, at the same time, to offer an olive branch; non-guild members, after payment and screening, could gain entry. But the olive branch was extended just so far. The bylaws were a clear attempt at establishing a monopoly, and those who continued to operate without the formal organization risked financial and ultimately physical penalty.

The bylaws are of interest for additional reasons. Rules were established for both individuals and corporations. All persons, masters, journeymen and householders, apprentices and servants, the last groups hired annually or by journey, were compelled to assemble at the Guildhall during the Feast of St. Edmund the King, Bury's patron. This allowed in theory for an annual check over everyone weaving cloth, and provided the opportunity for the guild fathers to elect from their ranks their leaders, "four appropriate freemen, to be chosen as guild wardens." All wardens had to be masters, and had to be presented for approval before the town bailiffs in the Tollhouse. They were given full powers over all guild business, and when elected were expected to devote their full attention to the job. Indeed, there was little choice; those elected who refused to serve were said to be negligent in their duties and forced to pay a steep fine. Members too had responsibilities. Socially, they were expected to play a large role in the annual town pageant and procession of *Corpus Christi*. Politically, it was their duty to attend guild assemblies, to pledge to abide by all rules and regulations of the craft, to open their homes for search or service by the guild wardens, and to rally whenever necessary to oppose merchant attempts to limit their power.

At the heart of the weavers' bylaws were economic regulations. No person was allowed to set up new looms or to accept apprentices unless they were fully recognized members of the craft. This was a key demand of the senior guild partners, determined to preserve their monopoly and control. Newcomers had to pay entry fees, and demonstration of expertise was required of those seeking wage work, even at the journey level. It would be nice to think of this procedure as a sort of quality control, but this was a secondary consideration. Its primary function was restrictive; it was another way in which senior members controlled cloth production, and was in part directed against the experienced and highly skilled Flemish and Dutch immigrants who settled in increasing numbers in East

Anglia in the fifteenth century.[94] Despite these obstacles, Netherlandish weavers would eventually work their way into the guild, and their presence must have been another element in Suffolk's late medieval textile boom.

Economic limitation, the essence of guild monopoly, applied to members of the guild, as well as to outsiders. No one was allowed to have more than four looms in operation on any given day.[95] There were restrictions on the time periods in which assistants could be hired, and all hired help, whether by day or long term, were subject to the approval of the omnipresent and omniscient guild wardens. Violators as always could be fined, and under all circumstances workers were taxed on their wages. Apprentices were also strictly regulated. No one was allowed to take one on for less than a seven-year term, nor to receive an apprentice at journeyman's rates. From the mid-fifteenth century onward, there was tremendous demand for weavers, and the guild fathers may even have tried to beat back clothiers hoping to tempt individuals to work for them on a more direct and perhaps higher scale. There are other hints to this possibility. Journeymen were forbidden to pick up and leave their masters under any circumstance. They were bound for the duration of their contracts by the initial terms, however unfavorable these terms may have been. Further, all work had to be guaranteed by their masters, under penalty of the guild's fine system. To cut down on internal competition, masters were forbidden to bid against one another for journeymen; and, to foster a spirit of cooperation, one day before Lent groups of twelve members or fourteen masters were sworn to an oath of allegiance before

[94] The best work on aliens has been done by S. L. Thrupp. See her: "A Survey of the Alien Population in England in 1440," *Speculum*, xxxii, 1953; and "Aliens in and Around London," in A.E.J. Hollaender and William Kellaway, eds., *Studies in London History* (London: Stodder and Houghton, 1970). Also of use is K. Ranson, *Lavenham* (Lavenham, Suffolk: L. Ranson, n.d.).

[95] The looms were of obvious importance and the object of great pride among the weavers. They appear prominently in many testamentary bequests; men passed their tools to wives and sons and daughters on a scale and with a passion that suggests more than a mere working interest. In 1495, for example, Beneyt Wareyn (P.C.B.S.E., Pye, f. 34) left two looms to his wife, on the condition that she actively continued to weave. In 1503, Edmund Goodhale (P.C.B.S.E., Pye, f. 130) left his two looms, one for wool and one for linen.

other members of the craft and the town bailiffs. Almost a type of urban frankpledge, this oath was followed by still another calling for mutual support among all guild members. If outside pressures were to be resisted successfully, internal solidarity had to be absolute.

The 1477 weavers guild bylaws, a reiteration of an earlier act of incorporation, are evidence of a powerful and prospering corporation, put on the defensive by new capitalistic groups, but able to resist because of their domination of the key industrial process. This had not always been the case. As late as the twelfth century, when most Suffolk cloth production was restricted to towns like Bury, the abbot controlled all weaving and fulling rights on the Lark and the Linnet.[96] Fulling privileges were leased, with craftsmen paying steep fines from their profits. The weavers fought long and hard to resist these sorts of encroachments, but were forced to pay some tolls until Dissolution, and had to swear annual oaths of fealty to the abbey's bailiffs. In some textile crafts, the abbot's hold was never severely challenged; the fullers, for example, continued to pay tolls throughout the sixteenth century.[97] But even among the less advantaged, some forms of proprietary rights developed, and in 1507 one Bury clothmaker felt sufficiently secure in his property rights to bequeath to his son a complete fulling mill.[98] Theoretically, all mills and perhaps all looms were held by the abbot, but this began to change in the fifteenth century as the importance of textiles increased.[99] By 1450 at the latest, most mills and looms were regarded by individual craftsmen as their own, regardless of the fees that they had to pay. Strong guilds like the weavers and dyers had fought hard to preserve their rights against one overlord, the abbey; they would organize in the fifteenth and sixteenth centuries to resist another, the new "capitalistic" clothiers.[100]

[96] Jocelyn, pp. 58-60.
[97] L. Redstone, "First Ministers' Account."
[98] P.C.B.S.E., John Gardiner, Pye, f. 196.
[99] Lobel, *The Borough*, p. 159.
[100] Weavers comprised the major segment of Bury's textile workers, but textile merchants and other craftsmen also played major roles. Among the merchants, mercers and drapers were the most important, and were among the richest and most powerful groups in the entire borough. Among other occupational groups involved with marketing were linendrapers, woolmen

We can summarize the development of the wool and cloth industries in late medieval Bury St. Edmunds and its hinterlands. The borough had important industrial and commercial functions. Some sheep were raised in the vicinity; the abbot's sheepfolds were considered to be among the finest in East Anglia, and the wool fields in northeast England were accessible enough to the ports along the Wash to ensure a steady supply. Bury stood at the center of a comparatively good river-and-road system, allowing for both waterpower and transportation. It was close enough to the Low Countries to make export feasible. Until the fifteenth century, industry in West Suffolk was settled primarily within the borough, but by 1450 had spread throughout the Stour River Valley, at the southern perimeter of the Bury urban region. Similarly, until some point in the fifteenth century, most production was geared to a local, primarily West Suffolk market. This was profitable but limited. As Lavenham and other cloth villages developed, production was stepped up for a wider East Anglian, eastern English, and finally overseas market. By late century, cloth production was of sufficient importance to attract London's Merchant Adventurers to Bury's Great Market.

Production was initially at the craft guild level, tightly controlled first by the abbey and then by the guilds themselves. By the end of the middle ages, this system was being challenged by a new capitalistic system wherein lone entrepreneurs—drapers, mercers, or clothiers—dominated and supervised all levels of the industrial and commercial process. In the face of this new challenge, many of the town's older guilds, just recently successful in gaining some measure of autonomy from St. Edmunds, saw their social and economic positions erode. Among the losers were shermen, fullers, combers, and carders. But the most powerful and best-organized craft guilds, such as the weavers and dyers, managed to maintain

---

or middlemen, and clothiers, a word used increasingly from about 1480 to describe the new entrepreneurs who combined all aspects of retailing and wholesaling under their auspices. Of all textile occupations, the most difficult to describe were tailors, the third most frequent occupation listed by testators. In London, tailors were incorporated as merchant tailors, and were one of the great livery companies of the city. It is not likely that they played such a large role in Bury St. Edmunds. Bury's tailors were involved in retailing on a small scale, but their principal role remained that of craftsmen making garments from cloth, and selling them in their shops and to the monks in the abbey.

their positions by organizing themselves more tightly than ever, and then eliminating all competition.

The borough of Bury St. Edmunds was not an industrial center of the first rank. And, while it was a major market, it had to compete with Colchester, Ipswich, King's Lynn, and London. Even with Lavenham aggregated in, Ipswich and Colchester proved to be strong textile rivals. But wool and cloth were crucial to the economic well-being and even rise of Bury, and were an integral part of the town's general economic prosperity.

GUILDS, OCCUPATIONS, AND NON-TEXTILE INDUSTRIES

Most of the rest of Bury St. Edmunds' industries functioned within the auspices of a guild structure. Guilds are among the most complex of all medieval socio-economic institutions.[101] Their functions encompassed an enormous array of activities, and, while their economic role is best known, their social tasks may well have been more important. Social aspects will be considered below; herein, I will concentrate on the economic.

Craft guilds can be traced back to the eighth and ninth centuries, but did not become a significant force in England until the eleventh century.[102] They thrived in environments like that offered by Bury St. Edmunds—small to middling-sized provincial towns, not ports, but centers whose industries served primarily local and regional markets. Bury was close to the demographic minimum for full guild development, and probably would have been hard-pressed to support as many crafts as it did, had it not been for its wider urban function of serving the West Suffolk urban region, and the presence of that large-scale customer, the abbey.

Like the weavers' and linen-drapers' guild, other craft guilds for which evidence has survived were monopolistic in structure, designed to place almost total control in the hands of the guild wardens. Bylaws exist from the bakers' and cordwainers' guilds.[103]

---

[101] For English guilds, see: George Unwin, *The Gilds and Companies of London* (Oxford: Oxford University Press, 1908). For a broader perspective, see S. L. Thrupp, "Gilds," in M. M. Postan, ed., *The Cambridge Economic History of Europe*, iii; and her "Gilds," in *The International Encyclopedia of the Social Sciences*, 1968. Also, Thrupp, "Medieval Gilds Reconsidered," *Journal of Economic History*, 2, 1942.

[102] Lujo Brentano, *English Gilds* (London: E.E.T.S., 40, 1878).

[103] For the cordwainers, see C.U.L. Ms. Mm, 4, 19; for the bakers, see C.U.L. Ms. Ff,2,33. Also, Lobel, *The Borough*, p. 52.

Both were drawn up in a similar though more elaborate fashion than the weaver's regulations. Both recognized the power of the abbot and his lieutenant, the sacrist, and paid recompense for the privilege of incorporation. But both were careful to ensure that daily operation and control of their respective skills lay solely with the guild fathers. Guild aldermen—a hereditary position in the case of the bakers—were appointed and they in turn selected the wardens. These wardens inspected all work, and had the power to levy fines against those whose work was judged inferior. They also controlled entry into the guilds. Entry could be made in two ways, the first of which was the well-known, well-discussed path of apprenticeship. Theoretically, the apprentice would learn the skills, serve through his allotted term, and move up into journeyman status. Here he would be more directly involved in craft production, doing the bulk of the manual labor. Journeymen in the bakers' and cordwainers' guilds were hired at low wages for fixed and often extended periods, and were crucial in the larger industrial process. In both guilds, the masters limited the mobility and salaries of these journeymen, thus solidifying their own control over production and marketing.

The road to master was an arduous one, and it is likely that just a few of those who entered the craft from the bottom actually made it to the top. There were several obstacles. One was the fundamental fact of high mortality rates, running in the high 30s/1,000 for the apprentice/journeyman age cohorts; life expectancy was sufficiently low so that perhaps 20 percent to 25 percent of those who started as apprentices would have died before they reached their 30s, about the time at which they might expect to become masters. But, assuming survival, it still took large sums of money and a great deal of luck to make it.[104] Given the low wages they drew, most journeymen would have found it virtually impossible to raise sufficient capital to pay off the right people and to buy a shop and tools, even in the high wage era which followed the Black Death. Perhaps the best chance was to have the good fortune to be born into a family of means, to have a father who was himself a craft's master, or to make a fortuitous marriage. If this happened and a current master died prematurely, the ascent to the top might be realized.

---

[104] This is discussed in detail for London merchants by S. L. Thrupp, in her *The Merchant Class of Medieval London* (Chicago: University of Chicago Press, 1948).

Another road to mastership was quicker, easier, and probably more relevant to Bury St. Edmunds' craft guilds. It was possible for aliens, foreigners, and those who lived outside the borough limits to buy entry into their respective guilds. In the mid-fourteenth century, Edward III opened the gates to large-scale Netherlandish immigration.[105] As Flemish industry ran into difficulties and Dutch and Brabantine industries were still in their nascent stages, more and more men from the Low Countries came to East Anglia. The alien registry rolls indicate that many settled in Bury, and, while the majority were weavers, dyers, and fullers, a good many were involved in victualing and other crafts. It has even been suggested that Dutchmen revolutionized English brewing.[106] These aliens were protected by the Crown, and, despite the efforts of the denizen guild fathers, could not be denied altogether. It has been stressed that the weavers' wardens provided entry at all levels of their craft upon payment of a fee; such too was the case with the bakers, cordwainers, and presumably most other guilds. Definitive data are not available, but a good many fifteenth- and sixteenth-century masters were probably outsiders who had bought their way in.

Like those of the weavers, the masters of the bakers' and cordwainers' guilds sought to maintain the structures that so favored them; the very existence of the bylaws confirms this. Some of the most severe sanctions and heaviest fines were assessed against those masters found tampering with the journeymen and even apprentices of their peers. Guild power was extended from production to marketing—if not quite monopoly then monopsony, as it has been called.[107] To ensure this required solidarity and sanctions against those who broke ranks in quest of higher profits. It is likely that such actions exercised upward pressure on prices, and no guild could ever have a complete monopoly on the making and selling of its commodities. Unorganized producers from surrounding villages in the urban region always presented some moderating force, even if they were barred from dealing directly in the Great Market. In a community like Bury it would have been relatively easy for

[105] For more information, see C.P.R., Henry VI, 1436, pp. 548-581.

[106] Brewing has not yet been discussed in detail for the middle ages. See H. A. Monckton, *A History of English Ale and Beer* (London: Bodley Head, 1966); and Mia Bell, *The Worshipful Company of Brewers* (London: Hutchinson, 1977).

[107] S. L. Thrupp, "Gilds," *Cambridge Economic History*, iii, pp. 247-249.

most basic food and service crafts to do business outside the borough. But, whatever the cracks in their solidarity, guilds dominated industry as well as the marketing of their goods.

Guild bylaws tell a great deal about the organization of certain crafts and trades, but in trying to discern the intricacies of the town's economy, we need evidence more revealing of the towns' social and economic operations. Guild records rarely describe the industrial or commercial processes themselves, and, because regulations survive for only about a half dozen of their number, they cannot provide a complete or even balanced picture of Bury's craft-level economy. Here we are at something of a loss; the best non-guild records come almost exclusively from the textile industry. There is one source—the testamentary evidence—on which to fall back. Many craftsmen listed occupations in their wills, and assessments of these occupations and how they changed through time reveal a great deal about Bury's industrial makeup.

The data are presented in Tables 3.5 through 3.9. Table 3.5 lists all occupations, along with their collective mean level of testamentary wealth, as outlined in Table 3.4. Of special interest are those occupations which had more than ten recorded members. Six were textile-related, three connected with victualing, three with the leather trade, and the rest with various services. Textile occupations have been discussed; their totals are listed in Table 3.7, and are divided into merchants and craftsmen. Aside from their large numbers—total textile affiliates make up one-third of the entire sample—the most important feature is their chronological frequency. The bulk of the textile workers and merchants came in the second part of the survey, from the 1440s, with the heaviest concentration from the 1480s. Without belaboring the point, Bury St. Edmunds always had a textile industry, like all towns and market villages in East Anglia, but full development did not come until late in the fifteenth century.

The chronology of testamentary occupations helps to indicate the presence and role of late medieval industries. Early in the period, fishing was of major importance.[108] Bury had relatively

---

[108] Fishing too has been strangely ignored. See A. R. Bridbury, *England and the Salt Trade* (Oxford: Oxford University Press, 1955); J. T. Jenkins, *The Herring and the Herring Fisheries* (London: P. S. King and Son, 1927); and Herman van der Wee, *The Growth of the Antwerp Market and the European Economy*, 3 vols. (The Hague: Mouton, 1963).

TABLE 3.5: OCCUPATIONS BY FREQUENCY

Occupation	n	Mean Group Bequest to High Altar	1354-1440	1441-1530
Weavers	50	18 pence	10	40
Corvisers	43	15 pence	28	17
Tailors	43	16 pence	10	33
Mercers	31	20 pence	8	23
Fullers	29	11 pence	14	15
Drapers	27	12 shillings	7	20
Bakers	21	2 shillings	7	14
Carpenters	21	6 pence	4	17
Tanners	21	3 shillings	8	13
Butchers	21	10 shillings	9	12
Chandlers	20	4 shillings	14	6
Smiths	16		7	9
Masons	15		5	10
Saddlers	12		7	5
Dyers	11		4	7
Scriveners	11		2	9
Cooks	11		3	8
Barbers	10		5	5
Fishermen	10		9	1
Skinners	10		3	7
Laborers	9		—	9
Thatchers	9		2	7
Wrights	9		6	3
Cloth-makers	8		2	6
Coopers	7		2	5
Curriers	7		2	5
Glovers	7		1	6
Bedweavers	6		—	6
Bladesmiths	6		—	6
Fletchers	6		—	5
Grocers	6		1	5
Shermen	6		2	4
Spicers	6		4	2
Woolmen	6		—	6
Brasiers	5		2	3
Coverlet-weavers (Chaloners)	5		2	3
Fishmongers	5		—	5

TABLE 3.5 (Cont.)

Occupation	n	Mean Group Bequest to High Altar	1354-1440	1441-1530
Goldsmiths	5		1	3
Tylers	5		1	1
Carvers	4		1	2
Cutlers	4		3	2
Merchants	5		3	3
Parchment-makers	4		2	2
Brewers	3		—	3
Card-makers	3		—	3
Haberdashers	3		—	3
Hardwaremen	3		1	2
Innholders	3		—	3
Stainers	3		1	2
Linen-drapers	3		3	—
Watchmen	3		1	2
Wheelwrights	3		1	2
Bowyers	2		—	2
Broiderers	2		1	1
Collar-makers	2		—	2
Furriers	2		2	—
Glasswrights	2		—	2
Hosiers	2		—	2
Limners	2		—	2
Millers	2		—	2
Net-makers	2		—	2
Painters	2		—	2
Physicians	2		—	2
Plummers	2		—	2
Ropers	2		—	2
Sewsters	2		—	2
Spurriers	2		—	2
Stationers	2		—	2
Sukors	2		—	2
Trumpeters	2		1	1
Bell-founder	1		—	1
Capper	1		—	1
Clog-maker	1		—	1
Clothier	1		—	1
Eelmonger	1		—	1

TABLE 3.5 (Cont.)

Occupation	n	Mean Group Bequest to High Altar	1354-1440	1441-1530
Freemason	1		—	1
Hayre-maker	1		1	—
Lattener	1		1	—
Malster	1		—	1
Notary	1		—	1
Payteyn-maker	1		—	1
Potter	1		1	—
Sawyer	1		—	1
Shear-grinder	1		—	1
Vintner	1		—	1
Wiredrawer	1		—	1

TABLE 3.6: FREQUENCY BY SOCIAL CLASS

Class	n
Clerics	113
Armigerous	33
Yeomen	12
Husbandmen	10
Burgesses	4
Servants	3
Alderman	1
Freemason	1

large numbers of fishermen and fishmongers, as well as a few eelmongers and netmakers. The largest proportion of these characters appeared before 1440, especially men who called themselves fishers. The Lark, the Linnet, the Tay, and other nearby fens provided a variety of freshwater fish, and local fishing was encouraged by the abbey. The cellarer, as discussed above, held the rights to fishing throughout the banleuca, and the abbey gleaned a share of every catch. Most townsmen probably fished at one time or another in attempts to supplement their diets, but those calling themselves fishermen must have worked regularly at the task, at least on a seasonal basis. Fishmongers were prominent in Bury's markets, and it is likely that fishing was a major industry in Bury St. Edmunds until the mid-fifteenth century.

Why did the fishing industry apparently collapse after 1440? Thereafter, virtually no fishermen and fewer and fewer fishmongers appear among Bury's testators. A possible explanation might lie in over-fishing, or a change in the nature of the waterways in and about the banleuca. The demise might also be the result of increased competition from saltwater fishermen, facilitated by better roadways and easier access in and out of West Suffolk; when salted, a technique perfected by the Dutch late in the fourteenth century, fish will keep for a long time. Both explanations are plausible, but there is a more likely one. The rise of the textile industry probably spelled the end for large-scale industrial fishing. Textiles were a safer investment, yielding higher profits for investors and better wages for workers. Moreover, with population levels generally declining through at least the first half of the fifteenth century, the need for fish as a food supplement was probably a bit less pressing. Most important, the textile industry needed precisely what the fishing industry did—fresh, running water. But, unlike fishing, certain aspects of the textile process, such as fulling, did not leave the water undisturbed. Fulling mills and dyes produced noxious materials that could not be washed away easily, quickly, or completely enough by slow-moving streams like the Lark and Linnet. The abbey, which held the rights over the waterways, had the option of leasing them for fulling or fishing, and fifteenth-century evidence suggests that the monks rather predictably opted for the former, which was far more profitable and yielded greater rents and farms. Coupled with the continual dumping of human and animal waste and refuse by the townsfolk, who used their waterways as a sewage system, fulling, dyeing, and other industrial textile processes may well have killed off most of the fish. The streams and fens of late medieval Bury St. Edmunds seem to have suffered from industrial pollution.

Large numbers of craftsmen worked in leather and leather related industries. Occupations concerned with them—skinners, tanners, and especially corvisers or cordwainers, to name the most important—totalled over 10 percent of the testamentary sample.

Further, if glovers and cappers are added, the proportion rises to close to 12 percent. Like fishing, leather was of relatively greater importance before the middle-fifteenth century. While the leather business did not fade as dramatically as fishing, many of its crafts-men, especially shoemakers, were far less common after 1440. It is likely that here too the pressure of higher profits and wages in textiles, plus the fact that sheep were easier to keep than cattle, was sufficient to lure money and men from an older craft into the new.

There were other industries in town. Building and metal related occupations formed a relatively large part of the sample, especially when compared with their counterparts from other provincial towns (Tables 3.8-3.9).[109] This may in part have been due to the presence of the abbey, a generous patron always repairing or erect-ing something. The abbey also supported some very unusual vo-cations, including a few generally found only in monastic, univer-sity, or very large towns. Bury had a number of bedweavers and coverlet weavers. Beds were the object of considerable pride and personal prestige, and became more common in the course of the fifteenth century as standards of living rose. Other unusual occu-pations included parchmentmakers, cardmakers, stainers, limners, latoners, bell-founders, and even two sixteenth-stationers, both sell-ing books. Bury had many medical men, surgeons, and barbers as well as physicians. There were several cooks, working in the thriving cookshops on Cooks' Row, and two innholders, catering not only to townsfolk but to pilgrims and visitors to the abbey. The borough was unique among late medieval provincial towns. It was an in-dustrial and commercial center, and, because it had an abbey, hos-pitals, and schools, was able to support specialized crafts and profes-sions that ordinary provincial towns of similar size could not. It was this combination of crafts, textiles, leather-working, an assortment of bowyers, fletchers, bladesmiths, and others, along with the usual amalgam of butchers, bakers, and candlestickmakers that made Bury such a prosperous place. In proportion to its size, the diversity of its craft industries may have rivalled that of London.

[109] The data are taken from W. G. Hoskins, *Provincial England* (London: Macmillan, 1965). Also of interest are the data in David Herlihy, "Distri-bution of Wealth in a Renaissance Community," in Philip Abrams and Wrigley, E. A., eds., *Towns in Societies* (Cambridge: Cambridge University Press, 1978), p. 148.

THE WEALTH OF THE TOWN AND THE TOWNSMEN

It is possible to measure with some precision the wealth of both the corporate borough of Bury St. Edmunds and of many of its individual residents, and to place them in a temporal, comparative framework. This can be done by using a series of regional and national taxes, lay subsidies, and testamentary sources.[110] In 1282, Edward I levied a subsidy to defray the costs of his campaigns in Wales.[111] It was a direct assessment that covered all the major towns in East Anglia. The data are presented in Table 3.10, and indicate that at the onset of the later middle ages Bury was of only middling prosperity, even in regional terms. The abbey and its vast wealth were exempted, which adds to the subsidy's importance. Had the abbey been included, Bury may well have approached and perhaps surpassed Norwich, but, without it, the borough was just one of several market centers of local importance. Great Yarmouth, the major port in eastern England in the thirteenth century, and Norwich, the *de facto* capital of East Anglia, were taxed at considerably higher levels, and presumably were far wealthier. Bury folk did pay more than those from Lynn and Ipswich, the major towns in West Norfolk and East Suffolk, and no other West Suffolk town was deemed important enough even to be included in the survey. But Bury St. Edmunds was merely the third town of East Anglia, and in comparison with London a veritable dwarf, its assessment running to one-seventeenth that of the kingdom's capital.

In 1327, the entire kingdom of England was levied under a lay subsidy. County Suffolk showed 11,720 taxpayers under 9,150 different names.[112] The names represent property; several men had less than a single piece of property, and certain individual names may represent many landholders. The 1327 results for the four Suffolk boroughs assessed in 1282 are listed in Table 3.11, and show a significant change. Ipswich, the center of East Suffolk, had passed Bury in numbers and in total secular wealth assessed. The

[110] For a general discussion of late medieval taxation, see M. W. Beresford, *Lay Subsidies and Poll Taxes* (Canterbury: Phillimores, 1963).

[111] Edgar Power, "The Taxation of Ipswich for the Welsh Wars in 1282," *P.S.I.*, xii, 1906. For a discussion of the source, see below, Appendix A.

[112] "Suffolk in 1327. Being a Subsidy Return," *Suffolk Green Books*, IX, ii (Woodbridge, Suffolk: George Booth, 1906). For a discussion of the source, see below, Appendix A.

TABLE 3.7: OCCUPATION CLASSIFICATION

Group	Components	Numbers	Mean Group Bequest to High Altar
1. Textiles (n = 220)			
a. Merchants (n = 68)			
	Clothier	1	20 pence
	Drapers	27	
	Mercers	31	
	Linen-drapers	3	
	Woolmen	6	
b. Workers (n = 152)			
	Broiderers	2	
	Clothmakers	8	
	Dyers	11	
	Fullers	29	
	Sewsters	2	
	Shear Grinder	1	
	Shermen	6	
	Tailors	43	
	Websters/Weavers	50	
2. Merchants (n = 105)			
a. Textiles (n = 68)			
b. Non-textiles (n = 37)			
	Eelmonger	1	14 shillings
	Fishmongers	5	
	Furriers	2	
	Goldsmiths	5	
	Grocers	6	
	Haberdashers	3	
	Hardwaremen	3	
	Merchants	5	
	Spicers	6	
	Vintner	1	
3. Crafts (n = 430)			
a. Textiles (n = 152)			
b. Building (n = 100)			
	Bladesmiths	6	11 pence
	Brasiers	5	
	Carpenters	21	
	Glasswrights	2	

TABLE 3.7 (Cont.)

Group	Components	Numbers	Mean Group Bequest to High Altar
	Lattoner	1	
	Masons	15	
	Netmakers	2	
	Painters	2	
	Ropers	2	
	Sawyer	1	
	Smiths	16	
	Thatchers	9	
	Tylers	5	
	Wheelwrights	3	
	Wire-drawer	1	
	Wrights	9	
c. Others (n = 178)			
	Bedweavers	6	9 pence
	Bell-founder	1	
	Brewers	4	
	Bowyers	2	
	Capper	1	
	Card-makers	3	
	Chandlers	20	
	Clog-maker	1	
	Collar-makers	2	
	Coopers	7	
	Corvisers	45	
	Coverletweavers	5	
	Curriers	7	
	Cutlers	4	
	Fletchers	6	
	Glovers	7	
	Hayre-maker	1	
	Hosiers	2	
	Maltster	1	
	Parchment-makers	4	
	Pateyn-maker	1	
	Plummers	2	
	Potter	1	
	Saddlers	12	
	Skinners	10	
	Spurriers	2	

TABLE 3.7 (Cont.)

Group	Components	Numbers	Mean Group Bequest to High Altar
	Tanners	21	
4. Service and Professionals (n = 118)			
	Bakers	21	5 shillings
	Barbers	10	
	Butchers	20	
	Carvers	4	
	Cooks	11	
	Fishermen	10	
	Innholders	3	
	Laborers	9	
	Limners	2	
	Millers	2	
	Physicians	2	
	Stainers	3	
	Scriveners	12	
	Sukors	2	
	Stationers	2	
	Trumpeters	2	
	Watchmen	3	

wealth of St. Edmunds was again exempted, and many of Bury's richest men seem also to have won exemptions. But, if Bury's notables did not have to pay the tax, it is likely that their Ipswich counterparts would not have done so either. Further, among those who were taxed, the richest from Ipswich were generally wealthier than their Bury counterparts. There is another trend of some significance. The two older boroughs, Orford and Dunwich, which had ranked relatively close to Bury and Ipswich in the Doomsday survey, were slipping rapidly. By the early fourteenth century, their borough status was more legal than socio-economic, and they were soon to be challenged by a number of unincorporated but thriving market villages. Caution must always be exercised when using tax rolls in trying to assess numbers of rankings of wealth. No one wants to pay taxes; evasion is always a strong possibility; and conclusions must be tempered accordingly. But it appears that early in the fourteenth century Bury St. Edmunds was still only the center

TABLE 3.8: LEADING OCCUPATIONS OF THREE MIDLAND
TOWNS IN THE EARLY SIXTEENTH CENTURY

Coventry	Northampton	Leicester
1. Cappers	Shoemakers	Butchers
2. Weavers	Bakers	Shoemakers
3. Shermen	Tailors	Tailors
4. Butchers	Weavers	Mercers
5. Shoemakers	Tanners	Weavers
6. Drapers	Mercers	Bakers
7. Dyers	Butchers	Tanners
8. Bakers	Glovers	Glovers
9. Mercers	Fullers	Smiths
10. Tailors	Drapers	Millers
11. Tanners	Dyers	Barbers
12. Smiths	Millers	Shermen

TABLE 3.9: PERCENTAGE OF TRADERS IN THE THREE
MIDLAND TOWNS

Trades	Coventry	Northampton	Leicester
Clothing	14	15	15
Food and Drink	15.5	15	21
Building	4.5	7.5	4
Leather	11	23	19
Textile	33	13.5	8.5
Metal	8	3	3
Others	14.5	23.0	29.5

of the West Suffolk market region, and any national importance or exceptional wealth it had was predicated on the presence and influence of the Benedictine Abbey.

This trend is confirmed by the 1334 Lay Subsidy.[113] On a county

---

[113] This has been taken from R. E. Glasscock, "England circa 1334," in H. C. Darby, ed., *New Historical Geography of England* (Cambridge: Cambridge University Press, 1973).

TABLE 3.10: THE WELSH WARS SUBSIDY OF 1282; RANKING OF
LONDON AND THE LEADING EAST ANGLIA TOWNS

Town	Assessment in £	Assessment as % of London
London	4,000	100.0
Great Yarmouth	666	16.6
Norwich	333	8.3
BURY ST. EDMUNDS	266	6.7
King's Lynn	200	5.0
Ipswich	100	2.5
Orford	100	2.5
Dunwich	66	1.6

TABLE 3.11: THE LAY SUBSIDY OF 1327; THE RANKING OF THE
SUFFOLK TOWNS

Town	Number of Names	Assessment in £
Ipswich	210	29,9 shillings
BURY ST. EDMUNDS	154	23,19s
Orford	35	6,7s
Dunwich	69	5,8s

level, Suffolk stood in the middle, with an overall assessment of
£14 per square mile. By contrast, Middlesex, containing London,
stood at the top, at £57, 71 shillings, and Northumbria at the bottom, at £2, 5 shillings. The urban data for the national and regional
assessments were presented in Tables 3.12 and 3.13. Bury St. Edmunds ranked but twenty-eighth in the kingdom, with its great
rival, Ipswich, wealthier and, at least in purely secular terms, of
greater consequence. It is worth reiterating everyone's distaste for
paying taxes, and the fact that all abbey property was exempted,
but the latter serves to remind us of the borough's dependence on
the abbey for its wider role in the kingdom.

With the exception of its market service, Bury had not yet de-

TABLE 3.12: THE LAY SUBSIDY OF 1334; THE TEN LEADING
TOWNS IN ENGLAND

Town	Rank	Assessment in £
London	1	11,000
Bristol	2	2,200
York	3	1,620
Newcastle	4	1,333
Boston	5	1,100
Great Yarmouth	6	1,000
Lincoln	6	1,000
Norwich	8	946
Oxford	9	914
Shrewsbury	10	800

TABLE 3.13: THE LAY SUBSIDY OF 1334; THE RANKING OF THE
LEADING EAST ANGLIAN TOWNS

Town	National Rank	Assessment in £
Great Yarmouth	6	1,000
Norwich	8	946
Lynn (King's and South)	11	770
Ipswich	14	645
BURY ST. EDMUNDS	28	360

veloped an independent economic base by the end of the first third
of the fourteenth century. It was the second town of Suffolk and
the leading center of West Suffolk, but was beginning to lose
ground even in its traditional home area. Sudbury, the seat of the
West Suffolk archdeaconry, was assessed at £281, and, lest this
comparative decline be attributed entirely to the exemption of the
abbey, it is worth noting that Ely, a rival, smaller monastic town to
the northwest, was assessed at £358, almost the same as Bury, presumably with its Benedictine house also excluded. Exemptions that
might have been won by leading secular figures still cannot be

accounted for, and we can be sure that everyone tried to pay as little tax as possible. But if these factors are presumed to have affected all towns in approximately equal fashion, it appears that Bury was losing ground early in the fourteenth century—at about the time of the most violent and destructive of the town-abbey riots.

Bury's apparent financial decline in the early fourteenth century was all the more remarkable when contrasted with its ascent from mid-century onward, a rise that picked up pace and became more pronounced in the fifteenth and sixteenth centuries. The 1377 poll tax indicates that Bury had not only met the challenge of Sudbury, but had passed Ipswich, and in little more than a generation had again become the leading town in Suffolk.[114] The poll-tax data are listed in Table 3.14. Overall, the county yielded more than £1,100, with Bury paying £40,15s, by far the largest single amount. This takes on added significance because the poll tax was sufficiently comprehensive to include most adults, albeit at a flat rate. On the surface, it appears as though Bury had undergone a vigorous period of commercial and industrial development, and to a degree this was probably true. But part of its recovery was the result of the Black Death and of the subsequent depopulation caused by the second plague pandemic. In the economic dislocation following a population reduction of perhaps 50 percent, areas best able to recover were those with the strongest financial bases and the most readily available capital. This describes Bury, a town with a still prosperous abbey. St. Edmunds was a *rentier*, and in time would

TABLE 3.14: THE POLL TAX OF 1377; THE RANKING OF THE
EAST ANGLIAN TOWNS

Town	National Rank	Assessment in £
Norwich	6	65, 17 shillings
King's Lynn	9	52, 2s
BURY ST. EDMUNDS	15	40, 15s
Great Yarmouth	20	30, 13s
Ipswich	27	24, 9s
New Market	—	19, 12s

[114] P.R.O., E179, E359. Also, see Beresford, *Lay Subsidies*, pp. 7-13.

be crippled by the high wages and low food prices that depopulation brought. But all of this lay several generations beyond the 1377 poll tax; in the years immediately following the Black Death, the abbey, with much of its liquid wealth intact and municipal controls still relatively firm, must have appeared as one of the economic stalwarts in eastern England. Significantly, the 1377 poll tax included secular clerics, and, with this segment of its large ecclesiastical population supplementing that of the burghers, Bury appears far wealthier than it had forty years earlier.

No lay subsidies or poll taxes were assessed in East Anglia for the next one hundred and fifty years, but the 1523-1524 lay subsidy suggests that Bury St. Edmunds continued to prosper through the fifteenth century, aided by the development of the Suffolk textile industry.[115] The data are presented in Table 3.15, and show the rise into the ranks of major provincial towns not only of Bury but also of a half dozen other East Anglian urban centers. In the 1334 lay subsidy, only Great Yarmouth and Norwich ranked among the kingdom's top ten towns, with King's Lynn and Ipswich in the next ten. Two hundred years later, Yarmouth had declined, but Norwich, Ipswich, and Lynn had all moved comparatively higher, and were joined by Bury, Lavenham, which I have suggested was part of "greater" Bury, and nearby Colchester. The borough of Bury St. Edmunds had fallen behind Ipswich and King's Lynn, but in an absolute sense the aggregate urban region of Bury and Lavenham was the seventh wealthiest conglomerate in early sixteenth-century England. Significantly, the combined populations could not possibly have ranked seventh, suggesting that, on a *per capita* level, Bury St. Edmunds and its hinterlands were among the wealthier regions in the kingdom. Since the abbey was again exempted from lay subsidy payments, Bury's financial ascent was clearly based on its secular wealth. By the sixteenth century the burgesses had built an independent economic base.

The general prosperity of Bury St. Edmunds was reflected not only in lump borough assessments, but by the broad-based and well-distributed wealth of its individual inhabitants. In the greater urban region, Thomas Spring III paid more tax in 1523 than any other laymen in England, and a number of Bury merchants ranked

---

[115] "Suffolk in 1524. Being a Return for a Subsidy Granted in 1523," *Suffolk Green Books*, x (Woodbridge, Suffolk, George Booth, 1910). For additional discussion, see below, pp. 257-258.

TABLE 3.15: THE LAY SUBSIDY OF 1523-1524; THE FIFTEEN
LEADING TOWNS IN ENGLAND

Town	Rank	Assessment in £
London	1	16,675
Norwich	2	1,704
Bristol	3	1,072
Coventry	4	974
Exeter	5	855
Salisbury	6	852
(BURY AND LAVENHAM)		807
Southwark	7	790
Ipswich	8	657
King's Lynn	9	576
Canterbury	10	532
Reading	11	470
Colchester	12	426
BURY ST. EDMUNDS	13	405
LAVENHAM	14	402
York	15	379

among the most highly taxed in East Anglia.[116] By using the bequest
in each will to the high altar of the parish of burial, we can get
some sense of the extent, levels, and distribution of personal wealth
among the borough's adult male population. Table 3.16 lists individual levels of wealth for Bury testators, and Table 3.17 shows
comparative wealth measured from a wider sample drawn from
other will-makers in East Anglia, Hertfordshire and London.[117] A
consistently high proportion of testators bequeathed something to

[116] For example, of all weavers, those from Bury had a mean wealth of
level C, as compared with D for weavers from Ipswich and Norwich. For
skinners and bakers, the Bury men had mean wealth levels of C for both,
compared with C and D respectively for Ipswich, and D and D for Norwich.
Bury did at least as well as Ipswich and Norwich for samples selecting
bachelors, widows, mercers, and gentlemen.

[117] The data are taken from Robert S. Gottfried, *Epidemic Disease in Fifteenth Century England* (New Brunswick, N.J.: Rutgers University Press and
Leicester University Press, 1978). For criticism of the wealth measure,
among other things, see Alan Morrison's review in *The Journal of Modern
History*, September 1979.

TABLE 3.16: THE WEALTH OF INDIVIDUALS IN BURY ST.
EDMUNDS

	A	B	C	D	E	Unknown
A. *Entire Sample*						
1354-1530	15.8	12.3	26.5	37.2	2.4	5.8
1354-1400	24.9	13.2	25.8	26.6	2.2	7.3
1400-1436	21.5	17.8	35.4	22.5	1.1	1.7
1436-1480	12.7	13.0	23.7	47.8	2.0	.8
1480-1530	11.0	8.3	24.9	40.3	3.6	11.9
1441-1450	12.0	12.7	23.9	47.9	.7	2.8
1451-1460	16.6	13.3	17.8	51.1	1.1	—
1461-1470	13.0	16.0	19.1	50.4	1.5	—
1471-1480	13.1	10.0	23.1	49.3	3.9	.4
1481-1490	9.1	6.1	30.3	42.4	—	12.1
1491-1500	10.9	6.8	22.5	52.4	3.4	4.1
1501-1510	10.6	11.6	20.6	40.7	3.5	13.1
1511-1520	10.1	6.0	26.8	37.6	6.7	12.8
1521-1530	13.2	8.2	29.6	30.2	1.9	17.0
B. *Males less Clerics*						
1354-1430	16.7	11.8	26.9	36.7	2.5	5.5
1354-1400	25.3	12.5	26.0	27.2	2.3	6.8
1400-1436	23.8	17.5	35.8	19.8	.8	2.3
1436-1480	13.2	12.9	24.5	46.5	2.0	.8
1480-1530	11.8	7.3	25.2	40.4	3.9	11.4
1441-1450	12.8	13.8	24.8	45.0	.9	2.8
1451-1460	15.9	17.4	18.8	46.4	1.4	—
1461-1470	14.1	15.2	19.2	49.5	2.0	—
1471-1480	13.7	8.2	23.1	51.1	3.3	.5
1481-1490	9.1	—	27.3	45.5	18.2	—
1491-1500	11.4	5.7	21.9	52.4	3.8	4.8
1501-1510	10.4	12.4	21.4	40.0	3.4	12.4
1511-1520	10.5	4.8	24.8	39.0	6.7	14.3
1521-1530	15.8	6.1	33.3	29.8	2.6	12.3
C. *Males Only*						
1354-1530	16.4	12.1	27.0	36.2	2.3	5.9
1354-1400	25.0	12.2	26.8	26.8	2.4	6.8
1400-1436	22.6	18.3	35.8	20.4	.7	2.2
1436-1480	13.2	13.3	24.4	46.4	1.9	.8
1480-1530	11.8	7.7	25.0	39.5	3.5	12.5
1441-1450	12.7	13.6	24.6	45.8	.8	2.5

TABLE 3.16 (cont.)

	A	B	C	D	E	Unknown
1451-1460	16.9	16.9	19.7	45.1	1.4	—
1461-1470	13.2	15.1	19.8	50.0	1.9	—
1471-1480	13.5	9.4	22.9	50.5	3.1	.5
1481-1490	11.5	3.8	26.9	42.3	—	15.4
1491-1500	11.0	5.5	22.9	52.3	3.7	4.6
1501-1510	10.2	12.2	20.5	42.3	3.2	11.5
1511-1520	11.1	6.0	25.6	37.6	6.0	13.7
1520-1530	14.8	6.7	31.1	26.7	2.2	18.5
D. Females Only						
1354-1530	13.2	12.9	24.2	41.1	3.2	5.5
1354-1400	22.7	18.6	22.0	23.7	1.7	10.2
1400-1436	16.3	15.9	31.9	31.9	2.9	—
1436-1480	12.0	12.0	19.3	53.0	3.6	—
1480-1530	8.6	10.7	24.3	42.1	4.3	10.0
E. Special Groups						
Clerics	13.5	15.8	27.8	31.6	.8	10.5
Gentry	33.3	16.7	30.0	10.0	2.4	5.5
Testators w/servants	31.6	15.8	28.4	20.0	2.1	2.1
Textile workers	10.5	5.3	22.1	50.5	8.4	3.2
Craftsmen	12.7	14.0	28.7	40.0	2.0	2.7
Stated occupations	17.9	11.0	26.0	37.9	2.7	4.3
Testators w/gsons.	26.7	13.3	26.7	30.0	3.3	—
Testators w/gdaus.	40.1	10.0	20.0	26.7	3.3	—

Key: A = 10/ or more
     B = 6/-9/
     C = 2/-5/
     D = 5d-20d
     E = 5d

the high altars, but this changed through time. Bequests reached an apex between 1400 and 1480, and in one 50-year period, 1430 to 1480, over 99 percent of the Burians contributed something. This pattern slowed considerably in the last 50 years sampled; the largest proportion of will-makers still contributed, but close to 12 percent did not. One the eve of the Reformation, at a period when

St. Edmunds and perhaps even the parish churches of St. James and St. Mary were struggling to make ends meet, one traditional source of income was falling.[118]

Mean testator wealth fell between categories C and D, representing a bequest level of between 5 pence and 5 shillings. Here too there are some interesting secular trends, primarily in the lower reaches of the tables. In the first testamentary period, 1354 to 1400, mean wealth fell within level C, a bequest of between 2 and 5 shillings, but categories A and B, respectively showing bequests of over 10 shillings and from 6 through 9 shillings, were fairly close in their general distribution. This might be expected; the will registering population was less complete before the fifteenth century. But from 1400 the comparative portion of very rich among the

TABLE 3.17: WEALTH OF INDIVIDUALS, EAST ANGLIA, 1430-1480

A. *County*						
All counties	11.0	11.9	22.9	39.5	5.0	9.7
Norfolk	10.6	11.8	23.8	38.5	3.3	12.1
Suffolk	11.5	12.4	23.3	40.4	4.9	7.0
Hertfordshire	10.6	7.9	16.7	40.5	12.2	11.9
B. *Decade*						
1430-1440	13.0	14.4	21.8	33.7	2.8	14.3
1441-1450	12.6	15.6	23.0	35.3	3.3	10.1
1451-1460	13.5	12.2	23.2	38.2	4.2	8.7
1461-1470	9.6	11.4	24.6	42.3	5.6	6.4
1471-1480	9.2	9.4	21.6	42.0	6.5	11.2
C. *Urban Areas*						
All towns	13.9	14.6	20.3	35.9	5.3	10.0
Norwich	21.2	18.3	21.1	21.1	2.0	16.3
Ipswich	14.6	19.6	21.2	30.6	3.7	10.2
St. Albans	7.2	9.6	14.4	42.7	13.3	12.8
BURY ST. EDMUNDS	12.0	12.9	23.9	47.4	2.0	1.2

[118] I have postulated in Chapter 2, pp. 55-63, that perhaps 25 percent of the adult male population did not feel it necessary to ensure will registration. Most of these men would undoubtedly have fallen into the poorest segment of the wealth sample, and we might get a fuller picture of wealth distribution by padding category E accordingly.

testators dwindled, slowly in the first four decades of the fifteenth century, and then more rapidly from 1440 onward, until by 1520 more than half the wealth sample fell within category D, representing a bequest of between 5 and 20 pence. Overall, the sample skewed toward the lower-middle portions of the population. The sole exception to this concerned the poorest testators, those in category E, who contributed less than 5 pence. Although a donation of a mere penny qualified testators for inclusion in the wealth hierarchy, totals in category E rarely exceeded 5 percent. It is possible that Bury had proportionally few very poor people, but it is more likely that those at the bottom of the town's economic scale just did not bother to register their wills. Category E does increase in the sixteenth century, to about 6 percent in the 1510s. While this figure is not empirically significant, it does hint at a broadening of the testamentary sample to a late fifteenth- early-sixteenth century high, perhaps representative of the region's growing prosperity. It is only in the late 1520s, when the will population begins to fall off in total coverage of the adult male population, that category E again slips back.

The financial fortunes of Bury testators can be compared with those of urban contemporaries from Norwich, Ipswich, and St. Albans, and rural populations in Norfolk, Suffolk, and Hertfordshire between 1430 and 1480. Upon initial inspection Bury's will-makers appear poorer than those from rural areas, particularly in the prosperous region Bury served in West Suffolk. Since larger proportions of rural wealth were rooted in the land, the figures could take on even added significance. Further, wealth levels of Bury testators were often lower than the aggregates from the other urban areas surveyed. It is possible that other parts of East Anglia were indeed wealthier, but this is not likely. Rather, we are probably seeing the very broad base of Bury's testamentary population, the high incidence of will registration among the town's lower and middling folk. When select occupational and social groups from Bury are isolated and compared with their counterparts from Ipswich and Norwich, the Bury inhabitants are always wealthier.[119] Further, a catalogue of select movables extracted from the wills, including bullion, furs, silk, brass, and pewter, shows greater numbers of Burians in possession of such valuables than any other East Anglians, urban or rural.

[119] See above, note 116.

There is another way to measure the distribution of wealth in Bury St. Edmunds. An index of concentration can be constructed, using a Lorenz Curve. A figure of 1 on the index indicates perfect equality of the distribution of wealth among the entire population, while a figure of 100 would mean that all of Bury's movable testamentary wealth was concentrated among the richest 1 percent of the burgesses.[120] For Bury, the index comes to 55 percent, a remarkable statement of the relatively equal distribution of wealth. By comparison, the index figures for similar samples surveyed for Ipswich, Norwich and St. Albans come, respectively, to 62 percent, 77 percent, and 64 percent. If broad general statements about the extent and distribution of wealth can be made from taxation and testamentary evidence, Bury St. Edmunds and West Suffolk were among the richest parts of the realm, with the wealth touching an extensive part of the population.[121]

The economic development of Bury St. Edmunds was the most crucial element in the rise of the secular community. Based on changing demographic patterns, the borough's role as a key market distribution center, the rise of south and western Suffolk as a major textile producing area, and the continuing strength of smaller craft industries such as leatherworking and the metal crafts, the burgesses succeeded by the late fifteenth century in building a financial base independent of St. Edmunds Abbey.

[120] To make the index, the following procedure was used. A frequency distribution was run on 2,300 wills, and the data divided into centiles, in order to make the graphing process more manageable. The data were then plotted on a Lorenz Curve, which actually indicates what percentage of households control what percentage of wealth. The index is taken from two curves, a theoretical one that shows an even distribution, and a second which shows the real distribution.

[121] See R. S. Schofield, "The Geographical Distribution of Wealth in England, 1334-1649," *Ec.H.R.*, 2nd series, xviii, 1965.

Chapter Four

THE BURGHAL ÉLITE
AND THE FOUNDATIONS OF
BOROUGH POWER

CIVIC OFFICE AND PROMINENT ALDERMEN

Power and influence in late medieval Bury St. Edmunds were vested primarily in the hands of a small group of wealthy men, whose riches came from landed and mercantile sources.[1] The extent of their power often rose and fell in direct relationship to the position of the abbot and his officers, and social distinctions within the secular community were sometimes blurred by the common opposition toward St. Edmunds. But the ascendancy in the borough of this élite, whom I shall call burgesses to distinguish them from the commons, remained essentially unchallenged from the late thirteenth through the early sixteenth century. When the abbey was dissolved in 1539, these burgesses took complete control of town governmental, social, and economic affairs. Who they were, where they came from, how they remained distinct from the commons, how they accumulated and maintained their wealth and power, and

---

[1] It is no longer fashionable to write biography, and in a social and economic history that has pretence toward empirical analysis this may be justifiably so. Further, given the lack of detailed personal information, it is extremely hard to write a biography of any late medieval figure. Nevertheless, some social and economic historians have shown what can be done with limited sources. I shall try to follow the splendid models of Thomas Betson and Thomas Paycocke drawn by Eileen Power in her *Medieval People* (London: Methuen, 1916). Also, see A. R. Myers, "The Wealth of Richard Lyons," in T. A. Sandquist and M. R. Powicke, eds., *Essays in Medieval History Presented to Bertie Wilkinson* (Toronto: University of Toronto Press, 1969); and Caroline M. Barron, "Richard Whittingdon: The Man Behind the Myth," in A.E.J. Hollaender and Kellaway, William, eds., *Studies in London History Presented to Philip Edmund Jones* (London: Hodder and Stoughton, 1969). For an account of some of the difficulties in doing late medieval biography see P. M. Kendall, *The Art of Biography* (London: George Allen and Unwin, 1965), pp. 50-91.

what became of their progeny are of paramount importance in trying to understand broader political, social, and economic relationships within the community. Many scholars have confronted such problems, and developed a number of theories to explain the legitimization of the rule of urban élites. Weber stressed charisma, traditionalism, and legal factors; Sjoberg emphasized appeal to absolutes, tradition, and expertise; while Pirenne and Hibbert stressed economic factors, especially the control of the wholesale and long-distance trades within given urban regions.[2] Dealing with the same problem in a rural community, LeRoy Ladurie stressed the general role of the family, with particular emphasis on wealth, family connections, and regional and local authority and influence.[3] I will try to assess the applicability of these and other theories of the power of ruling élites, examine the burgesses both as individuals and as a loosely defined corporate group, and look at the offices that they developed to help them to maintain their privileged positions.

The economic and social power of Bury's great merchants and landholders was institutionalized into political power through the public offices of aldermen, bailiffs, and town burgesses.[4] The alderman performed functions that in other towns earned the title "mayor," and was far and away the single most influential lay figure in Bury. When the office was held by a particularly dynamic and capable individual, its powers approached those of the prior, the sacrist, and even the abbot. The alderman's influence was derived largely from his leadership of the Alderman's or Town Guild, the richest and most powerful secular corporate body in West Suffolk. The position was initially created in 1292 as a substitute for an earlier office of civic leadership, the port reeve. But the prerogatives and responsibilities of the port reeve lay entirely within the jurisdiction of the abbey, and in the heady political atmosphere of

[2] Max Weber, *The City* (New York: The Free Press, 1958); G. Sjoberg, *The Preindustrial City* (New York: The Free Press, 1960); Henri Pirenne, *Medieval Cities* (Princeton: Princeton University Press, 1925); Pirenne, *Early Democracies in the Low Countries* (New York: Harper and Row TB edition, 1963); A. B. Hibbert, "Origins of the Medieval Town Patriciate," in P. Abrams and Wrigley, E. A., eds., *Towns in Societies* (Cambridge: Cambridge University Press, 1978).

[3] E. LeRoy Ladurie, *Montaillou: The Promised Land of Error* (George Braziller, 1978).

[4] A more detailed account can be found in Lobel, *The Borough*, pp. 59-95.

the late thirteenth century he was considered too subservient to be able to represent adequately town interests. The burgesses' search for an alternative led to the head of the Town Guild, established late in the twelfth century. Following the riots of 1292, they proposed that he be substituted for the port reeve and called mayor, the title vested with the chief official of the city of London and several provincial boroughs.[5] The abbot, John of Northwold, agreed to the substitution, but refused to grant the new title. The term "mayor," he claimed, implied powers that only he, the abbot, had. Further, John noted that the leader of the Town Guild was traditionally selected solely by the guild members, and, while all of these members were prominent citizens, the abbot was excluded from the process. As long as the guild played a comparatively limited role, such an election procedure could be tolerated. But if the office were now to be expanded to incorporate all the secular executive powers of the borough, the abbot wanted to have a say in the determination of its occupant. The guild members objected; they countered by claiming that the abbey already had several agents responsible to it in the borough, most notably the bailiffs. The burgesses said that they needed their own agent, and, since the Town Guild dealt primarily with non-governmental commercial questions, the abbot should not interfere. The guild itself was exempted from most abbey controls; should not its leader have similar independence? John of Northwold retorted that the question of independence was no longer germane. If the burgesses wanted to replace the port reeve with their own officer, the new officer would be undertaking broad civic responsibilities. His powers would extend well beyond commercial issues to questions of political jurisdictions, and these were surely within the interests of St. Edmunds. Had external political affairs been relatively stable, John probably would have resisted even more, but, because of the political disturbances discussed in Chapter 6, he accepted a compromise. Guild members would select from their ranks three candidates and present them to the abbot, who would then choose one from among them. This new arrangement, which lasted until Dissolution, favored the commune. Ultimately, the burgesses could offer the abbot three disagreeable characters and present him with little option. Backed by civic and commercial power, the new office proved to be formidable. When occupied by an aggressive and capable per-

[5] See Arnold, ii, pp. xlii-xlvi.

son—and most late medieval aldermen seem to have been both—
it and the guild, now named after the office, could resist and even
encroach on long-standing abbey powers.

The position of alderman was clear and well defined; that of a
burgess was not. If at times the term has been used rather vaguely,
it is because its precise role and functions are obscured by a distinct
lack of contemporary records. We might try to apply the term as
it was used in other late medieval boroughs, but it appears to have
meant different things in different places.[6] All the Bury sources
use it in the broadest, vaguest possible sense, and it seems quite
literally to have encompassed all the "great men" in social and
economic, rather than political and jurisdictional, terms. It may
even have held a similar meaning to the title "citizen," as used in
London; in late medieval Bury, the latter was rarely used, and then
usually in the set phrase "citizen and burgess." In the twelfth and
thirteenth centuries, the term "burgesses" may have carried some
technical requirements, possibly even the holding of the traditional
burgage tenure on land within the banleuca. But by the later middle
ages such distinctions had fallen into disuse.

Burgesses also had no specific roles to perform in civic government. All appear to have been members of the Alderman's and St.
Nicholas' Guilds, but they did not meet in the Guildhall or Tollhouse, and had no formal connection with the abbey or even with
the bailiffs. They derived no visible perquisites or income from
their titles, and had no fixed tenements from which they might
draw rents as an institutional body, as did the aldermen and bailiffs.
What they did have, however, was a sense of corporate identity
apart from the commons of the town. They were members of an
élite group that controlled the secular affairs of the town, from
which the alderman was selected and always remained only *primus
inter pares*. Ultimately, burgess was a social designation, a position
to which the *nouveau riches* might aspire, and one whose power
came through the prestige of its corporate influence.

The position of the bailiff was better defined and served a more

[6] Four sources for further information are: Helen M. Jewell, *English
Local Administration in the Middle Ages* (New York: Barnes and Noble, 1972);
S. B. Chrimes, *An Introduction to the Administrative History of Medieval England*
(Oxford: Basil Blackwell, 1952); James Tait, *The Medieval English Borough*
(Manchester: Manchester University Press, 1936); May McKisack, *The Par-
liamentary Representation of the English Boroughs During the Middle Ages* (Lon-
don: Frank Cass Reprint, 1962).

exacting function.[7] Bailiffs, usually two non-clerics drawn from among the residents of the town or suburbs, were the abbot's representatives in the borough. In the thirteenth and fourteenth centuries, the office was considered to be of middling prestige and prospects, and most holders came from the ranks of the lesser merchants or prosperous craftsmen. They collected abbey rents, heard complaints from the townsfolk, watched out for the abbot's interests in the marketplaces, and held court in the Tollhouse, his center for business in the borough. As long as the sacrist, the chief Benedictine officer assigned in the town, remained strong, the bailiffs had limited power. But in the fifteenth century, as revenue from the town proper began to shrink, the abbey sacrists started to concentrate more on their office's rural holdings. Consequently, the position of bailiff was allotted more responsibility. The salary was raised, and, even more important, the opportunities for corruption became almost unlimited. By 1450, with an annual salary of over £16 and potential income from graft three to four times higher, more and more of Bury's leading lights began to seek the office. By the sixteenth century, it was regularly held by only the greatest merchants and gentlemen. Bailiffs were elected, with the burgesses selecting and the abbot having final veto power. The office seems to have been rotated fairly frequently, and was a way for the great men to augment their fortunes at public expense. Ultimately, this was the case with all borough offices, major and minor; they legitimized, confirmed, and added to the positions of their holders.

While only limited information survives on the rituals of corporate offices in Bury St. Edmunds, a great deal remains on the men who held them. The wealthy merchants were a literate, articulate group, who left personal artifacts, deeds, charters, and, above all, long and detailed wills and last testaments that provide considerable insight into their private lives. From such personal records it is possible to get a collective picture of the individual aldermen and burgesses and their families. Some work has already been done. Lobel, for example, has written extensively about John de Berton, the alderman who led the 1327-1328 revolt.[8] He emerges as a dashing and romantic rebel, acting in part for his fellow burgesses,

[7] Lobel, *The Borough*, pp. 60-72.
[8] M. D. Lobel, "A Detailed Account of the 1327 Rising at Bury St. Edmunds and the Subsequent Trial," *P.S.I.*, xxi, 3, 1933.

and in part in self-interest. But de Berton was atypical; most of the aldermen, burgesses, and bailiffs were conservative, civic-minded, and rather staid figures. They were primarily interested in trade, in increasing the power of the burgess élite, in maintaining the *status quo* and their positions for themselves and their progeny, and in furthering the glory of Bury St. Edmunds. In doing so they enhanced their own self-images.

A list of aldermen from the mid-fourteenth to the early sixteenth centuries is presented in Appendix B.[9] I shall focus on four of the most outstanding, the first of whom was the draper Richard Charman, alderman during the reign of Edward III.[10] His will, proved in 1390, that of his wife, proved twelve years later, and the town deeds from their inception in the 1350s until the 1390s provide extensive information on his personal and professional life. He seems rather grudgingly to have begun his broader civic career, but, once selected, served the borough and his king, having been one of the royal tax collectors in Suffolk for 1379.[11] What most distinguishes Richard Charman, however, was neither his public office nor his activities as a draper. Rather, it was his land dealings. Charman was the most successful property speculator in the history of late medieval Bury St. Edmunds. A recent historian writing about late medieval burgesses claims that there were very few bourgeois *rentiers* before the sixteenth century. If his observation has general applicability, then Charman and all the other great men of Bury were marked exceptions.[12]

[9] The table, presented in Appendix B, was compiled from the following: M. D. Lobel, "A List of Aldermen and Bailiffs of Bury St. Edmunds," *P.S.I.*, xxii, 1934-1936; J. C. Ford, *The Aldermen and Mayors of Bury St. Edmunds from 1302* (Bury St. Edmunds, bound and compiled by the author, no date); C.U.L., Ms. G g 4 4; and the British Library Card Catalogue, The Manuscript Room, The British Museum, under "Bury St. Edmunds, Aldermen." This table differs slightly from that presented by Lobel. Other individuals who seem to have been aldermen but cannot be placed in time include: Thomas Bunning, William Bunting, Robert Burgess, Simon Clerk, William Coping, Robert Crepping, Clemens Drury, Thomas Emmys, John Forster, John Furseney, John May, John Riggemen, John Salmon, Laurance Smith, and William Thwait.

[10] His will can be found in P.C.B.S.E., Osbern, f. 58.

[11] C.F.R., Richard II, 1379, p. 152.

[12] Colin Platt, *The Medieval English Town* (London: McKay, 1976), pp. 181-182.

The Charmans lived on Churchgate Street, one of the more expensive streets in Bury, and, unlike many of their less prominent contemporaries, had several children who lived until adulthood. Indeed, biological success and comparatively large stem families were another of the dominant characteristics of the burghal élite. There were two sons, William and John, a daughter Joan, a household that included a dozen servants, and a private chaplain. Some of this wealth came from activity in the draperies, but Charman was far more prosperous than the rest of his draper peers; the bulk of his wealth was accumulated from land transactions. The records for these dealings come not from his wills, but rather from town deeds.[13] Charman held more property than any other layman in fourteenth-century Bury. Little indication of these vast holdings is given in Charman's last testament. His family was provided with a series of tenements, and Alice was left with the Churchgate Street house in which Richard died. This was because the bulk of the holdings were used not for personal, residential, or commercial purposes, but as real estate to be let to the highest bidder, usually on short-term leases.

Charman first appears in the town deeds in 1353, in one of the earliest records that has survived. In his twenties at the time—he would live until age 60, longevity being one more feature of the burghal class—he and Thomas Denham, himself a prominent citizen and long-serving alderman, bought five acres of arable outside of South Gate. Prime farmland, it was situated next to the holdings of the almoner, one of the abbey's major officers. Charman realized the importance of centralizing his holdings in order to enhance their commercial attraction. Accordingly, he entered into negotiations with the abbey, swapping fragments of widely scattered lands to make compact but contiguous segments that would be easier to cultivate. Richard also held extensive lands outside of West Gate, and exchanged these for more abbey property in the South Fields. By his late twenties, he was already one of the wealthiest men in the banleuca.

The land-deed records are by no means comprehensive; they show only the tip of the land speculators' iceberg. But, in Richard

[13] The Hengrave Deeds, i, Bury St. Edmunds and West Suffolk County Record Office, Bury St. Edmunds, 449. The deeds in which Charman is encountered include: 2/11; 2/12; 2/13; 2/14; 2/15; 2/529; 2/530; 2/531; 2/532; 2/533; 2/534; 2/535; 2/557.

Charman's case, even the partial evidence is impressive. After a flurry of records from 1354, no deeds survive until 1373. When they do again appear, Charman was still prominent. At the peak of his social prestige as well as of his economic power and influence, he continued to consolidate scattered holdings throughout the banleuca and West Suffolk. He got quitclaim of one Thomas Ganen for all lands and tenements in Bury held by William Charman, a very significant acquisition.[14] There is some question about the precise identity of this William; Richard had a son of that name who was in his twenties by the 1370s, and it may well have been he. Perhaps Richard was using him as a vehicle of enfeoffment. Alternatively, the aforementioned William may have been Richard's father, and the lands Richard's by inheritance. Whatever the exact relationship, Richard continued to acquire property. In 1374 he took possession of the Churchgate Street tenement in which he and his wife were to spend the rest of their lives, a large lot stretching back a full eighty feet to Hog Lane, containing one of the finest mansions in town.

Many of Bury's burghal élite were great merchants, and most tried to convert their mercantile wealth into landed investments. But there was another notable feature that distinguishes Charman's career; he made use of the capital from his mercantile and landed wealth to become a financier. Richard was one of the major money-lenders in late fourteenth century Bury St. Edmunds, and there are a number of records from the 1370s which show him plying his trade. At several junctures he went to court to seek recompense against those whom he felt had failed to repay him according to the terms of his contract.[15] By the 1390s, money-lending had become the principal part of the Charman family business, with son William playing the most active role. When William retired early in the fifteenth century to life as a country squire in nearby Hopton, the money-lending business passed to his son John, a prominent citizen and fishmonger in London, who still controlled considerable property in West Suffolk.[16] Indeed, Richard's position as county tax collector may in some way have been linked to his very profitable financial activities.

[14] *Ibid.*, 449, 2/13.
[15] C.P.R., Edward III, 1375, p. 196; C.P.R., Richard II, 1379, p. 411; C.P.R., Richard II, 1380, p. 440.
[16] Hengrave, 449, 2/561.

Richard Charman remained active in business and community affairs through the final years of his life. Toward his end, he began to donate lands and movables to the town corporation, and in 1390 applied for license in mortmain to leave four messuages in the borough to the abbey. As late as April 1390, three months before his death, he was called to act as a witness in a major land transaction.[17] The other witnesses were the alderman and bailiffs, and Richard's presence was testimony to his enduring reputation and prestige. Richard Charman was the great man *par excellence*: alderman, burgess, draper and merchant, landholder and land speculator, financier and philanthropist, patron and supporter of civic causes. Always upwardly mobile, Charman began his life as a merchant, saw his son pass into the ranks of the gentry, and his grandson become a citizen of London.

Charman's example was closely followed by another distinguished alderman, John Nottingham.[18] Nottingham was more civic-minded than Charman, serving as alderman on at least five different occasions under two kings; there are even indications that he went on campaign in France with Henry V. We do not know precisely what his occupation was, but it was probably in the draperies, and, like Charman, Nottingham was quick to convert the capital that he acquired through trade into more stable landed investments. Like Charman, he was the "new" sort of late medieval burgher, the urban realtor, and merchant prince, with status among the traditional landholding gentlemen. With his brother-in-law, John Jerveys, he was involved in high finance, including the funding of a royal fleet, and he spent a great deal of time in litigation, suing, and being sued for repayment of debts.[19] But, mostly, Nottingham held property, in Bury, where by 1440 he had more tenements and messuages than any other individual, in London and throughout West Suffolk. Virtually all of it was leased directly on a cash basis to whomever could meet his terms. Unlike Richard Charman, Nottingham would always remain primarily a *rentier* rather than a speculator, and his fortune rested on income from prime holdings that were in demand even in the renters' market of the early and mid-fifteenth century.

[17] *Ibid.*, 2/15.

[18] The will is reprinted in Tymms, pp. 5-11.

[19] See below, pp. 150-153. Also, see B.M. Harl. Ms. 27; C.P.R., Henry VI, 1423, p. 146.

Nottingham demonstrated his financial power in several ways. He seems to have had a great deal of cash at hand, and several times doled out large sums to his daughter, brother, and brother-in-law. He had extensive valuables in the form of brass, silver, and furs, and, like Charman, maintained a prestigious symbol of private prosperity, a personal chantry priest. But his principal vehicle for demonstrating his wealth came through acts of charity and private benevolence. He loved Bury and contributed large sums to the town, including the major share of the rebuilding costs of St. Mary's Church, which was destroyed by a series of fires early in the century. To celebrate his generosity, two porches were built in his honor, one of which stands today.[20]

Fellow burgess John Edward was alderman at least three times in the late 1430s, and was probably in office when he died in 1441.[21] Edward styled himself a "merchaunt" in his will, but other sources narrow this to "mercer." Early in his adult life, he concentrated on the sale of finished woolen cloth, but by the 1430s had broadened his mercery to include production as well as marketing, and he probably traded in other commodities. Like most of his peers, Edward had a large family, including three sons and three daughters alive at the time of his death, and, like the others, had sufficient property to endow each one, including his younger daughters. He was important enough to be called by royal commissioners to deliver Bury's gaol, and was a judge in the incident of the Saracen's Head Inn, one of the borough's most important law cases in the fifteenth century.[22] And, like so many other burgesses, Edward's accumulation of wealth meant a departure of sorts from the means by which it was initially accrued. John Edward took his commercial equity and invested it in land, enabling him to compile a larger fortune than he could possibly have accumulated solely through the wool and cloth trade. In the end, his legacy too was of sufficient size to allow his children to abandon commerce entirely and move into the ranks of the landed gentry.[23]

[20] They were on the north and west sides; the former is dedicated to wife Isabella, and stands today. For more information, see M. P. Statham, *The Church of St. Mary, Bury St. Edmunds, Suffolk* (Bury St. Edmunds, pamphlet, n.d.).

[21] *Ibid.*, Osbern, f. 253.

[22] Information on this fascinating incident can be found in C.P.R., Henry VI, 1435, pp. 470, 475.

[23] P.C.B.S.E., Osbern, f. 253. Also, C.P.R., Henry VI, 1433, p. 351.

Most prominent of all of Bury's aldermen was John (Jankyn) Smith.[24] From the 1420s, Smith served as alderman at least nine times in a forty-year period, and, if the records for the 1440s were more complete, they might supplement this tally. A sixteenth-century portrait of him hangs in the town Guildhall, and the only other medieval lay personages who compare with him in stature are Richard Charman and Sir Robert Drury. By mid-life, Smith was armigerous, an urban *rentier* of the highest order, holding more local property than even Charman had a century earlier, and having supplementary estates in all four East Anglia archdeaconries.

Although Smith left numerous personal documents and *testamenta*, several of which are enrolled with the town muniments, there are surprisingly few details surviving which tell of his personal life. He had a wife and daughter, both of whom pre-deceased him; herein, his small-stem family distinguishes him from most of the other burgesses. A son John is mentioned fleetingly in one of his wills and was provided with a small parcel of land, but this single reference is not substantiated elsewhere. With the bulk of his property being otherwise disposed, son John might have pre-deceased his father or been illegitimate. In any circumstance, John Smith's estates were so extensive that he probably would not have bequeathed all of it to a single heir, legitimate or otherwise. This was his singular claim to prominence; he was by far the greatest benefactor of late medieval Bury St. Edmunds. He made his fortune in land and trade, and gave most of it back to the town corporation at his death.

Smith's charity extended to all local ecclesiastical foundations, to the friars at Babwell, the borough's hospitals, the Dominicans at Thetford, the sister house of the monks of St. Edmunds, and the nuns of Redlingfield and Broyard. These bequests were never random contributions, but rather personal donations to specific members of each house, all of whom appear to have been personal friends. Even so, the Church received far less than his beloved town. His lands were to become the core of the endowment of the Alderman's Guild, and a major reason that it was able to resist the abbey late in the fifteenth century. Much of the money used in the litigation battles of the 1480s and 1490s came from the rents from what had been Smith's estates. He also made a substantial addition to the endowment of Bury's other key guild, the Dusse of St. Nich-

[24] Tymms, pp. 55-73. Also, C.P.R., Henry VI, 1443, p. 199.

olas, and created a new guild, "The Sweet Man Jesus," to sing perpetual masses for himself, his family, and his friends.[25]

Smith provided for prisoners and the poor, and most of the other guilds in Bury. But, above all, he left the bulk of his enormous land holdings, messuages, tenements, fields, meadows, rents, services, *et alia*, in Bury and throughout East Anglia to the people of Bury St. Edmunds. The lands were to be administered by the town guild, but were to be used for the general good of all the denizens. So great were these holdings that Smith's legacy was still being cited in the 1539 Court of Supervisor's accounts reporting to Henry VIII—despite the fact that he had been dead for close to sixty years.[26]

The late medieval aldermen were selected from among the greatest of the burghal élite, and their power was institutionalized by their office. Although no evidence survives to substantiate it, it is likely that while in office, aldermen used their official prerogatives and perquisites to enhance further their already considerable positions. All were initially merchants, but soon moved to land holding, and it was from the latter that the bulk of their income was ultimately derived. Some farmed themselves, others rented out, and a few speculated on their value, but all held extensive tracts of property. Even in a period of rather moderate inflation, contemporaries understood that land held its value far better than most commodities, and clearly carried more social status. All married well, and most had large families. The burghal élite were basically conservative, and many of the changes that affected them came from exogenous factors. But they had a strong sense of public responsibility, believed that political rights, power, and obligation stemmed from ownership of property, and played active roles in regional and national as well as local politics. This too tended to ensure their economic and social positions. And for all, the impetus of upward mobility was passed on to their progeny. The goal of most Bury merchants, like that of their London counterparts, was to move into the ranks of the landed gentlemen, and draw the bulk

[25] C.P.R., Edward IV, 1481, p. 259. The guild was styled a "college," designed to sing masses every day. It was given an annual trust yielding the considerable sum of £71 for warden, chaplains, lay men and women, and property for the warden.

[26] L. J. Redstone, "First Ministers' Account of the Possessions of the Abbey of St. Edmunds," *P.S.I.*, xiii, 3, 1909.

of their income not from their own labors, but rather that of others.[27]

THE GREATER BURGESSES

Many but by no means all of Bury's social and economic élite, or patriciate, as they might be called, were aldermen. Richard Charman's initial reluctance to serve in office has been mentioned; many other burgesses preferred to remain publicly anonymous and concentrate instead on their personal careers. Among the contemporaries of Richard Charman, four such characters stand out: Thomas Sutton, Nicholas Fornham, Thomas Hammond, and John Schapman.

Sutton died in 1361, probably a victim of the *pestis secundus*.[28] Information on most of these earlier burgesses is somewhat sketchy, and we do not know precisely what he did for a living. But Sutton did have shops on Skinners' and Butchers' Rows, both of which were passed on to his sons, and he probably traded livestock and their byproducts. Whatever his craft or trade, Sutton displayed that most outstanding characteristic of the burghal élite: he was a large landholder, both within and without the borough, a *rentier* of the highest magnitude. Most of his properties were situated around the Great Market in Risbygate Ward, and, in proportion to the number of tenants he had, his *per capita* returns may well have been higher than those of his contemporary Charman. Overall, there were sufficient holdings to provide for all his sons, and additional rural lands to provide for friends, a very unusual occurrence. Sutton himself lived on Gildhall Street, just becoming fashionable in the mid-fourteenth century, in a tenement with a large garden touching the west wall of the borough. On a slightly lesser scale, he followed the pattern set by his friend Richard Charman.

Fornham and Hammond both died in 1392.[29] Fornham was atypical among the great men in that he was a bachelor and had no immediate family. Apart from the natural desire to have heirs to perpetuate one's wealth and memory, a family was part and parcel

[27] Sources for comparison are: Gwyn Williams, *Medieval London* (London: Athlone Press, 1963), pp. 50-75; and S. L. Thrupp, *The Merchant Class of Medieval London* (Chicago: University of Chicago Press, 1948), pp. 321-376.

[28] P.C.B.S.E., Osbern, f. 26.

[29] *Ibid.*, f. 63 for Fornham; *ibid.*, f. 66 for Hammond.

of burghal respectability. It provided security and stability and served as a shelter against political and economic pressures, but, for whatever reason, Fornham elected to remain single. His economic life, however, was more like that of his peers. In addition to trade in the mercery, he was a major landholder in the banleuca, concentrating primarily on farmlands in the suburbs, which he let out directly. His property must have included the best arable in greater Bury, for even with the glut of farmland available in the late fourteenth century, Fornham never had difficulty getting tenants. When he died, all the major figures in the town and the abbey appeared at his funeral, with the leading burgesses acting as executors.

Thomas Hammond was a butcher. Along with the weavers and dyers, butchers formed the craft élite of late medieval Bury, and at times certain of their number were able to crack the ruling circle of merchants and gentlemen. Butchers in particular were successful because it was possible for the more enterprising of their lot to corner the marketing as well as the production aspects of their craft, much as the London spicers had done in elevating themselves to the level of merchant grocers. Unlike spicers, butchers could not engage in long-distance trade, which somewhat limited potential profits. But in a major regional market like Bury a great degree of control and prosperity was still possible. Thomas Sutton may well have risen via this route, and, in the fluid years immediately following the Black Death, Thomas Hammond unquestionably did. In most ways, he was typical of the suggested pattern of the burghal élite: he had three sons and three daughters, and by middle age had converted his trade capital into landed investments. Like the great merchants, Hammond owned shops and tenements in town, and fields and meadows in the suburbs. He bequeathed to each of his sons sizable chunks of property, and apparently all three jumped right from craftsman to gentleman status.

John Schapman was another craftsman who proved very successful.[30] Initially a cordwainer, Schapman was a member of that pre-cloth-era leather industry so important in fourteenth-century Bury. Like all the other dominant figures in the borough, he quickly transferred his liquid capital into property, which he then rented out and eventually passed on to his children.

The careers of Hammond and Schapman suggest a high degree

[30] *Ibid.*, f. 71.

of mobility in the upper strata of fourteenth-century Bury society. It was relatively easy to come up through the ranks and make one's fortune. This would be less the case in the fifteenth century; from 1400, fewer and fewer craftsmen made their way into the burgess élite. Mobility always existed, but by the fifteenth century was primarily the result of attrition caused by high mortality and the failure of over one-half the borough population to produce male heirs, rather than to social and economic opportunity.[31] In the fifteenth century, the great men came mostly from the ranks of the major merchants, from the grocers, drapers, mercers, and clothiers in the early years, and by the 1480s increasingly from the gentry.

In the first two-thirds of the fifteenth century, Bury's mercers enjoyed a period of particular prosperity, as the Suffolk cloth industry developed. Among those who made their marks was John Edward, who has been discussed in his capacity as alderman. Another was Richard King, himself a one-time alderman in the fifteenth century, but best known for his role in the mercery.[32] He was an influential character, with the familiar trademark of a large family to help in his commercial endeavors and succeed to his landed holdings. Much of King's property stood around the Great Market, and included Bury's most famous tenement, Moyses Hall.[33] While income from cloth sales and rents may have sufficed to keep such a splendid residence, his will suggests another potential source of income. King stored large quantities of grain, apparently marketing and speculating on their value. Further, much of the grain came from his own property in the suburbs, and here King differed from his peers; while they were almost exclusively speculators or *rentiers*, he appears to have actively cultivated parts of his arable, a throwback to an earlier era.

King was interesting for another reason. His lineage can be traced

[31] See above, pp. 56-57. Also, see Thrupp, *Merchant Class*, pp. 191-224. Some assessment of fertility differentials can be made from the indirect evidence of replacement ratios. No matter how the burghal élite are surveyed, through time or occupation, replacement rates for males and females never come close to unity. The highest figures are 82 percent for males and 61 percent for females. The distribution of sons was consistently low, and numbers of families with two or more sons was never more than 25 percent of the total.

[32] P.C.B.S.E., Osbern, f. 71.

[33] A. R. Edwardson, Moyses Hall Museum (Bury St. Edmunds, pamphlet, n.d.).

both back through time and forward for several generations. Later members of the King family also made their marks as prominent members of the burghal élite. Richard and his wife Katherine had two sons, both merchants of middling success and importance. The second, Edmund, along with his spouse Agnes, occupied Moyses Hall, and then passed it to another Richard King, probably Richard III, the son of Richard II, eldest child of Richard I and Katherine.[34] Richard III proved more successful than even his grandfather, and when he died his will was proved in the archbishop's court in Canterbury, an indication of great personal prestige and prosperity. Richard III and his wife Cicely had a son and three daughters, and sufficient property to endow each quite handsomely. He was a mercer, but gained most of his wealth through an inheritance from his elder brother, Sir Nicholas, the eldest child of Richard II. Sir Nicholas left Richard III two townhouses on the Long Brakelond and Guildhall Street, by the early sixteenth century the most fashionable avenues in the borough, and farmlands in Essex, Norfolk, Suffolk, Kent, and Cambridgeshire. On Richard III's death, spouse Cicely moved to London, where she remained for the rest of her life, living off her West Suffolk income, in a manner similar to that of the grandson of Richard Charman.[35] Ultimately, Richard III's eldest son retained Moyses Hall, but passed into the ranks of the gentry, marking the final departure of the Kings from the merceries.

Richard King III had another distinguishing mark. Like John Smith, he was one of the great benefactors of late medieval Bury St. Edmunds. His pious charity touched all the major institutions and needy groups, and in the case of several ecclesiastical foundations, helped to relieve the financial strain many experienced in the sixteenth century. King left funds for the abbey church, both parish churches, several hospitals, the Benedictines' sister nunnery in Thetford, the friars in Babwell, the gaol, the town's poor, a series of masses for the souls of family and friends, and the high altars of a half dozen surrounding parish churches. So great was the scope of these bequests that King's will was enrolled by the Al-

[34] For information about Agnes King, see Archdeaconry of Sudbury Wills, West Suffolk Record Office, Bury St. Edmunds, Baldwyn Register, f. 186. In 1539 Moyses Hall was held by Thomas Kynge for 6 shillings, 8 pence, per year. See L. Redstone, *First Ministers' Account*, p. 11.

[35] P.C.C. Fetiplace, f. 32. Also, see P.C.B.S.E., Hoode, f. 1.

derman's Guild with its regulations, in order to ensure certification.[36]

Other mercers among the burghal élite included William Bunting, another one-time alderman who came from a family of prosperous mercers, with shops on Hatter Street, the garment center of fifteenth-century Bury St. Edmunds.[37] He held the usual array of property throughout the banleuca, including a series of tenements on the ever-popular Long Brakelond. Still more prominent mercer burgesses included John Thurston, Laurance Smith, and Thomas Bruning, all of whom lived in the middle part of the fifteenth century.[38] All were active participants in the cloth trade; held sizeable tracts of land in the country and derived considerable income from them; lived in mansions around the Great Market, close to their shops; had large families; and participated in limited fashion in civic affairs. And by late in the fifteenth century their sons had moved up into the ranks of the landed classes, abandoning trade in the process.

Drapers and grocers were nearly as successful as were the mercers. Among the most influential of them were William Rycher, John Ridges, and William Bass.[39] Rycher, a draper, was the son of an alderman, but never aspired in his own right to high public office. Late in life he delivered the borough gaol, always a position reserved for the rich and powerful, but most of his career was spent procuring supplies of raw wool and shipping them to the Netherlands.[40] Ridges and Bass, both grocers, each died in 1465. Both were large landholders, and for a time, Ridges leased parts of Moyses Hall from the King family. Another important draper was John Parfay, who traded in a number of things besides woolen

[36] B.M. Harl. Ms. 4626. Also, see Oxford University, Bodleian Library, Suffolk Ms., Bury St. Edmunds, 515, for the Account of the Supervisors' Report, which confirms this.

[37] See above, pp. 30-33. William's will can be found in P.C.B.S.E., Hawlee, f. 262.

[38] Smith's will is in P.C.B.S.E., Hawlee, f. 325; Brunning's will appears a page later. Thurston's is in Hawlee, f. 63. A generation later, another John Thurston, also a mercer, burgess and man of prominence, appears in the Pye Register. Their relationship is not clear.

[39] Rycher's will is in P.C.B.S.E., Hawlee, f. 68. Ridges' is in P.C.B.S.E., Hawlee, f. 65; and Bass, Hawlee, f. 84.

[40] See: C.C.R., Henry VI, 1439, p. 349; C.P.R., Henry VI, 1444, p. 282; C.C.R., Henry VI, 1449, p. 135.

cloth, was wealthy enough to have had his will proved in the Prerogative Court of Canterbury, and who with his wife Katherine was another of the greater benefactors of the borough.[41] All traded and leased large tracts of land, all were at various times referred to as burgesses in official notarial documents, and all were members of the Alderman's and St. Nicholas' Guilds.

Most of Bury's dominant figures were men. Women were rarely given full freedom or opportunity to exercise their talents.[42] Lobel contended with some justification that a husband might alienate lands that were his wife's by dowry, even without her consent.[43] She asserted that a husband could sell his wife's property without permission; that a woman needed her spouse's consent to make a will; and that, if anything, Bury's patriciate adhered more closely to Common Law restrictions on women than most other late medieval municipalities. Lobel further declared that only five unmarried women left wills in the course of the fourteenth, fifteenth, and sixteenth centuries.[44] While the Bury women were clearly second-class citizens, their positions were never as restricted as Lobel claimed. More than five unmarried women left wills. Women could and did become members of town guilds, including the most prestigious, that of the alderman. On several occasions they used regional and royal courts to judge their rights over property. In 1295, for example, in a famous trial, Common Pleas confirmed the rights of a Bury woman to hold a tenement on the same terms as her husband had, despite strong lobbying against her by the abbot of St. Edmunds.[45] Certainly, many women felt vulnerable, especially widows with large holdings, and several placed themselves under the protection of the Alderman's Guild or the abbot. In the fourteenth century, for example, one widow left all her lands to the abbey, in return for protection and a lifetime pension.[46] But women could hold property, and function as had their husbands. At times, certain unmarried females were even able to carve for themselves singular places in the merchant community. In the mid-fifteenth century, Emma Goldsmith, self styled "singlewoman," was one of

[41] P.C.C., Bennett, f. 22.

[42] A reference is Eileen Power, *Medieval Women* (Cambridge: Cambridge University Press, 2nd ed., 1976).

[43] Lobel, *The Borough*, pp. 106-107.

[44] *Ibid.*, p. 107.

[45] C.U.L. Ms. E e 3 60, f. 192b.

[46] *Ibid.*, F f 2 33, f. 67.

Bury's most prominent *rentiers*, and throughout the accounts of all the major rentals from abbey officers there are women holding property, paying rents, and enjoying the profits of landed estates.[47] By and large, whatever their personal prejudices, St. Edmunds' abbots were less concerned with the gender of their tenants than whether they paid their rent.

Individual women made particular marks, including a few in the West Suffolk underworld. In the 1330s, Agnes Goldying was at various times accused of assault, arson, robbery, trespass, and even criminal offenses against the Crown. She was a member of a no-torious outlaw band, and was the *bête noire* of borough authorities. Curiously, she was granted royal pardon for all crimes in 1333 after making a personal plea to Queen Philippa.[48] Goldying was not the only woman criminal of note in the turbulent fourteenth century, and not the only woman to receive royal pardon for her crimes in a society not known for its sexual evenhandedness or leniency. In 1351, Katherine of Lackford, a woman of dubious reputation, murdered her husband, a prominent mercer.[49] When confronted with the crime, she pleaded temporary madness, and in a trial with an all-male jury was acquitted.

Other women made their marks in more orthodox fashion. One was Emma Cheyne. While old women were generally viewed in the worst of all lights, with contempt for them slightly less venomous than that reserved for Jews and lepers, such was not to be Emma's fate. Known for years as the recluse of Bury St. Edmunds, re-nowned for her piety and kindness, at age 68, 22 years a widow, she was granted a royal pension and given a formal position of honor.[50] At the other end of the social scale was Margaret Ode-ham.[51] Margaret was married to John Odeham, an important draper and burgess, who himself rose in the familiar pattern of trade and landholding.[52] He was a close friend of several important people, including John Smith, but as a Bury personage was out-

[47] For evidence of Emma, see *ibid.*, ff. 67-68. For information on the rentals, see 272-277.
[48] C.P.R., Edward III, 1333, p. 408.
[49] *Ibid.*, 1351, p. 175.
[50] C.P.R., Henry VI, 1449, p. 304.
[51] Tymms, pp. 73-81. Also, see B.M. Harl. Ms. 4626.
[52] For reference to John Odeham, see: C.C.R., Henry VI, 1448, p. 61; *ibid.*, 1449, p. 179; C.C.R., Edward IV, 1461, p. 85; C.P.R., Edward IV, 1473, p. 385.

classed by his spouse Margaret. Well connected, travelled, and educated, she had friends throughout England and the Low Countries, and financial dealings of her own in Norwich, Great Yarmouth, Ipswich, King's Lynn, Cambridge, and Colchester. She travelled to the Continent several times, at least once on business, and left funds after her death for an annual pilgrimage to the Netherlands. From her mansion on Skinners' Row, Margaret collected extensive rents from properties in town and throughout West Suffolk. She was upwardly mobile. Her husband died armigerous, and both her daughters married gentlemen. But all of this was secondary to her philanthropy. Odeham left a broad sampling of pious charity, much of which went to friends in hospitals and nunneries. She provided for the poor, for widows and orphans, for prisoners, education, virtually every guild in town and the abbey—in all, a wider range of bequests than any other individual save John Smith.

Like Smith and many other benefactors, Margaret Odeham's generosity may have been motivated in part by a dearth of heirs. Her two daughters were given sizeable dowries, but neither was provided with sufficient property to reduce significantly the bulk of the Odeham estate. There was a stepson from an earlier marriage of John, but he was provided for by his father, and Margaret left him only bits and pieces of rural lands. In effect, she found herself with a great deal of property and no pressing needs to bequeath it privately. The bulk of the estates, lands in the borough, the east and south fields of the suburbs, farms in Nowton, Barton, Horningsheath, even her house with its appurtenances on Skinners' Row, went to the town and people of Bury St. Edmunds. So important was the legacy that among her executors were Alderman Walter Thurston and Richard King III. Her will, like those of John Smith and King, would be enrolled with the charters of the Alderman's Guild, and helped to provide a substantial portion of the latter's endowment.

Most of Bury's burgesses took a low public profile, and submerged their individuality in the amorphous personality of the larger corporate group. A major exception was John Jerveys.[53]

[53] The author was not able to find Jerveys' will in the records of the Peculiar Court of Bury St. Edmunds, the Archdeaconry Courts of Norwich, Norfolk, Sudbury, or Suffolk, the Consistory Court of Norwich, or the Prerogative Court of Canterbury. Perhaps his problems with the law were partly responsible for a lack of probate.

Linked by marriage to John Nottingham, Jerveys was a man of many talents, several residences, and, in some respects, dubious honor. He took advantage of his brother-in-law's position, won entry into Bury's inner circles, and used his connections to make profits in the woolen trade. In 1438 Jerveys bought property with capital raised in several land deals by using Nottingham's prestige and good name, and, again borrowing on his brother-in-law's security, leased the lands out at a substantial profit.[54] Yet these local Bury deals formed but a small part of Jerveys' overall businesses. He dealt not only in Bury St. Edmunds and West Suffolk, but throughout East Anglia and all of eastern England, and had an office in London, where he lived for extended periods of time with his brother Thomas, himself originally from Bury.[55] John moved continually back and forth from London to Lincoln, and for a time lived in Bildeston, Norfolk, a halfway point for him.[56] But, wherever he was, the bulk of his property remained in West Suffolk, and the focal point of his operations was the Great Market in Risbygate Ward; at one time or another, the name of John Jerveys appears in most of the major land deals of the mid-fifteenth century.

Jerveys was also an arms dealer and procurer. In 1435 agents of Henry VI commissioned the Jerveys brothers to outfit two fleets for the French wars.[57] Evidently both king and the Jerveyses were content with the arrangement, for in the following year John was assigned to outfit two more ships.[58] This time, however, some doubt arose over his methods. As a financier, Jerveys both held debts and owed considerable sums.[59] Just as he tried to call in his outstanding loans to help to finance his ventures, so too was he asked to pay off his own commitments. Jerveys managed to avoid his creditors and raise the necessary cash, but in 1439 he was in trouble again. Despite the considerable profits from the arms deals, he continued to default, was arrested, and forced to appear in royal court.[60]

[54] C.P.R., Henry VI, 1438, p. 180.

[55] *Ibid.*, 1439, p. 389.

[56] *Ibid.*, 1437, p. 57; C.C.R., Henry VI, 1436, p. 112. Also, see C.C.R., Henry VI, 1442, p. 66.

[57] C.C.R., Henry VI, 1436, p. 57.

[58] C.P.R., Henry VI, 1436, p. 82.

[59] C.C.R., Henry VI, 1437, p. 112. Also, *ibid.*, 1433, p. 297; and *ibid.*, 1435, p. 366; *ibid.*, 1437, p. 112.

[60] C.P.R., Henry VI, 1439, pp. 358-359.

There, further allegations were laid against him; he had defaulted before and jumped bail. In all, the great speculator was charged with owing the staggering sum of £260. For some months in 1439, John and Thomas were hunted outlaws, until late in the year when they surrendered themselves and were thrown into the Fleet, London's debtor prison.[61] But the Jerveyses were not to remain in gaol for very long; their wealth and connections were sufficient to obtain for them royal pardon, and within a year they were back in operation with a letter of protection from the king.[62] John moved to Bildeston, and transferred his activities to Norfolk for much of the 1440s. Still, he was unable to keep out of trouble; the shadier side of speculation seems to have fascinated him. In 1455, problems, perhaps political, struck again, and royal commissioners sent out writs asking that he be brought before the king's justices to answer unspecified criminal charges. Unfortunately, we do not know how this affair was resolved; it is one of the last records of John Jerveys' activities.[63]

Despite his difficulties with authorities, Jerveys gained considerable wealth and power in the course of his lifetime. He held extensive properties throughout eastern England, and was called a gentleman as early as 1442.[64] So extensive were his lands and movables that by the mid 1430s he was placing much of it in enfeoffment. Few details or his personal or family life survive except the presence and activities of his brother and brother-in-law. John may have had a son, since by 1451 he was called John the Elder, but, because of his almost total absence from the local civil service, there are no additional documents that can shed more light on several unanswered questions.[65]

As the prosperity of Bury St. Edmunds increased from the late fifteenth century, the number of prominent and wealthy burgesses rose proportionally. They followed the established pattern of accumulating early fortunes in trade, graduating to ownership of

[61] *Ibid.*, p. 389.

[62] *Ibid.*, pp. 388-389.

[63] C.P.R., Henry VI, 1455, p. 255. The final reference is C.P.R., Edward IV, 1462, p. 109. It concerns land, mentions heirs, is vague, and may well be posthumous.

[64] C.C.R., Henry VI, 1442, p. 66.

[65] *Ibid.*, 1451, p. 264. As noted above, note 63, he is said in 1462 to have heirs, but their nature is never specified. The references to senior and junior may have no family context; on the continent, they were often used only to distinguish folk with the same name.

land and activity as financiers, and the lending of capital at usurious rates. Among the more interesting of the later figures were John Worliche and Robert Brett.[66] Like John Jerveys, Worliche found it profitable to operate in both London and Bury. A goldsmith by trade, he turned by the 1480s to pawn-broking and money-lending on a very large scale, and became one of the wealthiest men in Suffolk. His contemporary Brett was a highly innovative mercer, a member of that new breed of cloth dealers who styled themselves clothiers and dominated all aspects of woolen cloth production, from the shearing of sheep to the marketing of the finished commodity. Brett held considerable property in West Suffolk, much of which was used in his cloth production process. If he and his Bury counterparts such as Stephan Gardner were not quite as wealthy or as famous as the Springs of Lavenham, they were among the leading burghers in town, and had sufficient wealth to have their wills enrolled in the Prerogative Court of Canterbury.[67] The early sixteenth century also marked the emergence of more craftsmen into the burghal élite. Most prominent among these was William Honeybourne.[68] A dyer, Honeybourne was prosperous enough to have had his will, like those of Brett and Gardner, proved by the archbishop. He, wife Katherine, and daughter Anne lived in an expensive mansion on Northgate Street, which he purchased from no less a personage than John Smith, with whom he had regularly done business. There were others from the lesser trades, such as Edmund Clarke, a haberdasher, with shops in Bury and Thetford, in Norfolk; and Oliver Hall, a tailor who held property in West and East Suffolk, Norfolk, Essex, and Kent.[69] All show the same characteristics as the other great burgesses: wealth initially accrued through trade or craft, invested next in land and finance, and movement by their progeny into the ranks of the gentry.

THE GREAT FAMILIES: THE EXAMPLES OF THE BARETS AND DRURYS

Most of late medieval Bury's leading figures were individuals who made their fortunes and provided their heirs—if they had heirs—

[66] P.C.B.S.E., Pye, f. 99, for Worliche; for Brett, P.C.C., Porch, f. 27.
[67] P.C.C., Wattys, f.4.
[68] Tymms, pp. 81-83.
[69] Clark's will can be found in P.C.B.S.E., Hoode, f. 12; Hall's is Hoode, f. 88.

with substantial incomes. This and the biological difficulties of producing sons who managed to live to adulthood tended to limit the
number of prominent burghal figures from any given family. Some
filial groups, however, did make collective marks. There were the
Jerveys brothers, and the three generations of Richard Kings.
Among the aristocracy, the de Veres, the earls of Oxford, owned
land in West Suffolk and often made their presence felt in local
Bury affairs.[70] But the two outstanding families in the development
of late medieval Bury St. Edmunds were the Barets and the Drurys.
By studying their fortunes, we can learn much about the borough's
corporate ruling class. Both families started out as *bourgeoisie* and
both were firmly ensconced among the Suffolk gentry by the sixteenth century. They intermarried at least twice, and, at a time
when only about one quarter of all burghal families survived
through three generations, both had direct descendants throughout the entire later middle ages.

The Barets first came to prominence through trade in the draperies and merceries. The first of the line to leave extensive records
was Galfrid (see Table 4.1).[71] He died in 1416, a prosperous burgess
who left extensive property to both the Alderman's Guild and to
his family. He seems to have been a first-generation immigrant, for
his funeral monument stated that he originally came from Cratfield, in East Suffolk, near the market town of Halesworth. He was
a close friend of Abbot William of Cratfield, and the abbot may
well have helped in his compatriot's rise.

Galfrid and his wife Joan had four sons and at least one daughter.
His oldest son, also named John, and spouse Joan, who died in
1424, left testamentary records.[72] From them, additional information on the early years of the family is available. Galfrid was
between fifty and sixty years old at his death, an advanced age for
most men in the later middle ages, but surprisingly common among
the burghal élite. And, like many of his peers, Galfrid made a
fortunate marriage; Joan brought with her a considerable dowry,
including lands that she was empowered to dispose of at her dis-

[70] For example, C.C.R., Edward I, 1296, p. 495. There are several references in V. C. Redstone, "St. Edmund's Bury."

[71] See the genealogy in B.M. Harl. Ms. 294, f. 158. Galfrid Baret's will
is in P.C.B.S.E., Osbern, f. 142.

[72] P.C.B.S.E., Osbern, f. 168 for Joan. Information on son John I can
be found in the will of John II, Tymms, p. 15; and P.C.B.S.E., Osbern,
f. 201.

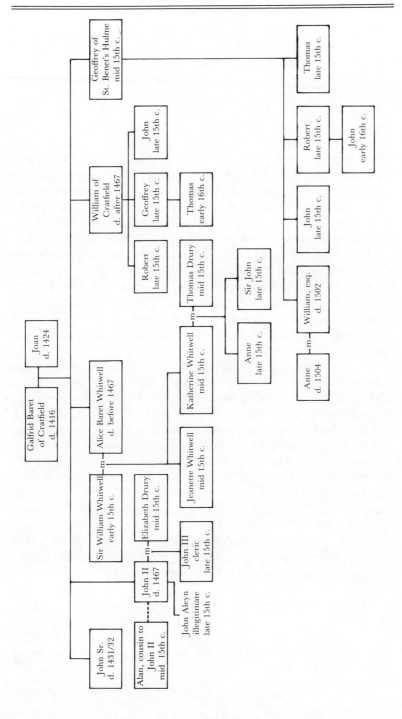

cretion. Hence, the second generation of Barets born in Bury St. Edmunds came into wealth from both sides of their family, an attribute that contributed to their continuing success in the later fifteenth and sixteenth centuries. It was at this stage, after the first generation of prosperity, that the progeny of many burgesses left the trades for life as *rentiers*. Some of the Barets did, but this was not the case with Galfrid's second son, John II.[73]

Perhaps John II elected to pursue a mercantile career because the bulk of his parents' estate was passed to his elder brother, John I. But when both John I and Joan pre-deceased him, most of the family lands did come to John II, making a life of leisure a possibility. But he continued to trade actively in wool and woolen cloth, and by his death in 1467 had surpassed the achievements of his father, becoming one of the greatest figures in Bury's history. More information survives about this Baret than for any other member of the clan, primarily through the long, detailed wills and *testamenta* he drew up and revised throughout the last 10 years of his life. Like John Smith, Margaret Odeham, and Richard King III, John Baret II was a major benefactor of Bury; for a time his portrait hung in the Guildhall, alongside that of John Smith. John II was an active member of the Alderman's Guild, the Dusse of St. Nicholas, and the local drapery. So great was the scope of his wool dealings that by the 1450s he had moved from the more restrictive field of draper proper into the broader ranks of the entrepreneur clothier. Ironically, as second son, John II elected not to sit back and play the role of country squire; his younger brothers William and Geoffrey, the latter the last and favorite son of old Galfrid, did choose such a life. William moved back to Cratfield and collected rents from his inheritance in East Suffolk and Norfolk; Geoffrey remained resident in Bury, but lived entirely from property rents in West Suffolk. A sister, Alice, also passed into the higher echelons of society, marrying a local knight named William Whitewell. And, for all his mercantile habits, even John II took a coat of arms. Within a generation, the progeny of a Suffolk immigrant had become members of the West Suffolk gentry.

Successful clothier, landowner, financier, and civic leader, John Baret II married into the other major fifteenth-century Bury family, the Drurys. He took as his bride Elizabeth, daughter of Sir

[73] Tymms, pp. 15-44. Also, see C.P.R. Henry VI, 1443, p. 199, for record of his commercial activities.

Roger I, who died about 1420. By all accounts it was a happy marriage, lasting several decades. But, despite the domestic bliss, the Barets produced but a single legitimate son, John III, who decided on a career in the church. While John III was to become a great success in his own right, his holy orders ensured that he could not perpetuate the family name. John II had a natural son, John Aleyn, but he was barred by the circumstances of his birth from inheriting the bulk of his father's estate. Hence, John II's situation was similar to those of John Smith and Margaret Odeham. He had a great deal of land and no one in particular to whom he might leave it; consequently, he gave the bulk of it to the town and people of Bury St. Edmunds, St. Mary's and St. James' churches. In the former he commissioned an elaborate chantry chapel named after the Virgin Mary, containing a large cadaver monument made up in his lifetime, after his own image and likeness. It depicts a lean, gaunt man, wearing the tonsure made popular earlier in the fifteenth century by Henry V and the Dukes of Burgundy, which may indicate the travels of a clothier to the markets of the Low Countries. The monument was sculpted under the direction of Simon Clerk, the most noted mason of the day, and the inscription on it may have been provided by St. Edmunds' most famous fifteenth-century monk, the poet John Lydgate. Both bear testament to John II's position and prosperity. At the cadaver's side is the Baret coat of arms, personally given to John II by Henry VI, another indication of the social progress of the family.[74]

Limited information survives on John II's son, John III.[75] As a cleric, he had less reason than his father to ensure probate of his will, and this potential source of personal information cannot be found. He entered the Benedictine abbey against his father's wishes, but, as the result of either his innate ability or of John II's influence, rose rapidly to high office. When he died he was *thesaurius et camerarius*, effectively, treasurer of the abbey hoard, one of the most powerful positions in the monastery. At his death, John III was living in a fine townhouse, the *Erquinquim*, on Southgate Street. In his own way, John Baret III left a mark in Bury St. Edmunds.

John II's will tells of the progress of his siblings and their chil-

[74] All of this can be seen on the monument. He also commissioned two angels to be sculpted on the roof of the church, bearing his mottoes, "Gode me Gyde," and "Grace me Governe."
[75] B.M. Harl. Ms. 58.

dren. Sister Alice had two daughters by William Whitewell, Jeanette and Katherine. Jeanette was given a few tenements in Bury by her uncle, but he seemed to prefer his younger niece. Katherine White-well married, as John II had, to a Drury. Husband Thomas was an influential and popular gentleman, and he, Katherine, and their children were provided with a rich array of lands throughout the banleuca. John II's brother William was active and prosperous in 1467, living a leisured life in Cratfield. Two of his sons, John and Robert, already provided for by their father, were given additional property by their uncle. But the bulk of John II's property not left to the town went to another nephew, William Baret, esquire, son of Galfrid's youngest child, Geoffrey. William was given most of the tenements in town, including the manse overlooking the Great Market in which John II lived, and the best fields in the suburbs. Despite his philanthropy, John Baret II had a keen sense of his clan, and, with no son who could leave legitimate issue, he picked nieces and nephews to perpetuate the family name and tradition. He laid extensive contingency plans to ensure that a Baret would take possession of the better part of his estate. If William were to die without heirs, his land would pass to Geoffrey and Robert, sons of William of Cratfield, and then to Geoffrey's son Thomas, another grandnephew. So it went, even to an obscure relative named John Claye, through one branch to another, all to make certain that the Baret tradition would be carried on.

By the last third of the fifteenth century, most of the Baret family had settled outside Bury proper. There were two exceptions. One was Alan Baret, a gentleman and clothier, who was a younger cousin of John II.[76] Extensive personal details of his life and career do not survive, but he was a burgess, and fairly active in civic affairs. More important was John II's nephew William.[77] A wealthy man in his own right, he inherited estates from his father and married well. By 1500 William had parlayed all of this and his uncle's legacy into one of the largest patrimonies in West Suffolk. John II selected well. William was an important member of the Alderman's and St. Nicholas' Guilds, and was one of the molders of town policy in the 1480s and 1490s. Along with his wife, Anne, he was a prominent patron, leaving funds for pilgrims, the poor, prisoners, and most

[76] C.C.R., Edward IV, 1461, pp. 65-66; *ibid.*, 1467, p. 447. He has not been included in Table 4.1 because I do not know where to put him.

[77] Tymms, pp. 93-95.

of the borough's ecclesiastical foundations.[78] His most important contribution was to the rebuilding of St. James's Church, which was severely damaged by fire in 1465.[79] As John II was a principal rebuilder of St. Mary's, so his nephew would provide for Bury's other parish church.[80]

There was a final irony in the life of William Baret. He died after increasing the value of the estates bequeathed to him, and keeping the Baret name in the forefront of Bury's civic and commercial circles. But he and wife Anne failed in one crucial aspect; they died without legitimate heirs. Accordingly, their estates, including the bulk of John II's legacy, ultimately passed to the cadet branches of the Barets, by the sixteenth century scattered throughout East Anglia. The Baret family was to survive in great numbers well into the seventeenth century, but exclusively as gentry, coming to Bury only as occasional visitors. In three generations the Barets went from the land to town, where they made their fortunes, and back to the land, richer than ever. The role of the Baret family in Bury St. Edmunds from 1510 onward was assumed by their inlaws, the Drurys.

The Drurys eclipsed even the Barets in wealth and influence. As with the Barets, it is often difficult to identify precise family relations, but attempts to do so have been made in Table 4.2. By late medieval standards, their numbers were considerable, and they were connected by marriage to just about every important person or family in the banleuca, including the aforementioned Barets, the Kings, the Lees, the Carews, and the de Veres. Drury was a very common West Suffolk surname, and some folk who appear so-named in notarial records probably were not members of the famous clan. Robert Drury, a carpenter whose will was proved in 1462, can likely be discounted, even as a younger son of a cadet

[78] Anne's will is in Tymms, pp. 95-99.

[79] For additional details, see the two pamphlets on Bury's parish churches: Statham, *The Church of St. Mary's*; and no listed author, St. Edmundsbury Cathedral [St. James], (Bury St. Edmunds, no press or date listed). Also see two entries by A. B. Whittingham, "St. Mary's Church, Bury St. Edmunds"; and "St. James' Cathedral," in *The Archaeological Journal*, cviii, 1951.

[80] Tymms, pp. 93-96. Also see M. R. James, *On the Abbey of St. Edmund's Bury* (Cambridge: Deighton Bell, 1895), pp. 208-212; and Whittingham, "St. James's Cathedral."

Table 4.2: **THE DRURYS**

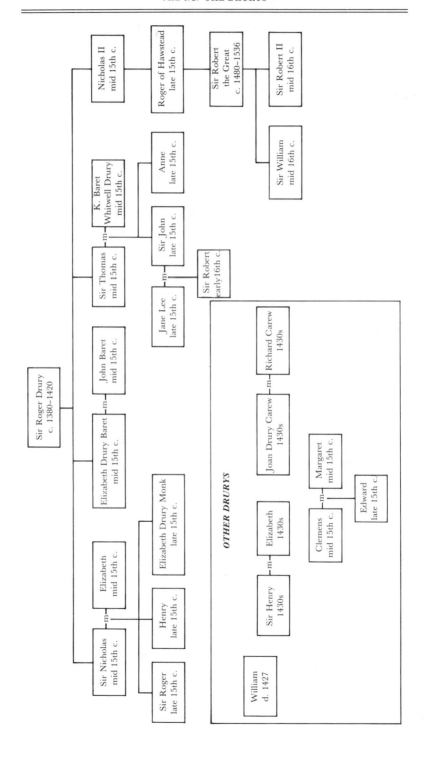

branch.[81] By the later fifteenth century it is improbable that any members of the great house were craftsmen. On the other hand, William Drury, a priest whose will was proved in 1471, cannot be so easily discounted, although it is difficult to establish exact relations since his will mentions no relatives or designated heirs.[82] There are other problems in dealing with the clan. The Drurys held a great deal of land in many places. Initially from Thurston, about five miles northeast of Bury, they held estates throughout East Anglia, and, while Bury remained paramount to their interests, it was never the sole focal point of their property. It was a big family, and many of its members had interests scattered about England; I shall concentrate on those Drurys living or dealing in Bury.

An early glimpse of the family comes through the Barets; from the will of John II we learn that the father of his wife Elizabeth was Sir John Drury, a large landholder and knight of countywide importance in Suffolk. From similar sources we learn that Sir Thomas Drury, who married the niece of John II and Elizabeth Baret, would come to share in considerable portions of both family fortunes.[83] The precise relation between Sir Thomas and Sir Roger is impossible to establish, except to cite the generational disparity; Roger flourished early in the fifteenth century, while Thomas was in his prime in the middle years, and must have been a son, or more likely a nephew. The Drurys who dominated family affairs late in the fifteenth century was Sir Thomas' son, Sir John. Sir John is mentioned in several records, and had the local presence to be selected as an executor for John Smith. It was he who led the family fortunes into the sixteenth century, and made a sagacious marriage with the Lee family. Sir John had at least one male heir, Sir Robert, who carried on family operations in and around Bury for a fourth generation. Few details survive about this Sir Robert's life, but he apparently tired of town living soon after coming into the bulk of his father's legacy, and moved permanently to the countryside.[84]

The greatest of the Drurys was another Sir Robert Drury, originally from the Hawstead branch of the family, located about four

[81] P.S.B.S.E., Hawlee, f. 71.

[82] *Ibid.*, f. 141.

[83] Tymms, p. 26.

[84] P.C.B.S.E., Hawlee, f. 84. Also, see C.P.R., Henry VII, 1486, p. 106; C.C.R., Henry VI, 1445, p. 311.

miles south of Bury. He was the son of a different Roger Drury, a contemporary of Sir John, and a considerable landholder in his own right. This Roger may have been a son of Sir Thomas, or perhaps of a contemporary of Sir Thomas named Nicholas Drury, and was almost certainly the grandson of Sir Roger.[85] Whatever the extent of his personal influence and the nature of his lineage, Roger's son Sir Robert was one of the great figures of medieval Bury St. Edmunds, and eventually became nationally renowned, serving as a speaker of the House of Commons and Privy Councillor to Henry VIII.[86] Sir Robert always played an active role in local West Suffolk politics, and served as royal agent in Bury, several times delivering the borough and county gaols.[87] Much personal information is provided in his will, which was proved in the Prerogative Court of Canterbury in 1536. Since governmental records of his public service begin in 1513, we might surmise that he was born in the 1480s, which places him in his fifties, a considerable age, at the time of his death. He represents the fifth generation of Drurys prospering in Bury, a remarkable achievement in its own right.

Sir Robert had many distinguishing characteristics. He had a large family that survived him, including two adult sons, Sir William and Robert.[88] He also had the single largest personal fortune in the history of the late medieval town, Richard Charman and John Smith notwithstanding; however rich mercantile wealth might make one, it could not compare with a family fortune rooted in landed estates and extending back for several generations. And, like the other great men, Drury donated much of his wealth to the borough. Sir Robert made all the usual contributions to town lay and ecclesiastical institutions, but in denominations larger than anyone else, including Margaret Odeham. What makes this more re-

[85] His will is in P.C.C., Hogan, f. 25. I will not devote great space to him because he is included in *The Dictionary of National Biography* (New York: Macmillan, 1888). See also: Lobel, *The Borough*, pp. 66-70; P.C.C. Bennett, f. 33, in the will of Thomas Ryndale.

[86] For some examples of Drury in service, see *Letters and Papers . . . of Henry VIII* (London: H.M.S.O., 1920), 1509, pp. 14, 54, 153, 161, 255, 341, 438. He was also ambassador to Scotland.

[87] *Ibid.*, 1511, p. 486. According to Lobel, *The Borough*, p. 167, he put down the 1528 rising of the poor men in Bury.

[88] Reference to William can also be found in *The Dictionary*, pp. 60-62. Also, Redstone, "First Ministers," p. 8, 44, 49, 52.

markable is that, of all the great town benefactors, only he had a number of direct heirs for whom he had to provide. He left a large number of books, furs, and bullion, and provided funds for a huge funeral party to celebrate his passing into the next life. Perhaps the best testament to Sir Robert's wealth, centered as it was around Bury St. Edmunds, was his possession of over £100 of silver plate, a huge sum that, if converted into modern value, might by itself represent the median income of a contemporary Suffolk family. As the Drurys were Bury's greatest clan, so Sir Robert was both its richest and most influential member.

Other Drurys made their marks. Jane Drury was the first wife of the prominent Suffolk knight William Carew.[89] She was active in guild affairs, and another of the family's generous philanthropists. There was another Sir Nicholas Drury, not to be confused with Sir Robert's grandfather, who was one of Bury's major landlords in the mid-fifteenth century.[90] This Sir Nicholas is a frustrating character. He was obviously a man of great importance, but only bits and pieces of personal records and governmental service survive, and he cannot be placed precisely in the Drury spectrum. He was assigned to gaol delivery in 1440, and the list of movables and lands in his last will is testament to his power and wealth.[91] He had a sister and wife, both named Elizabeth, and a married daughter named Elizabeth Monk; his sister might have been the wife of John Baret II. Sir Nicholas also had two adult sons surviving at his probate, Sir Roger and Henry. Here we are at something of an impasse. Given his title and the extent of lands he inherited from his father, this Sir Roger must have been a man of some significance in Bury's inner circles. Unfortunately, little information about him survives except that he delivered the Bury gaol in 1486, and we can only guess that he was a cousin of Sir Roger of Hawstead, father of Sir Robert the Great, and perhaps spent most of his life in the country.[92]

Details of the life of second son Henry are also shrouded in mystery. There was a Sir Henry Drury who was named tax collector and county assessor in 1436, and, while this Sir Henry may have

[89] Archdeaconry of Sudbury, Boner, f. 36. For William Carew, see C.P.R., Edward IV, 1471, p. 293.

[90] For Sir Nicholas, see P.C.B.S.E., Hawlee, f. 54.

[91] C.P.R., Henry VI, 1440, p. 373.

[92] C.P.R., Henry VII, 1486, p. 106.

been the son of the aforementioned Sir Nicholas, it is unlikely because of the time disparity.[93] The Sir Henry who was a tax collector had a wife named Elizabeth, who left in her will an impressive range of movables, including silver, gold, brass, linen, furs, and bedding, as well as livestock and property in Norfolk and Suffolk.[94] But nothing else about them is known, including their position in the Drury family tree. Another prominent Drury was William, one of earliest to make a mark, not to be confused with the priest of the same name who died in the 1420s.[95] Another William, a knight, purchased lands in Howton, Sapiston, and Faken Aspis, all excellent arable, and leased them out.[96] Land purchase was not limited to male Drurys; in 1451 Joan Drury, wife of Richard, sued in court for £100 to gain recompense for lands owed to her deceased husband yet not provided for her.[97] But, again, few personal details survive on the lives of any of these characters, and it is difficult to fit them into the larger Drury family tree.

Perhaps the most interesting of all the Drurys was Clemens.[98] He must have been a younger son, for, like Sir Roger of Hawstead, great-grandfather of Sir Robert the Great, he started his career in Bury as a merchant and burgess. A mercer, Clemens was able by mid-life to transfer his wealth into landed investment, get a coat of arms, and move his family into the ranks of the local gentry, alongside their cousins. Clemens knew all the "right" people, was mentioned several times in connection with John Smith, John Baret II, and Richard King, and from the vantage point of his house on Hatter Street, still in the heart of the borough's garment district, moved quickly up the social ladder. In many ways, Clemens Drury's was the archetype of a successful career in the late medieval town, a mixture of wealth resulting from an early mercantile career and later income from landed sources, combining in an age when it was said that "money maketh the man."[99]

[93] C.F.R., Henry VI, 1436, p. 288.
[94] P.C.B.S.E., Hawlee, f. 219.
[95] *Ibid.*, Osbern, f. 202.
[96] C.P.R., Henry VI, 1427, p. 413. For his activities in the wool trade, see *ibid.*, 1445, p. 199; for reference to him as a knight, see *ibid.*, 1442, p. 45.
[97] C.P.R., Henry VI, 1451, p. 397. Her husband Richard seems to have been a merchant.
[98] P.C.B.S.E., Hawlee, f. 207.
[99] This quotation is from Thrupp, *Merchant Class*, and reads:

Bury's aldermanic and burghal élite, made up of merchants, gentlemen, and the occasional very prosperous craftsmen, controlled the social, economic, and political fortunes of the secular community. They were never as strictly or formally organized as were their counterparts in London, or even provincial capitals like Norwich, York, Coventry, or Bristol. If well-defined rules of entry into the élite—we are not really able to call them a class—ever existed, they no longer survive. But they did have a clear sense of distinct identity that was galvanized through membership in the Alderman's Guild, and congealed by a steady resistance of the abbot and abbey officers. Less formally, the burghal élite had a series of common characteristics and traits, and a life-style and pattern that set them apart from other lay members of their community. Most started rather humbly, and then made early fortunes through trade or industry. This mercantile wealth was invested in property, so that most of the great figures enjoyed landed income in their later years. While all had some sense of "merchant identity," most strived to move up in society into the gentry class, and tried to marry their children into the squirearchy. Many were involved in textiles, the commodity primarily responsible for the prosperity of late medieval Bury St. Edmunds. Some played an active role in local governmental affairs, but at the very least all participated in the affairs of the corporate guilds, which struggled to free themselves from abbey control. Virtually all married, the majority had comparatively large families, including adult sons to carry on the family fortunes. But few of the sons followed their fathers' mercantile careers, opting instead for a more comfortable, easier, and more profitable life as proprietary *rentiers*. This upward mobility helped to ensure a high degree of fluidity among Bury's burghal élite. It was generally possible for an aggressive and enterprising immigrant like Galfrid Baret to come from the countryside and make his way through Bury society. Such fluidity might not have been intended, but it existed throughout most of the late medieval period, and provided the burghal élite with continuing new vitality.[100] It was this vitality,

---

Yt ys all ways sene now a days
That money makethe the mane.

[100] Lobel, *The Borough*, p. 93, writes: "It is evident that by the fifteenth century the whole burgess class had become very small." This is not evident at all. In absolute terms, the number of burgesses may have dropped along with total town population, but, in proportional terms, there were probably more burgesses than in the fourteenth century.

along with their wealth and their assumption of civic office that allowed the aldermen and burgesses to assume leadership in the town and suburbs, and win increasing freedom from the ancient prerogatives of the Abbey of St. Edmunds.[101]

[101] For an attempt at a computer assisted, statistical analysis of the burghal élite, see below, Appendix F.

Chapter Five

THE EXTENT AND DIVISION
OF BURGHAL CORPORATE POWER

THE PRIVILEGES AND POWER OF ST. EDMUNDS ABBEY

In their quest for political autonomy, the burghal élite of Bury St. Edmunds first had to secure their social and economic positions in the borough. They then needed to establish a broader commercial and industrial presence throughout eastern England. Finally, they had to convert these advantages into real control over at least some of the corporate institutions that governed Bury. This was a formidable task. The abbey had been vested by successive kings with almost total executive and judicial control over the entire banleuca, and was not willing to part with many of its prerogatives or much of its power.[1]

The single principal source of the abbot's power rested in control over the liberty of the eight and one-half hundreds (Map 10). Established by Canute early in the eleventh century and confirmed and defined by Edward II in 1326, the liberty included most of West Suffolk, and by itself made the abbot a great feudal lord.[2] There were three aspects to the abbot's jurisdiction: the franchisal, the baronial, and the domainial. The franchisal covered the seigneurial rights administered over the entire liberty, and, as such, directly concerned the banleuca.[3] It consisted of such things as frankpledge, trials of pleas from the king, the return and execution

[1] Many of Bury's governmental institutions have been discussed in great detail. Three excellent references are: D. C. Douglas, *The Social Structure of Medieval East Anglia* (Oxford: Oxford University Press, 1927); A. Goodwin, *The Abbey of St. Edmundsbury* (Oxford: Basil Blackwell, 1931); and Lobel, *The Borough*. Where others have already ventured in great detail, as Lobel has for the borough courts, I shall merely skim the surface.

[2] *The Calendar of Charter Rolls* (London: H.M.S.O., 1921), pp. 487-488. Also, see *C. Charter Rolls*, 5, 1352, p. 125; and L. J. Redstone, "The Liberty of St. Edmunds," *P.S.I.*, xv, 1914.

[3] Goodwin, *The Abbey*, p. 10.

of royal writs, and the imprisoning and hanging of felons. These powers were to last until Dissolution, and, as Goodwin noted, "not one, or four, but the whole of the six forfeitures usually reserved to the king—fiht-wite, fyrd-wite, grith-bryce, forsteal, hamsocn and ebberethef—also belonged to the abbot."[4]

Baronial powers were those of knight service, which rested with the abbot in his role as tenant-in-chief of the liberty. As tenant-in-chief, the abbot had the right to hold a baronial court; therein, he dealt with questions of tenure and service, inheritance, and feudal incidents like homage, fealty, relief, and wardship. The court and its officials, about which more will be written shortly, were presided over and supervised by the abbot's steward, whose relationship to his master was much like that of the sheriff to the king.

Because they serve as a principal example of the abbot's duties, his military obligations are worth additional explanation. Extensive knights' fees were owed for virtually all St. Edmunds' lands. By the later middle ages much of the direct burden was commuted through cash payments, but there were occasions when more ancient services were still required. In 1378, for example, a royal edict was sent to the town bailiffs ordering them to array and arm in the name of St. Edmund a ship to be used in the defense of the Suffolk coast.[5] In 1385 a command came from Richard II himself, asking Abbot John of Timworth to appear with all his household, armed in force according to his baronial obligation as the lord of the manor of Elmswell, to defend the Suffolk coast against French raiders.[6] The command was reiterated in 1386, and whether the abbot actually appeared in person, hired mercenaries, or paid a version of scutage is immaterial; the abbot's military obligations on land and sea lingered on into the later middle ages, and were occasionally called upon.[7] Successive abbots never failed their kings, a reason no doubt for continued royal support.

The third type of abbey jurisdiction was domainial, or manorial. As such it concerned the abbot's rural tenants outside the banleuca, and touched the burgesses only tangentially. Some of them held property beyond the suburbs and were affected by domainial au-

[4] *Ibid.*, p. 11. In theory, the borough was also exempt from royal taxes.
[5] C.P.R., Richard II, 1378, p. 43.
[6] *Ibid.*, p. 11.
[7] See, for example, C.C.R., Richard II, 1386, p. 174; C.F.R., Edward III, 1346, p. 501.

thority in peripheral fashion, but they were always a minority. For most of the burghers, domainial and baronial jurisdiction were far less important than franchisal jurisdiction.

Hence, the abbot was one of the most powerful figures in late medieval England. But the townsfolk also had to deal with the abbey's most important officials—the cellarer and the sacrist—and much of the patriciate's struggle was directed toward them. Technically, the town was held not by the abbot but by the convent; the sacrist was the chief official of the convent in the borough, and, as such, the key monastic figure in the eyes of the burgesses.[8] Among other things, the office controlled rent levels and collection, the borough courts, the right to levy taxes, and received homage from the alderman and the burgesses. The font of this power was control over the bailiffs, who actually collected such taxes as the *hadgoval* and *relevia*, and supervised all court actions. The sacrist controlled frankpledge in the leet court, criminal jurisdiction, and most rights to the town gaol. He dominated the marketplaces through his power over weights and measures, assizes and tolls. When foreign merchants, such as the butchers from Malmsbury, in Wiltshire, wished to trade in the Great Market, they had to pay the sacrist a fee.[9] Indeed, through stallage, even denizen merchants paid the sacrist for the privilege of doing business in the abbey's town.[10] The office controlled probates, and, when an individual died intestate, the sacrist was allowed to dispose of the goods. He controlled pavage (tolls toward fixing roads), picage (tolls toward breaking ground for building or setting up a market stall), and tronage (tolls on goods weighed for market), and surpervised all guild activity. When so powerful a guild as the Weavers and Linendrapers wished in the late fifteenth century to have their rights confirmed by Edward IV, its wardens first had to pay a fee to the sacrist.

As lord of the abbey's manors, the cellarer had less direct control in the town than did the sacrist. Nevertheless, the office held most of the suburbs and had considerable overall powers. These even included some land and tenements in the borough, and the rents and rights that went with them. Along with his suburban lands, a great deal of which was held of him by the burghal élite, the cellarer had all rights to mills, sheepfolds, manure, white clay, chalk, ani-

[8] Lobel, *The Borough*, p. 16.
[9] *Ibid.*, pp. 48-49. Also, see C.P.R., Edward I, 1304, p. 283.
[10] C.U.L. Ms. Gg 4 4. Also, Lobel, *The Borough*, p. 18.

mals that strayed on to his demesne, fishing, and multure. There was income from labor services, including ploughing and the old *arura*, and a host of related items. Like those due to both the abbot and the sacrist, many of the cellarer's service obligations had been commuted to cash by the middle part of the thirteenth century. But many obligations persisted, confirmed by lawsuits in the fourteenth and fifteenth centuries, reiterating the established political and constitutional power of St. Edmunds and its officers.

One of the most important sources of abbey power was control and maintenance of the judicial system. Bury's judiciary has been studied by others; and herein will be dealt with only briefly.[11] Bury had a complex hierarchy of courts by 1290, and they were firmly under abbey control. The most important was the portman moot.[12] It was the principal borough court from at least the eleventh century, meeting first in the Moothall, on *Le Mustowe*, and then in the Tollhouse. Among other things, the portman moot dealt with questions of property, debts, and felonies. It was always popular among the burgesses and often used juries. But, with it all, the court paid homage to the authority of the sacrist and was in some way always under his influence.

The leet court met when the portman moot was not sitting, usually twice a year; even in the thirteenth century, it remained the court of frankpledge.[13] It dealt with a variety of commercial issues, including the assizes. There was also the *curia mercatoria*, the Merchant's or Little Court, so named to distinguish it from the Great Court, which the abbot held for the entire liberty. The *curia mercatoria* met in the Tollhouse on market days, and dealt almost exclusively with commerce. The Great Court met once every three weeks, and concerned itself with issues almost exclusively from the liberty; consequently, it had little to do with the town, and the burgesses usually avoided it.

There were other courts. The abbot seems to have held his own

[11] This is especially the case with Lobel, *The Borough*, pp. 95-117. Unfortunately, there is little information about the role of the justices of the peace from the 1380s. In other areas, they compromised existing judicial powers, and they might have had a similar effect in Bury St. Edmunds and West Suffolk.

[12] *Ibid.*, p. 96. It is worth noting that Lobel and Goodwin, the latter as cited above in note 1, disagree on the precise timing and function of the courts and meetings.

[13] *Ibid.*, pp. 96-98.

court as a feudal baron for oyer and terminer, gaol delivery, and other aspects of royal justice. There was the Piepowder or Wayfarers' Court, of importance to denizen and alien merchants, held during the Fair of St. Matthew, in late September, and throughout the month of November.[14] And there were manorial courts, dedicated to the tenants of the abbey's estates, and, as such, of some concern to the many burgesses who held rural property.[15] The precise limitations and privileges of each court are somewhat obscure, and many jurisdictions must have overlapped. Further, the effects on this system of the establishment in the late fourteenth century of the justices of the peace—and in Bury St. Edmunds the J.P.s were usually the borough bailiffs—is unclear. Ultimately, the burgesses tended to patronize whichever court charged the lowest fees and was most autonomous from the sacrist. But all the courts had one thing in common throughout the later middle ages: they were controlled to varying degrees by the abbot and his officers, and served to reinforce and perpetuate abbey power. Jurisprudential powers were of great importance in control of town government, and, if the burgesses were ever to gain political autonomy, they had to make encroachments on these long-standing prerogatives.

St. Edmunds had many other privileges, obligations, and responsibilities. Some were profitable, others onerous, but all underscored its role of leadership and lordship over the borough and its hinterlands. By the thirteenth century, the burghers had escaped most of their rural obligations, from ploughing the lord's demesne and fertilizing his fields with their livestock, to carting eels from nearby Lakenheath. From the twelfth century onward, Abbot Samson set a precedent of commutations, and cash relationships.[16] In the course of the thirteenth century, the monks gradually lost power to the abbot and to his major officers, and the pattern for the fourteenth and fifteenth centuries was set. The major subject of the conflict was to be the control over borough institutions, and the major combatants were the abbey officers and burghal élite. They had built social and economic bases of power, but before they

[14] See above, pp. 84-94. The abbey's control extended to the fair's location. It was held in the open spaces across from the Great Gates of the abbey complex, rather than in the Great or Horse Markets.

[15] Bacon, 1 and 20, are examples.

[16] Lobel, *The Borough*, pp. 30-35.

could be truly autonomous the patriciate had to wrest control over at least some of the town's corporations.

THE CONTROL OF THE GAOL

Sources that describe the institutional conflict between the abbot and the burgesses in the later middle ages are limited and generally inadequate. Only a few, often incongruous institutions can be studied in any detail. One of the best and most fascinating is a particular aspect of justice: imprisonment. Bury's gaol was one of the most important in late medieval England, and its location astride the Great Market added to the borough's regional importance. Its delivery, maintenance, and profits were key aspects in Bury's corporate struggle, and its detailed history seems illustrative of the larger institutional conflict between town and abbey.[17]

Prisons played a rather large role in late medieval English society, but in some respects their general functions were more limited than those of their modern counterparts.[18] Gaol was seen less as a vehicle of punishment than as a method of coercion that might force prisoners to make recompense for their crimes. Virtually everything could be expiated by payment; indeed, a Venetian observer of late fifteenth century England suggested that all crimes were redeemable through some sort of cash payment.[19] But, if not redeemed, felonies were ordinarily punishable by death; this meant that most prisons were filled with civil offenders, especially debtors. Bury's gaol housed men and women whose families and friends were trying to raise funds to free them.

Scholars have delineated several types of late medieval prisons: royal and county gaols, supervised by sheriffs; municipal gaols

[17] A full record of the listings of gaol delivery rolls can be found in *A Guide to the Contents of the Public Record Office*, i (London: H.M.S.O., 1963). For a fuller list, see *List of Gaol Delivery Rolls in the Public Record Office*, London. The author looked through twenty series, with approximately twenty-five folio pages in each. For a complete listing, see below, in the bibliography.

[18] Ralph B. Pugh, *Imprisonment in Medieval England* (Cambridge: Cambridge University Press, 1968); John Bellamy, *Crime and Public Order in the Later Middle Ages* (London: R.K.P., 1973).

[19] C. Sneyd, ed., *A Relation . . . of the Island of England . . . About . . . 1500* (London: Camden Society, 37, 1848). Also, see Helen Jewell, *English Local Administration* (New York: Barnes and Noble, 1972), Chaps. 5 and 6.

serving their particular boroughs; and franchisal gaols, given over
to authorities with special powers. Bury's prison was exceptional,
and did not fit precisely any of these patterns. Gaol delivery records
clearly show that it did not service the county. Norfolk and Suffolk
shared a single sheriff and county prison, and, while its location
shifted several times, it was never in Bury St. Edmunds.[20] Pugh
believed that the Bury gaol was initially designed to serve the abbey's franchise, and later was broadened to include offenders from
the borough.[21] Lobel disagreed. She stressed the broader franchisal
functions, pointing out that control was always vested with the abbot
and never with municipal authorities.[22] It was supervised by abbey
officials, with the prior and cellarer taking responsibility for ap-
prehending criminals, and the sacrist caring for them once they
were incarcerated. Lobel is partially correct, but her focus is too
restricted. There is some evidence of a second prison in town, as
Lobel seems to imply, which served municipal and secular needs,
but it is unconvincing.[23] It is more likely that the franchise gaol was
used by the entire urban and regional community, and therein lay
its institutional significance.[24] With both burgesses and abbot using
the gaol, and with most of its prisoners incarcerated for civil and
financial rather than criminal or social offenses, its control was
representative of the larger town-abbey struggle.

Crucial to the question of who controlled the prison is a more
precise understanding of its penal jurisdiction. Pugh and Lobel
have probably drawn these jurisdictions too narrowly. While records of gaol delivery indicate that Bury was never a county prison,
these same records and others from royal calendars suggest that it
was a royal gaol.[25] In addition to its franchisal, municipal, and

[20] Pugh, *Imprisonment*, pp. 58-59, 78. In the twelfth and thirteenth centuries, the location seems to have switched back and forth from Thetford
and Ipswich, but by the fourteenth century it was settled in Norwich Castle,
where it remained through the fifteenth century.

[21] Pugh, *Imprisonment*, pp. 298-299.

[22] Lobel, "The Gaol of Bury St. Edmunds," *P.S.I.*, xxi, 1913.

[23] V. B. Redstone, "St. Edmunds Bury and the Town Rental for 1295,"
P.S.I., xiii, 1909.

[24] Pugh, *Imprisonment*, p. 262.

[25] For example, see: C.P.R., Edward I, 1283, p. 80; C.P.R., Edward II,
1314, p. 138; C.C.R., Edward I, 1273, p. 26; C.C.R., Henry V, 1414, p.
55; C.C.R., Henry VII, 1492, p. 191; C.P.R., Richard II, 1388, p. 467. In
L. J. Redstone, "First Ministers' Account," *Suffolk Institute of Archaeology*

liberty functions, Bury's prison was delivered dozens of times by the sheriff, the Crown's agent in East Anglia. It may not have been officially designated as a royal prison, but it clearly served as a repository for prisoners involved in actions against the king. Further, while it was under the *de jure* control of the abbot and his subalterns, and while the abbot's general authority in the liberty was usually honored by the Crown, there are records of periodic royal intervention.[26] The king may have been cautious about overriding a decision of the abbot, but he could and did do so on several occasions. And although the abbot theoretically had authority to appoint his own officers to gaol delivery, it was the king who did so in practice from the late thirteenth century onward. Lobel has argued against royal intervention in the affairs and operation of Bury's gaol, but she is probably incorrect.[27] Herein lies another key aspect of the gaol's importance in the struggle between town and abbey. The men whom the king appointed to deliver it were invariably the same local gentlemen or burgesses who ran the Alderman's Guild and supervised the secular affairs of the borough. Among them were John Baret, John Smith, and Sir Robert Drury. By the late fourteenth century, *de facto* control of at least a single aspect of the town gaol, its delivery, lay in part with the burgesses.

The prison thus had a tripartite function, which gave it considerable regional significance. It served the borough and banleuca in municipal cases, the greater West Suffolk urban region, and the Crown. On select occasions, it probably even supplemented the county gaol in Norwich or Ipswich. Evidence indicates that in the fourteenth and fifteenth centuries it held men from Norfolk, Essex, Cambridgeshire, and Lincolnshire, as well as Suffolk, making the borough something of a penal center. Hence, while the burgesses were never able to wrest away from the abbey all the profits or privileges of the judicial system, they did gain at least partial control over the prison.

Information survives on the gaol's inmates, staffing, and maintenance. The best evidence as to location indicates that it was sit-

---

and Natural History, xii, 3, 1909, p. 6, it is referred to as "the King's gaol of Burye." Also, see P.R.O. Gaol Delivery Rolls, Suffolk, Nos. 63, 64, 65, 106.

[26] For example, see *Letters and Papers . . . of Henry VIII* (London: H.M.S.O., 1920), 1510, p. 352.

[27] Lobel, *The Borough*, pp. 21-22; and her "The Gaol."

uated in the west side of the Great Market, near the Tollhouse, and used part of the town walls for its security.[28] The gaoler was appointed by the sacrist. It has been suggested that this was an unpaid position, which thus required the gaoler to make a profit from his keep, a situation guaranteed to breed corruption.[29] This may have been true at one time, but by the 1350s the gaoler was receiving a respectable annual salary of over fifty shillings.[30] Further, this was just the beginning; the sacrist's rental from 1357 shows that there were additional ways to turn a profit, and that annual gross income from the gaol amounted to £13, 11 shillings, 8 pence, over one quarter of the entire reported income of the sacrist's office.[31] Supplies were purchased on account, the sums for which often ran quite high. In 1369, for example, the gaoler claimed 18 shillings for purchase of candles and oil.[32] Energy costs seem to have been rising by the turn of the century; in 1429, the sacrist claimed that 52 pounds of candles were needed to light the prison, with candles alone costing 6 shillings, 6 pence.[33] Clearly, the position could be one of the more lucrative public offices in Bury. In the sixteenth century the gaoler was paid 53 shillings in salary, plus 10 shillings for clothing, and 8 shillings, 8 pence, and 3 shillings, 7 pence, in salary and clothing for an assistant.[34] And to all of this was added income as it had been procured in the old days, before the office was salaried. Most gaolers proved to be expert practitioners of bribery and extortion from both prisoners and their outside relations; an adept one might double his income in such a fashion. Entering prisoners were expected to pay an initiation fee, and many services were available at the right price. Weekly schedules of extortion rates survive from other East Anglian prisons; Bury's inmates may have had similar scales.[35] The Crown felt obliged to try to stop such abuses, but late in the fourteenth century was forced to accept them as part of the contemporary penal system. Henceforth, royal efforts at reform were aimed at controlling, or

[28] Lobel, "The Gaol."
[29] Redstone, "St. Edmunds Bury."
[30] C.U.L. Ms. Ff 2 29, f. 15.
[31] *Ibid.*
[32] Lobel, "The Gaol."
[33] *Ibid.*
[34] *Ibid.* In 1539, gaol profits were going directly to the gaoler. See L. J. Redstone, "First Ministers' Account."
[35] Pugh, *Imprisonment*, p. 175.

more properly limiting, the extent of such corruption. The position
of gaoler became so lucrative by the early sixteenth century that it
was usually held by a gentleman. At Dissolution, it was the prerogative of Sir John Holt, who was receiving the handsome wage
of 73 shillings, 4 pence.[36] And to this had been added another
attractive perquisite, the confiscation of the property of all convicted felons.[37]

A fifteenth-century inventory describes the equipment of the
gaolhouse in some detail. Among the items listed were: 49 pairs of
fetters, 1 "fevere called the stufforde," 7 collars with chains and
staples, 4 pairs of manacles, 6 pairs of stocks, and 13 locks and
keys.[38] Such things conjure up images of poor wretches chained
interminably to dungeon walls; while this must have occasionally
occurred, it does not seem to have been very common. Because
virtually all crimes were cash-redeemable and most services could
be purchased, life in gaol must have been tolerable for those with
some money. The real danger for Bury inmates was not the fetters
but rather the possibility of being forgotten by friends on the outside. Furthermore, overcrowding could be a problem. Although
most prisoners were debtors, Lobel has shown that the prison was
filled with wrongdoers of almost every stripe.[39] At certain points,
conditions must literally have approached standing room only.
Overcrowding proved especially acute during the protracted political disturbances of the fourteenth century, and in 1327 the numbers of incarcerated grew so large that many of the accused had
to be released on bail.[40]

More serious than the problems of space was that of provisioning;
how were the prisoners to be fed, clothed, and cared for? This was

[36] L. J. Redstone, "First Ministers' Account."

[37] We must not lose sight of the fact that even with the fringe benefits,
the position did not yield income comparable to that of a great merchant
or royal official. In 1429, when the gaoler was receiving profits of 18
shillings, 4 pence, it cost £47 merely to provide and to light candles for
the abbey complex. Further, it appears that the position proved something
of a financial millstone around the neck of the sacrist, the gaoler's patron.
It was the sacrist who had to pay the gaoler's salary, bear the continual
costs of gaol fabric repair, and, in return, received little profit. In the best
of circumstances, the position was held plurally. Its true worth was through
patronage, as a job the sacrist could dole out to those who cultivated him.

[38] Lobel, "The Gaol." In *The Borough*, p. 101, she claims that Bury prisoners were put in chains more frequently than inmates of other gaols.

[39] Lobel, "The Gaol."

[40] Arnold, ii, p. 348.

one of the issues facing the sacrist throughout the fourteenth century; the high costs of maintenance, shown in part above by increased energy costs, may have prompted the abbey to allow greater town control. Limited funding was available, but it was never enough, even when the prison had a small number of inmates. The wealthy and fortunate might rely on friends outside, but what of the bulk of prisoners? How were they to fare on their allotted pittance? To some extent, they did not, and, during periods of serious overcrowding, there must have been extensive physical abuse, malnutrition, and perhaps starvation, or at least extraordinary morbidity stemming from resulting consumptive, pulmonary, and enteric diseases. But some additional funds were provided through the *largesse* of the townsfolk, especially after 1470, when the burgesses played an increasing role in gaol management. Indeed, bequests to the prisoners became a major outlet for private benevolence.[41] Sometimes the benefactors were middling folk who left modest sums, but many were members of the patriciate. In 1467, for example, John Baret provided meat, bread, and drink, and a cash bequest of one pence per prisoner.[42] Baret, as befitted a successful draper, was realistic about how Bury's penal system worked. Having provided for the prisoners, he gave another, even larger sum of two pence per prisoner to the gaoler, to ensure that his charity would be implemented.

Despite the availability of many items, prison life was obviously basically unpleasant, and in the course of the later middle ages

[41] For more details on private benevolence, see below, pp. 182-186. Two books of interest are: Joel Rosenthal, *The Purchase of Paradise* (London: R&KP, 1972); and W. K. Jordan, *Philanthropy in England, 1480-1660* (London: George Allen and Unwin, 1956).

[42] Tymms, pp. 15-44. Another great benefactor was Margaret Odeham. She left meat, drink, and bread, plus a penny cash, to each individual in gaol (Tymms, p. 74). In 1493 John Plandon bequeathed "wood and other necessities" to all prisoners, and to four special but unnamed souls the considerable sum of £4, 3/4 [P.C.B.S.E., Pye, f.16]. In 1496, Robert Hervey bequeathed four yards of wood and "star" for winter, cloth, and a penny in cash, perhaps by the fifteenth century the traditional bequest (P.C.B.S.E., Pye, f.48). Five years later, John Coote gave two pence of meat and drink, and Alice Bumstead bread, ale and victuals, both on the date of their burials (P.C.B.S.E., Pye, f. 123 for Coote; and Hoode, f. 36 for Bumstead). And, in 1505, Anne Baret, member of the famous family, gave the considerable sum of four marks, to be used for general prison needs (Tymms, p. 95). Coupled with smaller bequests from humbler people, popular piety helped carry many prisoners through their leanest times.

there were a number of unfortunate incidents. Felons were generally held only until the gaol was delivered, but a few were detained
as part of their punishment and others were kept until they could
be hanged. The abbot had his own gallows in nearby Westley, which
for a time served the entire hundred; it was heinous enough to be
burned to the ground in 1306 by William de Beresford and William
Howard.[43] Overall, prison life was sufficiently otiose at times to
cause an occasional suicide among the inmate population, and
whenever someone managed to escape there was considerable chor-
tling and beaming in many quarters.[44]

Gaol breaks were fairly common. In 1306, the year the abbot's
gallows were burned down, William Pugg, imprisoned on a charge
of trespass on the abbey's fishponds, broke the gaol.[45] Such events
were particularly common in the early fourteenth century, when
the gaol fabric was in dilapidated condition; there are records of
escapes coming after prisoners actually kicked down their cell walls.
But there was—quite literally—another side to the gaol breaks. A
Bury laborer named Matthew Wyseman was being held in a Cambridgeshire gaol when he managed to escape.[46] He fled back to his
native town, presented himself to Bury's gaoler, paid his entrance
fee, and was detained there until his case came up for appeal in a
royal court.[47] This process of fleeing to, rather than from, Bury's
prison was repeated several times. In 1372, for example, a burglar
named Roger Haberdon escaped from the county gaol in Norwich
castle, fled to Bury, and had himself incarcerated while he too
appealed his case.[48] Flight to the Bury gaol might indicate that,
relatively, it was regarded by its native sons as a fairly benevolent
institution, or, more likely, that felons at least preferred to be delivered by their fellow townsmen.

Bury's most interesting late medieval gaolbreak came in the fourteenth century, and involved a husband and wife. In 1334, Nicholas
Brandon, described simply as a felon, escaped from "the king's
prison of St. Edmunds" with the help of his spouse Joan.[49] No
details are given of the mode of escape, but Nicholas was successful,

[43] C.P.R., Edward I, 1306, p. 472.
[44] C.P.R., Edward III, 1343, p. 31.
[45] C.P.R., Edward I, 1306, p. 416.
[46] C.P.R., Henry IV, 1417, p. 69.
[47] Wyseman was eventually acquitted.
[48] C.P.R., Edward III, 1372, p. 185. Haberdon pleaded benefit of clergy,
was able to get a change of venue, and was eventually acquitted.
[49] C.P.R., Edward III, 1344, p. 212.

and, quite incredibly, seems to have spent the short balance of his life in royal service. Joan was less fortunate. Her role was soon discovered, and she was apprehended and imprisoned. Women were not given special treatment in Bury's prison, and, although the gaol had separate quarters for the sexes, all were kept in similar conditions. Joan languished for several years, unaided because her husband died about a year after obtaining his freedom. But she continued to appeal to the Crown for pardon and what she perceived as justice. Finally, several years later, she got what she had been waiting for when "the king, pitying her for the long time she had sued in his court, in consideration for the good services of [husband] Nicholas, who died in service to the [royal] Butlery . . . has pardoned [Joan]. . . ."[50]

Gaol breaks and escaped prisoners were the responsibility of the gaoler and ultimately the sacrist, who in turn answered to the abbot. This seems to have been the case even in the late fifteenth and early sixteenth centuries, when the burgesses took over the principal role in gaol maintenance. Both the gaoler and the sacrist had to pay fines to the abbot, and a series of escapes could be an expensive proposition. Hence, officials did their best to prevent them, and often set out personally to apprehend those who got away. In 1439 John Clynton, described as porter of the gaol, sued in royal court over the escape of John Tiptoft.[51] Tiptoft had been delivered to the Bury gaol, and was held until trial under fine of 100 marks. When he escaped, the fine, which had been given over for "the keeping" to gaol officials, was taken back. Clynton, upset by the prospect of such a financial setback and threatened with the loss of his job, set out to track down Tiptoft. This he did, and, when the prisoner was back in gaol, the porter got back the 100 marks, another earlier forfeiture, and kept his position.

Detailed lists of prisoners in Bury's gaol, such as those used by Pugh, Bellamy, and others to determine criminal makeup, do not survive from the later middle ages. There is, however, a mid-sixteenth-century calendar of detainees, and, despite its late date—about a generation after Dissolution—it may be applicable to at least the last years under study.[52] Overall, the total number of prisoners was rather low, 17 in all. This might be a reflection of Dissolution *per se*, of new methods of Tudor punishment, or even of a drop in crime from an era that some observers consider to be

[50] *Ibid.*
[51] C.P.R., Henry VI, 1439, p. 240.
[52] B.M. Harl. Ms. 368.

the most violent and lawless in English history. Among the population was a female prisoner, a wife gaoled with her spouse. She may have been her husband's partner in crime, or simply living with him, but her mere presence must have been a source of considerable disruption. Since most serious felonies were still being punished with hanging, it is not surprising that most of the prisoners were jailed for larceny, comparatively minor acts of theft, and other crimes against property. Of these, one deserves particular mention; Thomas Parker was imprisoned for stealing silk, symbolic of the newest drapery in town.

Bury's gaol was a significant part of the local and regional judicial system, and, as such, an important part of late medieval government. In the thirteenth century, its control was vested in the abbot and his agents, but by the sixteenth century much of this control, especially gaol delivery and the power to name the gaoler, passed into secular hands. Still, as important as was control of this individual corporation, it is overshadowed by what it represents in the larger institutional struggle between abbey and burgesses. Ultimately, the gaol was of limited importance. The patriciate never gained control over any other important aspects of Bury's system of justice, and had to settle for partial control over what was ultimately a lesser corporation. Despite their newfound economic success, their larger political and judicial ambitions were not realized.

FRATERNITIES, CHARITY, AND SOCIAL SECURITY

Frustrated in their attempts to gain control over other established institutions, Bury's patriciate turned increasingly in the fifteenth century to their own indigenous corporate bodies and concentrated on increasing their power. The most important of these bodies were the socio-religious fraternities. The fraternities are well researched yet still remarkably misunderstood organizations; it remains virtually impossible to explain succinctly just what they did.[53]

[53] The following are recommended: S. L. Thrupp, "The Gilds," in M. M. Postan and E. E. Rich, eds., *The Cambridge Economic History of Europe*, iii (Cambridge: Cambridge University Press, 1963); Thrupp, "Gilds," in *The International Encyclopedia of the Social Sciences*, 1968; Thrupp, "Medieval Gilds Reconsidered," *The Journal of Economic History*, 2, 1942; George Unwin, *The Gilds and Companies of London* (London: Methuen, 1938); and T. and L. T. Smith, *English Gilds* (London: Early English Text Society, o.s., xcl, 1870).

The fraternities existed from the late Roman period onward, were more common than guilds formed or incorporated for commercial or industrial purposes; were organized at the parish level, from which they drew most of their members; and were usually dedicated to a particular saint or religious commemoration.[54] Members cared for the fabrice of their patron's church, paying the saint special attention, and occasionally assuming quasi-religious roles. Candles were lit in the saints' names, alms distributed on the appropriate day, and processionals organized for *Corpus Christi*, Easter, and Christmas pageants. But the fraternities had other more important functions. They assumed the roles of social, or, as the name implies, fraternal organizations, whose members filled key positions in the community and often controlled special aspects of town life. Fraternities probably served as drinking clubs in that day before public houses were common, and this must have been part of their basic attraction. But more important were their broader social roles, particularly as guarantors of social security, which made them so essential to daily life. Ultimately, these predominantly secular corporate bodies would provide formidable opposition to the institutional domination of St. Edmunds.

Foremost among Bury's fraternities was the Town or Alderman's Guild, also called the Candlemas from the 1330s onward.[55] Dedicated to the Virgin Mary, it was the most powerful, exclusive, and wealthiest of all Bury's fraternities. It was founded in the twelfth century and incorporated in 1305, and for close to two hundred years its membership was restricted to town burgesses. By the fifteenth century, however, as the very term burgess had become nebulous and ill-defined, membership was determined by one's ability to pay the initiation fee and the annual dues. Members included gentlemen; major merchants such as drapers, grocers, mercers, clothiers, and goldsmiths; and perhaps some of the weal-

[54] H. F. Westlake, "The Origins and Purposes and Development of Parish Guilds in England," P.S.I., xvii, 1921.

[55] H. F. Westlake, *The Parish Guilds of Medieval England* (London: The Society for Promoting Christian Knowledge, 1919). Also, P.R.O., Star Chamber Proceedings, Henry VIII, Bundle xxii, 6, reprinted by Lobel, *The Borough*, pp. 182-186. Lobel, *The Borough*, p. 75, note 2, and pp. 147-148, argues that Candlemas was a separate guild, probably called St. Mary and St. James (see below, p. 189), and took over many of the duties of the Alderman's Guild after the later was banned in the 1330s. I disagree. However, even Lobel admits that the functions of the two guilds were virtually identical, and that, ultimately, is what counts.

thiest craftsmen, all along with their wives. The dues were high, up to fifteen shillings per year by 1450, far exceeding those of any other guild. Indeed, some long-standing members found the annual fees too great, and by the 1470s lesser schedules were provided for a few relatively indigent members of special social distinction.[56] But even with these problems the Alderman's or Candlemas Guild always included the most influential burghers in the late medieval town, and remained sufficiently broad-based so that the larger urban community recognized it as the leading non-monastic institution in Bury.

The Alderman's Guild had no formal economic functions. It probably sponsored a cycle of mystery plays, but it was primarily political and social in purpose and outlook, and its guiding regulations were set up to promote fraternal obligation and brotherhood. The concept of duty was crucial in building the communal and fraternal experience. Funeral arrangements were to be organized in the event of the death of a member, followed by processionals and elaborate feasts that might best be compared with certain twentieth-century wakes. Food for these feasts and extensive series of trentals, said to hasten the departed's soul to heaven, were undertaken at guild expense. Fraternal bonds were built in life, as well. Common feasts were arranged so that members of the brotherhood might "join together." Widows and orphans of members were to be provided with food, fuel, and shelter; indeed, this was an integral implication of fraternity membership at all levels. In the absence of more formal organizations of social security, such services were in part provided by the guild.

This is illustrated by another major phase of guild activity: public benevolence. Charity was an important part of late medieval social life, a tenet of Christianity that played an important role in urban communities.[57] Ecclesiastical and private benevolence also figured in the public role of charity, supplementing guild activity. The church encouraged private donations and even required that a certain portion of each testator's estate should be so assigned. In one form or another, all testaments contained lists of pious donations; in order to show their distribution and the extent to which they buttressed local institutions of social security, an illustrative sample has been taken from the wills of the Peculiar Court of Bury

[56] Lobel, *The Borough*, pp. 147-148.
[57] See above, note 41.

St. Edmunds. The data are presented in Table 5.1. Most interesting is the direction of charity. Close to 60 percent of the sample provided something for the Franciscan friars of Babwell, just outside the northern boundary of the banleuca. Try as they might, the Benedictines of St. Edmunds were never able to discredit the Grey Friars. Even in the late fifteenth and early sixteenth centuries, over a hundred years after the friars had turned out to aid the townsfolk in their revolts against the abbot, and at a time when popular enthusiasm in England for other mendicant orders such as the Dominicans and Austin Brothers had diminished sharply, feelings toward the Franciscans remained high.[58] Significantly, and in contrast with the bequests pattern of the Franciscans, St. Edmunds' Benedictines fared less well. Despite its looming, dominating presence, the abbey ranked a poor third in popularity. Many people provided for the high altar of the abbey church or other parts of the abbey complex during their lifetimes. But on their deathbeds, perhaps because of resentment towards sacrist's fees for will reg-

TABLE 5.1: PIOUS BEQUESTS FROM THE TESTAMENTARY EVIDENCE, 1440-1530

Bequests	*Frequency*	*% Total (n = 1358)*	*Mean Group Bequest to High Altar*
Franciscans (Babwell)	772	56.8	11 pence
Poor	413	30.4	20 shillings
St. Edmunds	407	30.0	12 shillings
Guilds*	367	27.0	19 shillings
Education, books	135	9.9	3 shillings
Unspecified	122	9.0	6 pence
Civic projects	97	7.1	16 shillings
Hospitals	78	5.7	12 shillings
Gaol and prisoners	65	4.8	10 shillings
Pilgrimages	53	3.9	2 shillings
Private masses	50	3.7	5 shillings

* Guilds are also figured separately, below, p. 191.

[58] About 50 wills mentioned the Dominicans, and 16 the Austin Friars in a similar period.

istration and probates, or because of dissatisfaction with the tolls, tithes, and rents exacted throughout a lifetime, fewer testators than expected gave to St. Edmunds.

Bequests can be divided into two basic groups, those to ecclesiastical institutions and groups and those to lay persons and organizations. At first glance, it appears that bequests to church groups were numerically superior, even when guilds are taken to be secular. But closer inspection suggests that this result is heavily influenced by the presence of the Grey Friars. And if the general bequests to secular institutions lagged behind those to the church, they made up for it in diversity. Many testators showed considerable imagination in doling out their alms. Gifts to the poor appear in over 30 percent of the sample, ahead of those to the abbey. Their scope was wide-ranging, from a few pence, to bread and wine, to elaborate and handsome sums contingent upon the performance of special acts. One of the more interesting was money to the indigent if they attended the funerals of the rich. The funeral of a great person was a notable occasion, complete with parties and material benefits for all who came. For the simple task of singing a requiem mass a poor man might receive a new set of clothing and food to last several weeks. In 1467 John Baret provided a cash gift of a penny to all those who attended his funeral.[59] He also bought black costumes for those in attendance, and provided a grand *fête* for the entire town. Margaret Odeham asked for two feasts on the day of her interment, one for relatives and friends, and the other for "the poor folke of the town."[60] Nor was this the extent of her charity to the less fortunate. Money was left for bread and for the purchase of blankets. John Coote, another prominent burgess, gave 6 shillings, 8 pence, to the impoverished. He also left funds for funeral feasts, but outdid both Smith and Odeham; there were to be three, one for his friends, a second in the abbey for the Benedictines, and a third in the Guildhall for the town's poor, after they had celebrated a mass for his soul.[61]

At times the scope of pious charity went beyond borough limits. In 1499 John Mannyng provided cash for beggars in Bury, the

[59] Tymms, p. 15. The entry reads: "I will the alderman, the burgesses, gentlemen and gentlewomen have a dinner the same day that I am entered, with other folk of worship, priests and good friends, and also my tenants."

[60] *Ibid.*, p. 73.

[61] P.C.B.S.E., Pye, f. 123.

suburbs and four surrounding villages.[62] Gifts were not always in cash; at times they were left in bread, finished cloth, or, more commonly, one of the most precious of medieval raw materials, wood. In 1519 Katherine Parfay, widow of the prominent draper, John, provided for the residents of Bury's almshouses one quarter of wood for six years.[63] Among the general poor, special individuals or groups were often singled out. Most prominent among these were lepers. Bury was an important medical center, with leper hospitals and hostels outside its borough gates. Considered dead by the rest of society, reduced to the most wretched existence of begging and supplication, Bury's lepers at least had the solace of the sustenance and generosity of private benevolence from the townsfolk.

Other secular institutions that received a share of testamentary charity included education, libraries, civic projects, hospitals, gaols, and prisoners. Civic projects have been discussed; they were a principal target for the wealthier burgesses, and were used to express municipal pride. Schools, libraries, hospitals, and the gaol were of sufficient importance to merit individual discussion. Pilgrimages were not as essential to the institutional and corporate foundations of the town, but are worth a fleeting look.[64] Bequests for pilgrimage took two forms: money provided for clerics to take long trips, and funds for the poor to journey to local West Suffolk or East Anglian shrines. The most common overseas destinations were Rome and Jerusalem. In 1475 John Nicole gave cash to a group of rectors to go to the Holy See in Rome and sing a series of masses in his name.[65] In 1498 Edmund Stanton went a step beyond. He left funds for a pilgrimage to Rome, to be followed by another to the Holy Land.[66] Once there, the pilgrims were to convert the pagan Turks to the true faith.[67] More frequent were the domestic trips. Canterbury and the shrine of Thomas Beckett were the favorites, fol-

[62] *Ibid.*, f. 88.

[63] *Ibid.*, Hoode, f. 55.

[64] Not much has been written on pilgrimage. In many respects, the prologue of Chaucer's *Canterbury Tales* provides the best account. See J. Sumptien, *Pilgrimage: An Image of Medieval Religion* (Totowa, N.J.: Rowman and Littlefield, 1975).

[65] P.C.B.S.E., Hawlee, f. 210.

[66] *Ibid.*, Pye, f. 63.

[67] There was surprising awareness in provincial Bury of the East, and one of the most popular taverns in town was called "The Saracen's Head."

lowed by St. Mary's at Walsingham and Our Lady in Ipswich. In a sense, the entire concept was limited for Bury benefactors because they lived in one of the major pilgrimage centers in eastern England. The relics of the abbey drew folk from throughout the kingdom, but proximity eliminated it from the native pilgrim's itinerary. Pilgrimage in general was very common; there even seems to have been a group of professional pilgrims in Bury, perhaps unbeneficed clergy, anxious to pick up whatever material support came their way.

Overall, the scope of charity in late medieval Bury was impressive, in both variety and financial extent. Charitable bequests were a major part of the town's social foundation, and in general were closely connected to the fraternities, the principal secular outlet for social security. The fraternities were often asked to act as executors for individual bequests, and made many donations as corporate entities. Indeed, the social guilds were to become inexorably identified with popular charity, something that helped them to establish their reputations as essential secular social institutions.

Crucial to the ongoing success of the fraternities was their internal organization. The best source of information describing such organization comes from the fifteenth-century regulations of the Alderman's Guild. All members were pledged to uphold one another, with strict fines levied against those who broke ranks. Curiously, for all their projected civic spirit, members seemed reluctant to do the one thing that might most logically be expected of them—maintain their meeting place, the Guildhall.[68] Controversy between the guild and the abbot over responsibility for its upkeep occurred throughout the fourteenth century. The abbot held it as landlord and received rent for its use. But it was devoted exclusively to guild affairs, which by the late fourteenth century were as often as not directed against St. Edmunds. Neither side would acknowledge responsibility, and the old Guildhall along the Great Market steadily deteriorated. So bad had things become by the late 1370s that Richard II's advisers were forced to intervene, ordering guild members to repair the building.[69] Only in the fifteenth century, as the Alderman's Guild rose in prestige and power, did its members assume full responsibility for maintaining their hall. Upkeep had

[68] Margaret Statham, "The Guildhall of Bury St. Edmunds," *P.S.I.*, xxxi, 1967-70.

[69] C.P.R., Richard II, 1378, p. 57.

by then become a point of pride, a symbol of their success and prosperity, and a token of their aspiration to secular independence.

Money was never the major issue in the maintenance of the Guildhall. The Alderman's Guild was quite prosperous. In addition to the initiation and annual membership dues already mentioned, the guild had several other reliable sources of income. It was licensed to hold an annual trade fair, and, while details of the scope and ultimate success of this fair do not survive, it was convened several times and must have been reasonably profitable.[70] The guild was the recipient of numerous private bequests, some of which were quite considerable. In the fifteenth and sixteenth centuries, three of the great lay figures of Bury—John Smith, Margaret Odeham and Richard King III—left such considerable endowments that guild leaders appended each of their wills to reiterations of the guild regulations, lest anyone, especially the abbey, challenge their authenticity.[71] Such bequests, of which these are but the outstanding examples, provided the guild with cash, assorted movables, and, most important, property. Ultimately, the principal source of its income was the landed endowment, which by the sixteenth century had grown larger than that of any local institution except the abbey. By the 1520s these holdings extended well beyond the banleuca, throughout West Suffolk, East Suffolk, Norfolk, Essex, and Cambridgeshire—overall, lands in over 200 parishes, with indications that even this represented only part of the total endowment.[72]

In all, the abbey must have felt threatened by this wealthy, secular corporate institution made up of prominent figures from the boroughs and suburbs, and viewed by many of the poorer and middling elements as the defender of their rights. The guildsmen themselves were conservative and cautious. They never became directly involved as an organization in the civic difficulties of the fourteenth century, fearful perhaps that their extensive privileges might be abrogated on just such a pretext. The guild benefited enormously from the thirteenth-century restrictions on bequests in mortmain,

[70] Lobel, *The Borough*, p. 72.

[71] B.M. Harl. Ms. 4626. For the individual wills, see Tymms, P.C.C., as cited in Chapter 4.

[72] B.M. Harl. Ms. 4626. The list of lands runs on for a half dozen folio pages, despite the fact that at least as many pages have been ripped out of the manuscript. If the full endowment could be pieced together it might well run to over 400 parishes.

and from its incorporation in 1305 right down to Dissolution was the most influential secular body in Bury St. Edmunds.

Information about other secular, corporate fraternities in Bury comes from a smattering of individual guild records and the 1389 response to a royal writ requesting accounts from all fraternities in the kingdom.[73] From Charlemagne onward medieval kings seem to have been suspicious of organizations that required alternative oaths of loyalty, and Richard II and his advisers were no exception. Whether they were also suspicious of craft and merchant guilds is not clear, but the 1389 returns, listed in Table 5.2, show mostly social fraternities. In all, 507 returns were filed from throughout England, 164 of which were from Norfolk, 39 from Suffolk, and 17 from Bury St. Edmunds. All the fraternities show characteristics similar to those described in the Alderman's Guild. They were primarily social organizations, with some religious or social affiliation. The Guild of *Corpus Christi*, for example, situated in the abbey church, had the rather typical role of lighting candles for its patron, and putting out the lead float in the important pageant honoring its day and name.[74] Members were expected to attend the funerals not only of their fellows, but those of all townsfolk. *Corpus Christi* was not an élite or especially prestigious guild. It had low entry fees, which helped to keep it popular, and drew many members from the town's humbler folk. Indeed, so popular was it that in 1317 a second *Corpus Christi* was founded. Apart from membership, the only distinction between the two was that the original continued to meet in the abbey church, and the second in St. Mary's.

Other guilds in the 1389 list had similar functions: lighting candles for their patrons, providing care for his or her parish shrine, organizing processionals on appropriate days, attending funerals and wakes, caring for sick fellow members, and distributing alms. Some guilds had special additional functions. The Guild of the Clerks in neighboring Glemsford, which numbered among its members many Bury folk, was especially designed to care for the sick and poor.[75] In 1481 a priest named Henry Herdeman was

[73] Westlake, *Parish Guilds*.

[74] V. B. Redstone, "Chapels, Chantries and Gilds in Suffolk," *P.S.I.*, xii, 1906.

[75] *V.C.H.*, ii, p. 311. Also, see F. W. Warren, "A Pre-Reformation Village Gild," *P.S.I.*, xi, 1903. Lobel, *The Borough*, p. 73, note 1, says: "The fraternity was also known as the clerks of Glemsford, because it held property there." I am not as certain.

TABLE 5.2: PARISH GUILDS IN BURY ST. EDMUNDS, 1389

Name of Guild and Parish	P.R.O. #	Principal Duty	Earliest Reference to Incorporation, if known
Alderman (Virgin Mary, Candlemas)	399	Maintain Guildhall	1305
Assumption, St. M.	400	Lights for St. M.	
Corpus Christi, St. Ed.	401	Lights, funerals, processionals	
Corpus Christi, #2, St. M.	402	Annual Masses	1317
St. Anne, St. J.	403	Lights, masses at funerals	1309
St. Christopher, St. Ed.	405	Honor patron,	1349
St. Mary, St. J.	406	Honor patron, perform on Assumption	
Passion St. Edmund *Rex*, St. Ed.	407	Lights, funerals, masses	1329
St. Edmund Bury, St. Ed.	408	Honor patron	1385
St. George, St. Ed.	409	Honor patron, St. Edmund	1369
St. James, St. J.	410	Honor patron	
St. John Baptist, St. Ed.	411	Honor patron, funerals	
St. John Baptist, St. J.	412	Honor patron, funerals	
St. Margaret, St. M.	413	Honor patron, funerals	1346
St. Mary Mag., St. M.	414	Honor patron, funerals	1282
St. Nicholas, St. M.	415	Funerals	1282
St. Peter, St. M.	416	Funerals	1309

St. M. = St. Mary's Parish
St. J. = St. James' Parish
St. Ed. = St. Edmund's, the Abbey Church

granted royal license to found a chantry, and within it a perpetual guild called "The Sweet Man Jesus," complete with wardens, chaplains, and associated lay folk.[76] The sole purpose of "The Sweet Man Jesus" was prayer, apparently the only guild in Bury to be so devoted. Its members were to sing a daily mass for the king, his queen, the entire royal family, and the great benefactor of Bury St. Edmunds, John Smith and his wife, an indication of the source of the endowment.

Perhaps the most intriguing of all the town's guilds was that dedicated to St. Nicholas, also called the Dusse, Douse, or Douze.[77] With the Alderman's and first *Corpus Christi*, it was one of the major fraternities in Bury St. Edmunds. The Dusse was established in 1282, and had multiple functions that combined the duties of all the other fraternities. As in the Alderman's, membership required social and financial standing, and its members included the greatest of the burgesses.[78] Named after its guilding council of twelve, it administered to the poor and provided important contributions for all local pageants. The Dusse was also charged with caring for the needs of alien merchants who came to Bury, a function that encouraged all major denizens merchants to seek admission. Most important, the Dusse maintained the college of Songschool Street. Redstone has used the sacrist's rental of 1317 to show how the guild paid the rent on the tenement abutting St. Mary's Church in which the school was situated, wedged between the abbey compound and the grammar school.[79] The school will be discussed in some detail, but patronage of education can be added to the list of guild services. Membership in the Dusse, like that in the Alderman's Guild, was expensive and time-consuming. Its members were expected to contribute frequently and vigorously to corporate activities. Yet, despite this, membership was considered a mark of prestige and honor, and was highly sought. One of the first acts of a merchant just recently successful was application for admission. All of this suggests a growing sense of responsibility and civic pride within the burghal community.

[76] C.P.R., Edward IV, 1481, p. 259.

[77] The Dusse has been discussed by many scholars, including: Lobel, *The Borough*, pp. 46, 73; *V.C.H.*, i, pp. 657659; and Redstone, "St. Edmunds Bury," p. 16. Redstone calls it the Dulse.

[78] The guilds were by no means mutually exclusive. Many, in fact, most of the members of one belonged to the other.

[79] Redstone, "St. Edmunds Bury."

Additional evidence of the popularity and importance of the social fraternities comes from the testamentary evidence; data for a select sample from 1440 to 1530 are presented in Table 5.3. Both pious bequests and statements of parish and burial often contain information about guild memberships and affiliations. Unlike many other aspects of testamentary benevolence, no records of guidelines explaining the conditions of such charity survive. It is impossible to judge whether law or custom dictated that a given amount should be left to a fraternity, but it is most likely that there were no formal criteria. For all these reasons, plus the added burden of more formal demands from other public sources, it is difficult to put guild bequests in exact focus. Some general observations, however, can be made. First, 27 percent of the testators sampled provided something to one of the fraternities. Considering that such bequests seem to have been completely voluntary, this is a considerable proportion. Second, fraternal benefactors were among the wealthiest testators in the town. The donors to all the guilds except one had estates large enough to rank them in the wealthiest fifth of the testamentary population. The exceptional guild was the Holy Name, probably *Corpus Christi*, renowned for attracting middling and poorer members. It was the wealthiest burgesses who identified most closely with the fraternities and who had the most to gain from their activities. In part, their generosity reflects the extra cash they had. But in part it also suggests that the rich—perhaps just because they

TABLE 5.3: GUILD TALLY FROM TESTAMENTARY BEQUESTS, 1440-1530

Guild	Frequency	% Total (1358)	Mean Group Bequest to High Altar
St. Peter	231	17.0	15 shillings
St. Botolph	229	16.9	19 shillings
Holy Name	190	14.0	3 shillings
St. Nicholas (Dusse)	111	8.2	18 shillings
Candlewick	93	6.8	10 shillings
Blessed Mary	85	6.3	13 shillings
St. John Baptist	84	6.2	11 shillings
Alderman's (Candlemas)	61	4.5	20 shillings

were wealthy—were the most active of all guild members. Finally, it might be noted that the testamentary record of the guild does not coincide with the 1389 account. In the late fourteenth century, there were no formal records of a guild dedicated to St. Botolph, thus indicating a later foundation or the possibility that it might have been a particularly well-organized fraternity in a surrounding village, patterned after the clerks at Glemsford. And even assuming that the Guild of the Holy Name was that of the *Corpus Christi* fraternities, the Candlewick Guild cannot be precisely identified. But, overall, the testamentary data provide additional evidence showing the role of fraternities in the emergence of the secular community. Because of their broad application and activities, they combined many of the social, governmental, and institutional functions of the commune outside of the auspices of St. Edmunds.

THE MEDICAL COMMUNITY

Another example of the rise of independent or quasi-independent institutions in late medieval Bury St. Edmunds was the town's hospitals and related medical community. Established by the abbey, the six hospitals were generously endowed; while never strictly secular, they developed apart from St. Edmunds through much of the later middle ages. Most important, by 1400 the hospitals were of sufficient account in their own right so that, whatever their formal affiliation, they attracted people to Bury through their intrinsic merits and services. The six hospitals made Bury a major regional medical center and provided the town with another base apart from the abbey.[80]

Medieval hospitals were considerably different from their counterparts in industrial societies. In England most of them did not seek to cure, or at times even minister to, the needs of the sick as much as they tried to isolate them from the mainstream of society and prevent the spread of their diseases. Alternatively, they functioned as almshouses, places where the poor and those infirm from

---

[80] A general survey of medieval hospitals is R. M. Clay, *Medieval Hospitals of England*, 2nd ed. (London: Frank Cass, 1966). Also, see *V.C.H.*, i, pp. 133 ff.; and Joy Rowe, "Medieval Hospitals of Bury St. Edmunds," *Medical History*, 2, 1958. Of general interest is Margaret Pelling and Charles Webster, "Medical Practitioners," in Charles Webster, ed., *Health, Medicine and Mortality in the Sixteenth Century* (Cambridge: Cambridge University Press, 1979).

old age might go.[81] Bury's hospitals, however, were somewhat different. For one, the town had separate almshouses, supplemented by additional abbey facilities designed to care for the clerical poor. More than most of their contemporary counterparts, Bury's hospitals were established with some medical *raison d'être*. And, second, Bury had six hospitals in a population that never exceeded 7,000, a ratio far greater than necessary to care solely for the sick from the borough, suburbs, or even the greater urban region. The hospitals served all of East Anglia and perhaps even eastern England. If caution is taken to appreciate the meaning in its medieval context, late medieval Bury St. Edmunds can be seen as a medical center, with a steady stream of the sick and infirm making their way to the town.

Bury's medical tradition preceded the establishment of hospitals *per se*. St. Edmunds had its own medical history. It was widely believed that the chief shrine of the abbey had the power to heal.[82] Miracles were alleged to have been performed there, and infirm pilgrims flocked to it as early as the tenth century. In addition to the shrine of The Martyr, the abbey possessed the cup of St. Edmund, also believed to hold the power to cure all those who drank from it. Since Bury was so situated geographically that travellers to and from London and Norwich or Cambridge and Ipswich inevitably passed through it, many passers-by combined a "cure" with business or pilgrimage. Hostelry was an obligation of the abbey, and its *Liber Consuetudinum Monasterii* contained 46 clauses that carefully defined housing responsibilities.[83] Further, several of St. Edmunds' early abbots were physicians who emphasized the abbey's growing medical role.[84] It had a large infirmary, which from the twelfth century took in secular patients, and later supplemented the external hospitals. So pervasive was this medical influence that St. Mary's parish church was decorated with a number of medical or quasi-medical themes, including a physician inspecting a urine flask, and patron saints of surgery, Cosmas and Damian.[85]

[81] *Ibid.* Also, see Charles Creighton, *History of Epidemics in Britain*, i (London: Frank Cass Reprints, 1965).

[82] *V.C.H.*, ii, pp. 133-136.

[83] B.M. Harl. Ms. 1005. Also, see Dugdale, iii, p. 116.

[84] Samuel Tymms, "Notes: Towards a Medical History of Bury St. Edmunds," *P.S.I.*, 1, 1853.

[85] Calvin Wells, "Fifteenth Century Wood Carvings in St. Mary's Church, Bury St. Edmunds," *Medical History*, 91, 1965. I believe Wells carries his argument too far.

Extensive records survive describing the endowments and organization of Bury's hospitals. To a lesser extent they tell something about their staffing and patients. The founding charters make clear that each hospital was originally designed to deliver souls rather than to cure bodies, and was assigned to take in travellers as well as the sick and the poor. In the eleventh and twelfth centuries they served as hostelries, housing pilgrims and travellers on a cash basis. Some may even have begun as guest houses, caring for the infirm who sought cures at abbey shrines, and it may well have been only after an extended period of time that these sick pilgrims were treated on a more regular basis. Bury's hospitals also profitted from the same road network that helped the town's merchants. All stood on the major highways into the borough, the same roads that crisscrossed between London, Norwich, Ipswich, and Cambridge, and all other major points north and east. They were near the road to East Anglia's other major healing shrine, Our Lady in Walsingham. How convenient for the sick pilgrim, going to one shrine, to stop for the cure at the other, and stay in one of Bury's hospitals! Through the twelfth century the hospitals served an almost inn-like function that supplemented their medical role.

By the mid-thirteenth century the banleuca's hospitals had developed more narrowly defined medical functions. With greater numbers of sick coming into the borough, the need to isolate them became more pressing; gradually, this became the hospital's major function. The largest and most important of the early groups to be treated was lepers.[86] Leprosy was quite common in the high middle ages, and was believed to be highly contagious. Given the close quarters and contacts of medieval urban life, contemporary medical opinion held that lepers had to be isolated. Along with Jews they were society's supreme pariahs. Upon diagnosis, the victim was counted among the dead, and a requiem mass said for his soul.[87] Earth was shoveled on the leper's feet to symbolize departure from the mainstream of society, and the patient removed to one of the town's leper hospitals. In the fourteenth century the number of lepers at the hospitals began to dwindle, perhaps because plague had eliminated many from their ranks, but some persisted and they

[86] Creighton, *History of Epidemics*, i, pp. 69-113; S. N. Brody, *The Disease of the Soul: Leprosy in Medieval Literature* (Ithaca, N.Y.: Cornell University Press, 1974).

[87] Rowe, "Medieval Hospitals," p. 256.

more than anyone else represented the isolation service of Bury's hospitals.

Surviving records tell a great deal about the administration of the local hospitals. Daily control was vested with a master or warden. He was a cleric, usually a Benedictine from St. Edmunds, responsible until the fourteenth century for all his actions to the abbey hosteler. Accordingly, hospital life was closely modelled on the Benedictine Rule. Masses were sung several times a day, and a special liturgy for the afflicted was adopted for everyday use. The master was given almost total authority over the hospital community, and inmates were required to subordinate their own needs and desires to those of the larger hospital population. Despite these monastic connections, all of the hospitals maintained very close ties to the secular community. Like the abbey, they needed material sustenance and technical and commercial skills that could come only from the townsfolk. Individually, hospital patients rarely made a great impact on the borough markets, but, taken as a group from six institutions complete with staff, they proved to be an important addition.

Hospital funding came from several sources. Many patients paid entry fees and continued payments according to financial ability throughout the duration of their stay. Charity was another source, although, if last bequests in wills are a fair indication, it must have represented a small portion of total income. There was a smattering of royal and aristocratic support, but the bulk of hospital revenues came from landed endowments. Five of the six built up large holdings of estates throughout the fourteenth and fifteenth centuries, extending beyond the banleuca into much of East Anglia. Most of the lands were provided by St. Edmunds, and later supplemented through royal and private generosity, and their scope was sufficient to make each hospital an important factor in local land markets. Management of these estates, however, was another question. Some masters were fiscally adept and made substantial profits for their institutions; others were not, and drove their houses into bankruptcy. Herein lay part of their larger significance. Because the hospitals were large landholders of differing economic success, they were to become important factors in the town-abbey conflict. Whoever controlled these institutions, which contributed so much to Bury St. Edmunds' regional importance, would gain an important advantage.

A series of rentals allows closer investigation of the extent and management of hospital estates. The 1295 collective rental indicates that after the sacrist the wardens of St. Nicholas and St. Saviour Hospitals were the largest property holders in the borough, and that, along with St. Peter's and St. Petranilla's, were among the largest holders in the suburbs.[88] All were exempted from municipal tithings, and, despite the considerable share of their income skimmed off by the abbot, remaining funds should have been adequate to insure solvency. But this was not always the case. Hospital masters rarely exploited their estates directly, even in the thirteenth century, when food prices were quite high and many landlords reaped exceptional profits by cultivating their demesnes. Instead, they opted to lease out property and live as *rentiers*. Hence, as the land market declined in the fourteenth century, the hospitals suffered, and at least four of them fell into bankruptcy. Sometimes there were mitigating factors. St. Saviour had too many patients, many of whom were royal pensioners, and had to petition the abbot for more money. The abbot himself was short of funds, and had to make entreaties to the king. But generally, the hospitals' financial woes were the result of their own fiscal mismanagement and high living.[89] Between 1300 and 1325 St. Peter's, St. Nicholas, and *Domus Dei* all went broke. These and the other hospitals were in turn bailed out at various times in the fourteenth and fifteenth centuries, in some cases by the abbey or Crown, in others by private citizens or guilds. But in the process each paid the price of a loss of some of its independence. The hospitals retained their medical prestige and regional attractions throughout the later middle ages, but the penalty assessed by those who restored solvency was a voice in hospital management and part of the income from the lands. For St. Edmunds, it merely represented additional property that had initially belonged to it in any case. But for the townsfolk it had far more value; it represented new areas of power and responsibility.

Varying bits of information survive on the individual hospitals. Least well known and documented was St. Stephan's, and there is some doubt about its continuing presence as an active institution in the late middle ages.[90] Two principal things are known. First, it

[88] Redstone, "St. Edmunds Bury," pp. 31-32.

[89] C of I. Henry VII, 1495, p. 430, is illustrative of the problems.

[90] Information can be found in: Rowe, "Medieval Hospital"; and Clay, *Medieval Hospitals; V.C.H.*, i; Tymms, "Notes"; C.P.R., Richard II, 1395, p. 676.

was supposed to have drops of the blood of its patron, taken when he was stoned to death. This would have provided it with alleged curative powers, much like those of the relics of St. Edmunds, and no doubt attracted many pilgrims and patients. And, second, it was at some time located between Eastgate Bridge and St. Nicholas' Hospital, without Eastgate Ward. But it was rarely mentioned, and there is virtually no information on its management. While St. Stephan's surely existed as an autonomous institution in the twelfth and thirteenth centuries, it may well have collapsed because of a lack of funds in the fourteenth or fifteenth, or have been absorbed by one of its neighbors, perhaps the larger and wealthier St. Nicholas.

More information survives on the other five hospitals. St. John the Evangelist, better known as *Domus Dei*, was founded in the thirteenth century. There is controversy over the precise date, with various authorities claiming 1216, 1248 and 1256.[91] The abbey was its principal patron, and its warden directly supervised by St. Edmunds' prior and cellarer, who accordingly reaped a share of the landed income. This dependence, which had not been the intention of the hospital's thirteenth-century founders, was the result of a financial crisis early in the fourteenth century that brought *Domus Dei* to the brink of bankruptcy. For the rest of the later middle ages, a large share of its income went to abbey officers.[92]

Considerable information survives on the organization of *Domus Dei*, primarily from its foundation deeds.[93] The hospital's original purpose was as an almshouse to care for seven destitute men, with provisions if necessary for a few more. But circumstances destined it for broader things. *Domus Dei* was situated on a very busy stretch of highway, running through South Gate, and pilgrims from the south stopped by and often provided donations. By the 1270s it had grown sufficiently to require new quarters; Southgate Street tenements were exchanged for a position closer to the gate itself. A chapel and cemetery were added, and *Domus Dei* became more "medically" oriented, taking in infirm travellers and patients from the urban region. Hence, its fourteenth century financial crisis was

[91] The *V.C.H.*, i, claims 1248, Clay 1256. and Rowe, 1216.

[92] *V.C.H.*, ii, pp. 133-134.

[93] B. M. Arundel Ms 1. The following also provide information: Rowe, "Medieval Hospitals"; Clay, *Medieval Hospitals; V.C.H.*, i; Tymms, "Notes"; C.P.R., Richard II, 1395, p. 676.

primarily due to the small size of its original endowment, initially intended for a handful of poor people. After the abbey took over management its fiscal base was enlarged by the addition of a number of fields in the suburbs, and several stalls in the Great Market; by 1340 the hospital was rich enough to be assessed by the Crown for 12 acres of arable.[94] *Domus Dei* was to find another benefactor late in the fourteenth century. As income from the landed estates began to fall after the Black Death, the hospital was again faced with financial crisis. This time, its savior was secular. The Cockerels, a prominent West Suffolk family, became patrons, and in 1373 provided sufficient funds to allow the wardens to expand the hospital complex and to build a separate, free-standing chantry along Southgate Street. The chantry had its own chaplain, who was given room, board, and an annual stipend of over 33 shillings.[95] The example of *Domus Dei* illustrates the evolution of a hospital from an almshouse-hostel to a hostel-medical institution deeply involved in town affairs.

St. Petranilla's was associated with *Domus Dei*. Its patron was a popular West Suffolk figure, and her alleged skull was among the abbey's relics.[96] A twelfth-century foundation, it too stood on Southgate Street, near *Domus Dei*, with an original purpose of housing female lepers. This it did through the thirteenth century, but in the fourteenth century, having established closer ties with *Domus Dei*, it expanded first to house lepers of both sexes, and then to include the poor. After 1349 St. Petranilla's had increasing financial problems, but it had a very large endowment and was one of the more important *rentiers* in Bury. In the 1535 *Valor Ecclesiasticus*, its gross worth was placed at over £10, plus £4 rather mysteriously specified for the poor.[97]

St. Nicholas' Hospital was founded in the 1250s by Abbot Hugh of Northwold, and located outside East Gate.[98] St. Nicholas was a

[94] P.R.O. E2/41/4; "Cartulary of the Hospital of *Domus Dei*," from B. M. Arundel Ms. 1.

[95] Rowe, "Medieval Hospitals," p. 258.

[96] The following provide information of St. Petranilla's: Clay, *Medieval Hospitals*; Rowe, "Medieval Hospitals"; and Richard Yates, *The History and Antiquities of the Abbey of Bury St. Edmunds* (London: J. B. Nichols and Son, 1843).

[97] Rowe, "Medieval Hospitals," p. 258.

[98] Information on St. Nicholas can be found in: Rowe, "Medieval Hospitals"; Clay, *Medieval Hospitals*; *V.C.H.*, i; Tymms, "Notes"; and H. A.

patron of lepers, and hospital origins were probably so connected. But, as with the others, it developed well beyond its original purpose. The hospital always had well-defined medical functions. It was firmly linked with practicing physicians, including one of Bury's most famous doctors, Henry Rudde of Cambridge University, and seems to have been dedicated to the treatment of infectious disease. St. Nicholas was also closely connected with charitable causes; in the thirteenth century, it established an independent almshouse, which was maintained until the sixteenth century. Its routine was the most rigidly monastic of Bury's six hospitals, with a master warden, a chaplain, and several officially designated lay brethren.[99] St. Nicholas was well endowed. Along with *Domus Dei* and St. Saviour's, it held much property, and along with St. Saviour's was allowed to hold an annual trade fair to supplement its income. Further, it was the most popular of the hospitals among the townsfolk, consistently receiving more charitable bequests than the next two combined. Of all the hospitals, St. Nicholas was best able to stay solvent, and needed external stewardship only for a brief period in the fifteenth century.[100] Consequently, it was the most independent of them, and was able to play a considerable role in local social, economic, and administrative developments. In a royal assessment of 1340 it accounted for 44 acres of land, and the hospital was given its own coat of arms.[101]

Although it would become most famous for its role in the plague epidemic of 1637, St. Peter's Hospital was also an important medieval foundation.[102] The official leper hospital of West Suffolk, it stood outside Risby Gate, and was founded by Abbot Anselm in the mid-twelfth century, first for leprous clerks and then for the wider leper population.[103] Like St. Nicholas and *Domus Dei*, from its inception it was generously provided with landed estates, and

---

Hariss, "Notes: The Site of St. Peter's Hospital Chapel," *P.S.I.*, xvii, 1921; C.P.R., Richard II, 1392, p. 147; C.C.R., Henry V, 1414, p. 55.

[99] Rowe, "Medieval Hospitals," p. 258.

[100] *Ibid.*

[101] In the 1535 *Valor Ecclesiasticus*, its wealth was measured at £7. Obviously, the hospital must have declined in the 1520s. See C.P.R., Richard II, 1392, p. 147.

[102] Information of St. Peter's can be found in: Rowe, "Medieval Hospitals"; Clay, *Medieval Hospitals; V.C.H.*, i; and Hariss, "Notes: The Site"; *C of I*, Henry VII, 1495, p. 430.

[103] Rowe, "Medieval Hospitals," p. 258.

as late as the 1530s was assessed for about £15. Its master drew separate income from a manor at Lackford, Suffolk, and the hospital itself had an attached chantry worth £10.[104] St. Peter even had its own almoner to help to raise funds in St. Mary's and St. James' parish churches, collecting whatever he could exact from regular churchgoers.

The richest and best known of Bury's hospitals was St. Saviour's.[105] It was founded in the twelfth century by Abbot Samson, and remained the abbey favorite throughout the later middle ages. Its endowment was supplemented several times in the thirteenth century, until the hospital complex became one of the most impressive collections of buildings in the banleuca, and provided for a warden, 12 chaplains, 6 clerks, and 12 poor men and 12 poor women. St. Saviour was situated on the Fornham Road, just outside North Gate, where its ruins remain, across from the British Railway Station, opposite St. Thomas' Chapel. In its heyday, it constituted with the Franciscan settlement in Babwell a small, flourishing suburban community just outside the banleuca, an impressive enough conglomeration to attract as a resident in 1446 the "Good Duke," Humphrey of Gloucester.[106]

St. Saviour's was initially more autonomous than any other hospital. In 1186 its warden succeeded in obtaining a papal bull granting it virtual independence from town and abbey, and at the same time providing it with additional income from the tithes of abbey lands at Redgrave and Rickinghall, two of the most profitable manors in West Suffolk.[107] In 1190 another friend, the Bishop of Norwich, confirmed to it two-thirds of the tithings from Icklingham Manor.[108] This meant that St. Saviour's had a splendid endowment held apart from the abbey, in addition to whatever property was provided by St. Edmunds.

[104] Yates, *History and Antiquities.* The chantry was established by a townswoman with the unlikely name of Scientia de la Gaye.

[105] Information on St. Saviour's can be found in: Clay, *Medieval Hospitals*; Rowe, "Medieval Hospitals"; *V.C.H.*, i; E. R. Burdon, "St. Saviour's Hospital, Bury St. Edmunds," *P.S.I.*, xix, 1925-27; C.U.L. Ms. Ee 3 60; *ibid.*, Mm 4 19; C.P.E., Edward III, 1336 p. 265; C.P.R., Edward II, 1318, p. 199; C.P.R., Richard II, 1390, p. 179; Lobel, *The Borough*, pp. 142-143.

[106] Humphrey died there, awaiting trial. See E. F. Jacob, *The Fifteenth Century* (Oxford: Oxford University Press, 1960), pp. 483-484.

[107] Burdon, "St. Saviour's Hospital," is the best source on the landed endowments.

[108] *Ibid.* Also good is Rowe, "Medieval Hospitals," pp. 259-262.

Given such favor, St. Saviour's should have remained a strong autonomous foundation throughout the later middle ages, but this was not to be. In the thirteenth century its administrators made a series of financial blunders. In the 1290s the hospital became insolvent, and had to be bailed out by the abbey. The price it paid was the loss of much of its property and self-determination. Apparently, the monks who rescued the hospital failed to make the essential reforms, and mismanagement continued. By the early fourteenth century, fiscal disaster threatened again. A warden appointed by the abbot went on a pilgrimage to the Holy Land with a large share of St. Saviour's ready cash and never returned.[109] In his absence, other monks—the same brothers initially installed to prevent corruption—siphoned off much of its annual income for their own purposes. In the 1310s they began to sell off parts of its endowment. The inmates and hospital administrators objected, and, getting no satisfaction from Abbot de Draughton, first began to expel alien patients and then appealed to the burgesses. The burgesses in turn petitioned Parliament, which appealed to the king. Royal agents were sent to Bury to supervise St. Saviour's, and by the 1340s it had been returned to solvency and resumed its position of influence. The hospital continued to be an important factor in local affairs until the sixteenth century.

The quick royal response to St. Saviour's fourteenth-century problems can be explained by special royal interests. Successive monarchs used it as a pensionary. Its initial role combined that of isolation, almshouse, and hostelry, but, unlike the hospitals, whose social roles broadened in the course of the fifteenth and sixteenth centuries, St. Saviour's actually became more restricted. Increasingly, it was treated as a retirement home, ironically a ramification of its great wealth. The major consequence of royal intervention in the 1320s was that the hospital would henceforth be required to take in and care for large numbers of royal pensioners. It had already been designated in the 1290s by the abbot as an old-age home for his monks, and in the fourteenth century, as the Crown tried to free itself from increasing financial obligations, the opportunity to slough off one cost on an autonomous foundation was not overlooked.[110] Abbey, hospital, and town officials united in protest, but to no avail. St. Saviour's continued to be a dumping ground for anyone the king wished to place in it, and by the fif-

[109] *Ibid.*
[110] Clay, *Medieval Hospitals.*

teenth century was so popular that new inmates had to be approved by a committee of burgesses and Benedictines.

Information survives on the internal life at St. Saviour's.[111] Upon entering, the patient received food, board, and clothing for the rest of his life. In return, the entrant was expected to contribute to his upkeep with an almost dowry-like donation. At times the contributions were quite large; one wealthy pensioner provided 29 marks. Daily life was well regimented. There were always a great many monks and clerics in St. Saviour's, and they closely followed the Benedictine routine. But, despite both financial and religious restrictions, life in the hospital was much freer than that in the abbey. Expenses were always high, and St. Saviour's inventories following the 1327 riots show why.[112] Building and farm maintenance costs were considerable. There were wages to be paid, and the basics of food, clothing, and shelter to be provided. Unfortunately, the latter often proved to be greater than that which had been originally budgeted. Upkeep is a relative term, and in St. Saviour's it went well beyond the basic necessities. Some pensioners were provided with silk tablecloths, latten basins, silver knives and spoons, elaborate sets of bedding, and silk and linen clothing, hardly things which might be expected in a hospital-almshouse. Many of the monks probably found themselves enjoying in retirement a higher level of material comfort than they had had in the abbey. And, despite eventual financial woes, the wardens of St. Saviour's never cut back on their own high level of personal comfort.[113] In the early sixteenth century the hospital listed among its possessions Flemish wall-hangings, silk coverlets, and scarlet window curtains. The master's goods included three "good" cloaks, one of bright red, and two of royal purple, both of which were trimmed in fur. Indeed, so well were St. Saviour's officials living in 1528 that the Medici Pope Clement VII, never noted for his frugality, was sufficiently shocked at the inmates' life-style to set out yet another hospital reform plan. He placed tight restrictions on the officers, who in the years just before Dissolution seemed determined to milk St. Saviour's dry. But, despite Clement's efforts, they were successful. By 1539 the hospital buildings were in ruins, and a few years later, when Sir Nicholas Bacon purchased the entire complex,

[111] Rowe, "Medieval Hospitals," pp. 119-120.

[112] Arnold, iii, p. 346.

[113] V.C.H., i, pp. 133-135. Also, see Tymms, "Notes."

it was so dilapidated that he took stones from its walls in order to build up his newly acquired estates at Redgrave.[114]

The role of Bury's six hospitals can be summarized by emphasizing their position in the larger life of the urban community. Six hospitals existed initially because St. Edmunds Abbey was a pilgrimage attraction and because part of its appeal rested with the alleged medical and curative powers of its relics and shrines. Many of the pilgrims were old or infirm, and needed accommodation; the abbey could provide for a few, but not for all tourists. Consequently, the hospitals evolved as inns for the sick. Because the abbey was a rich, landed institution, it was able to endow them with sizable estates, a situation found in only a few other important ecclesiastical towns, such as Canterbury and St. Albans. In time, the hospitals expanded from their pensionary purpose to become nascent medical centers and, on the strength of their endowments, attained a degree of autonomy from their creator. As long as they remained solvent, they retained independence. But when the hospitals ran into financial difficulties—and at least five of the six did at one time or another in the later middle ages—they had to seek financial support from the abbey or secular sources. The price paid for this support was increased external interference in the hospitals' affairs, and a further division of corporate institutional power between town and abbey.

The hospitals had another important function in the emergence of the commune. They gave continuing impetus to Bury's rise as a regional medical center. This extended beyond the institutions to individuals, to include a comparatively large resident community of medical practitioners. Concentrations of doctors were not unusual in large medieval towns like London and Norwich, but in a middling-sized provincial borough such as Bury this was quite remarkable.[115] The medical professionals included a few university-trained physicians, several surgeons and barber-surgeons, and even a few butcher-surgeons. As was the case with the hospitals, their rise was aided and encouraged by the long medical tradition of the abbey. Abbot Baldwin had been the court physician to Edward the Confessor, and became one of the most prominent doctors in eleventh-century Europe. He continued as royal medical adviser under

[114] Bacon, 2440. Also, see Rowe, "Medieval Hospitals," pp. 261-262.

[115] Pelling and Webster, "Medical Practitioners," emphasize this, but clearly underestimate the number of practitioners in Bury St. Edmunds.

William I, and dispensed advice to the papal *curia*.[116] A century later, during the abbacy of Samson, Jocelin of Brakelond noted the connection between St. Edmunds and the famous physician Walter of St. Albans. Walter was provided with abbey funds to establish an almonry-clinic, and, while little information about it has survived, we might conjecture that it prospered at least through the balance of his lifetime.[117] It is also likely that the abbey had its own resident physician, or at least an in-house monk with some medical training to treat his fellow Benedictines and perhaps select townsfolk. St. Edmunds had a well-established infirmary, and its curator-infirmarer was one of the richest abbey officers. The Court of Arrears statement of 1539 lists the office as drawing rent from tenements on eighteen streets in the borough.[118] The infirmary itself was located in semi-isolation on a corner of the abbey complex. It was a stone building with apartment-like components designed to separate folk with infections from those who had broken bones and minor respiratory infections.[119] Apparently business was booming, for the infirmary expanded in the twelfth and again in the thirteenth centuries. As with so many other facets of social life, impetus for Bury's medical community came from St. Edmunds.

Less information survives on the individual members of the community. Everyday aches and pains and bone settings were probably serviced by surgeons rather than by physicians. Most of these surgeons were essentially craftsmen, with minimal philosophical or theoretical but a great deal of practical training. In Bury, most barbers appear to have been at least part-time practitioners, and they occupied an important place in the larger community. Tymms claims that they were incorporated in 1461 by Edward IV, and reincorporated under more favorable circumstances by Henry VIII early in the sixteenth century.[120] Their fee schedules seem to have

[116] For details on Baldwin, see C. H. Talbot and Hammond, E. A., *The Medical Practitioners of Medieval England: A Biographical Register* (London: Wellcome Historical Medical Library, 1965), pp. 19-21. Two general studies are: Talbot, *Medicine in Medieval England* (London: Oldbourne, 1967); and Stanley Rubin, *Medieval English Medicine* (London: David Charles, 1974).

[117] Jocelin, *The Chronicle*, p. 114. Also, see Talbot and Hammond, *The Medical Practitioners*, p. 364.

[118] L. Redstone, "First Ministers' Account," pp. 14-15.

[119] Yates, *History and Antiquities*, p. 197.

[120] Tymms, "Notes." I have looked extensively for records of incorpo-

been quite reasonable, and they were probably consulted by the lesser tradesmen and merchants, workers, and peasants of the urban region. Finally, the poorest strata of greater Bury society may well have had their own medical system, relying primarily on unlicensed practitioners who offered cruder surgical services at even lower rates.[121]

Barbers and barber-surgeons left few details about the actual practice of their craft. Their wills yield very limited information. In his last testament, proved in 1497, Richard Wryth left to his apprentice John Woode all his tools, described as a barber's bag, knives, cloth and basin.[122] In the 1523-1524 lay subsidy the wealthier men and women of Bury were allowed to pay a reduced anticipation. Among them was the surgeon John Wacy, paying £4.[123] There was a Barbers' Row on the south side of the Great Market, and there is evidence of medical practice there.[124] Beyond these meager bits and pieces, and the presence of large numbers of barbers and butchers in the borough throughout the later middle ages, there is little additional personal information.

Bury's university-trained physicians were not an incorporated craft, and little is known of the actual nature of their medical practice. They were all clerics, primarily from Cambridge University. A reference from the will of John Bakere, proved in 1358, refers to his shop on Leches' Hill.[125] Leche was a common description for physician, and the presence of such a place, used in popular if not formal topographical terms, is significant. Three physicians left probated wills. The first was John Brinkele, whose will was proved in 1443. He gives few personal or professional details, save to mention a very large bequest to St. Saviour's Hospital, and to write that he was married and lived on the Long Brakelond.[126]

---

ration for Bury barbers and have not found them. Presumably, Tymms is referring to the London barber-surgeons. See Sidney Young, *The Annals of the Barber Surgeons of London* (London: Blades, East and Blades, 1890).

[121] Pelling and Webster, "Medical Practitioners," deal with this in great detail.

[122] P.C.B.S.E., Pye, f. 60.

[123] *Suffolk in 1524, Being the Return for a Subsidy Granted in 1523, Suffolk Green Books*, x (Woodbridge, Suffolk: George Booth, 1910), pp. 352-358. As noted above, p. 41, surgeon Thomas Stacy was also assessed.

[124] Redstone, "St. Edmunds Bury," p. 27.

[125] P.C.B.S.E., Osbern, f.6.

[126] *Ibid.*, Hawlee, f.6; Talbot and Hammond, *Medical Practitioners*, p. 127.

John Denham's will was proved in 1459 in London, but he was originally from Bury and maintained a practice there.[127] A third will survives from Henry Rudde, "master doctor," who died in 1509.[128] Rudde was one of the more prominent figures in late medieval Bury. He was wealthy and generous, and left numerous provisions for the poor and infirm, perhaps a reflection of his professional experiences. He was a Cambridge graduate, and retained extensive links with the university after he left. One of his executors was a Master Doctor Candelyn of Cambridge, apparently another East Anglian physician.[129] But, except for this and the fact that he was associated throughout his life with St. Nicholas Hospital, he left no personal information.[130]

There are fragments of information about other physicians. John de Bury, for example, was personal *medicus* to Richard II, but left few details of his private life.[131] The 1523-1524 lay subsidy lists a few doctors, and is of additional interest because it delineates the social and economic superiority of the physician over the surgeon.[132] John Kempe, a leche, claimed at the time of the assessment to be in London and a resident of Lackford, perhaps hoping for a better tax rate. But the assessors listed him as a Bury resident, and he paid £13, 4 shillings. There was a Master Doctor Rede, claiming to live in Beccles, but also being assessed as a Bury burgess, at a rate of £10. Two other men may have been physicians. Richard Smythe styled himself a "horseleche." He too claimed residence elsewhere, in Sudbury, but paid tax in Bury. It was £12, less than that of most mercers and drapers, but well above the craftsmen and yeomen who appear at the bottom of the anticipation. Finally,

He may have had a son who was a Cambridge M.D. See Talbot and Hammond, *Medical practitioners*, p. 26.

[127] London Guildhall Ms. 9171/5, Sharpe, f. 26lb; Talbot and Hammond, *Medical Practitioners*, p. 140.

[128] Tymms, pp. 106-113. There was no information in Talbot and Hammond, *Medical Practitioners*.

[129] Talbot and Hammond also do not list him.

[130] Tymms, pp. 106-113. According to the royal rolls of account of the Treasurer of Cambridge University, Rudde was employed by the university, and served as a mediator in a town-gown conflict. More information can be found in Tymms, "Notes."

[131] For de Bury, see Talbot and Hammond, *Medical Practitioners*, p. 128.

[132] For more details on the subsidy, see above, pp. 39-41, and below, Appendix A.

there was someone named Newman who called himself a "fissis-shener," in the middling ranks of the assessment, and probably a medical doctor.[133]

The evidence is spotty, but suggests an active and busy medical population in late medieval Bury, supplementing its hospitals. Together, doctor and hospital made the town a medical center of regional and perhaps of national importance.[134] Like so many other local institutions in Bury St. Edmunds, those pertaining to medicine were given life by the abbey. But they soon became self-perpetuating, and as independent organizations added to the attraction and rise of the secular community.

EDUCATION

Among the most important institutions in late medieval Bury St. Edmunds were its schools and libraries. Indeed, Bury's role as a regional center of education was as important as its medical, legal, and perhaps even commercial roles. Burgesses and gentlemen throughout West Suffolk sent their children to the borough to be educated. Consequently, control of the schools was a crucial element in the larger issue of control of the town. Here again, it is possible to see the oft-repeated dichotomy of the late medieval town. The schools and the library all initially developed under the auspices of the abbey and its patronage.[135] But, in time, on their

---

[133] There was one final medical, or at least quasi-medical group in late medieval Bury St. Edmunds. These were the masters of the six hospitals. Once again, I am frustrated in my attempts to gain details of their professional lives, and must rely on bits and pieces, primarily from testamentary records. In 1504 Simon Burgeon, clerk and master of the Hospital of *Domus Dei*, died; within three months, his successor as master, William Place, also died. I do not know why, and neither will provides extensive details, save to tell that Place had a fascination of sorts with the image of death, and provided funds to have men berobed in "blak vestament and blak cloth steyned with an ymage of deth" at his funeral. In 1481, John Burbruddge, an earlier master of *Domus Dei*, died with similar invocations. A will also survives for Thomas Crowe, rector of Elvedon and master of St. Nicholas, who died in 1504. All were probated in the P.C.B.S.E., except Place's, which is in Tymms, pp. 105-106.

[134] As stated above, note 115, Pelling and Webster seem to underenumerate them.

[135] A. F. Leach, *The Schools of Medieval England* (London: Methuen, 1915),

own and apart from the abbey, they would to varying degrees attract support from outside sources, become powerful institutions, and draw students to Bury on the strength of their own intrinsic merits. And, ultimately, as quasi-independent institutions, they would serve the townsfolk in their struggle for autonomy.

Like all large Benedictine houses, St. Edmunds had a monastic school within its cloister to educate its oblates. Such monastic schools were part of the foundation of early and high medieval education, and it is probable that before the eleventh century the school took in selected non-oblates. Not much detailed information survives about it, and some scholars have confused it with the town grammar school. But most authorities believe that the monastic school was rather small, with perhaps 12 or 13 students in the mid-thirteenth century, when the abbey had about 80 monks.[136] From the twelfth century the monastic school had little to do with the town; its sole job was to produce Benedictine monks for St. Edmunds, and it would continue to do so until Dissolution. As such, it was the school that remained most firmly in control of the abbey.

This was not the case with the grammar and Song School. The grammar school, also called the collegiate school, was the most important in the borough. Its development has been the subject of considerable controversy. Leach, one of the leading authorities on medieval education, has written two rather contradictory accounts. In his great opus, he dates it from a foundation by Canute, early in the eleventh century.[137] But, writing some years later, he was more cautious, claiming that there were no definitive records of its existence until the twelfth century.[138] There is evidence suggesting that Canute endowed a school in Bury, and that in the mid-twelfth century Abbot Samson attended a non-monastic school before seeking the Benedictine vocation. Whether these records refer to a single school is open to question, but it is clear that Bury had but one grammar school, and that in 1181 Samson provided it with a new school building that it would occupy until the sixteenth cen-

---

is rather dated but still the principal authority. Nicholas Orme, *English Schools in the Middle Ages* (London: Methuen, 1973), adds very little to Leach. Also useful for Bury is Leach's entry in *V.C.H.*, ii, pp. 301-314.

[136] *Ibid.* Also, see C.U.L. Ms Ff 2 29, ff. 47, 58-59.

[137] Leach, *The Schools*, p. 91.

[138] *V.C.H.*, ii, pp. 306-314.

tury.[139] The building was at the corner of Reyngate and Schoolhall Streets, perhaps in a house confiscated from one of the Jews whom Samson had expelled from Bury, and was provided with a small, landed endowment.

Leach believed that Bury had some sort of secular school extant from the reign of Athelstan in the tenth century.[140] If this were so, it probably preceded the foundation of the monastic school. He also claimed that it was always expressly designed for secular priests, and never for oblates. Then, in the twelfth century, with a wider demand for secular education, it opened its doors to the sons of local burgesses and gentlemen. Indeed, he went so far as to call it the public school of the borough, and claimed that by the thirteenth century it emerged virtually independent of St. Edmunds, despite the nature of its endowment. Parts of its income continued to go to the abbey, but once this obligation was fulfilled the school operated under its own initiative.

Lobel, who studied Bury's educational system as closely as she did its gaol and administrative development, disputed several of Leach's contentions.[141] She claimed that the monastery did indeed have control over the collegiate school, particularly its fabric and finances. The only areas in which some autonomy was asserted were those concerning curriculum and admissions. Masters and pupils had some degree of intellectual freedom, but material support, the foundation of independence, was firmly controlled by St. Edmunds. Ultimately, the grammar school's master was responsible to the sacrist.

Sources that might definitively resolve the questions of dates of foundation and origins of the school do not exist, but there is information pertaining to its degree of autonomy. In his *Gesta*, Jocelin of Brakelond states the following: "The Abbot [Samson] bought some stone houses in the town of St. Edmund and assigned them to the master of the schools, in order that the poor clerks might be quit of hiring houses for which each scholar, whether he could or could not, was forced to pay a penny or halfpenny twice a year."[142] Presuming that Jocelin was describing *hadgoval* com-

[139] Jocelin, *The Chronicle*, pp. 43-45.
[140] *V.C.H.*, ii, p. 301.
[141] Lobel, *The Borough*, pp. 45-46.
[142] Jocelin, *The Chronicle*, p. 45.

mitments, further information shows that by the fourteenth century other areas of autonomy had been severely circumscribed. An excerpt from the 1326 cellarer's rental indicates that all rents the school took in and accounts of what it spent were to be scrutinized by the abbot.[143] Perhaps the collegiate school was like St. Saviour's Hospital; its independence varied with its financial state, and fluctuated dramatically in the later middle ages.

Whatever the school's origins and fiscal responsibilities, the function of the grammar school is not in doubt. It was clearly non-monastic, designed primarily for secular priests, and, later, the children of prominent townsfolk. It was, in the English sense, a public school. Its masters were always secular clerics, and there appears to have been no interference by abbey officials in pedagogical affairs. Unlike the hospitals, the school's endowment was modest, and if it had any major properties to be let in the town or suburbs, no evidence survives. Ultimately, the grammar school had its building and a salary of £2 alloted to its master.[144] This small endowment may have been the reason the school went "public." While those studying for the clergy were given scholarships, the sons of burgesses and local gentlemen had to pay tuition. With the influx of these town students from the thirteenth century, things in the collegiate school began to change. It became quite wealthy, and by the sixteenth century its master's income had been raised to £40.[145] With this independent source of funds, the grammar school became increasingly autonomous. And autonomy proved to be a self-perpetuating financial boon; as a secular institution the school received more and more support from private secular sources in the banleuca. Certain distinguished folk had bequeathed cash as early as the twelfth century, but the financial extent of such benevolence did not become significant until after 1400. By Dissolution, such bequests formed a major part of the school's budget. The number of free students had grown from 12 to 40, the number of fee-paying students to at least that number, along with an usher, the head master, and at least five submasters. By the mid-sixteenth century, Bury St. Edmunds' collegiate school was the best and most famous in Suffolk.

[143] C.U.L. Ms. Gg 4 4, f. 249.
[144] *V.C.H.*, ii, pp. 306-309.
[145] *Ibid.*

Bury's third school, the Song School or *Scola Cantus*, was from its inception autonomous of St. Edmunds. It was sponsored by the Dusse Guild, which included the most important secular figures of the commune, and always had sufficient funds.[146] The *Scola Cantus* had clearly defined functions; it was to teach song, namely the rudiments of the mass and psalter, along with reading and grammar to secular clerics. Its origins are obscure, but Leach claims they were pre-Norman. It was located on Song School Street, adjacent to but not contiguous with abbey grounds.[147] Because it was well supported by a powerful secular sponsor, the Song School remained solvent throughout the later middle ages, with its influential patrons assuring freedom of educational policy and admissions. The abbey obviously resented such independence on the part of a tenant, especially one concerned with something at least tangentially in its own interests, and several abbots attempted to curb the Song School master. In 1290 John Harrison was backed by St. Edmunds in an attempt to establish a rival song school. But the Dusse's burgess members objected vociferously, and Abbot John of Northwold withdrew formal abbey support, causing the new school to collapse.[148] By the mid-fourteenth century, the Song School had become a venerable local institution, entrenched in the hands of the townsfolk.

There are a few other aspects of education in late medieval Bury St. Edmunds that further emphasized the town's role as a regional cultural center. Some came from St. Edmunds. The abbey was not a lavish patron of the arts, but it did make some important contributions.[149] One of the most significant was its library.[150] Like

[146] *Ibid.*, pp. 309-311.

[147] The geographical placement comes from a reference from one Sara Sturbite, who gave her son Michael and his children half a house at the entrance of the School Hall. See C.U.L. Ms. Gg 4 4, f. 249.

[148] Leach, *The Schools*, p. 188; *V.C.H.*, ii, p. 309.

[149] The cultural life of the abbey is a broad topic that cannot be discussed herein. Two works of interest come from Elizabeth Parker McLachlan: "The Bury Missal in Laon and Its Crucifixion Miniature," *Gesta*, xvii, 1978; and her "The Scriptorium of Bury St. Edmunds in the Third and Fourth Decades of the fifteenth Century," *Medieval Studies*, xl, 1978.

[150] The best reference to the library, along with a listing of its books, is Dugdale, iii, p. 132. Also, see Lobel, *The Borough*, p. 120; and *V.C.H.*, ii, pp. 56-57.

many Benedictine houses, St. Edmunds had a sizable collection of manuscripts, partly owing to copying and partly from purchase. This library was to help to produce several first-rank scholars from the abbey community, including the poet Lydgate. But more significant as far as the townsfolk and the general state of secular education and learning were concerned, the library was to become almost a civic, public institution. As early as the twelfth century, select townsfolk were permitted to borrow books. By the fifteenth century, their numbers had grown to the point where records suggest that they used it more frequently than did the monks. With the advent of printing and the spread of literacy late in the fifteenth century, this process continued to accelerate and in the 1520s the town numbered among its merchants two booksellers.[151] Dugdale has listed many of the books in the library. The collection was not extraordinary in its scope, but the fact that it was opened to at least the town burgesses was quite significant.[152]

St. Edmunds was a patron of higher education. The 1535 *Valor Ecclesiasticus* indicates that it provided over £26 *per annum* in alms to help to support four Benedictines in Oxford; Bury brothers were resident in Gloucester Hall from its early-thirteenth-century inception.[153] The abbey maintained strong links with Cambridge as well, supporting a hall there and keeping close ties with several colleges and masters. Henry Rudde, the physician, is a case in point. But support of higher education was also to fall increasingly on the townsfolk from the fifteenth century onward.[154] In 1433, with local expenses on the rise, Abbot William Curteys decided to abandon the Cambridge hall, which had been patronized since the thirteenth century. Correspondingly, the burgesses' interests increased. Before 1440 there are virtually no bequests in wills to the universities; thereafter, they become the fifth most frequent donations.[155] In 1502, for example, James Hammond left five shillings for Cambridge scholars.[156] In 1504 John Hedge left money for a secular priest to attend college there to study "in arts and non other sciens."[157] This priest was to be a Norfolk or Suffolk man, further

[151] See above, pp. 111-113.
[152] Also of use is Yates, *History and Antiquities.*
[153] Dugdale, iii, p. 116.
[154] C.U.L. Ms. Ff 2 29, f. 29.
[155] See above, p.
[156] P.C.B.S.E., Pye, f. 120.
[157] *Ibid.*, f. 146.

indication of the regional pride that Bury folk showed in so many of their activities, and was expected to stay at the university until funds ran out. In addition, Hedge left additional money if his sons decided on academic careers.

There were many other "cultural" bequests. John Wastrell left money to King's College, Cambridge, and books to the university.[158] Agnes Orlow left the considerable sum of £4 to Edward Skinner, so that he might stay at Cambridge, and numerous other provided funds for poor scholars to say masses in their names; the latter must have been a major source of income for fifteenth- and six-teenth-century university masters and students.[159] In 1494 John Benale left £20 per year, a fine living, if either of his sons went to Cambridge or Oxford.[160] Anne Baret, one of Bury's most generous benefactors, provided a trust for poor scholars "to help them in their exhibition to learning . . . so that they be good and honest."[161] John Hedge specified that the funds he left to his sons, should they go to university, be transferred to others if the sons elected to pursue non-academic careers.[162] And there were some, like William Place, who simply left all his money and all his books.[163] In many places in England, secular education would not become widespread until late in the sixteenth century. In Bury St. Edmunds it became common one hundred years earlier.

In many ways, education is symbolic of the townsfolk's attempts to gain autonomy from the abbey. Denied access to the central institutions of executive and judicial power, the burgesses tried to gain control or even create lesser but still important corporations and turn them toward their own needs and ends. These corpo-rations grew increasingly important in secular hands, and added to the town's intrinsic non-monastic attractions. From the mid-fifteenth century at the very latest, immigrants, merchants, and capital were drawn to Bury more by its secular than by its religious attractions. The town was a regional center of complex, multi-faceted significance. But, at the same time, this new corporate in-stitutional power should not be overestimated. Actual control over the most crucial governmental institutions such as appointments of

[158] *Ibid.*, Hoode, f. 15.
[159] *Ibid.*, f. 64.
[160] *Ibid.*, Pye, f. 25.
[161] Tymms, pp. 99-105.
[162] P.C.B.S.E., Pye, f. 146.
[163] Tymms, pp. 105-106.

the bailiffs and control of most of the judicial system was still in the hands of the abbey. Despite its faltering financial fortunes, St. Edmunds remained firmly in control of the most important instruments of power. Direct political action would be necessary before the abbey would loosen its controls.

Chapter Six

THE POLITICAL IMPLICATIONS: THE RISINGS OF THE BURGESSES

The dominant fact of political life in late medieval Bury St. Edmunds was that the Benedictine abbey ran the town; the dominant activity was the struggle of the town's burghal élite to assert their independence. In the early days, until the mid-thirteenth century, the borough owed its prosperity to the presence of St. Edmundsbury, one of the five wealthiest monastic houses in England.[1] But, as I have tried to show, from about the middle part of the thirteenth century, gradually at first and then at an ever-quickening pace, the burgesses who dominated the town began to grow uneasy. And, as their economic power grew, they began to seek corresponding political strength. Had successive abbots and their advisers been more sensitive to the growing economic power and restiveness of the burgesses and gradually loosened some controls over municipal government, Bury's political crises might have been considerably eased. But the abbey establishment remained rigid. Rather than loosen the ties, they tried to tighten them through new restrictive legislation. Frustrated, the townsfolk, led by the aldermen and burgesses, moved to rebellion.[2]

The first confrontations preceded the general political crisis of the later middle ages; they came, indeed, during the halcyon days

[1] There are many studies of the comparative fortunes of English ecclesiastical houses. One of the best is N. M. Trenholme, *The English Monastic Boroughs* (Columbia, Mo.: University of Missouri Studies, 1927), ii, 3. Also of use are: Dugdale; and the various works of D. D. Knowles, especially *The Religious Orders in England*, 2 vols. (Cambridge: Cambridge University Press, 1950-1955).

[2] Two good references to the political development of Bury St. Edmunds that will be consulted throughout this chapter are: A. Goodwin, *The Abbey of St. Edmundsbury* (Oxford: Basil Blackwell, 1931); and Lobel, *The Borough*, pp. 118-170. Also of use is the *V.C.H.*, ii, pp. 56-72, and 157-181.

of Abbot Samson, late in the twelfth century. When in the 1180s and 1190s London merchants claimed to be exempt from all tolls in all local markets throughout England, including Bury, Samson objected.[3] The abbot suspected that if the Londoners could substantiate their claims, their Bury counterparts would press for similar privileges. He resisted strenuously, calling into play all his royal influence. Finally, a compromise was reached between all three parties, and in this early instance serious civil problems were averted. For the next seventy-five years, the abbey remained firmly in control of town government and economy; indeed, by the early thirteenth century, the monks of St. Edmunds had clearly come to regard the borough as existing primarily for their pleasure and convenience. But, in the 1260s, the abbey's complacency was given a severe jolt, and Bury St. Edmunds entered a century of violent confrontation.

The bitter town-abbey troubles of the fourteenth and fifteenth centuries were exacerbated by a general background of social violence. The later middle ages was an era of transition and change, one in which many traditional lay and ecclesiastical institutions were breaking down. Contemporaries bemoaned what they perceived as an enormous upswing in crime.[4] Men often went about their daily activities armed, and when provoked showed considerable inclination toward using their weapons. Bury St. Edmunds proved no exception to these general trends. A sampling of letters patent—

[3] For the economic aspects of this dispute, see above, pp. 85-86. The source is Jocelin, pp. 75-84. Jocelin fascinated Thomas Carlyle, who wrote extensively about him and Samson in his *Past and Present*. The definitive edition is H. E. Butler, ed., *The Chronicle of Jocelin of Brakelond* (New York: Oxford University Press, 1949). Also of use and germane to virtually all references in this chapter are the three volumes of Arnold. Much of the narrative was taken from the *Cronica Buriensis, 1020-1346*; and the *Depradatio Abbatie Sancti Edmundi*, both reprinted therein.

[4] A general survey is J. G. Bellamy, *Crime and Public Order in England in the Later Middle Ages* (London: Routledge and Kegan Paul, 1973). Crime has been the subject of a number of recent studies; one of the newest is Barbara Hanawalt, *Crime and Conflict in English Communities* (Cambridge, Mass.: Harvard University Press, 1979). One authority, Richard Kaeuper, argues that the increased references to crime really reflect changes in the judicial machinery. See his "Law and Order in 14th Century England," *Speculum*, 54, 1979.

and these usually just mention pardons—from the late thirteenth through the early fifteenth century yields 54 homicides in a town whose population in the same period averaged about 4,000.[5] Added to the murder toll were numerous larcenies, burglaries, robberies, rapes, assaults, horse thefts, and rustlings, and other felonies.[6]

The homicides cut across class divisions. Murders were committed in "cold" and "hot" blood. Merchant slew peasant, and peasant slew hunter. Brother killed brother, and father killed son, husband stabbed wife, and wife strangled husband.[7] Nor was crime restricted to lay society. Perhaps the most intriguing of all crimes occurred in the Benedictine abbey. In 1369 three monks—John de Norton, John de Grafton, and William Blundeston—quarrelled among themselves for unknown reasons.[8] That night, as most of the monks slept, Grafton crept through the abbey dormitory and stabbed Norton to death. When the other monks awakened and discovered the body, they panicked. Instead of informing civil or even church authorities, perhaps fearing a scandal at a low ebb in the abbey's popularity, they decided to bury the body without calling in the coroner, a violation of the law. But the body was poorly hidden in a shallow grave in the church cemetery, and Abbot John de Brinkeley soon discovered it. Fearing town reaction, he investigated the crime. Both Grafton and Blundeston were discovered and imprisoned, the latter having acted as an accessory. The imprisonment, however, proved to be a sham. Both men were pardoned by Edward III without ever having been brought to trial, based on the assumption that the crime was committed in "hot blood"; the implication of the pardon is that such violent actions occurred with some regularity. Similar instances of violence and inadequate punish-

[5] The figures were taken by scanning all of the above volumes of the C.P.R. and the C.C.R. from 1272 to 1420.

[6] For the same period noted above the figures were as follows: larceny, 3; burglary, 5; robbery, 11; rape, 10; assault, 13; horse theft, 3. Other pardons included: false oath, gaol break, and smuggling. It is important to remember that these are pardons, and in absolutely no sense make up a "crime rate."

[7] For some examples, see: C.P.R., Edward III, 1340, p. 547; *ibid.*, 1343, p. 15; *ibid.*, 1351, p. 173; *ibid.*, 1363, p. 387; C.P.R., Richard II, 1392, p. 221; and *ibid.*, 1396, p. 696.

[8] C.P.R., Edward III, 1369, p. 186.

ment were common. Men learned that they could take the law into their own hands and, as often as not, avoid the consequences.[9]

It is not surprising, then, that the town-abbey quarrels would eventually erupt into violence. The first major series of riots occurred in 1264, stemming from a charter presented by Samson to the townsfolk in 1194.[10] In it, ancient liberties and customs granted to the abbey by Henry I were confirmed, but custody of the borough and the wardship and watch of the town gates, important for the tolls they yielded and the prestige and symbolism involved in their keep, were given to the town for four gates and the abbey for one. While this appeared to be a major concession, in reality it was a very limited one. The abbot retained power to veto any warder appointments not to his taste, in effect negating the essence of the privilege. Custody of the gates and this veto power were to become the tokens for all future town-abbey conflicts, but they were just two of the sore points. Samson's new charter contained several others. It compelled the burgesses to conduct all their legal affairs in the borough court, the portman-moot, which met in the Tollhouse and was controlled by the abbot, rather than in their own court, meeting in the Guildhall, or the shire or royal courts.[11] This meant that their litigation had to be conducted in front of the portreeve, an appointee of the abbot, and that the profits of justice would accrue to the abbot. In the 1190s, this was resented, but there was little that the burgesses could do. Three generations later, with the burgesses richer, stronger, and more confident, many of them were determined to effect change, one way or another.

The troubles of 1264 began when a group of younger burgesses—"hotheaded," the abbey's chroniclers called them—confronted the abbot, Simon of Luton, with a series of demands.[12] In

[9] Bellamy, *Crime and Public Order*, pp. 89-120. The connection between private and public violence is, of course, rather more complex than this passing allusion allows. See Michel Foucault, *Discipline and Punishment*, trans. Alan Sheridan (New York: Pantheon, 1977).

[10] The best general discussions are: Goodwin, *The Abbey*; Lobel, *The Borough*; and the various chronicles in Arnold. A good source for comparison is Gwyn Williams, *Medieval London* (London: Athlone Press, 1963), pp. 219-242.

[11] Lobel, *The Borough*, pp. 95-117, discusses Bury's court system in some detail. Also, see above, pp. 170-171.

[12] The best description from this point can be found in the chronicles collected in Arnold.

retrospect, these demands appear rather restrained, but to Simon they were a threat to the very foundations of his rule, and he was determined to resist them. Their gist was that the burgesses and citizenry of Bury, in essence the borough's upper crust, be recognized as a corporate secular guild or horn, in which all power over town secular affairs would be vested. For a time, the young rebels were successful; acting quickly, they took over municipal control and restricted the monks to the abbey. But, notwithstanding their energetic efforts, the revolt of 1264 was doomed to failure because of hesitant and sporadic support from those who had the greatest influence, the older burgesses. Abbot Simon reacted to the takeover promptly, appealing to the Crown for a commission of inquiry into the guild's demands. The mere threat of such a commission was sufficient to frighten the senior burgesses into action against their younger colleagues. Fearing that their existing privileges might be compromised or even abrogated, they withdrew even token support, and the horn was dissolved. The senior burgesses then entered into conference with the abbot, and agreed to pay a fine of £40 silver in damages for violation of the abbey's ancient prerogatives. Thus, in 1264, as in the 1190s, it appeared as though the abbey had won a resounding victory. But, while its privileges remained intact, considerable damage had been done. For one, the young burgesses had shown how simple it was to threaten and intimidate the monks. And, second, they had set a precedent for violent action, one that was to be repeated several times in the course of the later middle ages.

The next town-abbey conflict erupted in 1292.[13] It concerned the custody and control of the town gates, now clearly the symbols of the struggle. But this time another issue was involved, a more fundamental one concerning the right of the burgesses to elect their own alderman without the abbot's interference. In 1292 physical confrontation was limited to a few isolated incidents, and the issue was settled in a compromise. The burgesses were now to gather once a year at Michaelmas to hold elections, selecting the alderman and bailiffs from among the leading citizens of town, and choosing four persons to be keepers for all the gates vested to town control. The abbot was to have veto power over the choices, but

[13] As with the events of 1264, the best detailed descriptions can be found in Goodwin, *The Abbey*; Lobel, *The Borough*; and Arnold.

beyond that ultimate selection rested with the citizens. The burgesses had made their initial inroad into abbey power.

As Bury St. Edmunds' social and economic growth continued
unabated in the fourteenth century, troubles flared up again. In
1305 there was another confrontation, which was solved only
through royal intervention.[14] The abbot charged that the alderman
and chief burgesses had withheld fines and tolls due him, and
resisted monastic officials when they tried to collect them. Less
important financially but perhaps more significant symbolically, the
abbot also charged that certain men and women had stoned the
roofs of abbey buildings, causing considerable damage, and then
harrassed workmen trying to make repairs. Further, he claimed
that certain monks had been assaulted while carrying out their civic
duties, especially rent collections. Royal officials were eventually
called in, the settlement being implemented along lines similar to
those of 1292. But, the settlement aside, the troubles of 1305 left
a bitter legacy. Physical harassment of the monks continued, and
as late as 1314 certain townsmen were fined £200 for taking arms
against the king's bailiffs, beating monks in town, and bothering
work crews as they repaired the fabric of the abbey. The bitterness
of the long-term struggle was intensified by the more general political problems of early fourteenth century England, and would
erupt in 1327 in the greatest of all town-abbey conflicts.

The events of 1327-1328 were also complicated by an internecine
church conflict dating from the thirteenth century.[15] Almost immediately after its establishment in England in the 1220s, the Franciscan order attempted to settle its friars in a house in Bury. This
was vigorously resisted by the Benedictine monks, who feared en-
croachment on their long-standing privileges, and for a few years
the friars were banned.[16] But the Franciscans were persistent and
appealed to Pope Alexander IV, who gave them special dispen-
sation to settle within the abbot's liberty. The friars finally entered
Bury in 1257, planting themselves on a farm within Northgate.

[14] *Ibid.*

[15] In addition to the references listed in note 10, see: M. D. Lobel, "A
Detailed Account of the 1327 Rising at Bury St. Edmunds and the Subsequent Trials," *P.S.I.*, xxi, 3, 1933; and N. M. Trenholme, "The Rising
in English Monastic Towns in 1327," *The American Historical Review*, vi,
1905.

[16] Knowles, *The Religious Orders*, is another source of information on the
Benedictine-Franciscan quarrel.

Abbey officials continued to balk at their presence, however, and within a few weeks expelled them once again, papal objections notwithstanding. The Franciscans made yet another appeal to the pope, who stood firm in his support. Because the Bishop of Norwich, who had local jurisdiction, was reputed to be in league with the abbot, Alexander enjoined the neighboring Bishop of Lincoln to help the Grey Friars to find a suitable house in the borough. A tenement was rented, but the monks remained adamant in their opposition. They annoyed the friars continually and late in 1257 literally drove them and the episcopal legates from Lincoln out of town.

The Franciscans remained determined. Having failed to gain satisfaction from pope or bishop, they resorted to a new strategy: appeal to the king. Again the friars were successful; Henry III, urged on by Queen Eleanor, who was sympathetic to the entire mendicant movement, ordered that the Franciscans be reinstalled in Bury under royal protection. Back to Bury went the friars, this time raising their own buildings to avoid added rents from the abbey. They managed to stay for a few years, but in 1261 their patron, Pope Alexander, died, and was replaced by Urban IV. For reasons that are unclear, after Urban received a delegation of Benedictines from St. Edmunds, he ordered the Franciscans to pull down their buildings and leave town. This they did in November 1262, never to return. But the Franciscans still had royal support, and were determined to establish themselves somewhere in West Suffolk. Eventually a compromise was worked out, and the friars were permitted to erect new buildings at the village of Babwell, just outside the northern cross of the Banleuca. On the surface, all seemed well, and there was limited cooperation between the orders. But mutual resentment continued to simmer, especially among the Grey Friars, who remained locked out of civic affairs, and could enter the borough only with the abbey's permission. They gradually began to take the townsfolk's side in their conflicts with the abbey.

Another factor in the intra-church dissension was the resentment against the Benedictines felt by secular clerics, primarily rectors with livings, who resided in Bury St. Edmunds. They too were treated by the abbey monks as second-class ecclesiastical citizens, and tended in any crisis to side with the townsmen. In effect, the burgesses were generally able to find energetic and articulate clerical allies to help their cause. Added to this were a series of self-inflicted woes within St. Edmunds itself. Increasingly, the Benedictines were straying from their vows and misusing their privileges. It may well have been that, from the thirteenth century, fewer recruits had the true monastic vocation, but, whatever the cause, matters had deteriorated sufficiently so that when the revolt of 1327-1328 erupted, thirty-two monks out of a total of eighty were away from the abbey "*praedicto fuerent extra ad spatiandum per diversa loca. . . .*"[17]

The 1327-1328 revolt coincided with the political troubles of the reign of Edward II. In September 1326 Queen Isabella, her paramour Roger Mortimer, and the king's son Prince Edward landed on the River Orwell, and began the process that would end with the deposition and murder of the king. From this stemmed chaos and disorder, which spread throughout the realm. It is likely that people in Bury heard of the political troubles quite early, since East Anglia was a crossroads for travellers coming to and from the Low Countries, and because Isabella and Mortimer came via nearby Orwell. But, ultimately, the disturbances in Bury were touched off by news of a series of riots in another monastic town, Abingdon.

The outbreak began on 15 January 1327.[18] A mob reported at 3,000 strong (almost certainly too high a figure, since it would have required most of the town's adult population) began to mill around the abbey gates. It grew restless, and then, whipped up by agitators alleged to have been villeins and the "baser" elements of the town—as contrasted with the young burgesses of 1264—attacked the abbey. They easily broke through the gates opposite Cooks' Row, and began to loot. The more headstrong sought out the monks themselves, seizing and beating about a dozen, including the prior and several of his assistants. The rooms of the sacrist, the abbey's liaison with the townsmen, and those of the chamberlain were broken into and sacked. By the next morning nine more hapless monks had been rounded up and imprisoned, the convent's treasury repeatedly raided, and the town charters taken from the abbey vaults and secured in the Guildhall.

The rebels held the upper hand for several months. In the early heady January days, leadership passed from the villein rabble-rousers to the senior burgesses, who had been unwilling participants

[17] Arnold, iii, p. 39. This might loosely be translated as: "in the country at the time, on holiday."

[18] Dugdale; and Yates, *History and Antiquities*, provide additional information on the events of the revolt.

in 1264. They named as alderman the merchant John de Berton, and did not submit his name to the abbey for final approval.[19] De Berton's first act, perhaps in order to secure support of the mob, was to authorize another pillaging foray inside the abbey, specifically directed against the abbot's personal treasury, which as yet had not been touched. Bury's inhabitants were clearly in an anti-monastic mood, and de Berton, who was to prove an opportunist and something of a scoundrel, was quite prepared to play to their whims. He summarily cancelled all debts, and, more importantly, rents due the abbey, of great significance since everyone in town owed something to the abbot and his officers. He also completed the secular takeover of all aspects of Bury's municipal government, excluding the abbot from any role. In the meantime, the violence continued. Anti-monastic feeling ran so high that a group of monks travelling past the town on the road south to London were stopped, robbed, and beaten, although they had no connection with the abbey. De Berton and his rebels took over custody and collections at all town gates, including East Gate, which had always been the special prerogative of the abbot, and periodically permitted new forays into the various treasuries of the partially ruined abbey complex. The monks were completely intimidated by the physical violence of the town mob, which de Berton seemed able to incite at will. He set up a block complete with headsmen and axe in the Great Market, and in a short time, through persuasion, threats, and intimidation, won the support of virtually everyone in Bury St. Edmunds.

During the first days of the crisis, Abbot Richard de Draughton was in London attending Parliament. When news of the rebellion reached him, he hastily returned to Bury, arriving in town on the 28th of January. De Draughton was a competent and forceful man, and de Berton and his henchmen did not welcome him. On 29 January the two antagonists met within the abbey gates, and de Berton presented the abbot with a charter of rebel demands, which if approved would have ended all monastic control over municipal government. De Draughton perforce acquiesced.

The Charter of 1327 marks a crucial point in the political relationship of town and abbey.[20] Despite the laments of monastic ob-

---

[19] For a detailed discussion of the life of John de Berton, see M. D. Lobel, "A Detailed Account."

[20] The entire charter is reprinted in Arnold, iii, pp. 302-318.

servers, it was, like the Charter of 1264, fairly restrained in its demands, the result of the caution of the senior burgesses, who had a vested interest in preserving their positions at the top of the existing social order. These men wanted to be free of monastic controls, but restraint now might mean lasting benefits later, in case the rebels were overthrown. The charter provided special privileges to the alderman, no doubt on account of the personal abilities and ambitions of the rebel leader de Berton. The alderman was to be made completely independent of monastic constraints, and to hold powers similar to those of the mayor of London. He would be elected by the burgesses, the leading lights of the town, and the concept of a single, independent merchant guild-horn of the great burgesses was to be implemented on the model of 1264. The townsfolk were to control all gates, and the tolls and privileges connected with them. The old system of town labor and monastic finance in maintaining the fabrice of Bury was retained, but any profits realized now accrued to the former rather than to the latter. The alderman was authorized to levy indirect taxes on merchandise traded throughout the town, and given considerable powers over the disposition of property of orphans, wards, and widows. Perhaps most important for the bulk of Bury's landholders, payments on lands liable to *hadgoval*, the old Anglo-Saxon hearth tax/ground rent due the abbey on virtually all property in town, were to be carefully monitored and kept within reasonable limits.[21] Significantly, *hadgoval* was not abolished; here again the innate conservatism of the burgesses can be seen. They were reluctant to abolish all income or privilege connected with landed wealth, for, if the abbey's property privileges were abrogated, theirs might next be called into question by the unprivileged mob.

There were other important parts to the charter. Besides the restraints on raising *hadgoval* assessments, the power to distrain goods of debtors was taken from the abbot and vested with the alderman and burgesses. No longer could the abbot's bailiffs seize the townsmen's houses if debts were not paid. None of these changes might be described as radical, because all of them left the vast holdings of the abbey intact throughout the banleuca. Land was wealth, and no attempts were ever made to encroach on the

[21] For additional information on *hadgoval* tenure, see Lobel, *The Borough*, pp. 7-9, 54-55.

abbey's patrimony, the one action which would have truly engendered "radical" change.

There were other clauses in the 1327 charter concerning property that reflected the upper-class, proprietary bent of the charter. A burgess who held any property or land within the borough for a year and a day without challenge was considered to have vested rights to it. The alderman and burgesses were to have physical possession of the town muniments and charter, which had formerly been held by the abbot and used as leverage to keep the townsmen at bay. The abbot was enjoined to provide sanctuary within the abbey, a traditional duty, but obviously one that the abbot was not consistently performing if the rebels felt the need to force formal approval. The charter also contained a series of economic demands that reflected the commercial orientation of the burgesses. It is worth reiterating that the 1327 charter was a conservative list of grievances, reflecting the interests of a propertied class, and in no way impinged upon the major endowments of St. Edmunds.[22] The traditional authority of the abbot and his officers was consistently upheld, and the fundamental right of the abbey to hold its power and privileges was never questioned. Basically, the burgesses were conservative businessmen looking for a larger personal share of the borough's wealth through a reduction of their financial obligations to the abbey.

The acceptance of the charter by de Draughton and his monks, albeit under duress, and its ratification by seal of the town warden, satisfied the burgesses, but there were still the personal ambitions of John de Berton and the whims of the mob to be dealt with. Meanwhile, de Draughton saw that he was helpless in Bury, and managed to slip out and make his way back to London. There he proceeded up river to Parliament, declaring before its members the misdeeds of the rebels, and claiming that his approval of the charter was non-binding because it was given under duress. Word of his actions filtered back to de Berton, who was furious. He raised the mob again, and turned them loose on the abbey. On 16 February, men described as villeins looted and pillaged the dormitories and wardrobes, and then paraded through the Great Market displaying their wares. This was sufficient to inspire more looting, until a mob described as thousands rampaged through the shat-

[22] This point is made by several observers, including Arnold, Dugdale, and Yates, the historian of the abbey.

tered abbey. Many looted for material gain, and brought carts to the abbey gates so that they might carry away more; others were just malicious, such as those who destroyed the conduits that brought fresh water into the abbey complex.

There are no records of activity in Bury St. Edmunds from February to May.[23] Presumably, de Berton and his burgesses restrained the mob after the February rioting had run its course, and continued to exercise real power while the mob was satisfied with its material bonanza. But, in May, violence erupted again. On the 19th, the abbey was sacked, this time with a new twist. Now it was not de Berton who incited the mob but the Franciscan friars from Babwell and the secular priests. The front doors of Bury's parish churches, St. Mary's and St. James's, inlaid and valuable, were ripped off and carried away. Most of the jewels went to the secular clerics, who claimed that their stipends were too miserable to live on, and that the abbey allowed them no rights in the town. Old frictions between secular clerics, friars, and townsmen were forgotten as all took revenge on the Benedictines. The burgesses even asked the secular priests to minister to the shrines of St. Edmund, as they had done three hundred years earlier, before the coming of the monks. Everyone saw the abbey, that arrogant *rentier*, as the common enemy.

By the spring of 1327, the monks remaining in the abbey had lived through a nightmarish series of events. They had seen their prerogatives and material wealth gradually whittled down, and they decided to resist. In mid-May, the young monks and their servants organized, armed, and sallied forth from the abbey to attack the mob. The monks fought well but were badly outnumbered and had to give way; in retaliation, part of the mob ransacked and burned the abbey church. The Benedictines' next effort was hardly more successful. Emissaries were sent to Abbot de Draughton, now comfortably situated in London, asking for aid; he in turn sent an envoy to Avignon for papal help. Unfortunately, the messengers never got there; they were said to have died on the road, though no causes of death were recorded. De Draughton planned to send another delegation, but news got back to the burgesses, who sent their own delegation of secular priests to the pope. They arrived

[23] The best information on this mysterious period can be pieced together from the chronicles in Arnold.

before the abbot's men, and were able to convince John XXII to support the town's position.

In the meantime, the monks continued to suffer at the hands of the mob. Tithes, offerings, and rents continued to be withheld, and any monk who ventured into the town was likely to face verbal or physical abuse. Several monks, unable to endure the strain, slipped out of Bury, further reducing the already depleted ranks. There appeared no end to the abbey's plight. The sheriff of Norfolk and Suffolk, Sir Robert Morley, attempted to settle the dispute, but, with the dynastic crisis, there was no royal authority to send troops. The deposition of Edward II and the minority of Edward III created a leadership void, and the rebels, aware of the sheriff's weakness, refused all pleas for negotiation and compromise.

Through the summer of 1327, the burgesses set about fortifying the town walls and solidifying their internal position. In the autumn, de Berton unleashed the mob again. The bells from the Tollhouse and the parish church of St. James were rung, calling for assembly at the ruins of the abbey's great gates. De Berton harangued them, and again they headed into the shattered abbey complex. More of the fabrice was set afire and destroyed. This time the mob turned on several non-abbatial structures in the complex, sacking and burning such buildings as Bradfield, the king's house in Bury St. Edmunds. Several outbuildings were burned, including the abbot's stables, after the horses had been rustled. And, with the abbey smoldering, the looters turned to the roofs, carrying away as much of the lead as was possible.

The remaining monks again responded vigorously and with courage. They gathered the remaining servants, who must have been a very loyal group, and armed them. Once again they led a series of sorties outside the gates to try to relieve the pressure on them, but were outnumbered and decisively beaten back. And, once again, the mob took revenge. With the abbey in near ruins, they concentrated on other tangible aspects of St. Edmunds' wealth in the banleuca. Since it was autumn, the barns were stuffed with grain, and were raided several times. Cattle were rustled, and unharvested crops stolen from the fields. Even the abbey ruins were not immune; in October a new raiding expedition sifted through whatever of value remained. John de Berton continued to dominate the mob and the burgesses. After the October raid, he summoned all the remaining monks, perhaps a score, to a meeting in St. Mary's Church. Stung by their continued resistance and recalcitrance, he

told them he wanted all monks restricted to a single place, where-
upon he had his retainers seize and imprison them. Now there was
no authority left in the abbey, and the mob moved in yet again. All
abbey lands in the banleuca and many of the abbot's twenty-two
manors in West Suffolk were pillaged. So extensive was the damage
that the grange alone allegedly suffered £1200 in losses. Lands of
lesser abbey officials were rifled, and the looting extended even to
the estates of erstwhile friendly and semi-supportive institutions,
such as the Hospital of St. Saviour, which suffered damages to-
talling £800.

In the autumn of 1327, things looked bleakest for the abbey.
Dramatically, the situation changed almost overnight. In November, Pope John, who a few months earlier had rejected the abbot's
entreaties for support, reversed himself. He backed de Draughton,
and excommunicated all those who had taken part in the riots and
violated the sanctuary of the abbey—that is to say, all who took part
in the looting, which must have included virtually every able-bodied
adult in town. Only the thirty wealthiest burgesses and their families
were exempted, perhaps in anticipation of fines.[24]

Now de Draughton had the spiritual sanction he wanted; material
and military support followed later in the month. The political
situation in England had begun to stabilize with the formation of
a royal council around the new king. De Draughton was able to
procure a royal writ directed to Robert Morley, the sheriff, and
John Howard, a prominent East Anglia landholder, ordering them
to raise an army, reestablish the abbot, and quell any more disturbances. At the sight of armed soldiers marching to their walls,
the burgesses surrendered without a fight. Thirty carts were needed
to carry the arrested townsmen to Norwich, where they were to
stand trial for treason before four royally appointed special justices.
All the accused, including the leaders, John de Berton and his
principal henchman, Gilbert Barbour, were convicted of treason
and imprisoned, and damages on monastic property ordered assessed, so that the townsfolk could pay compensation.

By the end of 1327, it appeared as though a year's rioting and

[24] This seems to have been a fairly common practice. Further infor-
mation can be found in: R. H. Snape, *English Monastic Finances in the Later
Middle Ages* (Cambridge: Cambridge University Press, 1926); and E. Savine,
English Monasteries on the Eve of Dissolution (Oxford: Oxford University
Press, 1909).

looting were over, with the abbot again triumphant and the *status quo* restored. But there was to be another chapter. Early in 1328 de Berton and Barbour escaped from their gaol, possibly aided by the Franciscan friars at Babwell, in whose house they took sanctuary. Now the ringleaders were free, within two miles of the abbey gates, and untouchable by the sheriff and the Benedictines. De Berton and Barbour stayed in sanctuary through the winter, spring, and summer of 1328. In August events took a new turn; the notorious outlaw Thomas Thornham came to Bury with his criminal band. Abbot de Draughton implored the townsfolk to lock the gates against the bandits, but they did not; instead, they opened them and provided a hero's welcome, complete with ceremonial procession through Risby Gate. Emboldened by this greeting, Thornham and his band feasted in the marketplace and then took up residence in Moyses Hall, the finest house in Bury. An armed party from the abbey sent to arrest them was attacked and scattered by a mixed band of outlaws and townsfolk, the latter still enraged by their defeat the previous year and by the resultant indemnity payments.

Encouraged by the mob's reëmergence, de Berton and Barbour decided that the time had come for action. Leaving their sanctuary, they were joined in town by a prominent burgess, Richard Froisel, some members of the Thornham gang, other men described as London outlaws, and two women from Bury. The group then marched to Chevington, about five miles southwest of Bury. They seized Richard de Draughton, and split up, one part of the band returning to Bury to raid the abbot's house in his absence. The other group, led by de Berton, stuffed the poor abbot into a sack, and smuggled him to London to the house of one John Coterel of Wood Street, possibly affiliated with the infamous outlaw band led by a Coterel of the same Christian name, which operated in the Peak District.[25] To avoid detection, they moved de Draughton from one house to another with the help of some prominent Londoners, including the famous fishmonger, Haimo Chigwell.[26] Chigwell ap-

[25] Details of the Londoners' role in the Bury uprising can be found in Williams, *Medieval London*, pp. 296-302. Neither Williams nor S. L. Thrupp, *The Merchant Class of Medieval London* (Chicago: University of Chicago Press, 1948), pp. 321-327, include Coterel in their appendices of important London people.

[26] Chigwell is a fascinating character, serving as an alderman and perhaps mayor of London. His will was enrolled in the Hustings Court of London in 1333, and provides personal information.

pears to have been in on the plot from the outset, and apparently on his suggestion it was decided to move the abbot from London to Dover, and then across the Channel to Diest, in Brabant. There de Draughton was hidden through the winter of 1329, while his captors laid plans to demand a ransom for his safety.

Meanwhile, a new series of disturbances had erupted in Bury. Although Thornham and the bulk of his gang left Bury by late 1328, the town was infected with a "criminal spirit."[27] In December men described as "criminous clerks," imprisoned for their roles in the great revolt, broke the town prison and headed west. They tried to make their way to Cambridge, hoping perhaps to find refuge among the student population, but most were taken and returned to the Bury gaol. There were a few additional street demonstrations outside the abbey gates, but the complex itself was not stormed. The violent aspects of the revolt had come to an end by late December 1328.

By January 1329 the tide of events had turned inexorably in the abbey's favor. The Archbishop of Canterbury, Simon Meopham, followed the pope in excommunicating all those alleged to have participated in the abduction of the still-missing Abbot de Draughton. Further, Edward III authorized a commission of four justices to investigate the kidnapping. It quickly bore fruit, uncovering the complicity of the Londoners Coterel and Chigwell. Coterel was brought before a jury in February 1329 and charged with committing robbery and "outrage" on the abbot. Found guilty, he was imprisoned for a time in the Tower of London, and finally hanged. Haimo Chigwell was more fortunate; he claimed and received benefit of clergy, and with his considerable wealth and well-placed friends managed to obtain complete acquittal. But de Draughton was still missing, and neither demand for ransom nor news of his whereabouts was forthcoming. The pope reiterated his ban of excommunication, but this too failed to pry the abbot from his captors. The mystery was to remain unsolved until April 1329, when, through an extensive network of royal spies and friendly clerics, de Draughton was discovered in his prison in Brabant. Little is known about the circumstances of his rescue, but it appears that his gaolers—and it is not clear as to whether they included de Berton or Barbour—were convinced by local authorities to release the abbot unharmed, without a shilling's payment in ransom. Per-

[27] Arnold, ii, pp. 349-350.

haps de Draughton was being held in remission of the £14,000 penalty which had been levied on the town. In any case, Richard de Draughton was back in Bury late in 1329, and remained as abbot until his death in 1334.[28]

The town-abbey troubles of 1327-1328 were temporarily laid to rest with a peace treaty in 1331.[29] The burgesses and abbot agreed that the town was to pay a fine of £14,000 over an extended period of time. This sum was staggering, probably in excess of the liquid wealth of the entire town, and it may well have been assessed only as a warning against future risings. This is implicit in the method of payment. Once 50 marks of the fine were collected, the defendants, in effect the entire town, were to receive a letter of quittance. The townsmen were not to be hindered in any way by ecclesiastical agents in collecting the fine, and at the same time had to pledge not to try to renegotiate its sum in another, presumably royal, court in hopes of securing lesser payment. If all these conditions were met in good faith, £10,000 of the fine was to be forgiven. Yet, from the town fathers' perspective, the settlement had one favorable feature. The methods of raising the money were not specified. Hence, the burghal élite might exempt themselves, or at the very least, pay less than their fair share, and squeeze all they could from the middling- and lower-income-level townsmen. In all, the settlement proved acceptable for the two elements that counted most, the abbot and the burgesses. Such was the course of the greatest of town-abbey conflicts. In 1332, with the Charter of 1327 revoked, it seemed quite futile, despite the ephemeral triumphs of a few years earlier. Once again, the abbey seemed to have won total victory. But an important legacy of violence was confirmed, and the mob was to take to the barricades once again.

The last major uprising came in the fateful year of 1381. England was swept up in its most famous medieval insurrection, the Peasants'

[28] There is considerable mystery over the fate of de Berton and Barbour. In her article, "A Detailed Account," Lobel cites the *Brevis Chronica*, reprinted in Arnold, which claims that de Berton was captured, tried in the Bury Tollhouse, and imprisoned in the borough gaol, where he later died. No comment or connection on his role in the kidnapping is discussed, and, as Lobel recognizes, the reference is a questionable one. Ultimately, there is no firm evidence as to the fate of either conspirator.

[29] The provisions of the settlement are discussed in detail in Arnold, ii, pp. 327-354, and 357-361.

Revolt.[30] Smouldering over their lords' attempts to reimpose pre-Black Death labor obligations, banalities, and wage levels, and disenchanted with the ruling clique surrounding the boy king Richard II, the peasants of eastern England, from Lincolnshire to Kent, rose in revolt in the spring of 1381. The immediate cause was the attempt of royal tax farmers to collect the third poll tax in four years. In Kent and Essex thousands of men and women, led by Wat Tyler and John Ball, the latter a vagrant priest, marched to London with vague notions of seeing their king, and clearer visions of the potential loot.

In East Anglia the leader of the revolt was alleged to be Jack Wrawe, and the Abbey of St. Edmundsbury, rich and resented, proved to be a favorite target for the rebels from throughout the region. Since the 1332 settlement, the abbey had fallen on hard times. In 1345 a special episcopal commission complained of scandalous immorality among the Benedictine monasteries of England, and singled out the abbey of St. Edmunds as one of the worst offenders. The abbot, William of Bernham, surely the least competent of all late medieval leaders of the abbey, objected and denied the charges to the Bishop of Norwich.[31] But his protests were rejected and the reputation of the abbey was severely tarnished. St. Edmunds' problems were compounded by the Black Death and subsequent era of depopulation. The abbey entered a period of economic hardship, as prices for its agricultural commodities fell and wages for its laborers rose. Income declined, but the abbey failed to cut back on expenses, which produced a financial shortfall that would persist into the sixteenth century. In addition to these economic misfortunes, the abbey once again had internal political troubles. The monks were divided by a bitterly disputed election.

[30] The best national coverage can be found in Charles Oman, *The Great Revolt of 1381* (New York: Haskell House Reprints, 2nd ed., 1968). Also worthwhile are: R. H. Hilton, *Bondsmen Made Free* (London: David Charles, 1973); and André Reville, *Le Soulèvement des Travailleurs d' Angleterre* (Paris, 1898). The best regional study is Edgar Powell, *The Rising in East Anglia in 1381* (Cambridge: Cambridge University Press, 1896). Local Bury aspects are covered in most of the books listed above, and in more detail by Lobel, in her *The Borough*; and "Some Additions to André Reville's Account of Events at Bury St. Edmunds following the Revolt of 1381," *P.S.I.*, xxi, 3, 1933; and Godwin, *The Abbey*.

[31] This assessment is not shared by all authorities. See Goodwin, *The Abbey*, pp. 56-57.

During the 1379 voting for abbacy, two factions developed. The pope nominated the proctor-general of the Benedictine order in England, Edward Bromfeld, but, before the pope's decision reached them, the monks had selected one of their own, the sub-prior, John Tymworth. Bromfeld had close connections with some of the leading burgesses in Bury, and this, coupled with their traditional opposition to any candidate favored by the monks, caused the townsfolk to rally behind the proctor-general. The alderman, Thomas Halesworth, claimed to be Bromfeld's cousin, and reviving memories of past injustices, managed to assemble Bury's ever-ready mob and win the support of the Alderman's Guild of leading merchants. Bromfeld came to Bury and pledged to make major concessions if he were allowed to take the abbacy. This was all the mob needed to hear; they reinitiated their old practice of physical pressure and harassment of the monks, and effectively prevented Tymworth from becoming abbot. The dispute simmered for a number of years, and would not end until it was discovered that Bromfeld was a felon, having earlier committed an offense against the Statute of Provisors. In time, he would be imprisoned and his supporters fined, but in 1381 this lay in the future. That year, Tymworth was still effectively barred from assuming his office, and the name of Edward Bromfeld served as a rallying cry. Meanwhile, leadership of St. Edmunds was in the hands of the prior, John de Cambridge, a well-meaning but inept muddler during the best of times, and quite helpless in a crisis.

On 14 June, 1381, Jack Wrawe entered Bury and led a band of peasants and townsmen down Cooks' Row to the Great Gates of the abbey, repaired in the 1340s and 1350s. Upon hearing of Wrawe's entry into the borough, de Cambridge and several other monks fled; those who remained wisely decided not to resist, and the rebels sacked and looted, following the pattern of behavior of earlier generations. With Wrawe at the head, the mob made its way to the townhouse of Sir John Cavendish, the king's chief justice. Like de Cambridge, Cavendish had fled in advance of the rioters, and his empty house was also pillaged and burned. Meanwhile, Wrawe sent bands of men to scour the countryside to try to find the fugitive officials. Cavendish, personally disliked and considered the symbol of the unpopular royal regency, was hunted down and captured near Mildenhall. He was hacked to death and decapitated on the spot, his head placed on a pike, carried back to Bury, and put on display in the Great Market. The rebels were initially less successful with de Cambridge. The prior managed to elude his pursuers for several days, but was finally betrayed by his guide, and taken in woodlands outside New Market, on the road to Cambridge. After a mock trial, de Cambridge suffered the same death as Cavendish; his head was then taken back to the borough and placed next to that of the chief justice. In a macabre twist of humor, one of the rebels took the heads of Cavendish and de Cambridge, and turned them so that the mouth of the former was opened and placed next to the latter's ear.

As in the earlier part of the century, things looked bleak for the abbey. Those few monks who had always supported Edward Bromfeld came to the fore, and for a few short weeks dominated St. Edmunds. Intimidated, the rest of the monastic community quickly acceded to the demands of the rebels. These were much the same as those of their predecessors, who wanted additional autonomy in commercial and industrial activities. And, like their predecessors, the 1381 rebels broke into the abbey complex, looted it, and beat up as many monks as they could find. The Charter of 1327, revoked in the 1331 settlement, was revived, and all charters and muniments pertaining to the town were again taken from the abbey's treasury and placed in the Guildhall. Without an abbot, and with their prior's head on a stake in the marketplace, the frightened monks made no attempt to repeat their resistance of 1327.

The rebels' triumphs proved to be shortlived. They were based on a temporary breakdown of regional and royal power, and, as soon as that power was restored, their efforts were doomed. Regular troops were raised in the spring, and by summer 1381 the Peasants' Revolt had been put down throughout England. In East Anglia, the instrument for restoration was Henry Despenser, the warlike bishop of Norwich, who personally led his forces in the field.[32] On 23 June his army appeared at the gates of Bury St. Edmunds, and the burgesses, always first concerned with their own necks and pocketbooks, ceased to support the rebellion, and surrendered the rebel leader Wrawe. After an elaborate staged trial, in which he vainly tried to turn king's evidence, Wrawe was convicted and given the traitor's death—hanging, disembowelment, emasculation, drawing and quartering. By the end of the summer, all prominent rebel leaders had been captured and dealt with.

[32] Henry Despenser's role in quelling the revolt has been described in detail in the monographs listed above, note 30.

Once again, the townsfolk were compelled to pay for their transgressions. The terms of the 1381 settlement were especially severe.[33] All reenacted provisos of the 1327 charter were unequivocally rejected, the monks claiming that they had agreed to it under duress. A fine of 2,000 marks was levied, 1,500 of which was eventually collected. The collection process itself is of some interest because it illustrates the tensions that existed within the borough. The burghal élite, the only strata of townsmen with whom the abbot dealt, were charged with appointing from their ranks a commission of twenty-four to supervise the payments. Headed by the alderman and his bailiffs, the twenty-four were themselves clearly intent on contributing as little as possible, despite their position as commercial and political leaders.[34] They directed their agents to sweep down on the houses of the lesser folk and carry off as much in movables as possible. So outraged were the poor that they appealed to the king's sergeant, who appointed special bailiffs to supervise the tax farmers. Two of Bury's most prominent burgesses, John Bernard and Geoffrey of Middleton, then broke ranks with the twenty-four and supported the lesser folks' demands, until Richard II himself finally intervened. By 1385, when most of the fines and indemnities had been paid off, the burden of payment had been so redistributed that the burghal élite were forced to contribute their fair share.

The rising of 1381 was the last major physical confrontation between the abbey and the burgesses. Violence was unnecessary in fifteenth-century resistance because the townsfolk were in an increasingly strong position. For the remaining 158 years of monastic presence, confrontations were generally restricted to words and to legal battles. Overall levels of animosity did not diminish, nor did the townsfolk lose interest in gaining autonomy, but the burgesses changed their approach.[35] Bury St. Edmunds was getting richer, and, while a series of able abbots, especially William Curteys, strengthened its political, administrative, and moral fiber, the com-

[33] For the full circumstances of the settlement, see Arnold, iii, pp. 177-182.

[34] They were Roger Rose, alderman, and James Marham and Edward Lucas, bailiffs; none has been discussed in Chapter 4. For additional information, see J. C. Ford, *The Aldermen and Mayors of Bury St. Edmunds from 1302* (Bound and compiled by the author: West Suffolk Record Office, Bury St. Edmunds, no date).

[35] Trenholme, *English Monastic Boroughs*; and Lobel, *The Borough*, provide information on post-1381 friction.

parative fortunes of St. Edmunds continued to falter. The disparity
between abbey and town grew smaller and smaller, the burgesses'
confidence grew accordingly, and they concentrated on improving
their *de facto* rather than *de jure* privileges. Existing guilds were
consolidated and expanded, with some, like the weavers and linendrapers, seeking and obtaining royal sanction for their charters.[36]
The borough's corporate groups now had money to pay for greater
prerogatives, which abbey and Crown, ever strapped for cash,
found hard to resist. Some difficulties arose during the troubled
reign of Henry VI, and there were a series of litigations in the
royal courts during the 1480s and 1490s.[37] But by the late fifteenth
century, with the town's economic position approaching a peak,
the trend was clear; the burgesses had triumphed.[38] When Dissolution came in 1539, the abbey was but a shadow of its former self,
holding less than half the tenements in town and needing only a
gentle push to topple its tottering frame.

There was considerable irony in the course of the town-abbey
struggle from the mid-thirteenth to mid-sixteenth centuries. Through
the thirteenth and fourteenth centuries, townsmen took to the barricades and battled for what they perceived as their just due; they
believed that the town existed as much for their glorification as it
did for the abbey's. They won brief and bloody battles, but inevitably lost the wars. It was only when Bury St. Edmunds began to
develop economically that it would forge ahead politically. When
the burgesses gained a larger share of the town's wealth and could
purchase privileges from abbey and king, they found ready takers.
Ultimately, it was the shilling rather than the club that won freedom. Irony is equally evident for the abbey's part. While firmly in
control, abbey officers never considered compromise. Despite the
violence, actual demands from Bury's rebels were rather restrained,
never threatening the abbey's rents or control of property in the
banleuca. Had the abbey been less rapacious, had it loosened its
reins ever so slightly, its end may well have been the same, but the
transition to secular municipal power would have been far less
violent.

[36] The text is in Arnold, iii, pp. 358-368.
[37] Goodwin, *The Abbey*, pp. 65-81. In 1480, the burgesses took the abbot
to court over several commercial questions, and lost on every one. There
were many other such cases in the 1490s, all once again won by the abbey.
[38] In 1528, a rising of "poor men" took place, but, as Lobel has indicated,
it was directed primarily against the Crown. For details, see Lobel, *The
Borough*, p. 167.

Chapter Seven

THE DISSOLUTION OF THE ABBEY
AND THE TRANSFER OF POWER

Dating can present serious problems for historians, but selecting a terminal point for this study was obvious. In 1539 Henry VIII dissolved the Abbey of St. Edmunds as part of his reformation of the English church. Good records survive that show the state of the abbey in its last two decades. It was clearly in decline, with only 60 monks in residence, as compared with over 80 during its thirteenth-early-fourteenth-century peak. Further, of the 60, only 44 were deemed sufficiently worthy to be pensioned off by the Crown. The level and value of pious bequests from private secular donors had been dropping from about 1500, and income from the landed endowment had also fallen. To make things worse, when dissolution did come in 1539, the abbey was in the midst of a serious plague epidemic.[1] In all, St. Edmunds was in poor shape in the 1530s. But it had experienced hard times before, and had always been able to recover. It might well have been able to come back once again if expenses were cut and landholdings and internal administration reorganized, as had been done in the mid-fourteenth century, after the devastation of the Black Death.[2] In order to do this in the 1530s, however, the abbey needed outside, probably

[1] Dugdale, *Monasticon*, iii, p. 170. Also of importance are: E. Savine, *The English Monasteries on the Eve of Dissolution* (Oxford: Oxford University Press, 1909); R. H. Snape, *English Monastic Finances in the Later Middle Ages* (Cambridge: Cambridge University Press, 1926); D. D. Knowles, *The Religious Orders in England*, 2 vols. (Cambridge: Cambridge University Press, 1950-1955); and A. G. Dickens, *The English Reformation* (New York: Schocken, 1946).

[2] A. Goodwin, *The Abbey of St. Edmundsbury* (Oxford: Basil Blackwell, 1931), pp. 65-84, disagrees with the general themes presented in this chapter. He believes the abbey managed to clean its own house, and was in a strong position at Dissolution.

royal, assistance. Such support was not forthcoming, and, as the Crown had first established the monastery in the eleventh century, so too would it supervise its demise in the sixteenth.

In the fourteenth century, St. Edmunds weathered its civil and political crises. But, while these difficulties were to diminish somewhat in the course of the fifteenth century, newer and ultimately more serious problems arose. These new woes were financial. For all its impressive income, the abbey was finding it harder and harder after 1348 to make ends meet; the abbot and his cohorts found it impossible to live within their considerable means and remain solvent. By the late 1400s they were continuously in debt.

Part of the abbey's insolvency can be traced to high living. The abbot was a great lord, and lived accordingly. Among other things, he had a private hoard of gold and silver, and a personal array of gold and silver smiths. He also had several personal silk merchants, and a string of the plushest private residences in East Anglia.[3] Abbey officers copied the style of their leader as closely as their incomes allowed, and seemed to live well beyond their individual means. At any given time, over half the officers and less exalted monks could be away from the monastery, "on vacation," as one observer phrased it.[4] Compounding this tendency was a notorious lack of administrative expertise; when, in the fourteenth century, the pope gave the abbot charge of St. Saviour's Hospital so that he might straighten out its fiscal affairs, there must have been considerable local bemusement. In a short time, the monks managed to plunge the hospital into financial chaos, as they had continually done with their own house.[5]

Despite their financial woes, the abbot and his officers refused to cut back on their levels of consumption. From the mid-fourteenth century, the abbot held a house in Aldgate, London, appropriately called "The Abbot of Bury and His Place," which cost £40 annually in rent, plus £20 more in maintenance—all for a residence in which he could not have spent more than a few weeks a year.[6] From the late thirteenth century, successive abbots were paying the considerable sum of over £13 per week for the labor,

[3] Dugdale, *Monasticon*, iii, pp. 116-117.
[4] This famous phrase is taken from Arnold, iii, p. 39.
[5] See above, pp. 194-203.
[6] Dugdale, *Monasticon*, iii, p. 117.

supplies, and operations of the abbey bakehouse and brewery.[7] Indeed, this figure is so high that it must have included some payoffs and kickbacks, perhaps to abbey officers or to local merchants at the expense of the larger Benedictine community. The wages of personal servants cost another £13, and the *Firma St. Edmundi*, also from the late thirteenth century, claims that feeding the abbot alone cost over £100 per year.[8] In all, domestic expenses for the abbey were estimated in the 1290s at close to £1407 *per annum*. In the thirteenth and early fourteenth centuries, with agricultural and land prices high, most abbots could meet such expenses. But in the late fourteenth and fifteenth centuries, with the advent of harder times and falling revenues, it became increasingly difficult to make ends meet.

Excessive spending, high living, and administrative mismanagement were the major causes of St. Edmunds' fiscal woes, but they were not the only ones. A peculiar inability to adapt to the more favorable economic conditions for great landlords that began late in the fifteenth century may have played as large a role as profligacy. As Suffolk population began to grow again, food prices rose and wages dropped, but the abbot and his officers seemed unable to implement the changes that allowed other great landholders to prosper anew. There were several agrarian solutions to falling revenues. One was rack-renting; most tenants surely would have suffered at least some rise in their rents and even shorter leases. Another answer would have been further concentration on livestock, especially the sheepfolds. With cloth prices high through much of the fifteenth and early sixteenth centuries, and the bulk of the abbot's estates on the northern perimeter of one of England's premier cloth-producing regions, land-intensive husbandry could have been quite profitable. Neither potential solution was applied. Instead, an easier but invariably crippling method was employed: the landed endowment was sold off. This process began in the midfifteenth century, and slowly increased until the 1520s, when it reached landslide proportions. Perhaps St. Edmunds was tied to long-term leases at low rates, but Hilton has shown that these leases rarely exceeded a generation, and there was adequate time under the new agrarian conditions of the late fifteenth century to offer

[7] Indeed, the figure is sufficiently high so that its veracity must be questioned, either in terms of period or the amount.

[8] Dugdale, *Monasticon*, iii. pp. 116-117.

new leases more favorable to management.[9] Ultimately, the abbey seems to have suffered from poor management, for reasons that are difficult to understand. Perhaps fewer able men sought to enter the Benedictine house, but this is not the impression of most observers, who suggest a surplus of secular and regular clerics in England in the two generations before the Reformation.[10] It is unlikely that a prosperous abbey such as St. Edmunds would have proved an exception to this general condition. There were other possible paths to fiscal solvency, including cutting back on consumption, apparently an alternative never seriously considered. In all, it is difficult to offer a definitive explanation for the abbey's continued fiscal crises. They were chronic and after 1450 quite severe, and, if the monastery was stronger than most other Benedictine houses at Dissolution, it was still far weaker than it had been one hundred and fifty years earlier.[11]

One ramification of St. Edmunds' lack of funds was its indebtedness.[12] Although the abbey played the role of lender to many merchants and craftsmen in the town, it was by necessity also a borrower. At times abbey officials may have borrowed from the greatest merchants in the borough, mercers and grocers like John Baret II, John Smith, or Richard King III. But, generally, it had to go farther afield. One source was the Crown, but the Crown itself was often short of cash, and had to ask institutions like St. Edmunds for anticipations in lieu of later, fuller taxes. In 1290 a large loan was negotiated by Abbot Simon of Luton from Henry III; subsequently, there are records of a half-dozen similar arrangements. More frequently, abbey officials sought out Italian sources. Like many other English monastic houses, St. Edmunds

[9] R. H. Hilton, *The Decline of Serfdom in Medieval England* (London: Macmillan, 1969), pp. 44-59. For details of late agrarian trends, a fine source is John Hatcher, *Rural Economy and Society in the Duchy of Cornwall, 1330-1500* (Cambridge: Cambridge University Press, 1970). For a study closer to Bury, see J. A. Raftis, *The Estates of Ramsey Abbey* (Toronto: The Pontifical Institute, 1957).

[10] The best source is Dickens, *The English Reformation*, pp. 38-58.

[11] Despite its role as a lender in town (see above, pp. 89-90), the abbey seems to have had relatively little cash. This extended to anticipations for royal taxes. Except for a period in the 1290s, St. Edmunds seldom seems to have taken advantage of Crown offers for quick payment in place of higher taxes later on.

[12] B.M. Harl. Ms. 230, f. 48b.

was often in debt to the great Tuscan and Lombard bankers.[13] In 1259 and 1260 Abbot Simon was forced to mortgage part of the abbey patrimony to pay off a note of 2,500 marks owed to the Bardi of Florence.[14] There was considerable opposition from many monks and townsmen to breaking into the endowment, but the abbot forced it through with the threat of excommunication for anyone who opposed him. This loan, despite its considerable size, proved to be insufficient to liquidate the debt; the abbey needed more cash within the year, and borrowed 2,300 marks from the same source.[15] In 1314 Abbot Richard de Draughton committed himself to pay off a loan of 1,000 marks to the Bardi, at a rate about 50 percent higher than that at which the funds had been borrowed initially.[16] Subsequent records of such loans are rare, but St. Edmunds continued to scour the national money market, and the absence of references to its presence on the international market may well reflect a paucity of surviving records rather than a lack of participation.[17]

It is important not to overstate the issues of indebtedness, especially in light of the still extensive revenues coming into St. Edmunds through the course of the fourteenth and even the fifteenth centuries. Definitive statements on the economic fortunes of the abbey must await detailed analysis of its vast rural estates. Life inside the abbey complex remained quite comfortable by contemporary standards. But, as expenses rose and income began to fall, as the abbey began to sell off its precious landed endowment, the abbot and his monks were living more and more from precarious sources. By the 1520s the situation had become particularly acute. St. Edmunds was on the verge of collapse, and some change was inevitable.[18]

A picture of abbey holdings in the 1530s comes from several sources. Accounts of total annual income are disputed, with the *Valor Ecclesiasticus* giving it as £1,659, Speed as £2,336, and a third

[13] C.U.L. Ms. Mm 4 19, f. 32b. Of interest is Richard Kaeuper, *Bankers to the Crown* (Princeton, N.J.: Princeton University Press, 1973).

[14] *Ibid.* For additional reference, see C.U.L. Ms Mm 4 19, ff. 61-63.

[15] *Ibid.*

[16] B.M. Harl. Ms. 230, f. 48b.

[17] The author has been able to find but a single reference, C.C.R., Richard II, 1397, p. 32. A Lombard living in London was lending unspecified amounts to the abbey.

[18] Again, Goodwin, *The Abbey*, disagrees.

independent source in the Norwich Public Record Office as £1,-669.[19] The 1539 report of supervisors to Henry VIII's commission to the treasury claims that there were more than 5,000 marks of gold and silver in the house, and much in the way of emeralds and other precious stones.[20] Whatever the accuracy of these figures, all were considerably less than the landed and material wealth held two centuries earlier.[21] This is further illustrated by the most comprehensive survey taken at Dissolution, the report of the Court of Augmentations.[22] The report is a detailed record of where income came from, in the borough, the banleuca, West Suffolk, and other areas in eastern England in which the abbey held estates. It shows the decline of the abbey's landed endowment even before 1539. From the fourteenth century, St. Edmunds had continually sold pieces of its landed property, but, at the same time, bought new land, effectively changing the shape rather than the size of its estates. By the 1520s and 1530s the latter practice had all but ceased, and, though the extent of abbey lands was still considerable, it was far smaller than it had been as late as the 1490s. In an effort to meet increasing expenses, the abbot and his officers were dipping into their ultimate source of wealth. In the 1520s and 1530s whole manors were sold to such notable lay figures as Thomas Kyton, Anthony Rouse, and Nicholas and Thomas Bacon, and smaller pieces of arable and meadow to lesser folks. In all, the estates of St. Edmundsbury in 1539 were less than half of what they had been in the 1290s.[23]

There was still a great deal for Henry VIII and his agents to dissolve. Holdings can be divided into broad groups: tenements within the borough and suburbs; the hospitals and their lands, control now divided between the abbey and lay sources; rural es-

[19] Dugdale, *Monasticon*, iii, p. 116. Most authorities believe that the *Valor* underestimates most monastic incomes, especially Bury's. It does not include colleges, chantries, and other foundations, many of which were dissolved in the mid-1530s. Many movables also escaped the survey. But, beyond the obvious fact of underenumeration, it is not possible to state which of the three estimates was most accurate.

[20] *Ibid.*, pp. 116-118.

[21] See Yates, *History and Antiquities*, pp. 195-201.

[22] Lillian J. Redstone, "First Ministers' Account of the Possessions of the Abbey of St. Edmunds," *P.S.I.*, xiii, 3, 1909.

[23] *Ibid.*

tates in West Suffolk; rural estates in the rest of East Anglia and the east coast of the kingdom; and a variety of banalities and traditional prerogatives surviving from the twelfth and thirteenth centuries. This income ranged from rabbit warrens and manure from a series of western Norfolk villages to over £100 pounds per annum in rent from a West Suffolk manor. For most lords, this would have represented a splendid patrimony, and the abbey of St. Edmunds must still have been one of the largest single landholders in Western Suffolk. But, given the extent of holdings of even a century earlier, with incomes drawn from over three hundred manors, it marked precipitous decline. And, to make matters worse, the pace of decline was accelerating rapidly.

The report of the Court of Augmentations indicates additional abbey troubles. Properties in the suburbs, once directly exploited, were now all being farmed out *en masse* through long-term leases at low rents. Included here were virtually all the arable, barns, meadows, sheepfolds, gardens, and orchards that at one time represented one of St. Edmunds largest sources of income. Even forges and mills were leased out on long-term, unprofitable bases. The land market in eastern England was getting tighter in the sixteenth century and rents were rising, but, for whatever reason, the abbot and his officers never took advantage of the new economic conditions. By Dissolution, the abbey had settled almost entirely into the life of a distant and detached *rentier*.

There were other problems. Profits were still taken from the courts and borough gaol, but by the 1530s were so low that they barely paid for the collection processes. Probate of wills, once a leading moneymaker, brought in no income at all by 1539. Again for inexplicable reasons, the abbey was selling wood from its forests at well below market value, at a time when prices for this crucial raw material were soaring throughout the kingdom. Even livestock and grazing rights were largely vested with outsiders; for example, in 1539 a London mercer named William Clayton was paying a mere £28 per annum for a monopoly of the sheepfolds throughout the banleuca.

The Court of Augmentations report shows another aspect of the abbey's plight. Much of the physical fabrice of its remaining holdings was deteriorating. There are lists of decaying and dilapidated tenements and houses, many uninhabitable and producing no rents, and consequently being written off by the court officers as total financial losses.[24] In the mid-1530s the abbot tried to raise funds for repairs on these tenements and various other structures around the borough, including the town walls and the Tollhouse, but none were forthcoming. By 1539 the Abbey of St. Edmundsbury was like a jaded dowager, a still rich but fading institution renting out everything and increasingly forced to sell parts of its patrimony in order to remain solvent.

I have attempted to describe the emergence of an important late medieval English town. Originally, the borough of Bury St. Edmunds developed beneath the walls of the abbey, which was essential to the very fiber and being of the town from its inception through much of the thirteenth century. But, from the late thirteenth century, the borough's own institutional, social, and economic development was such that it functioned, indeed, flourished on its own. By the early fourteenth century, Bury St. Edmunds had developed its own varied attractions. It stood at a natural geographic crossroads, and as such was a staging point for many travellers going to the Low Countries. It was an intellectual and cultural center with three schools, a library, and links with Cambridge University. It was, by late medieval standards, a medical center, with six hospitals and an active community of doctors, and an ideal place for the poor, with extensive almshouse facilities. It was a rich regional market center, with weekly and annual trade fairs selling a variety of goods from fresh produce to raw wool and finished cloth. This was supplemented by an additional rich consumer, the abbey, which helped to support a number of specialized craft industries. All of this meant prosperity and an integral town-abbey connection. Well into the fourteenth century, Bury was an important provincial town, but the borough was still dependent on the abbey.

But from the mid-fifteenth century, the town-abbey relationship began to change once again. The abbey stopped growing while the borough continued to develop. Given impetus by the monastic community, Bury's cultural, intellectual, judicial, and medical institutions developed from their own indigenous resources. Coupled

---

[24] *Ibid.* Charles Phythian-Adams, *Desolation of a City: Coventry and the Urban Crisis of the Late Middle Ages* (Cambridge: Cambridge University Press, 1979), stresses the ruin of many of the wards in the central areas of Coventry. As has been emphasized above, however, Bury St. Edmunds and Coventry shared little else in the sixteenth century.

with this was the exogenous expansion of West Suffolk as one of the major cloth-producing regions in England. Always a cloth market of local importance, Bury's Great Market developed into a major export center, attracting merchants from London and from the Continent. Accordingly, the borough became more prosperous than ever before, and by 1524 was among the leading provincial towns in the kingdom. By the 1460s, when the abbey began to experience financial difficulties, the town had attained importance on the basis of its intrinsic social and economic merits.

Had the abbey remained fiscally strong, it might have been able to temper the growing movements among the burgesses for autonomy and slow the movement to municipal independence, but it did not. The abbey was a large-holding institution dependent upon cheap, almost servile, labor, a commodity that disappeared after the Black Death. Consequently, St. Edmunds slipped into passive *rentier* status, and became rigidly conservative in trying to maintain its rights and privileges. As the town adapted to the new conditions, the abbey stagnated. Ultimately, the abbot and his monks became totally dependent on royal favor for their existence. When this was withdrawn, the Abbey of St. Edmunds fell, and the town of Bury stood alone.

Conclusions

BURY ST. EDMUNDS, THE URBAN CRISIS, AND LATE MEDIEVAL SOCIETY

Bury St. Edmunds was not like most late medieval towns. The consensus amongst historians that has developed for these towns, as outlined in the introduction, is one of general decline and decay. Some facets of life in Bury were in fact less pleasing in 1539 than they had been in 1290. Certain areas of the borough, particularly the streets immediately to the west of the abbey, were in disrepair and sometimes disuse. The fishing and leather industries, once staples of Bury's economy, had fallen almost to the point of insignificance. But, excepting these and a few other instances, daily living, work, and governance were better than ever. Bury was more prosperous, important, and free from external non-burghal controls than at any time since its foundation. Even at the nadir of development for most English towns, the early part of the sixteenth century, that acute observer John Leland remarked about Bury's success, as he commented on the general state of urban decay.[1]

Why was Bury St. Edmunds able to run counter to general national trends? The answer is best understood by looking at the many levels at which its prosperity and autonomy can be observed. The most graphic aspect of Bury's success was its increasing population. Like virtually all of England, and indeed of western Europe, Bury's population was diminished by the subsistence crises of the late thirteenth and early fourteenth centuries, and decimated by the second plague pandemic, which began in 1348. Bury's post Black Death, recovery, however, was much quicker than that of virtually all other urban areas. It fell from about 7,150 folk in 1340 to perhaps only 3,000 in 1440, but thereafter population stabilized and then began to increase. This was due not so much to a rise in fertility or even to a drop in mortality levels, but rather to steady

[1] John Leland, *Itinerary in England: In or About the Years, 1535-1543*, ed., Lucy Toulmin-Smith (London: George Bell and Sons, 1908), i, p. 156.

immigration from all over eastern England. By 1540 Bury, unlike virtually all other important provincial centers, probably had as many people living in it as it did before the plagues. In fact, Bury's late medieval demographic experience was similar to that of London, also the beneficiary of a constant stream of immigrants. While Coventry, York, Bristol, Southampton, even Norwich, were slow to recover their numbers in the fifteenth century and actually experienced new and concerted demographic decline early in the sixteenth century, Bury's population continued to rise apace.[2]

Bury was unusual, then, in its ability to attract the newcomers so crucial in an age of extraordinary urban depopulation. There were several reasons for this. First, the hinterlands for which it served as the marketing center included some of the most productive agricultural parts of Britain. Indeed, Suffolk's rural productivity helps to account for the concomitant rise of the county's other principal town, Ipswich, a second exception to the general late medieval paradigm of decay. A definitive analysis of West Suffolk's rural economy cannot be made until the abbey's estates are fully studied, but rentals from the Great Market and bits of evidence from the Redgrave estates, all discussed in Chapter 3, show high production and high demand. The call for grain products seems to have fallen somewhat after the Black Death, but, if market stallage fees are a reliable indicator, demand for dairy and meat products remained strong, bolstered by immigration and rising standards of living. Further, direct demesne cultivation dropped while the valuations for the banleuca's sheepfolds steadily rose. More and more farmers were turning from labor to land-intensive production, taking advantage of the continued high prices for non-corn crops, and many of the town's wealthiest burgesses kept investing in and at times actually working rural property. It may be too great an exaggeration to proclaim the triumph of capitalist agriculture in fifteenth-century Suffolk; some investors remained *rentiers*. But, while local food markets were floundering in most provincial towns—Coventry, Leicester, and Northampton, for example—that in Bury St. Edmunds remained strong.[3]

[2] The best summary article is Charles Phythian-Adams, "Urban Decay in Late Medieval England," in Philip Abrams and E. A. Wrigley, *Towns in Societies* (Cambridge: Cambridge University Press, 1978), pp. 159-185.

[3] W. G. Hoskins, "English Provincial Towns in the Early Sixteenth Century," in his *Provincial England* (London: Macmillan, 1975), pp. 68-85.

Wool and cloth provided the second important measure of Bury's economic success. Even the gloomiest observers of late medieval England's fortunes acknowledge the general prosperity of the rural cloth areas, of which West Suffolk was one of the most important.[4] Bury St. Edmunds was a principal retail market for Stour Valley cloth, and, ironically, late medieval depression notwithstanding, the Great Market attracted more non-denizen merchants in the fifteenth and sixteenth centuries than it had in the thirteenth and fourteenth. Even as the worsted industry of nearby Norwich and its Norfolk environs began to decline around 1500, Bury's woolen cloth industry continued to expand.[5] Rural cloth manufacture, along with agricultural production, show how closely Bury's vitality was connected with that of its hinterlands.

Economic success, especially that based on wool and cloth, had profound social and economic effects. In Bury St. Edmunds as in London—and there are striking similarities in the development of the regional and the national centers—a ruling élite or patriciate emerged in the fourteenth century.[6] In both centers, the initial source of much of the élite's wealth came from textiles; most of Bury's aldermen and burgesses, for example, were drapers, mercers, or members of that new entrepreneurial group, clothiers. And, as was the case in London, Bury's patriciate, whatever its intentions, was an open and fluid group. This was not the result of burghal largesse, but rather of biological attrition and attitudes toward wealth and class. High infant and child mortality made survival of heirs a haphazard affair. In Bury, London, and indeed virtually every other provincial town 75 percent of all families failed to produce male heirs for even three successive generations. Further, the 25 percent who did have sons tended, if successful in business, to buy land and move into the ranks of the gentry. For Bury's patriciate this had a positive side; it meant that the upper crust of society always had room for "new blood." Throughout the

[4] For example, M. M. Postan, "The Fifteenth Century," and "Agrarian Evidence of Declining Population in the Later Middle Ages," both in his *Essays on Medieval Agriculture and General Problems of the Medieval Economy* (Cambridge: Cambridge University Press, 1973), pp. 41-48, 186-213.

[5] Barbara Green and Rachel M. R. Young, *Norwich; the Growth of a City* (Norwich: City of Norwich Museum, 1972), pp. 18-19.

[6] The best comparisons can be made in Gwyn Williams, *Medieval London: From Commune to Capital* (London: The Athlone Press, 1963), pp. 285-314.

later middle ages, Bury St. Edmunds like London was a place where ambitious immigrants went to make their fortunes.[7]

Most provincial towns had élites who suffered from high mortality and wished to transfer their wealth from commercial to landed sources. But, while the élite dominated their towns, Hoskins, Dobson, Phythian-Adams, and others have perceived a change in their behavior by late in the fifteenth century.[8] There was an increasing reluctance in Coventry, Leicester, Northampton, Norwich, York, and other provincial centers to participate in the communal affairs of these towns, and to invest in urban property. In essence, their commitment and interest in urban life began to flag. In Coventry, for example, civic ceremonies such as the *Corpus Christi* pageants had long been used by the élite as a demonstration and reaffirmation of their position.[9] But, as the town's economy soured around 1500, the town fathers showed less and less inclination to participate in such ceremonies. Even more telling, many refused to hold public office, as the costs of being in office rose and their comparative financial positions fell. In Bury, quite the opposite took place. Not only did the burghal élite continue to sponsor public ceremonies and hold civic office, but they were joined by the gentry of West Suffolk. Families like the Drurys, major figures in East Anglian society, delivered the town gaol and served as bailiffs. Indeed, public office was considered more desirable in 1520 than it had been in 1290.[10]

The pride Bury folk had in their town is shown in other ways. In Coventry, many other midlands towns, and Norwich, the failure of the élite to invest in town properties caused a decline in tenement values and the dilapidation and ruin of large parts of these towns.

[7] S. L. Thrupp, *The Merchant Class of Medieval London* (Chicago: University of Chicago Press, 1948), pp. 191-233.

[8] Hoskins, "English Provincial Towns"; Charles Phythian-Adams, *Desolation of a City: Coventry and the Urban Crisis of the Late Middle Ages* (Cambridge: Cambridge University Press, 1979), pp. 170-179; R. B. Dobson, "Urban Decline in Late Medieval England," *Transactions of the Royal Historical Society*, 5th series, xxv, 1977, pp. 20-22.

[9] Charles Phythian-Adams, "Ceremony and the Citizen: The Communal Year at Coventry, 1450-1550," in Peter Clark and Paul Slack, *Crisis and Order in English Towns, 1500-1700* (London: R.K.P., 1972), pp. 57-85.

[10] This sense of public service may also have persisted in Southampton. See Colin Platt, *Medieval Southampton: The Port and Trading Community, 1000-1600* (London: R.K.P., 1974), pp. 63-64.

In Bury, things were different. Only those parts of the town which the abbey rack-rented were allowed to decay. Deeds and wills show that the élite and anyone else who could raise the funds were leasing low rent *hadgoval* tenements. In Bury, an active *rentier* class had developed by 1400, perhaps a century before it came to most other provincial towns.[11] When dilapidations did occur in tenements held or leased by townsfolk, and when public buildings and roads started to deteriorate in the sixteenth century, funds were raised to repair them. The town's greatest decade of rebuilding, to judge from the testamentary evidence, ran from 1510 to 1520.

The civic pride of Bury's élite was matched by the zeal of the commons. The prosperity of the late medieval town was broad-based and far-reaching; the lower orders were far more prosperous than their counterparts in surrounding towns like St. Albans, Ipswich, and Norwich.[12] Public office was restricted to wealthy middle-aged males. But guild records and wills show that throughout the later middle ages virtually all the men and women in Bury participated in borough pageants and ceremonies, and bequeathed what they could for the improvement of the town's fabric and institutions.

Bury's economic strength was just one reason for its residents' civic pride. A second was the abbey of St. Edmunds, and this, like the vitality of the food markets and of the rural cloth industry, was a key part of the town's late medieval history. Bury's local government was unlike that of most other provincial centers because of the extent of the abbey's powers and privileges. In 1290 St. Edmunds controlled virtually every aspect of the town's political life. One of the principal themes of this study has been the struggle between the burgesses and the abbot for civic autonomy. While other late medieval townsmen fought against various forces of extraneous authority, the abbey made Bury's struggle unusual. Total burghal autonomy came only with Dissolution; battles won before 1539, because of the charters which made the abbey *seigneur* of the liberty of eight and one-half hundreds, could never be complete victories. This had a galvanizing effect on burgesses and commons alike. Riots and rebellions in other English towns often matched

[11] Colin Platt, *The Medieval English Town* (London: MacKay, 1976), pp. 181-182.

[12] The best evidence for this is the data from the index of concentration and the Lorenz Curve, above, pp. 124-130.

one stratum of town society against another.[13] In Bury, this was never the case; frustration against St. Edmunds was always enough to overcome "class" conflicts. Indeed, so broad-based was popular revolt in Bury that townsmen were sometimes joined by secular clerics and Franciscan friars from nearby Babwell. All antipathies were submerged beneath the general distaste for the rich and privileged Benedictines.

The abbey was crucial to Bury's development in positive as well as negative ways. Its prestige and institutional and fluid wealth gave Bury a "leg up" on all other provincial towns except perhaps Canterbury and St. Albans. Reinvestment of some of this wealth was one reason for Bury's comparatively quick recovery after the Black Death. Moreover, St. Edmunds was crucial as a large-scale and high-living consumer; it was an important element in local market demand—no doubt its absence was felt after 1539—and it helped to support a wide range of crafts industries. Hoskins has described the diversity of crafts in the early sixteenth century in Coventry, Leicester, and Northampton.[14] Bury, as discussed in Chapter 3, seems to have had an even greater number of craftsmen, and in relation to its size had a diversity that matched that of London. Hence, the economic advantages that the abbey brought were considerable. Yet, for all of this, the greatest contributions St. Edmunds made to the town were educational, religious, and institutional. Key elements in late medieval Bury's prosperity were its library, three schools, six hospitals, and dozens of pilgrimage sites and items. St. Edmunds gave impetus to all of these things, but by 1450 control over them had passed largely into secular hands. Again, a comparison with London, albeit at a regional rather than a national level, is apropos. Bury St. Edmunds was one of the most important provincial cultural centers in England.

All of these things—a growing, dynamic and highly skilled population; a powerful, civic-minded, and fluid burghal élite; a strong, textile based industrial economy; one of the most important general markets in England; a rich institutional overlord that also served because of its wealth and power as a common foe that in turn all but eliminated other forms of internecine strife—help to explain Bury St. Edmunds' prosperity in an era of urban crisis. These strengths are well reflected in the progression of Bury's lay subsidy

[13] Phythian-Adams, *Desolation of a City*, pp. 281-290.
[14] Hoskins, "English Provincial Towns," pp. 74-82.

taxes. In 1334, when most provincial towns were either still growing or holding their own, Bury's assessment placed it twenty-eighth among the towns surveyed. By 1523 it ranked thirteenth, and if, as I have argued, "suburban" Lavenham should be figured into the Bury total, the borough rises to seventh.

There may well be another reason for the emergence of Bury St. Edmunds in the later middle ages. Although its economic and thus social and political success and stability were based to a great degree on its rural environs, Bury was also part of an international trading system. It is tempting but unwise to regard Bury's situation as unique, in large measure because there is insufficient evidence to make definitive statements. But, as argued in Chapter 3, Bury and indeed all of East Anglia had close connections with the Netherlands, particularly the northern parts, and in some ways this was more important than trade with the rest of the British Isles. As long as the Netherlands trade continued—and it seems to have grown in the fifteenth and sixteenth centuries—and local markets remained strong, Bury could prosper irrespective of general downward economic trends in other parts of England. In short, if late medieval England must be viewed "through the dark glass," Bury shines as a bright light.[15]

Finally, I might take a second and considerably deeper plunge into the morass of generalization. In his innovative study, Wallerstein has argued that three things were essential for the emergence of a capitalist world economy.[16] These were: an expansion of the geopolitical size of the world in question, the development of divisions and zones of labor, and the creation of strong state machines. At a micro-level, all of Wallerstein's elements were present in Bury St. Edmunds by 1500. It had consolidated its control over West Suffolk, was playing a greater role in English and Netherlandish markets than ever before, and entered into trading relations with partners as far afield as Iberia, Norway, and the Baltic. It had a cadre of skilled craftsmen, a well-paid labor force, and an aggressive mercantile élite. And, in the course of the later middle ages, abbey governance was replaced by stronger burghal leader-

[15] The quote is taken from J. R. Lander, *Conflict and Stability in Fifteenth Century England* (London: Hutchinson, 1969), p. 11.

[16] Immanuel Wallerstein, *The Modern World System: Capitalist Agriculture and the Origins of the European World Economy in the Sixteenth Century* (New York: Academic Press, 1974), p. 38.

ship, with greater resources to call on. Bury St. Edmunds, obviously, was not a major force in the emergence of world capitalism. It was not London, Antwerp, or even Nuremberg. But in an age when other important towns were in deep crisis, Bury had developed an aggressive and prosperous market economy. It had, at its level, reached the apex of success.

Appendix A

THE SOURCES

The sources dealt with in this appendix are those used most extensively and not discussed in depth in other studies of late medieval English towns.[1] The discussion will proceed roughly in the order in which the sources are encountered in the text.

Two categories of source materials stand out—rentals and probated wills. The rentals for the banleuca of Bury St. Edmunds are among the finest topographical records covering any late medieval urban region. Four have been used extensively: the 1295 comprehensive rental from the sacrist, cellarer, other abbey officials, and the hospitals; the late-fourteenth-century sacrist's rental; the 1433 sacrist's *hadgoval* listing; and the sixteenth-century Dissolution rentals. Closely related is the borough *relevia*, inclusive from 1353 to 1539. All are records of rent expectations by landlords—usually the abbot or his major officers—and the rents due them on particular banleuca properties. These properties are often described in considerable detail and always name the street and ward in which the holding is situated. Ideally, the rentals provide a total picture of who was holding what, how valuable the property was felt to be, and, in theory, the total number of established households in the borough.[2]

Unfortunately, while the rentals are a rich topographical, social, economic, and demographic source, they do not always answer all

[1] A good general description of late medieval English sources is G. R. Elton, *England, 1200-1640* (Ithaca, N.Y.: Cornell University Press, 1969).

[2] Unfortunately, rentals cannot be used for direct demographic purposes, except perhaps in gaining a sense of households. They never list family members, and often fail to mention what a particular tenement was used for. It may have been residential or agricultural, which means that a simple counting of manses may not even yield total number of manses actually being used at a fixed point in time.

the questions they were initially formulated to ask. In some cases, they merely list payment of a cash rent. Further, as with many late medieval English records, there is a problem with their completeness. Most of the rental manuscripts have blank pages or torn overleafs. And, most serious, there are problems in interpreting the fashion in which many of the properties in the banleuca were held. While all technically belonged to the abbot within his liberty, in practice the streets and fields were given over to various abbey officials as part of their incomes. No single abbey officer held all of the town or even a given ward in its entirety; consequently, in order to reconstruct holding patterns at any given time, the current holdings of every abbey officer must be determined. While this can often be approximated, it can never be outlined definitively, since the best record of such divisions of property comes from the very rentals themselves![3]

Clearly, no single rental from any given office, even that of the sacrist, the *de jure* holder of town property, provides a complete topographical picture of late medieval Bury St. Edmunds. For a balanced view, a comprehensive rental is necessary, and, fortunately, a reasonably complete one survives. This is the amalgam of landed incomes from a dozen monastic officials, including the sacrist, the cellarer, the almoner, the infirmarer, the warder of the Chapel of St. Mary, the prior, the hosteler, the subcellarer, and the wardens of the hospitals of St. Peter, *Domus Dei*, St. Nicholas, and St. Petranilla. Of all the officers of St. Edmunds, the only important absentee was the treasurer, and there is no hint that any of his income was drawn from local rentals. Yet even this is not complete; individual surveys surviving from the above-mentioned offices show that each had more extensive holdings than those included in the 1295 amalgam. Nevertheless, the 1295 rental is a long and complex survey, and provides the best-available topographical picture of late medieval Bury St. Edmunds.

Nothing as comprehensive as the 1295 survey survives for the town until the eighteenth century. There are, however, a number of issues from individual monastic officers, and, while many of these are too restrictive for general topographical application, some from the sacrist, the principal holder in the borough with the pos-

---

[3] For a discussion of what major officials did, see above, pp. 169-171. Perhaps the best account is in Richard Yates, *The History and Antiquities of the Abbey of Bury St. Edmunds* (London: J. B. Nichols and Son, 1843).

sible exception of Westgate Ward, can be used to chart the dynamics of change in the fourteenth and fifteenth centuries.

The earliest fragments of sacrists' rentals come from Robert of Denham, who held office during the reign of Edward II, but the first relatively complete survey is that of Thomas of Rudham, sacrist late in the fourteenth century.[4] It quite clearly does not include all holdings within the borough, but still provides a broad enough picture to compare with that of the town in 1295. The Rudham rental can also be used in conjunction with the 1433 sacrist's rental, the most comprehensive of the later middle ages after that of 1295. The latter purports to list all *hadgoval* tenants, those persons holding property developed before the Norman Conquest. In effect, *hadgoval* was a pre-Norman burgage rent of 1/2 pence per measure, per half year, per holding. It was hereditary, and could be bought or sold, and was thus a ground rent with additional and subsequent property rents heaped upon it. Some scholars, including Lobel, considered that all holders in town paid *hadgoval*; indeed, she commented on how *Le Mustow*, with few listed tenants, seemed uninhabited.[5] This is not likely, and she herself has explained that *hadgoval* was meant initially to apply only to the old Anglo-Saxon *burh*, Southgate Ward. Further, additional fifteenth-century rentals from abbey officers other than the sacrist list many non-*hadgoval* tenants. But, these objections notwithstanding, the sacrist's *hadgoval* of 1433 is fairly complete and provides the best post-1295 image of Bury St. Edmunds.

The various rentals are supported by another topographical record, the *relevia*, dating from 1353 to the Dissolution. It was a relief, literally an inheritance tax paid by heirs so that they might succeed to their patrimonies. *Relevia* was levied only on *hadgoval* tenants, and assessed above and beyond *hadgoval*, at about twenty shillings *per annum*. Because *relevia* was so assessed, and because record of it survives only when property is bequeathed, it cannot be used as a comprehensive topographical record, nor even assumed to be as complete as the better sacrists' rentals. But it covers a two-century time-span, and hence can be used as an independent, dynamic check on the projected spatial trends.

There are two series of records that can be used as topographical

---

[4] For a complete listing of this and all other sources discussed herein, see the bibliography, pp. 290-295 ff.

[5] Lobel, *The Borough*, p. 9.

and spatial analyses in the sixteenth century. These are the 1523-1524 Lay Subsidy and its anticipation; and the 1539 and 1553 Dissolution rentals. The former has been used and analyzed in great detail elsewhere, and can be discussed very briefly.[6] Its topographical significance stems from the method of its assessment—a ward-by-ward evaluation of individual wealth. Ultimately, it was a graduated tax on all persons of both sexes over sixteen years of age who had an annual income of £1 or more. For this reason, the lay subsidy has also been used in the judgment of comparative burghal wealth presented in Chapter 3. The subsidy was comprehensive enough to include aliens—hence, its additional use in Chapter 3—and by medieval standards rather equitable. There are few references to evasion, and, while clerics were exempted, Hervey believed that even manual laborers were caught in the taxmen's web.[7] While he may have been overly optimistic, records of payment from 17,000 Suffolk folk survive, making it second only to the 1377 Poll Tax in fiscal comprehension.

A key part of the lay subsidy was its anticipation. There were always gaps between taxes in theory and revenues collected, and many subsidies simply served as a starting point of negotiation from which actual rates might be arranged. In Bury, the wealthiest strata of townsfolk were allowed to pay discounted rates in return for cash advances. This was the anticipation, and could be paid by any individual assessed at about £40. Both the anticipation and the subsidy were levied by ward, thus providing a picture on the eve of the Reformation of the geographical distribution of the wealthiest folk in Bury.

The final late medieval topographical records are the 1539 and 1551 rentals. Both were taken after the demise of St. Edmunds and the sale of most of its endowment. Consequently, they show the effects of the selling by the abbey in the 1520s and 1530s of much of its endowment. The 1539 survey shows the sacrist presiding over those properties still not sold, the bulk having been purchased by Sir Nicholas Bacon, while the latter shows a diminished core, transferred by John Holt to the West Suffolk gentleman Sir John Eyer. Neither of these final rentals can be used in isolation

---

[6] See the appropriate articles in H. C. Darby, *A New Historical Geography of England* (Cambridge: Cambridge University Press, 1973).

[7] *Suffolk in 1524, Being the Return for a Subsidy Granted in 1523, Suffolk Green Books*, x (Woodbridge, Suffolk: George Booth, 1910).

because they represent less than half the tenements in the town. They are, however, a good account of the nadir of abbey holdings, and, when compared with the 1295 and even 1433 rentals, provide a good image of long-term landholding trends.

Taken individually, the surveys are useful in depicting most of St. Edmunds' and other ecclesiastical holdings in the abbey town at fixed time periods. Taken together, they provide a dynamic picture of a changing town. All in all, the rentals make for a superb survey of the changing topography of an important provincial center. They are among the best sources for the history of late medieval Bury St. Edmunds.

The other superb, perhaps unrivaled, source for late medieval Bury St. Edmunds is the probate records of the sacristry—wills and letters of admonition or administration. Testamentary jurisdictions in later medieval England rested with a hierarchal series of ecclesiastical courts.[8] The wealthiest testators registered their wills in the archbishop's court, the next wealthiest in the bishop's consistory court, and middling and poorer folk in the local archdeaconry courts, all according to a fairly strict schedule of property and non-movable assessments. From the mid-fifteenth century, East Anglia has an excellent series of testamentary records which cover well over half the adult male population. But Bury St. Edmunds has even better representation; perhaps 70-75 percent of its adult males registered their wills. There were several reasons for this remarkable coverage. First, Bury had a peculiar jurisdiction; its testators took their wills not to the archbishop's, bishop's or archdeacon's courts, but to that of the abbey sacrist. This was part of the abbot's prerogative, falling within his liberty of eight and one-half hundreds.[9] From 1354 to the mid-fifteenth century, registration was occasionally haphazard, but from 1440, perhaps because of the profits of the process and a series of very diligent officers, registration was at least three-quarters complete. Indeed, I have argued elsewhere that it was the most demographically comprehensive of all late medieval testamentary series.[10]

Wills provide detailed information on institutional, demographic,

[8] Robert S. Gottfried, *Epidemic Disease in Fifteenth Century England* (New Brunswick, N.J.: Rutgers University Press, and Leicester University Press, 1978), pp. 18-22.

[9] There are about a score of Bury testators in the Prerogative Court of Canterbury and twenty-two in the Norwich Consistory Court. The author found no *bona fide* Bury residents in the archdeacons' courts.

[10] Gottfried, *Epidemic Disease*, pp. 22-28.

economic, and social history. Herein, they have been used for all
of the above, as well as for topographical and biographical purposes, and, to these ends, 2,116 of them have been analyzed with
the aid of a computer for over forty variables. The method of
analysis has been discussed in depth elsewhere, and will not be
reiterated in detail.[11] Some additional description, however, is necessary because several new categories of computer information
have been added to the sample. These are charitable bequests; land
and inheritance information; guild information; place-name information; and lists of personal, movable possessions. All have been
coded on one-, two-, and three-digit bases, depending upon the
number of members in each fixed set. For example, when twenty
guilds were encountered, each guild was given a two-digit coded
number. When this guild was needed in analysis, it was programmed along with the larger set of information in a given will.
When the number of things in a set was potentially infinite, the
categories were fixed. This was the case with movable properties,
for example. They were thus grouped into twenty-five larger categories, such as livestock, bullion, textiles, etc. This allowed for
larger, more meaningful groups to be used in broader social and
economic analyses. When aggregated in this or similar fashion the
2,000 strong testamentary sample provides a fine base of quantifiable information.

Two aspects of the testamentary records have been the subject
of some debate. One is their accuracy for the study of population;
this has been discussed extensively elsewhere.[12] The second is their
use as a measure of assessing wealth; it too has been mentioned in
other works, but in far less detail, and deserves additional discussion. I have taken as representative of individual wealth testators'
individual contributions to the high altar of the parish of their
burial. Such bequests are found in about 94 percent of the Peculiar
Court of Bury St. Edmunds' wills, and by legal statute were supposed to represent a fixed portion of an individual's liquid wealth.
Obviously, the law was not always obeyed, and bequests may well
represent varied shares of personal fortunes. Further, property,
which accounted for a major share even of townsfolk's total estates,
is not included in the measure. But, despite these reservations, the
comprehensiveness of the proposed wealth measure provides an

[11] *Ibid.*, pp. 225-230.
[12] *Ibid.*, pp. 22-28.

unparalleled opportunity to gain some sense of the comparative wealth of individuals. Faced with no other workable alternative, when used with caution it provides a barometer of the financial status of large numbers of Bury residents.

Two records have been used in conjunction with the wills to measure Bury's population levels. These are the 1377 Poll Tax and the 1522 Suffolk Military Muster Rolls. The 1377 Poll Tax has been used by Russell and innumerable others to calculate late-fourteenth-century population.[13] For some counties, it provides nearly complete lists of all men and women over age 12, with minimal levels of evasion and omission. Unfortunately, Suffolk is exceptional; the village-by-village returns for the county have been lost, and only the aggregates can be used. While they cannot provide comprehensive demographic differentials, the county aggregates do allow measure of sex ratios, and, if total population can be extrapolated, age-specific mortality and fertility.

The 1522 Military Muster provides the percentage of males considered by agents of Henry VIII to be eligible for military service. In theory, this should allow for use of model life-tables to reconstruct population and calculate vital statistics. In practice, the reality is different and more difficult, for the musters present their own unique problems. It is often hard to find the limits of eligibility for military service. What was considered too old or too young; was it 16 to 60, as was the case with other surveys of Henry VIII? This problem can often be tracked down by checking the records that initiated the muster, but leaves another, more intractable, issue; the degree of evasion. It was common practice for upper and middling class men to purchase exemptions. Sometimes, this too can be figured, but it is never possible to discern the numbers who ran off to the forest, in a cruder but equally effective means of escape. Taken alone, the muster rolls, like all medieval demographic evidence, present severe drawbacks, but, when corroborated by other records, they can be used. In effect, this is the essence of late medieval demographic study.

The lay subsidies, discussed above in the context of their topographical value, are also helpful in studying population. Because they assess in lump sum rather than in flat head rates they provide less information than the 1377 Poll Tax. A county or borough was

[13] J. C. Russell, *British Medieval Population* (Albuquerque, N.M.: University of New Mexico Press, 1948).

expected to pay the tax, with the means or distribution left unspecified, and the local municipal officers distributing the burden
as they wished. This undoubtedly led to wide-scale evasion, and it
is difficult to select a denominator from which a total population
might be derived. Further, the extent of lay-subsidy population can
rarely be figured; it is likely that the entire lower strata of society
and considerable segments of the upper classes avoided the grasp
of the tax men. But the lay subsidies still have demographic value
when used comparatively. Bury's payments can be measured
through time against those of other boroughs or regions; if this
does not provide absolute population, it can help in determining
secular trends. Of use in a similar vein is the Welsh War tax of
Edward I, assessed in 1282, which prorates the six largest East
Anglian towns.

As helpful as tax records are for topographical and demographic
information, they are most useful in studying the financial and
economic aspects of late medieval Bury. Lay subsidies were levies
granted on assumptions made from the twelfth century that a certain part of an individual's or corporation's wealth could be distinguished as movable, apart from any land that was held. This new
interpretation of wealth was especially relevant for townsfolk, much
of whose wealth could be so regarded. Occasional assessments were
made in the twelfth and thirteenth centuries, and, as royal ex-
penditures rose steadily in the next two centuries, the Crown was
then forced to go to Parliament to ask for their approval. When
used to determine wealth, the subsidies contain, like all other medieval records, a number of flaws. By definition, they do not reflect
total income. Periodically and for various reasons, certain key towns
were exempted or omitted; such was the case for Newcastle, Durham and Chester in the Lay Subsidy of 1523-1524. But, if we
assume these and other inherent weaknesses, the lay subsidies can
be used to assemble lists of comparative urban wealth, and to place
Bury St. Edmunds in a national perspective.

The initial assessment pertaining to Bury is not national, but
regional; this is the aforementioned Welsh War tax of Edward I.
Townsfolk were required to pay in sums proportional to their assessed wealth, and it includes all the major East Anglian towns.
The earliest lay subsidy that survives for Bury was in 1327. It was
far more comprehensive than the Welsh War tax, and allows for
comparison on a much broader scale. The rate was 1/20, with two
gentlemen from each county appointed to supervise the collection

process. In Suffolk, these men were exempted from payment, and, despite royal proclamations to the contrary, it is likely that many others also acquired exemptions. Further, there was a base limitation of five pence for those paying the tax, and possibly an age limit as well. The editor of the *Suffolk Green Book*, in which the tax records have been preserved, was quite certain that "every holder of the upper class, every householder of the middle class, and a proportion of the poorest" were included.[14] This may be an exaggeration, but, presuming that exemptions and omissions were approximate throughout the towns of the realm, the subsidy might again be used for comparative purposes.

In 1334, another Lay Subsidy was assessed at 1/15 of movables in rural areas, and 1/10 from towns. The 1334 subsidy has been closely and expertly analyzed, and need not be discussed here in detail. It differed from that of 1327 in that it was assessed in lump sums for given towns, eliminating all forms of analysis but straight comparison.[15] The 1377 Poll Tax is also useful for comparative wealth analyses, but the next Lay Subsidy did not come until 1523-1524. As discussed above, it was the most comprehensive of all the late medieval subsidies. It was granted to Henry VIII for a proposed French expedition, was levied at 1/20 of all men's goods or land worth £20 or more, and graduated to higher levels for wealthier persons. It applied to all men and women over age 16, and, while it was not as comprehensive as the fourteenth-century Poll Tax, it was nevertheless a far-reaching assessment.[16]

Tax records are by far the best evidence for the economic and financial history of late medieval Bury St. Edmunds. Other sources which bear on these topics include: land deeds, royal calendars, a set of stallage fees, guild records, and the ubiquitous testamentary sources. Bury's land deeds are a rich source that can be used to determine the extent and direction of the local land market, single out those individuals and institutions most active in it, and, to some degree, help to determine what particular lands were being used for. Each deed provides a detailed description of the parties in-

[14] *Suffolk in 1327, Being a Subsidy Return, Suffolk Green Books* (Woodbridge, Suffolk: George Booth, 1906).

[15] R. E. Glasscock, *The Lay Subsidy of 1334* (London: Royal Historical Society, 1975).

[16] See John Sheail, *The Regional Distribution of Wealth in England as indicated in the Lay Subsidy Returns of 1524/25* (London: Unpublished University of London Ph.D thesis, 1968).

volved in the transaction, and very extensive descriptions of the property itself, including the surrounding area. As usual, the deeds present some inherent problems. First, they survive only in limited numbers for select time periods, being fullest in the late fourteenth and mid-fifteenth centuries. More important, while some deal with the borough and its suburbs, most concern the surrounding West Suffolk region, and are peripheral to the history of the town. Accordingly, I have used them primarily to discuss the economic activity of the burghal élite rather than to analyze the local land market.

Overall, the evidence for Bury's economic history is not as full as that for many other provincial towns. There are few direct aulnage records, and trade beyond the urban region is very difficult to measure. In an attempt to allay this problem, extensive use has been made of royal calendars of patent, close, and fine rolls. Because of the profitability of late medieval trade, most kings kept close tabs on it, and royal writs, correspondence, and court records provide some information on the scope, types, direction, and distribution of commerce. In all they provide a sampling of the activities of Bury's merchants, but unfortunately therein lies their major weakness. The calendars can never be more than a survey; they can never possibly describe the depth and extent of trade, and their completeness must always remain a mystery. It is possible that some important aspect of the trade of Bury has been omitted.

Evidence for local trade and industry is better. One source is the stallage market list from the fourteenth century. The stallage provides numbers and fees of those having Great Market stalls, in turn providing valuable information on local trade. Guild records are another useful source. Although not as extensive as those which survive for Norwich, Bristol, or Coventry, Bury's guild records include the rules and regulations of incorporation from the bakers, cordwainers, and weavers and linendrapers. They give information on the social, economic, and institutional aspect of this crucial part of town life. Wills provide additional information about guilds, and supplement this with excellent data on occupations; since the testamentary evidence is temporal by nature, guilds and occupations can be studied for changes through time.

Much economic evidence comes from abbey records. As master of most of the town and suburbs, from the marketplace to the sheepfolds, St. Edmunds was directly concerned in most of Bury's economic activities. While there are no statistical records extant, handbooks from the sacrist, cellarer, treasurer, prior, and others contain information on financial activities, market regulation, and industrial output. Indeed, one of the finest collections of records for the late medieval town comes from the abbey—the accounts, surveys, and manorial court records from the abbey estates.[17] As a cohesive unit, the rural evidence, especially the Bacon collection, ranks with the testamentary evidence and the town rentals as a superb source. They deal primarily with the economic list of rural West Suffolk, and, as such, have been used less frequently than wills or rentals. But invariably, they contain direct or indirect information on town life, especially the market and textile industry, and have been used where appropriate.

In general, the evidence of economic life in late medieval Bury is spotty and at times unreliable. Such things as Freeman's Rolls, a stalwart of the study of many other provincial towns, do not exist for Bury.[18] And, unfortunately, evidence for the social history of the town is even more fragmented and haphazard. There are data on several institutions and aspects of town social life, but they lack the depth necessary for use in writing a comprehensive social history. Among the social/institutional records are inventories; gaol delivery rolls; hospital records; lists and descriptions of social fraternities; some almshouse and medical records; school records and library lists; a smattering of additional cultural information; and a few royal records, such as Richard II's 1389 guild writ, which pertain to many of the above-listed topics. The testamentary and royal calendar data are also useful.

Among the most impressive of these are the Gaol Delivery Rolls. Numbering approximately 38, with about 200 references on each roll, they cover the entire period. The rolls have been scored as inadequate and filled with holes, but, together with the institutional records of Bury's gaol, including a few inventories, a sixteenth-century prisoner list, and some physical evidence, they combine to make a good picture of crime and punishment in town.

The records of the schools, almshouse, and fraternities are mostly institutional descriptions of rules and regulations, and are similar to the guild records discussed above. They describe the structure

[17] See the comments of Richard Smith, in *Bacon*.
[18] See, for example, Charles Phythian-Adams, "Urban Decay in Late Medieval England," in Abrams and Wrigley, eds., Towns in Societies (Cambridge: Cambridge University Press, 1978).

and function of the institution, and, although they often fail to discuss their internal components, some information on the latter can be gleaned from the testamentary records. Wills give considerable information about things like charity, fraternal membership, books, and the like, and fill out the drier constitutional records. Perhaps the finest sources on the social/institutional life of the town concern Bury's six hospitals; in many ways, these records are a microcosm of the pleasure and pain of trying to reconstruct late medieval urban history. There are data on numbers and types of patients, treatment, entrance requirements, hospital staff and administration, financial management and fiscal stability, and endowments. But all these records survive to a limited extent, for limited time periods, and often pertain to but one of the hospitals. They lack the cohesiveness that comes from a few central rather than many scattered sources, and the treatment of hospitals necessarily has been broadcast. When the project began, the author hoped to discuss the general social life of the late medieval townsfolk. Due to the nature of the sources, this had to be abandoned, and fragments of social life were incorporated in a rather rigid, institutional framework.

More success was met in the study of Bury's patriciate, or burghal élite, as they have been referred to. Many authorities have bemoaned the difficulties in trying to do late medieval biography, and, while this is surely the case for the prominent men of late medieval Bury, records exist from which a corporate or collective biographical study can be attempted.[19] Indeed, a great deal can be learned through a variety of sources, the most outstanding of which is the omnipresent will. With will registration running to perhaps three-quarters of the adult male population, most of the great figures left probate records. These in turn provide information about family, residence, movables, and even glimpses into personality, such as what charities particular men felt most inclined to endow. The testamentary evidence is supplemented by other sources, including artifacts and physical records. There are monuments in the churches, and in one case a portrait of a fifteenth-century alderman.[20] There are also references in national records,

[19] P. M. Kendall, *The Art of Biography* (London: George Allen and Unwin, 1965), is a good source of information.

[20] This portrait of John Smith, as Mrs. Margaret Statham of the West Suffolk Record Office in Bury St. Edmunds points out, is probably sixteenth or seventeenth century in composition.

such as the royal calendars, for it was the great men of Bury who were known beyond the banleuca and make some mark in East Anglia or even England. What is lacking is more personal information—letters, diaries, handbooks. Wills begin to open the lives of the burghal élite, but go only so far. Ultimately, we know a great deal about what and how certain things were done, but the whys remain a mystery.

Because of St. Edmunds, a relatively large body of literary and narrative evidence survives for the town. This evidence has been carefully and extensively discussed, and I need not go into it in detail. There are about eight fairly good narrative accounts of late medieval Bury, with the only major gap falling in the fifteenth century, a rather frequent problem.[21] Excellent records survive describing the political troubles of the fourteenth century, and for the 1327 riots there are several different sources. The chronicles are supplemented by various hagiographies and accounts of abbots' lives, letter books from two abbots, some private letters, and a few scattered codicils. The major problem with these narrative sources is that all are from the abbey's perspective, and are accordingly myopic. Little is told from the burgess' perspective, and virtually all the accounts restrict themselves to the political relationship of town and abbey, or to St. Edmunds' internal affairs. All are anecdotal, and say virtually nothing about the social, economic, or even institutional life of Bury. Further, the national chronicles that cover the later middle ages have little to say about Bury St. Edmunds, except in the riot years. These observations notwithstanding, they serve a distinct function, describing Bury's political crises and outlining the broader political history of the late medieval borough.

Finally, a few words are in order about the records that have not been used. My intention has not been to write a comprehensive social and economic history; as has perhaps been made clear, the nature of the source material precludes this. Rather, the text has tried to chart those aspects of Bury's social and economic development which contributed to the emergence of the commune as one of sixteenth-century England's leading provincial towns. Therefore, many of the fine records of the Abbey of St. Edmunds have been excluded entirely, or used only as they pertain to the

[21] Elton, *England, 1200-1640*, goes into the fifteenth century deterioration of literary sources, pp. 16-18. Also, see C. L. Kingsford, *English Historical Literature in the Fifteenth Century* (Oxford: Clarendon Press, 1913).

town, the suburbs, or the immediate issues of the town-abbey conflict. This includes the splendid array of rural economic evidence from the abbey's estates, as discussed above. It also includes an excellent series of administrative-institutional records that discuss the power and organization of the abbey itself. Further, they have been excluded not only because of the lack of direct involvement, but because they have already been discussed by Lobel and, to a lesser extent, by Goodwin and Yates, in their constitutional and abbatial studies. Perhaps the best of these abbey records are the registers of the abbey officers, in particular, those of the sacrist, which contain crucial information on the governance of the town, as well as of the abbey. They are a superb source, and have been used whenever they bear directly on town or town-abbey issues; in a true sense, the rentals I have relied on for so much and even the testamentary evidence are "sacrists'" sources. Unlike the history of the rural economy of the abbey estates, which awaits an author, these abbey institution and constitutional records do not need to be exploited. Lobel has used them quite well in her administrative history.

LATE MEDIEVAL ABBOTS AND ALDERMEN

1. ABBOTS	*Dates in Office*
Simon of Luton	1257-1279
John of Northwold	1279-1301
Thomas of Tottingham	1302-1312
Richard of Draughton	1312-1335
William of Bernham	1335-1361
Henry of Hunstanton	1361
John of Brinkeley	1361-1379
John of Timworth	1379-1389
William of Cratfield	1390-1415
William of Exeter	1415-1429
William Curteys	1429-1446
William Babington	1446-1453
John Bohun	1453-1469
Robert Ixworth	1469-1474
Richard Hengham	1474-1479
Thomas Rattlesden	1479-1497
William Codenham	1497-1513
John Reeve	1513-1539

2. ALDERMEN

Edward III (Regnal Year)

John De Berton	(1327)	Robert of Eriswell	(1336)
John De Berton	(1328)	Robert of Eriswell	(1337)
John De Berton	(1329)	Robert of Eriswell	(1338)
John De Berton	(1330)	John Osbern	(1339)
Henry son of Roger	(1331)	John Osbern	(1340)
Henry son of Roger	(1332)	Luke son of Edward	(1341)
Galfrid Arysk	(1333)	Richard le Taillour	(1342)
Robert of Eriswell	(1334)	Richard le Taillour	(1343)
Robert of Eriswell	(1335)	Luke son of Edward	(1344)

Robert of Eriswell   (1345)
Robert of Eriswell   (1346)
Robert of Paston   (1347)
Theo de Denham   (1348)
Theo de Denham   (1349)
John de Ewell   (1350)
John de Ewell   (1351)
John Gerard   (1352)
Roger Rose   (1353)
Roger Rose   (1354)
Roger Rose   (1355)
Roger Rose   (1356)
Roger Rose   (1357)
Thomas Denham   (1358)
Thomas Denham   (1359)
Thomas le Draper   (1360)
William Noreys   (1361)
Adam Poyk   (1362)
Adam Poyk   (1363)
Adam Poyk   (1364)
———— (1365)
Thomas of Denham   (1366)
———— (1367)

Edward III

Richard Charman   (1368)
Edmund son of Luke   (1369)
Edmund son of Luke   (1370)
Roger Rose   (1371)
Roger Rose   (1372)
———— (1373)
Thomas of Denham   (1374)
Richard of Ringham   (1375)
Richard of Ringham   (1376)

Richard II

Thomas Halesworth   (1377)
Harvey of Lackford   (1378)
———— (1379)
John Osbern   (1380)
———— (1381)
———— (1382)
Roger Rose   (1383)
———— (1384)

John of Bury   (1385)
Adam Waterwood   (1386)
Adam Waterwood   (1387)
Adam Waterwood   (1388)
Roger Rose   (1389)
Roger Rose   (1390)
John Toller   (1391)
Jacob Marham   (1392)
Adam Waterwood   (1393)
Adam Waterwood   (1394)
Adam Waterwood   (1395)
Adam Waterwood   (1396)
John Osbern   (1397)
Giles at the Pyrye   (1398)

Henry IV

Giles at the Pyrye   (1399)
Giles at the Pyrye   (1400)
———— (1401)
———— (1402)

Henry IV (Regnal Year)

Roger Frampton   (1403)
Roger Frampton   (1404)
Roger Frampton   (1405)
John Nottingham   (1406)
John Nottingham   (1407)
Thomas Halesworth   (1408)
———— (1409)
William Methwold   (1410)
William Methwold   (1412)

Henry V

———— (1413)
John Drinestone   (1414)
———— (1415)
Roger Lygrene   (1416)
Roger Lygrene   (1417)
Roger Lygrene   (1418)
William Methwold   (1419)
William Methwold   (1420)
Richard King   (1421)

Henry VI

—— (1422)
John Smith   (1423)
John Rothe   (1424)
John Nottingham   (1425)
John Nottingham   (1426)
John Nottingham   (1427)
John Maggys   (1428)
John Maggys   (1429)
—— (1430)
Roger Messenger   (1431)
John Edward   (1432)
John Edward   (1433)
John Edward   (1434)
John Gowtry   (1435)
William Rycher   (1436)
William Rycher   (1437)
Roger Messenger   (1438)
Roger Messenger   (1439)
John Smith   (1440)
John Smith   (1441)
John Smith   (1442)

Henry VI

John Smith   (1443)
—— (1444)
—— (1445)
—— (1446)
—— (1447)
—— (1448)
—— (1449)
—— (1450)
—— (1451)

John Thurston   (1452)
John Ayleward   (1453)
John Smith   (1454)
John Reggis   (1455)
John Reggis   (1456)
John Reggis   (1457)
John Reggis   (1458)
John Smith   (1459)

Edward IV

John Smith   (1460)
John Smith   (1461)
John Smith   (1462)
William Aleyn   (1463)
Thomas Bret   (1464)
Thomas Bret   (1465)
Robert Gardner   (1466)
Robert Gardner   (1467)
Walter Thurston   (1468)
Robert Gardner   (1469)
Giles at the Pyrye   (1470)
Giles at the Pyrye   (1471)
John Foster   (1472)
Walter Thurston   (1473)
Walter Thurston   (1474)
Robert Gardner   (1475)
Walter Thurston   (1476)
Walter Thurston   (1477)
Giles at the Pyrye   (1478)
Giles at the Pyrye   (1479)
Robert Gardner   (1480)
Robert Gardner   (1481)

Appendix C

THE TOWN RENTALS

1. THE 1295 RENTAL

Street	Number and Description of Holdings
1. Eastgate Ward	
Eastgate Street	25 ten.; 1 grange; 1 meadow
Le Mustowe	13 ten.; 1 mes.
East Fields	1 ten. on Sparrow Hill
2. Southgate Ward	
Smiths' Row (Churchgoval)	33 ten; 1 pentice
Ponchislane (Goldsmiths' Row)	3 ten.
Schoolhall Street	5 ten., 1 with garden
Horse Market	5 ten.; 1 mes.
Southgate Street	23 ten., 6 with gardens or meadow
Reyngate Street	4 ten.; 1 acre arable toft
Yoxforelane	9 ten.
Maydewater Street	4 ten.
Sparhawk Street	6 ten.
3. Westgate Ward	
Bernwell Street	5 ten., 1 with dovecote
Friars' Lane	3 rods arable
Gildhall Street	9 ten.
4. Risbygate Ward	
The Great Market	
Ironmongers' Row	17 ten., 4 on Void Place
Tollhouse	4 ten.
Skinners' Row	9 ten.
Risbygate Street	7 ten.; 5 granges, 2 with gardens
Tayfen Lane	1 ten.
Long Brakelond	6 ten., 4 of which are in 1 mes.
Brentgoval	3 ten.
Lomb's Lane	1 garden
Baxter Street	9 ten., 2 with gardens
Barbers' Row	9 ten., 3 in 1 mes.
Mustowe	2 ten.
Wells Street	1 ten.

Street	Number and Description of Holdings
Old Baxter Street	4 ten., 1 with garden
Net Market (Meat Market)	5 ten.
Cheese Market	3 ten., 1 on corner of Oyster Hill
Poulterers' Row	2 ten.
5. Northgate Ward	
Long Brakelond	6 ten., 1 with garden
Northgate Street	14 ten., 2 with meadows; 8 gardens; 2 tofts; 4 acres meadow
Burman's Lane	1 ten.
Garlond Street	1 ten.; 1 grange
Little Brakelond	4 ten.
Bow Lane	3 gardens; 5 acres meadow; 1 of pasture
Skorun Lane	4 ten.; 1 garden; 3 acres meadow

2. THE ST. PETER'S HOSPITAL
SUPPLEMENT TO THE 1295 RENTAL

Street or Field	Number and Description of Holdings
Risbygate Field	3 tenements
Wool Hill	1 tenement
Brakelond	3 tenements
Eastgate Street	3 tenements
Reyngate Street	3 tenements
Risbygate Street	2 tenements
Whiting Street	1 tenement
Maydewater Lane	1 tenement
Southgate Street	1 tenement
South Field	1 tenement
Eastgate Field	17 gardens, 1 dovecote
Burman's Lane	4 tenements
Smiths' Row	1 tenement
Little Brakelond	2 tenements

3. LATE 14TH CENTURY SACRIST'S RENTAL
OF THOMAS RUDHAM

Street or Tenement	Number of Holdings
Southgate Street	30
Reyngate Street	6
Maydewater Lane	9
Old Market	5

Street or Tenement	Number of Holdings
Sparhawk Street	14
Goldsmiths' Row	28
Inside West Wall	25
Outside West Wall	9
Gildhall Street	21
Whiting Street	18
Churchgate Street	3
Hennecote and Hatter Street	6
Bolaxe and Wells Street	5
Barbers' Row and Cooks' Row	15
Fishmongers' Street	2
Brentgoval	8
Garlond Street	1
Burman's Lane	1
Long Brakelond	13
Northgate Street	15
Little Brakelond	9
Mustow	18
Eastgate Street Without	19
Risbygate Street	10
Magna Fors	9
Smiths' Row	12
Skinners' Row	9
Linendrapers' Row	20
Spicers' Row	10
Le Mustow	19

4. THE SACRIST'S *HADGOVAL* RENTAL, 1433

Street	Total Holdings	Hadgoval	Non-hadg.	*Lobel totals*
Reyngate	39	24	15	23
Southgate	83	58	25	53
Horse Market	15	15	1	15
Sparhawk	6	3	3	2.5
Goldsmiths' Row**	12	10	2	11
Maydewater Lane	13	11	2	11
Westgate	25	15	10	14
Gildhall	49	35	14	33.5
Whiting	37	28	9	26
Hennecote and Hatter	33	23	10	14
Old Baxter	9	4	5	5
Churchgate	22	13	9	14.5
Versus portus cimitori	5	5	—	5
Master Andrew	5	2	3	3

Street	Total Holdings	Hadgoval	Non-hadg.	*Lobel totals
Le Mustow, Southgate	5	3	2	—
Mag. Fors ex. parte occ.	19	14	5	17
Long Brakelond	44	35	9	64
Little Brakelond***	33	25	8	—
Cooks' Row	3	2	1	1
Garland	19	10	9	9.5
Cryspen's Lane	6	3	3	3
Burman's Lane	4	2	2	2
Lomb's Lane	5	4	1	4
Brentgoval	6	5	1	5
Meat Market (Net)	11	7	4	11
Northgate	21	15	6	17
Le Mustow, Eastgate	17	14	3	—
Eastgate Within	3	3	—	6
Eastgate Without	15	11	4	12
Sparrow Hill	7	6	1	6
Skurf Lane	11	7	4	7
Totals	582	411	171	395

* The data presented by Lobel, *The Borough*, p. 8, differ considerably from the author's figures, for reasons I cannot explain. They are presented for comparative purposes.

** Referred to in the text as *Ad. Gab. Btre M.*

*** Totals include tenements on Wells Street.

5. THE BURY *RELEVIA*, 1353-1539

Street	Number of Fines
Le Mustow	39
Brentgoval	19
Gildhall	124
Long Brakelond	97
Reyngate	39
Bernwell*	31
Little Brakelond	61
Westgate	60
In Fors (Risbygate)	17
Eastgate	47
Whiting	74
Southgate	184
Horse Market	41
Maydewater	24
Northgate	37

Street	Number of Fines
Wells	8
Garland	31
Master Andrew	4
Churchgoval and *Gab. Btre. M.***	24
Elyngham***	1
Mercers' Row	2
Baxter and Old Baxter	13
Sparhawk	12
Pudding Lane	5
Mag. Fors	17
Veti Fors	1
Skinners' Row	9
Burman's Lane	4
Hatter	30
Churchgate	52
Lomb's Lane	13
School Hall	10
Brytes Lane***	1
Cheese Market	1
Risbygate	5
Cryspen's Lane	2
Cooks' Row	4
Loveshand***	22
Net Market	14
Skurf Lane	11

* Also listed as "*alius* Hennecotestrete."
** Goldsmiths' Row.
*** I have found no other listings for these streets.

6. THE DISSOLUTION RENTALS, 1539 AND 1553

Street	Number of Holdings
Reyngate	14
Hennecote, alias College	1
Northgate	5
Horse Market	13
Gildhall	20
Westgate	6
Sparhawk	1
Garland	1
Great Market	8
Whiting	15

Street	Number of Holdings
Churchgate	7
Hatter	4
Net Market	4
Long Brakelond	11
Gab. St. James	7
Little Brakelond	4
Mustow-Eastgate Ward	1
Eastgate	9
Skurf Lane	1
Maydewater	1
Lomb's Lane	1
Gab. St. Mary	4
Old Baxter	1
Burman's Lane	1
Cryspen's Lane	2
Southgate	41

Appendix D

PLACE-NAME SURNAMES
OF BURY ST. EDMUNDS' INHABITANTS

Village	Number	1354-1440	1441-1530
1. ARCHD. OF SUDBURY			
Aldham	2	1	1
Ampton	7	5	2
Babwell	2	2	—
Bacton	1	1	—
Bardwell	6	3	3
Barnham	3	1	2
Barningham	1	1	—
Barrow	7	7	—
Barton	1	1	—
Botesdale	2	2	—
Bradfield	5	4	1
Buxhall	1	1	—
Cavenham	4	3	1
Chilton	1	1	—
Chippenham (Cambs.)	1	1	—
Clare	3	—	3
Cockfield	2	2	—
Combs	1	1	—
Denham	1	1	—
Depden	2	—	2
Drinkestone	2	2	—
Elveden	1	1	—
Eriswell	2	2	—
Euston	1	1	—
Fornham	1	1	—
Gedding	5	4	1
Gislingham	1	1	—
Glemsford	1	1	—

Village	*Number*	*1354-1440*	*1441-1530*
Hargrave	1	1	—
Hawkedon	1	1	—
Herringswell	2	—	2
Horningsheath	1	1	—
Lackford	1	1	—
Lakenheath	1	1	—
The Lark	1	—	1
Mildenhall	5	5	—
Lindsey	2	1	1
Oakley	1	—	1
Pakenham	2	2	—
Preston	1	1	—
Rattlesden	1	1	—
Redgrave	1	1	—
Reed	5	—	5
Rickinghall	5	3	2
Rougham	7	5	2
Saxham	4	4	—
Soham	1	1	—
Somerton	1	1	—
Stanton	5	2	3
Thelnetham	1	—	1
Thurston	5	—	5
Whepstead	1	1	—
Total Sudbury	123	84	39

2. ARCHD. OF SUFFOLK

Battisford	3	3	—
Benhall	1	—	1
Boyton	2	—	2
Brandeston	1	—	1
Brightwell	1	—	1
Brundish	1	1	—
Burstall	2	2	—
Carlton	1	1	—
Clopton	1	—	1
Coddenham	2	—	2
Cratfield	1	1	—
Dennington	1	1	—
Elmham	1	1	—
Framesden	1	1	—

Village	Number	1354-1440	1441-1530
Halesworth	2	2	—
Hoo	1	1	—
Hoxne	1	1	—
Ipswich	1	—	1
Kenton	1	1	—
Kirton	5	4	1
Langham	4	3	1
Norton	2	1	1
Otley	2	—	2
Parham	1	1	—
Stratford	2	2	—
Suffolk	1	1	—
Sutton	4	4	—
Walpole	3	1	2
Walton	1	1	—
Weston	1	1	—
Worlingworth	1	1	—
Yoxford	2	2	—
Total Suffolk	55	39	16

3. ARCHD. OF NORWICH

Village	Number	1354-1440	1441-1530
Binham	1	1	—
Breccles	2	2	—
Caister	2	1	1
Cley	1	1	—
Harling	8	8	—
Hevingham	1	1	—
Houghton	2	1	1
Kelling	1	—	1
Knapton	1	1	—
Lopham	1	1	—
Methwold	4	2	2
Reddenhall	1	—	1
Stockton	2	—	2
Stoke	1	1	—
Swanton	4	3	1
Terrington	3	—	3
Thetford	1	1	—
Thompson	1	1	—
Tilney	1	—	1
Watton	1	—	1
Wellingham	4	4	—
Wells	1	—	1

Village	Number	1354-1440	1441-1530
Whitewell	2	1	1
Wretham	3	3	—
Total Norwich	49	32	17

4. ARCHD. OF NORFOLK

Bressingham	1	1	—
Brockdish	1	1	—
Brooke	4	2	2
Brumstead	1	1	—
Dereham	1	1	—
Dickleberg	2	2	—
Diss	1	1	—
Dunstan	1	1	—
Felbridge	1	1	—
Feltwell	1	—	1
Gooderstone	2	—	2
Heigham	1	1	—
Hempstead	1	1	—
Hilborough	2	2	—
Hockham	1	1	—
Langford	1	1	—
Mundham	1	—	1
Melton	1	1	—
Necton	1	1	—
Norfolk	2	1	1
Pulham	1	1	—
Riddlesworth	1	—	1
Rockland	1	1	—
Shelfanger	1	1	—
Shimpling	1	1	—
Shipdham	1	—	1
Sporle	1	1	—
Tilney	1	—	1
Walsham	1	1	—
Woodnorton	1	1	—
Total Norfolk	37	27	10

5. OTHERS (DOMESTIC)

Cambs.			
Castle	1	1	—

Village	Number	1354-1440	1441-1530
Caxton	2	2	—
Chesterton	1	1	—
Downham	1	1	—
Cornwall	1	—	1
Devon	1	—	1
Essex			
Belchamp	1	1	—
Bocking	1	1	—
Dunton	1	1	—
Horndon	1	—	1
Littlebury	1	1	—
Ramsden	1	1	—
Shelford	5	4	1
Hampshire			
Winchester	4	1	3
Kent	1	—	1
Lancs.			
Radcliffe	1	—	1
Leics.			
Welham	3	1	2
Lincs.			
Brougham	1	1	—
Coningsby	1	1	—
Corby	1	—	1
Frampton	1	1	—
Gedney	1	—	1
Horncastle	1	1	—
Lincoln	1	1	—
Spalding	1	—	1
Middlesex			
Belchamp	1	1	—
Ratcliffe	1	1	—
Nottingham	2	1	1
Northampton			
Helpstone	3	1	2
Rutland			
Overton	1	1	—
Shropshire			
Shrewsbury	1	—	1
Somerset			
Babington	3	1	2
Sussex			
Burton	1	1	—

Village	Number	1354-1440	1441-1530
Yorkshire			
Holtby	1	—	1
Skelton	1	—	1
Total	52	28	24

6. OTHERS (FOREIGN)

Bordeaux	1	—	1
Brittany	1	1	—
France	1	—	1
Gascony	1	1	—
Total	4	2	2

Appendix E

LANDHOLDING AND INHERITANCE

Landholding and inheritance patterns are among the most important and complex of all medieval topics, and require intensive study
to be explained in depth. Good information for both comes from
the Bury testamentary evidence. Unfortunately, this information
cannot be fitted into the particular theme of the struggle between
town and abbey; although the abbey held most of the property in
the borough, there do not appear to have been any temporal
changes in landholding and inheritance. At the same time, the
results of computer-assisted statistical analysis seemed of sufficient
interest to be presented. My intent is not to present a comprehensive or exhaustive study. Overall, the evidence is insufficient for
such purposes, and some of what is adequate has been analyzed
by Lobel.[1] Rather, my goal is a basic explanation of types of landholding and patterns of inheritance found in the large testamentary
sample.

   The terminology and procedures of late medieval urban land
tenure are complex and often inconsistent, with no absolute rules
applying to all will makers. The most common description for units
of property was *tenementum*, the Latin term for "holding." It was
used throughout the fourteenth, fifteenth, and sixteenth centuries,
but is never fully explained in contemporary legal literature, and
even Maitland is a bit unclear on it.[2] It describes a piece of property,
usually with a house or mansion on it; and, even in the banleuca's
rural environments, most tenements had people living on them,
rather than being devoted strictly to agrarian ends. The type of
housing was never specified, but the tenements clearly seem to have
been inhabited. *Tenementum* can be contrasted with *messuagium*, or

---

[1] Lobel, *The Borough*, pp. 2-60.
[2] S.F.C. Milson, ed., Pollock and Maitland, *The History of English Law*
(Cambridge: Cambridge University Press, 1968), i, p. 236.

messuage, yet another ambiguous term. *Messuagium* usually referred to property, but not always with a house, a curtilage or adjacent out houses for family use. It is generally difficult to distinguish between *tenementum* and *messuagium*; they were never used interchangeably, but it is hard to point out precise differences. Probably, tenement was used in a more restricted sense, for residential properties with people resident upon them, while messuage suggested property that was not always built up or improved. In his 1429 will, John Whitop listed a messuage with a tenement on it; from this, it appears that at least in the early fifteenth century, *messuagium* was a plot of land, and *tenementum* a developed property with a house.[3] A description of respective rents would be of great help in defining the distinctions, but none of the rentals are consistent in their listings. Ultimately, precise differences are obscured by a lack of proper evidence.

Inheritance patterns in Bury St. Edmunds were both partible and non-partible. Before the Black Death, with population at an apex, impartible primogeniture was most common, but this pattern diminished with the depopulation of the fourteenth and fifteenth centuries. The earliest reference to partible inheritance come in pre-plague 1331, but do not reach significant proportions until the fifteenth century.[4] By 1450 it was common not only for younger sons to get parcels of land but also daughters, and at times, even younger daughters.[5] Before 1450, fewer than 20 percent of the testamentary records show any form of inheritance other than wife and single son. After 1450, fully 75 percent of all wills mentioning inheritance provide for more than just wife and son; and, since many families would provide for younger children before the last testament, it may well be that many more families were providing for all their progeny, however small their estates might have been.[6] Eldest sons continued to inherit the bulk of the property, but, at least until the early years of the sixteenth century, large portions of movables were distributed more freely than they had been for the previous two hundred years.

With a few exceptions, all land in the banleuca was held by the

---

[3] P.C.B.S.E., Osbern, f. 190.

[4] Bacon, 805.

[5] The opinions are based on the data in Tables E.1 and E.2. Such trends of inheritance seem to have been the result of depopulation and not of any abbey policy.

[6] Bacon, 805.

TABLE E.1: INHERITANCE PATTERNS FROM THE
TESTAMENTARY EVIDENCE, 1354-1530

Heir Description	Frequency	% Total	Testators' Modal Wealth
No listing	1,050	49.6	10 pence
Wife only	622	29.4	12 pence
Son only	96	4.5	15 pence
Daughter only	48	2.3	20 pence
Wife, then child	124	5.9	11 pence
Disposition of will	117	5.5	5 shillings
Sold for cash	5	0.3	15 pence
Friends/Relatives	53	2.5	4 shillings

abbot or his officers, a pattern that persisted until the 1520s, when the abbey began to sell outright large chunks of its endowment.[7] But, while the abbot was recognized as the final holder of most property, renters had considerable rights and powers to buy, sell, alienate, and even sublet and partition what they in turn held directly. The principal concern of the abbot throughout the later middle ages remained the revenues which the property brought in. Further transactions on what was already held would simply bring in additional revenues, such as the *relevia*. Consequently, wills and deeds show considerable activity in the local land markets, and by the fifteenth century these activities were being undertaken without the traditional vehicle of disguise, enfeoffment. Aside from *hadgoval* ground rents paid on those pre-Norman holdings, the most common form of tenure in Bury was burgage tenure. Burgage tenure has been discussed in general terms for English towns by Tait and others, and Bury seems to have conformed to the general pattern.[8] As mentioned, it too was characterized by free transfer and bequest, although the abbot retained power to refuse sale to Jews and others considered undesirable. The only other restrictions

[7] A major exception, of course, was Maydewater Manor. See above, p. 29. Also, see C.C.R., Richard II, 1385, pp. 385-386.

[8] J. Tait, *The Medieval English Borough* (Manchester: University of Manchester Press, 1936). Pollock and Maitland, *The History of English Law*, is, of course, another source.

TABLE E.2: LAND DESCRIPTIONS FROM THE TESTAMENTARY
EVIDENCE, 1354-1530

Description	Frequency	% Total	Testators' Modal Wealth
No listings	1,035	48.9	5 pence
Urban Bury only	1,006	47.5	11 pence
Other urban	18	0.9	13 pence
Rural banleuca only	7	0.3	7 pence
Rural other	5	0.3	20 shillings
Combination of above	45	2.1	——

on such transfers was the preëmptive right of kin to purchase at or near the market price. But, given the general restrictions of medieval land markets, tenure in Bury St. Edmunds was comparatively free. This in turn probably contributed in a large measure to the flowing patterns of town settlement, and perhaps to the ultimate demise of the landed endowment of St. Edmunds.

Appendix F

STATISTICAL INFORMATION ON THE BURGHAL ÉLITE

In Chapter 4, the leading merchants, craftsmen, and gentlemen of Bury St. Edmunds were analyzed and discussed as the corporate, secular body most responsible for making town policy, and leading the borough in its struggle against St. Edmunds. While the power and influence of this burghal élite seems rather certain, the selection of representative individuals to illustrate their power necessarily favored figures about whom the evidence was fullest, and whose names occurred most frequently in the records. The possibility exists then that the selection of the members of this group, inherently unscientific as it was, may have omitted worthy or included unworthy characters. In an attempt to counterbalance this, the computer was programmed to select from the testamentary sample its great men. This too is a "prejudiced" sample, of course, since it may well reveal only those testators with the features arbitrarily deemed most important to be recorded in the coding process! But the method does have the advantage of chosing with no predestination, and should include any important figures missed in Chapter 4 and exclude others selected because of their prominent surnames. It must be emphasized that this is just a start to a collective, statistically oriented biography; much more will be done in the future, perhaps in comparison with similar folk from London and other provincial towns.

The criteria used for selection have been defined as broadly as possible. The sample includes all testators who were landed gentlemen, citizens or burgesses of the borough, all grocers, drapers, mercers, or clothiers. It also includes all testators whose bequests to the high altar of their parish of burial was twenty shillings or higher. This provides for a very broad-based sample—perhaps too broad—and the last qualification allows for the inclusion of any craftsmen, lesser merchant, or shopkeeper of great wealth, or an individual who failed to mention social class, position or occupation in his will. In all, 325 men and women, about 15 percent of the total sample, were included. I then developed statistics on the following characteristics: seasonal mortality, marriage and remarriage proportions, numbers of male and female progeny, age distribution, heirs and inheritance patterns, landholdings, and whether debts were held or owed. The single major variable not asked for was wealth, since it was one of the criteria for admission in the group.

The data for the burghal élite are presented in Table F.1, and can be compared with the data taken from the larger testamentary population and presented in Chapters 2 and 3. There are several interesting differences between the two populations. The burghal élite were "better" than the rest of the town's testamentary population; they had more of everything save debts. In a sense, this is a bit like the statement "the rich are just like everybody else but richer," but the difference between the great and common folk should still be underscored. Even their mortality patterns, largely controlled by plague, a disease generally considered to be oblivious to wealth and social class, showed unusual patterns. It had less of an autumnal and more of a spring skew. The burghal élite nuptial patterns ran about 10 percent higher, and remarriage was far more frequent. Male and female replacement ratios were greater, reflecting not only fewer families with no children, but more families with multiple numbers of sons and daughters. Their age distribution showed more young and more old in the testamentary populations, in part a reflection of the measure itself, which was based on numbers of progeny, but also indicative of real age differentials.

The contrast between burghal élite and ordinary folk extended from demographic to social categories. By definition, the élite were richer. Their inheritance patterns showed the effects of primogeniture, but high proportions of them were able to provide for more than one son, and often for daughters, relatives, and friends. They held far more land and owned many more movable goods, from bullion and jewels to clothing. And, while a good proportion of the élite owed debts, several held them. Until more work is done on the computerized sample, it is difficult to do more than underscore the distinction between the class in power and those whom they ruled. While they must have been richer and more prolific to enter

TABLE F.1: DEMOGRAPHIC AND SOCIAL CHARACTERISTICS OF THE ÉLITE

Season of Death	*Mode*	*Winter*	*Spring*	*Summer*	*Fall*			
	Fall	20.8%	23.6%	23.1%	24.9%			

Nuptiality	*% Ever Married*		*Mode*		*% Remarried*			
	83		1		1.1			

Male Progeny	*R.R.*		*% Distribution*					
		0	1	2	3	4	5+	
	.62	60.2	24.0	10.5	4.6	0.5	0.2	
Female Progeny	.49	70.3						

Age	*Under 25*		*25-50*		*Over 50*		*Unknown*	
	1.8		34.1		16.0		48.1	

Land*	*0*	*1*	*2*	*3*	*4*	*5*		
	38.2	54.7	1.8	0.5	0.5	4.3		

Heirs**	*0*	*1*	*2*	*3*	*4*	*5*	*6*	*7*	*8*
	39.1	33.6	6.2	3.2	9.2	4.8	0.2	0.2	3.4

Debts***	*0*	*1*	*2*	*3*	*4*			
	75.7	1.4	21.3	1.4	0.2			

* Land Code	**Heirs Code	***Debts Code
0 = no holdings listed	0 = none listed	0 = no listing
1 = urban Bury only	1 = wife or husband	1 = owed to person
2 = other urban	2 = son	2 = owed by person
3 = rural local West Suffolk	3 = daughter	3 = owes and owed
4 = rural other	4 = spouse/son/daughter	
5 = combination of any of above	5 = cash to will beq.	
	6 = cash to wife/progeny	
	7 = other relatives	
	8 = friends	

the élite, membership itself may well have helped to perpetuate their superiority. But one thing is certain: in a closed, highly structured society, they dominated the secular affairs of Bury St. Edmunds, and were accepted by the "lesser" townsfolk as their leaders, at least while the common enemy, the abbey, flourished.

Bibliography

A. PRIMARY SOURCES

1. Manuscript Records

Bury St. Edmunds. Suffolk Record Office, Bury St. Edmunds Office, Registered Probate Wills, Sacrist's Court, Osbern, 1354-1442.

———, Wills, Hawlee, 1442-1482.

———, Wills, Pye, 1491-1509.

———, Wills, Mason, 1510-1514.

———, Wills, Hoode, 1510-1530.

———, The Hengrave Deeds, 1, 449.

Cambridge. Cambridge University Library, Ms. Ee 3 60, "Pinchbeck Register."

———, Ms. Ff 2 29, "Book of Charters."

———, Ms. Ff 2 33, "Register of the Sacrist of Bury."

———, Ms. Ff 4 35, "The Liberty of the Abbot."

———, Ms. Gg 4 4, "Register of the Abbot of St. Edmunds."

———, Ms. Mm 4 19, *Nigrum Regis.*"

Chicago. The Joseph Regenstein Library, University of Chicago, The Sir Nicholas Bacon Collection.

Ipswich. Suffolk Record Office, Registered Probate Wills, The Archdeaconry Court, Baldwin, 1439-1476.

———, Wills, Hervey, 1476-1479.

———, Wills, Fuller, 1442-1480.

London. The British Library, The British Museum, Ms. Additional 10108, "Notes."

———, Ms. Arundel 1, E2/41/4, "Cartulary of the Hospital of *Domus Dei.*"

———, (Cotton), Ms. Claudius A x ii.

———, (Cotton), Ms. Titus Ms. B v, "Survey of the Benefits which Cometh from Wool and Cloth in Suffolk."

———, Ms. Harl. 27, "Roll of the Pitancer."

———, Ms. Harl. 58, "Rentals, *Relevia, Hadgoval.*"

———, Ms. Harl. 230, "Miscellaneous."

———, Ms. Harl. 294, "Genealogies, Will Abstracts."

London. The British Library, The British Museum, Ms. Harl. 368, "Kallander of Prisoners."

———, Ms. Harl. 638, "Rentals."

———, Ms. Harl. 645, "Rentals, Tolls, Stallage."

———, Ms. Harl. 1005, "Rents, Incomes."

———, Ms. Harl. 4626, "Alderman's Guild Statutes."

———, Ms. Lansdowne 114, "Wool Records."

———, Ms. Sloane 110, "Medical Recipe Book of the Spring Family."

London. The Public Record Office, Gaol Delivery Rolls, Nos. 63, 64, 65, 85, 105, 117, 118, 119, 125, 134, 152, 158, 164, 181, 182, 200, 206, 207, 212.

———, The Poll Tax Returns, E 179.

———, The Poll Tax Returns, E 359.

———, The Prerogative Court of Canterbury Registered Probate Wills. Those registers with Bury St. Edmunds, testators are: Marche; Stokton; Wattys; Moore; Blamyr; Adeane; Bennett; Fetiplace; Coode; Waynwarying; Porch.

Norwich. The Norfolk Record Office, Registered Probated Wills, The Consistory Court of Norwich. Those registers with Bury St. Edmunds' testators are: Hersyk; Briggs; Popy; Heydon; Herning; Aleyn; Surflete; Doke; Typpes; A. Caston; Spurlinge; Spyltymber.

Oxford. Bodleian Library, Oxford University, Ms. Suffolk, Bury St. Edmunds 515, "Account of the Supervisors."

2. *Printed Sources*

Arnold, Thomas, ed., *Memorials of St. Edmunds Abbey*, 3 vols., (London: Kraus Reprints, 1965).

Butler, H. E., ed., *The Chronicle of Jocelin of Brakelond* (New York: Oxford University Press, 1949).

Calendars of Charter Rolls, 1257-1516 (London: H.M.S.O., 1908-1927).

Calendars of Close Rolls, 1268-1509 (London: H.M.S.O., 1938-1963).

Calendars of Fine Rolls, 1272-1485 (London: H.M.S.O., 1911-1961).

Calendars of Inquisitions, 1,2,3,4, 1272-1377, 1485-1509 (London: H.M.S.O., 1904-1915).

Calendars of Papal Registers, 1342-1492. (London: H.M.S.O., 1896-1960).

Calendars of Patent Rolls, 1272-1494 (London: H.M.S.O., 1901-1941).

Clarke, Edward, *Bury Chroniclers in the Thirteenth Century* (Bury St. Edmunds: Bury Free Press, 1905).

Davies, R.H.C., ed., *Kalendar of Abbot Samson of Bury St. Edmunds* (London: Royal Historical Society, lxxxiv, 3rd series, 1954).

Douglas, D. C. "Fragments of an Anglo-Saxon Survey from Bury St. Edmunds," *English Historical Review*, xliii, 1928.

Dugdale, William, *Monasticon Anglicanum*, ed. J. Calley and Sir Henry Ellis (London: James Bohn, 1846).

Galbraith, V. H., "The Pinchbeck Register," *English Historical Review*, xli, 1963.

———, "The St. Edmunds Bury Chronicle, 1296-1301," *English Historical Review*, lviii, 1925.

Gasquet, F. A., *The Bosworth Psalter* (London: H. G. Bohn, 1908).

Glasscock, R. E., *The Lay Subsidy of 1334* (London: Royal Historical Society, 1975).

Grandson, Antonia, ed., *The Chronicle of Bury St. Edmunds, 1212-1301* (London: Nelson, 1964).

———, *The Letterbook of William of Hoo, Sacrist of Bury St. Edmunds, 1280-94* (Ipswich: Suffolk Record Society, v, 1963).

Hariss, H. A., ed., *The Household Book of Dame Alice de Bryene of Acton Hall, Suffolk, September, 1412 to September, 1413* (Ipswich: W. E. Harrison, 1931).

Hervey, Francis, ed., *The History of King Eadmund the Martyr and the Early Years of the Abbey* (Oxford: Oxford University Press, 1929). This is a transcription of Bodley Library, Oxford, Ms. 197.

———, ed., *The Pinchbeck Register*, 2 vols. (Oxford: Oxford University Press, 1925).

———, ed., *Suffolk in the Seventeenth Century. The Breviary of Suffolk by Robert Reyce, 1618* (Oxford: Oxford University Press, 1902).

Letters and Papers, Foreign and Domestic, Henry VIII, 1509-1530 (London: H.M.S.O., 1920-1965).

The Paston Letters, 5 vols., ed. Norman Davis (Oxford: Clarendon Press, 1971).

Redstone, Lillian J., "First Ministers' Account of the Possessions of the Abbey of St. Edmunds," *P.S.I.*, xiii, 3, 1911.

Redstone, V. B., "St. Edmunds Bury and the Town Rental for 1295," *P.S.I.*, 1909.

Suffolk in 1327. Being a Subsidy Return. Suffolk Green Books, ix (Woodbridge, Suffolk: George Booth, 1906).

Suffolk in 1524. Being the Return for a Subsidy Granted in 1523. Suffolk Green Books, x (Woodbridge, Suffolk: George Booth, 1910).

Thompson, R. M., *The Chronicle of the Election of Hugh, Abbot of Bury St. Edmunds and Later Bishop of Ely* (Oxford: Clarendon Press, 1974).

Toulmin-Smith, Lucy, *English Gilds: Original Ordinances of the Fourteenth and Fifteenth Centuries* (London: Early English Text Society, 1870).

Tymms, Samuel, ed., *Wills and Inventories from the Registers of the Commissary of Bury St. Edmunds and the Archdeacon of Sudbury* (London: Camden Society, 1850).

William of Worcestre, *Itineraries*, ed. John Harvey (Oxford: Clarendon Press, 1969).

Williamson, E. W., *The Letters of Osbert of Clare* (Oxford: Oxford University Press, 1929).

3. Select Listing of Calendars and Guides to Sources Used

Camp, A. J., *Wills and Their Whereabouts* (Canterbury: Phillimores, 1963).

Catalogue of Harleian Manuscripts in the British Museum, vols. i and ii (London: George Eyre, 1808).

Copinger, W. A., *Suffolk Manuscripts and Records*, 5 vols. (London: Henry Southeran, 1904).

Crisp, F. A., *Calendar of Wills at Ipswich, 1444-1606* (Privately Printed, 1895).

Ekwall, Eilert, *The Concise Oxford English Dictionary of Place-Names* (Oxford: Clarendon Press, 1940).

Farrow, M. A., "Index of Wills Proved in the Consistory Court of Norwich, 1370-1550, and Wills Among the Norwich Enrolled Deeds, 1298-1508," *Norfolk Record Society*, xvi-xviii, 1943-1945.

Gibson, J.S.W., *Wills and Where to Find Them* (Canterbury: Phillimores, 1974).

The Manuscripts of Lincoln, Bury St. Edmunds and Great Grimsby Corporations (London: Historical Manuscripts Commission, 14, Report 8, Eyre and Spottiswode, 1895).

Oswald-Hicks, T. W., *A Calendar of Wills. . .of Suffolk Proved in the Prerogative Court of Canterbury, 1383-1604* (London: Privately Printed, 1913).

Redstone, V. B., *A Calendar of Pre-Reformation Wills . . . at Bury St. Edmunds* (Bury St. Edmunds: Privately Printed, 1907).

Smith, Frank, *A Genealogical Gazetteer of England* (Baltimore: Genealogical Publishing Co., 1968).

Smith, Richard, *The Sir Nicholas Bacon Collection: Sources of English Society, 1250-1700* (Chicago: University of Chicago Library Publication, 1972).

Thompson, J. R., *The Records of St. Edmunds of East Anglia*, 2 vols. (London: Simpkin and Marshall, 1890).

B. SELECTED SECONDARY WORKS

Abrams, Philip and E. A. Wrigley, eds., *Towns in Societies: Essays in Economic History and Historical Sociology* (Cambridge: Cambridge University Press, 1978).

The Archaeological Journal, cviii, 1951, "Report of the Summer Meeting at Ipswich." Includes: H.J.M. Maltby, "Bury St. Edmunds"; J. T. Smith, "A Note on the Origin of the Town Plan of Bury St. Edmunds"; Margaret Wood, "Moyses Hall; A Description of the Building"; Maltby, "A History of the Building and the Museum Collection"; Maltby, "The Town Hall and the Guildhall"; A. B. Whittingham, "Bury St. Edmunds Abbey"; Whittingham, "St. Mary's Church, Bury St. Edmunds"; Whittingham, "St. James' Cathedral."

Baker, Alan R. H., "Changes in the Later Middle Ages," in H. C. Darby, ed., *A New Historical Geography of England* (Cambridge: Cambridge University Press, 1973).

Barley, M. W., ed., *The Plans and Topography of Medieval Towns in England and Wales* (London: C.C.B.A. Research Report, 14, 1976).

Bautier, R-H., "Feux, Population et Structure Sociale au Milieu du XVe Siècle: L'Exemple de Carpentras," *Annales E.S.C.*, 1959.

Bellamy, John, *Crime and Public Order in England in the Later Middle Ages* (London: R.K.P., 1973).

Beresford, M. W., *Lay Subsidies and Poll Taxes* (Canterbury: Phillimores, 1963).

——, *New Towns of the Middle Ages* (New York: Praeger, 1967).

Bergeron, D. M., *English Civic Pageantry* (London: Edward Arnold, 1971).

Blanchard, Ian, "Population Change, Enclosure, and the Early Tudor Economy," *Ec.H.R.*, 2nd series, xxiii, 1970.

Blunt, C. E., "The St. Edmunds Memorial Coinage," *P.S.I.*, xxxi, 3 1969.

Bloor, W. A., "The Proper of the Mass for the Feast of St. Edmunds," *The Douai Magazine*, vii, 4, 1933.

The Borough of Bury St. Edmunds, Official Guide, ed. H. R. Marsh (Norwich: Jarrold and Sons, 1976).

Bowden, Peter, *The Wool Trade in Tudor and Stuart England* (London: St. Martin's Press, 1962).

Breese, Gerald, ed., *The City in Newly Developed Countries* (Englewood, N.J.: Prentice-Hall, 1969).

Bridbury, A. R., *Economic Growth: England in the Later Middle Ages* (London: Unwin, 1962).

——, "English Provincial Towns in the Later Middle Ages," *Ec.H.R*, 2nd series, xxxiv, 1981.

Cam, Helen, *Liberties and Communities in Medieval England* (New York: Barnes and Noble, 1963).

Carus-Wilson, E. M., "The English Cloth Industry in the Twelfth and Thirteenth Centuries," in her *Medieval Merchant Venturers* (London: Metheun, 1954).

——, *The Expansion of Exeter at the Close of the Middle Ages* (Exeter: The University of Exeter, 1961).

——, "The First Half Century of the Borough of Stratford-upon Avon," *Ec.H.R.*, 2nd series, xviii, 1965.

——, "An Industrial Revolution of the Thirteenth Century," in *Medieval Merchant Venturers.*

——, "The Medieval Trade of the Ports of the Wash," *Medieval Archaeology*, vi-vii, 1962-63.

——, "Trends in the Export of Woollens in the Fourteenth Century," *Medieval Merchant Venturers.*

Carus-Wilson, E. M., and Coleman, Olive, eds., *England's Export Trade, 1275-1547* (Oxford: Oxford University Press, 1963).

Christaller, Walter, *Central Places in Southern Germany* (Englewood, N.J.: Prentice-Hall, 1966).

Clark, Peter, and Slack, Paul, *English Towns in Transition, 1500-1700* (Oxford: Oxford University Press, 1976).

——, eds., *Crisis and Order in English Towns* (London: R.K.P., 1972).

Clay, Rotha Mary, *Medieval Hospitals of England* (London: Frank Cass Reprints, 1966).

Coleman, Olive, "Trade and Prosperity in the Fifteenth Century: Some Aspects of the Trade of Southampton," *Ec.H.R.*, 2nd series, xvi, 1963-1964.

Colvin, H. M., "Domestic Architecture and Town Planning," in A. L. Poole, ed., *Medieval England* (Oxford: Oxford University Press, 1958).

Conger, M.R.G., "The Use of Town Plans in the Study of Urban History," in H. J. Dyos, *The Study of Urban History* (London: St. Martin's Press, 1968).

Cornwall, Julian, "English Country Towns in the 1520s," *Ec.H.R.*, 2nd series, xv, 1962-63.

———, "English Population in the Early Sixteenth Century," *Ec.H.R.*, 2nd series, xxiii, 1970.

Darby, H. C., ed., *An Historical Geography of England Before 1800*, (Cambridge: Cambridge University Press, 1936).

———, ed., *A New Historical Geography of England* (Cambridge: Cambridge University Press, 1973).

Davis, H.W.C., "The Commune of Bury St. Edmunds," *English Historical Review*, xxiv, 1909.

Davis, R.W.C., "The Monks of St. Edmunds, 1020-1148," *History*, xl, 1955.

Deich, Werner, *Das Goslarer Reichsvogteigeld* (Lübeck: Mattheison Verlag, 1974).

Desportes, Pierre, "La Population du Reims au XVe Siècle d'après le Dénombrement de 1422," *Le Moyen Age*, lxxii, 1966.

Dewey, R., "The Rural-Urban Continuum: Real but Relatively Unimportant," *The American Journal of Sociology*, lxvi, 1960.

Dickens, A. G., *The English Reformation* (London: Batsford, 1964).

Dickenson, R. B., "Town Plans of East Anglia," *Geography*, xix, 1934.

Dickenson, W. R., *The West European City* (London: R.K.P., 1951).

Dicks, T.R.B., "Network Analysis and Historical Geography," *Area*, 4, 1972.

Dietz, F. C., *English Public Finance*, 1485-1641, 2nd ed. (London: Frank Cass Reprints, 2 vols., 1964).

Dobb, Maurice, *Studies in the Development of Capitalism* (London: G. Routledge, 1947).

Dobson, R., "Admissions to the Freedom of the City of York in the Later Middle Ages," *Ec.H.R.*, 2nd series, xxv, 1973.

———, "Urban Decline in Late Medieval England," *Trans. of the Royal Historical Society*, 5th series, xxv, 1977.

Douglas, D. C., *The Social Structure of Medieval East Anglia* (Oxford: Oxford University Press, 1927).

Dulley, A.J.F., "Four Kent Towns at the End of the Middle Ages," in Margaret Roake and John Wyman, eds., *Essay in Kentish History* (London: Frank Cass, 1973).

Dyer, A. D., *The City of Worcestre in the Sixteenth Century* (Leicester University Press, 1973).

Dyos, H. L., *The Study of Urban History* (London: Macmillan, 1973).

Edwards, J. K., "The Decline of the Norwich Textile Industries," *Bulletin of Economic and Social Research*, xvi, 1964).

Edwardson, A. R., *Moyses Hall Museum* (Bury St. Edmunds, pamphlet, n.d.).

Everitt, A. M., ed., *Perspectives in English Urban History* (London: Macmillan, 1973).

Fisher, F. J., "The Development of London as a Center of Conspicuous Consumption in the Sixteenth and Seventeenth Centuries," *Trans. of the Royal Historical Society*, 4th series, xxx, 1948.

———, "The Development of the London Food Market, 1540-1640," *Ec.H.R.*, 1934-35.

Ford, J. C., *The Aldermen and Mayors of Bury St. Edmunds from 1302* (Compiled and Handwritten by the Author, n.d.).

Gade, J. A., *Hanseatic Control of Norwegian Commerce During the Late Middle Ages* (Leiden, E. J. Brill, 1951).

Gage, J., *The History and Antiquities of Suffolk Thingoe Hundred* (London: By the Author, 1838).

Galbraith, V., "The East Anglian See," *English Historical Review*, xl, 1925.

Ganshof, F. L., *Etude sur le Développement des Villes entre Loire at Rhin au Moyen Age* (Paris: Presses Universitaires de France, 1943).

Gasquet, F. A., *Henry VIII and the English Monasteries*, 2 vols. (London: J. Hedges, 1902).

Gillingwater, E., *Historical and Descriptive Account of St. Edmundsbury* (Bury St. Edmunds: J. Rackham, 1804).

Glasscock, R. E., "England circa 1334," in H. C. Darby, ed., *New Historical Geography of England*.

Gibson, Gail McMurray, "Bury St. Edmunds, Lydgate and the N-Town Cycle," *Speculum*, 56, 1981.

Goodwin, A., *The Abbey of St. Edmundsbury* (Oxford: Basil Blackwell, 1931).

Gottfried, Robert S., "Bury St. Edmunds and the Populations of Late Medieval English Towns," *The Journal of British Studies*, Autumn, 1980.

———, *Epidemic Disease in Fifteenth Century England: The Medical Response and the Demographic Consequences* (New Brunswick, N.J.: Rutgers University Press, 1978).

———, "Population, Plague and the Sweating Sickness: Demographic Movements in Late Fifteenth Century England," *The Journal of British Studies*, Autumn, 1977.

Graham, Rose, "A Papal Visitation of Bury St. Edmunds and West-minster, 1234," *English Historical Review*, xxviii, 1912.

Grandson, Antonia, "A Democratic Movement in the Abbey of Bury St. Edmunds in the Late Twelfth and Early Thirteenth Centuries," *The Journal of Ecclesiastical History*, xxvi, 1975.

———, "On St. Benets Holme and the *Chron. Bur.* and the Abbey," *Bulletin of the Institute of Historical Research*, 68, 1963.

Green, Mrs. J. R., *Town Life in the Fifteenth Century*, 2 vols. (London: Macmillan, 1894).

Haggett, P., and Chorley, R. J., *Network Analysis in Geography* (London: Edward Arnold, 1969).

Hanawalt, Barbara, "Crime in East Anglia in the Fourteenth Century," *Norfolk Record Society*, xliv, 1976.

Harper-Bell, Christopher, "A Late Medieval Visitation—The Diocese of Norwich in 1499," *P.S.I.*, xxxiv, 1, 1977.

Harris, H. A., "Notes: The Site of St. Peter's Hospital Chapel," *P.S.I.*, xvii, 3, 1921.

Hartshrone, C. H., "The Visits of Edward the First to Bury St. Edmunds and Thetford," *P.S.I.*, 1, 1858.

Hatcher, John, *Plague, Population, and the English Economy* (London: Macmillan, 1977).

Haward, W. I., "The Trade of Boston in the Fifteenth Century," *Reports and Papers of the Lincolnshire Architectural and Archeological Societies*, xli, 1932-33.

Heard, Nigel, *Wool: East Anglia's Golden Fleece* (Lavenham, Suffolk: Terrance Dalton, 1970).

Hill, Francis, *Medieval Lincoln* (Cambridge: Cambridge University Press, 1948).

Hills, Gordon M., "The Antiquities of Bury St. Edmunds," *The Journal of the British Archeological Association*, xxi, 1865.

Hilton, R. H., "The Small Town as Part of Peasant Society," in his *The English Peasantry in the Later Middle Ages* (Oxford: Oxford University Press, 1976).

Hofrath, Philipp, "Samson von Tottington Abt von St. Edmund," *Sitzungsberichte der kaiserlich Akademie der Wissenschaften: Phil. Hist. Klasse*, 48, 1846.

Hoselitz, B. F., "The Role of Cities in the Economic Growth of Underdeveloped Countries," *The Journal of Political Economy*, lxi, 1953.

Hoskins, W. G., "English Provincial Towns in the Early Sixteenth

Century," *Transactions of the Royal Historical Society*, 5th series, 1956.

————, "Harvest Fluctuations in English Economic History, 1480-1619," *Agricultural History Review*, xii, 1964.

Hunard, N. H., "The Anglo-Norman Franchises," *English Historical Review*, lxiv, 1949.

James, Montague Rhodes, *On the Abbey of St. Edmund Bury* (Cambridge: Deighton Bell, 1895).

Jewell, Helen M., *English Local Administration* (New York: Barnes and Noble, 1972).

Jones, B. C., "The Topography of Medieval Carlisle," *Trans. of the Cumberland and Westmorland Antiquarian and Archaeological Society*, n.s., lxxvi, 1976.

Jones, Emrys, *Towns and Cities* (Oxford: Oxford University Press, 1966).

Jusserand, J. J., *English Wayfaring Life in the Middle Ages* (London: Ernest Benn, 1889).

Krause, J., "The Medieval Household: Large or Small," *Ec.H.R.*, 2nd series, ix, 1956-57.

Le Goff, Jaques, "The Town as an Agent of Civilization," in Carlo Cipolla, ed., *The Fontana Economic History of Europe: The Middle Ages* (New York: Fontana, 1972).

LeRoy Ladurie, E., *Montaillou: The Promised Land of Error* (New York: George Braziller, 1978).

Lloyd, T. H., *The English Wool Trade in the Middle Ages* (Cambridge: Cambridge University Press, 1977).

Lobel, M. D., *The Borough of Bury St. Edmunds: A Study in the Government and Development of a Medieval Town* (Oxford: Oxford University Press, 1935).

————, "A Detailed Account of the 1327 Rising at Bury St. Edmunds and the Subsequent Trial," *P.S.I.*, xxi, 3, 1933.

————, "The Ecclesiastical Banleuca in England," in F. M. Powicke, ed., *Oxford Essays in Medieval History* (Oxford: Clarendon Press, 1934).

————, "The Gaol of Bury St. Edmunds," *P.S.I.*, xxi, 3, 1933.

————, "A List of the Aldermen and Bailiffs of Bury St. Edmunds from the 12th to the 16th Century," *P.S.I.*, xxii, 1934-36.

————, "Some Additions to Andre Reville's Account of the Events at Bury St. Edmunds following the Revolt of 1381," *P.S.I.*, xxi, 3, 1933.

————, ed., *Historic Towns: Maps and Plans of Towns and Cities in the*

British Isles, with Historical Commentaries, from Earliest Times to 1800 (London: Scholar Press, 1969).

MacCaffrey, Wallace T., *Exeter, 1540-1640: The Growth of an English Country Town* (Cambridge, Mass.: Harvard University Press, 1958).

McClenaghan, Barbara, *The Springs of Lavenham and the Suffolk Cloth Trade in the XV and XVI Centuries* (Ipswich: W. E. Harrison, 1924).

MacFarlane, Alan, *The Origins of English Individualism* (Cambridge: Cambridge University Press, 1978).

McFarlane, K. B., *The Nobility of Later Medieval England* (Oxford: Oxford University Press, 1973).

McKinley, R. A., *Norfolk and Suffolk Surnames in the Middle Ages* (London: Phillimore, 1975).

———, *Norfolk Surnames in the Sixteenth Century* (Leicester: Leicester University Press, 1973).

McLachlan, Elizabeth Parker, "The Bury Missal in Laon and Its Crucifixion Miniature," *Gesta*, xvii, 1978.

———, "The *Scriptorium* of Bury St. Edmunds in the Third and Fourth Decades of the Fifteenth Century," *Medieval Studies*, xl, 1978.

Marshall, T. H., "Capitalism and the Decline of English Gilds," *Cambridge Historical Journal*, iii, 1928.

Martin, G. H., *The Borough and Merchant Community of Ipswich, 1317-1432*, Oxford University D. Phil Thesis, 1955.

———, "The Registration of Deeds of Title in the Medieval Borough," in Bullough, D. A. and Storey, R. L., eds., *Essays in Honor of Kathleen Major* (Oxford: Oxford University Press, 1971).

Metha, S. K., "Some Demographic and Economic Consequences of Primate Cities: A Case for Reevaluation," *Demography*, i, 1964.

Miskimin, Harry A., Herlihy, David, Udovitch, A. L., eds., *The Medieval City* (New Haven, Conn.: Yale University Press, 1977).

Mitchell, S. K., *Taxation in Medieval England* (New Haven, Conn.: Yale University Press, 1951).

Morant, A. W., "On the Abbey of St. Edmunds," *P.S.I.*, iv, 1870-75.

Morley, C., "A Catalogue of Beneficed Clergy of Suffolk, 1086-1550," *P.S.I.*, xxii, 1934-36.

Mumford, Lewis, *The City in History* (New York: Harcourt Brace, 1961).

Oman, Charles, *The Great Revolt of 1381*, 2nd ed. (New York: Haskell House, 1968).

Orme, Nicholas, *English Schools in the Middle Ages* (London: Methuen, 1973).

Palliser, D. M., "The Borough of Medieval Staffordshire," *North Staffordshire Journal of Field Studies*, xii, 1972.

Pankin, W. A., "Medieval English House Plans," *Medieval Archaeology*, vi-vii, 1962-63.

Parker, V., *The Making of King's Lynn* (London and Chichester: Phillimore, 1971).

Patten, John, "Population Distribution in Norfolk and Suffolk during the Sixteenth and Seventeenth Centuries," *The Institute of British Geographers*, lxv, 1975.

———, "Village and Town: An Occupational Study," *Agricultural History Review*, xx, 1972.

Pelham, R. A., "Fourteenth Century England," in H. C. Darby, ed., *Historical Geography of England Before 1800*.

Pelling, Margaret, and Webster, Charles, "Medical Practitioners," in Charles Webster, ed., *Health, Medicine and Mortality in the Sixteenth Century* (Cambridge: Cambridge University Press, 1979).

Phelps-Brown, E. H., and Hopkins, Sheila, "Seven Centuries of Prices of Consumables, Compared with Builders' Wage Rates," *Economica*, 2nd series, xxiii, 1956.

Phythian-Adams, Charles, *Desolation of a City; Coventry and the Urban Crisis of the Late Middle Ages* (Cambridge: Cambridge University Press, 1979).

———, "Ceremony and Citizen: The Communal Year at Coventry, 1450-1550," in Clark and Slack, eds., *Crisis and Order in English Towns*.

———, "Jolly Cities: Goodly Towns. The Current Search for England's Urban Roots," *Urban History Yearbook*, 1977.

———, "Urban Decay in Late Medieval England," in Abrams and Wrigley, *Towns in Societies*.

Pirenne, Henri, *Medieval Cities* (New York: Doubleday, 1956).

Platt, Colin, *The Medieval English Town* (London: McKay, 1976).

Postan, M. M., *Essays on Medieval Agriculture and General Problems* (Cambridge: Cambridge University Press, 1973).

————, *Medieval Economy and Society* (Berkely, Cal.: University of California Press, 1973).

————, *Medieval Trade and Finance* (Cambridge: Cambridge Press, 1972).

Pound, J. F., "The Norwich Census of the Poor, 1570," *Norfolk Record Society*, xl, 1971.

————, "The Social and Trade Structure of Norwich, 1525-1575," *Past and Present*, 34, 1966.

Powell, Edgar, "Muster Rolls of the Territorials in Tudor Times," *P.S.I.*, xvi, 1915, 1918.

————, *The Rising in East Anglia in 1381* (Cambridge: Cambridge University Press, 1896).

————, "The Taxation of Ipswich for the Welsh War in 1282," *P.S.I.* xii, 1906.

Power, Eileen, *The Wool Trade in English Medieval History* (Oxford: Oxford University Press, 1941).

Power, Eileen, and Postan, M. M., eds., *Studies in English Trade in the Fifteenth Century* (London: Routledge & Kegan, 1933).

P.S.I., xxxi, 3, 1969, "St. Edmunds Commemorative Issue, 869-1969."

Pugh, Ralph B., *Imprisonment in Medieval England* (Cambridge: Cambridge University Press, 1968).

Ramsey, G. D., "Distribution of the Cloth Industry, 1561-1562," *English Historical Review*, 57, 1942.

Ranson, K., *Lavenham* (Lavenham, Suffolk, pamphlet, 1973).

Redstone, L. J., "The Liberty of St. Edmunds," *P.S.I.*, xv, 1914.

————, "Suffolk Limiters," *Suffolk Institute of Archaeology and Natural History*, xx, i, 1928.

Redstone, V. B., "Chapels, Chantries and Gilds in Suffolk," *P.S.I.*, xii, 1906.

————, ed., *Memorials of Old Suffolk* (London: Bemrose and Sons, 1908).

Reichal, O. J., "Jocelyn de Brakelond and the *servicum debitum*," *Trans. of the Devonshire Association for the Advancement of Science and Art*, 36, 1904.

Reynolds, Susan, *An Introduction to the History of English Medieval Towns* (Oxford: Clarendon Press, 1977).

Rigby, S. H., "Urban Decline in the Later Middle Ages," *Urban History Yearbook*, 1979.

Ritchie, Carson, "The Black Death at St. Edmunds," *P.S.I.*, xxvii, 1, 1956.

Rodgers, H. B., "The Market Area of Preston in the Sixteenth and Seventeenth Centuries," *Geographical Studies*, iii, 1956.

Rörig, Fritz, *The Medieval Town* (Berkeley, Cal.: University of California, 1967).

Rosenthal, Joel T., *The Purchase of Paradise* (London: R.K.P., 1972).

Round, J. H., "The First Charter to St. Edmunds Bury, Suffolk," *American Historical Review*, ii, 1898.

Rouse, Clive, *The Old Towns of England* (London: Batsford, 1936).

Rowe, Joy, "Medieval Hospitals of Bury St. Edmunds," *Medical History*, 2, 1958.

Rubin, Stanley, *Medieval English Medicine* (New York: Barnes and Noble, 1974).

Russell, J. C., *British Medieval Population* (Albuquerque, N.M.: University of New Mexico Press, 1948).

Salmon, Vivian, "The Other Elizabeth Drury," *P.S.I.*, xxix, 1964.

Savine, E., *The English Monasteries on the Eve of Dissolution* (Oxford: Oxford University Press, 1909).

Scarfe, Norman, "The Bury St. Edmunds Cross," *P.S.I.*, xxxiii, 1976.

Schofield, R. S., "The Geographical Distribution of Wealth in England, 1334-1649," *Ec.H.R.*, 2nd series, xviii, 1965.

———, "Historical Demography: Possibilities and Limitations," *Trans. of the Royal Historical Society*, 5th series, xxi, 1971.

Sennett, Richard., ed., *Classical Essays on the Culture of Cities* (New York: Appleton-Century-Crofts, 1969).

Sheail, John, *The Regional Distribution of Wealth in England as Indicated in the Lay Subsidy Return of 1523/24*, London University Ph.D. Thesis, 1968.

Sheehan, Michael, "Influence of Canon Law on the Property Rights of Married Women in England," *Medieval Studies*, xxv, 1963.

———, *The Will in Medieval England* (Toronto: Pontifical Institute of Medieval Studies, 1963).

Sherbourne, J. W., *The Port of Bristol in the Middle Ages* (Bristol: Port of Bristol Series, xiii, 1965).

Sjoberg, G., *The Preindustrial City: Past and Present* (New York: Free Press, 1960).

Slack, Paul, "Mortality Crises and Epidemic Disease in England, 1485-1619," in Webster, ed., *Health, Medicine and Mortality in the Sixteenth Century*.

Smith, A. H., "English Place Name Elements," *English Place Name Society*, xxv, 1956.

Snape, R. H., *English Monastic Finances in the Later Middle Ages* (Cambridge: Cambridge University Press, 1926).

Statham, Margaret, "The Guildhall of Bury St. Edmunds," *P.S.I.*, xxxi, 1967-1970.

Statham, M. P., *The Church of St. Mary, Bury St. Edmunds* (Bury St. Edmunds, pamphlet, 1976).

Stephanson, Carl, *Borough and Town* (Cambridge, Mass.: Harvard University Press, 1933).

Suckling, Alfred, *The History and Antiquities of the County of Suffolk* (London: J. Weale, 1846).

Sumptien, J., *Pilgrimage: An Image of Medieval Religion* (Totowa, N.J.: Rowman and Littlefield, 1975).

Tait, James, *The Medieval English Borough* (Manchester: University of Manchester Press, 1936).

Talbot, Charles, and Hammond, E. A., *Medical Practitioners in Medieval England* (London: Wellcome Historical Medical Library, 1965).

Talbot, C. H., *Medicine in Medieval England* (London: Oldbourne, 1967).

Thompson, Leonard, P., *Old Inns of Suffolk* (Ipswich: The Ancient House, 1946).

Thrupp, S. L., "The Alien Population in England in 1440," *Speculum*, xxxii, 1957.

————, "Aliens in and Around London in the Fifteenth Century," in A.E.J. Hollaender and William Kellaway, eds., *Studies in London History* (London: Hodder and Stoughton, 1969).

————, "The City as the Idea of Social Order," in G. Handlin and J. Burchard, eds., *The Historian and the City* (Boston: Beacon, 1963).

————, "The Creativity of Cities," *Comparative Studies in Society and History*, iv, 1961-1962.

————, "The Gilds," in M. M. Postan and E. E. Rich, eds., *The Cambridge Economic History of Europe*, iii (Cambridge: Cambridge University Press, 1963).

————, "Gilds," *The International Encyclopedia of Social Sciences*, 1968.

————, "Medieval Gilds Reconsidered," *The Journal of Economic History*, ii, 1942.

————, *The Merchant Class of Medieval London, 1300-1500* (Chicago: University of Chicago Press, 1948).

————, "Social Change in the Medieval Town," *Journal of Economic History*, i, 1941.

Trenholme, N. M., *The English Monastic Boroughs* (Columbia, Mo.: University of Missouri Press, 1927).

———, "The Rising of the English Monastic Towns in 1327," *American Historical Review*, vi, 1917.

Turner, Hilary, *Town Defenses in England and Wales* (London: John Baker, 1971).

Unwin, George, *The Gilds and Companies of London* (New York: Barnes and Noble, 1963).

———, ed., *Finance and Trade Under Edward III* (London: Frank Cass Reprint, 1962).

Urban History Yearbook, 1974-1980.

The Victoria History of the Counties of England: Suffolk, 2 vols. (London: Archibald Constable, 1907).

Warren, F. E., "A Pre-Reformation Village Gild," *P.S.I.*, xi, 1903.

Webb, G. F., "On Bury Excavations," *Archaeological Journal*, cvi, 1949.

Weber, Max, *The City* (New York: Free Press, 1956).

Wells, Calvin, "Fifteenth Century Wood Carvings in St. Mary's Church, Bury St. Edmunds," *Medical History*, 9, 1965.

West, S. E., "Excavations of the Town Defenses at Tayfen Road, Bury St. Edmunds," *P.S.I.*, xvii, 1973.

Westlake, H. F., "The Origins, Purposes and Development of Parish Gilds in England," *P.S.I.*, xvii, 1921.

———, *The Parish Gilds of Medieval England* (London: The Society for Promoting Christian Knowledge, 1919).

Whittingham, A. B., *Bury St. Edmunds* (London: H.M.S.O., 1971).

Williams, Gwyn A., *Medieval London: From Commune to Capital* (London: The Athlone Press, 1963).

Wrigley, E. A., *Population and History* (New York: McGraw-Hill, 1969).

Yates, Richard, *The History and Antiquities of the Abbey of Bury St. Edmunds* (London: J. B. Nichols and Son, 1843).

Index

abbots, list of, 269. See under individual names
Abingdon, 74, 222
aldermen, 130-143, 215-236; list of, 269-271
Alien Registry Roll of 1436, 93, 109
Anselm, Abbot, 199
Antwerp, 253
Asty, John, 91
Athelstan, 209
Avignon, 226

Babergh Hundred, 52, 76
Babwell, 16-20, 25, 141, 183-184, 200, 221, 251
Babwell Fen, 16-18, 25
Bacon, Sir Nicholas, 202, 242, 258
Bakere, John, 205
Baldwin, Abbot, 203-204
Barbour, Gilbert, 228-231
Bardi bankers, 89, 241
Baret family, 68n, 153-166, 213
Baret, Alan, 158
Baret, Galfrid, 154-156
Baret, John II, 77, 83, 98, 154-159, 174, 177, 184, 240
Baret, William, 158-159
Bass, William, 91, 147
Beccles, 77
Bellamy, John, 179
Benale, John, 213
Beodricsworth, 73
Beresford, William, 178
Bernard, John, 235
Bernham, Abbot William, 51, 82, 232, 268
Berton, John, 135-136, 223-231
Beverley, 95
Bildeston, 151-152
Black Death, see plagues

Blackbourne Hundred, 76, 79
Blackney, 93
Blundeston, William, 217
Bohun, Abbot John, 77
Bossohow, Richard, 92
Boston, 95, 122
Boxstead, 22
Brabant, 91, 94, 109, 230
Brakelond, Jocelin, 85-86, 204, 209
Brandons, Nicholas and Joan, 178-179
Brett, Robert, 153
brewing, 109
Bridbury, A. R., 9
Brinkele, John, 205, 217
Brinkley, Abbot John, 83, 268
Bristol, 87, 112, 125, 165, 247, 264
Bromfeld, Edward, 233-234
Bruges, 90
Bruning, Thomas, 147
Bunting, William, 147
Bury, John, 206
Bury St. Edmunds, banleuca, 18; *buildings:* gaol, 30, 172-180, 243; guildhall, 3-5, 30-31, 44-45, 86, 103, 156, 184, 186-187; housing, 30-32, 32-33n; mills, 19, 73-84, 243; mint, 26, 81-83; moothall, 26, 170; Moyses Hall, 3-5, 31-32, 44-45, 145-146, 147, 229; repair of, 43-45; rot of inner town buildings, 43-45; St. James' Church, 3-5, 44, 128, 156-157, 189, 226; St. Mary's Church, 3-5, 44, 128, 140, 156-157, 189, 193, 226, 227; Tollhouse, 3-5, 30-32, 87, 103, 170, 231n, 244
civic pride, 250
crosses delineating boundaries, 16-19
cultural role, 207-224
crime, 215-217

Bury St. Edmunds (*cont.*)
  demography, economic effect, 46,
  71-72; fertility, 49-60, 289-290; gender ratios, 48-51, 53-54, 289-290;
  general movements, 43, 50-55; immigration, 67-71, 109, 247; migration, 67-71; mortality, 49-72, 248,
  289-290; nuptiality, 60-63, 289-290;
  replacement ratios, 55-60, 71-72,
  289-290; sources for, 47-48
    education, 207-211
    emergence of ruling élite, 7-8,
  248-249
    geographic situation, 14-23, 106-
  107
  industry: 94-116; textiles, 94-116,
  247; leather, 114-115, 247; fishing,
  110-114, 247
  markets: 22, 84-94; Corn Market,
  30, 87, 88; Great (Risbygate) Market,
  7, 21-23, 29, 30-34, 84-90, 96-98,
  169-172, 225, 245, 248; Net (Meat)
  Market, 30, 87; Old (Horse) Market,
  29, 34, 84, 87; regional markets, 7,
  99-101; West Suffolk market system,
  20-23
    medical center, 7, 18, 40n, 192-
  207
    prosperity, 244-245
    rebellions, 176, 218-236. See re-
  volt for individual listings
    road system, 15-26
    secularization, 71-72, 153
  streets, 27, 272-277; Barbers' Row,
  27, 30-33, 34-38, 42-43, 272-277;
  Bertonway, 16-17, 24-27; Churchgate Street, 27, 38, 137-138, 272-
  277; Cooks' Row, 3, 27, 30-33, 34-
  38, 42-43, 87-88, 272-277; Crouchway, 16-17, 24, 26; Eastgate, 16-17,
  18, 24-27, 34-38, 42-43, 197, 198,
  272-277; Goldsmiths' Row, 3, 27, 28,
  34-38, 84, 272-277; Gildhall Street,
  27, 29, 34-38, 42-43, 143, 146, 272-
  277; Hatter Street, 3, 27, 31-33, 87-
  88, 272-277; Holeway, 16-17, 24-26;
  Horsecroftway, 16-17, 24-26; *Le
  Mustow*, 27, 34-38, 42-43, 257, 272-
  277; Little Brakelond, 27, 33-34, 34-
  38, 42-43, 272-277; Long Brakelond,
  27, 33-34, 34-38, 42-43, 143, 272-
  277; Master Andrew Street, 27, 38,
  272-277; Maydewater Manor, 29,
  286n.; Northgate, 16-17, 24-27, 33-
  34, 34-38, 42-43, 200, 272-277; Risbygate, 16-17, 18, 24-27, 30-33, 34-
  38, 42-44, 199, 272-277; road system, 16-17, 24-25, 44; Schoolhall
  Street, 27-29, 272-277; Smiths' Row
  (Churchgoval), 27, 33, 272-277;
  Southgate, 5, 16-17, 24-27, 34-38,
  42-43, 197-198, 272-277; Sparhawk
  Street, 27-29; Spinthilmillway, 16-17;
  Westgate, 24-27, 29, 34-38, 272-277;
  Whiting Street, 27, 38
    trade, 84-116
    village dependence on towns, 20-
  22
    walls, 16-18, 24-25, 43
  wards, 26-42, 272-277; assessment
  of wealth by, 28, 35, 37, 39, 42;
  Eastgate, 26, 28, 35, 37, 39, 42;
  Northgate, 28, 33-34, 35, 37, 39, 42;
  Risbygate, 28, 30-33, 35, 37, 39, 42;
  Southgate, 26-29, 35, 37, 39, 42;
  Westgate, 28, 29, 35, 37, 39, 42

Calais, 96
Cam, Helen, 52
Cambridge, John, 233
Cambridge, 4, 15, 22, 24, 150, 193,
  206, 212-213
Candelyn, Master Doctor, 206
Canterbury, 125, 185, 203, 251; Ca-
  thedral Priory, 74
Canute, 3, 166, 208
Carus-Wilson, E. M., 9, 14
Cavendish, Sir John, 233-234
charity, 141-142, 146-147, 150, 156-
  158, 182-187, 212-214
Charman, Richard, 77, 136-139, 141
Charman, William, 137-138
Charter of 1194, 215-216
Charter of 1327, 223-225
Chester, 262
Chevington, 229
Cheyne, Emma, 149
Chigwell, Haimo, 229-230
Chirche, Thomas, 40n
Clark, Peter, 7

Clarke, Edmund, 153
Clayton, William, 243
Clement VI, Pope, 51
Clement VIII, Pope, 202
Clerk, Simon, 157
Clever, John, 98
Clynton, John, 179
Coale-Demeny Life Tables, 48-50
Cockerel family, 198
Coft, 93
Colchester, 4, 15, 48, 100-101, 107, 124-125, 150
Coote, John, 184
Cornwall, Julian, 184
Corpus Christi processions, 103, 181, 188, 249
Cosford Hundred, 52, 76
Cosmas and Damian, 193
Coterel, John, 229-230
Cotswolds, 96
Court of Augmentations (arrears), 26, 43, 142, 204, 243-244
courts of West Suffolk, 170-171, 218
Coventry, 4, 6, 10, 23n, 43n, 50n, 67n, 120, 125, 165, 244n, 247, 249, 251, 264
Cratfield, Abbot William, 154, 268
Cratfield, 154, 158
crime and violence, 214-217, 228-231, 232-233
Curteys, Abbot William, 3-5, 212, 235, 268

Denham, John, 206
Denham, Thomas, 137
Denton, William, 8
Despenser, Bishop Henry, 234
Dobson, R. B., 10, 249
doctors, 203-207
Dover, 230
Draughton, Abbot Richard, 82, 201, 223-231, 241-268
Drury family, 68n, 77, 156-166, 249
Drury, Clemens, 160, 164
Drury, John II, 158, 160-161
Drury, Sir Robert the Great, 141, 160-163, 174
DuBoulay, F.R.H., 12
Dugdale, 7, 212
Dunwich, 91, 119

Durham, 262
dysentery, 65

Eckwall, Eilert, 68
Eden, Thomas, 41
Edinburgh, 92
education, 212-214
Edward, John, 140, 145
Edward the Confessor, 3, 26, 78, 203
Edward the Martyr, 82
Edward I, 3, 19, 23n, 81, 116, 262
Edward II, 167, 222, 227, 257
Edward III, 93-94, 96, 109, 136, 179, 222, 227
Edward IV, 102, 169, 204
élites, 131-132, 136-143, 248-249
Elmswell Manor, 168
Elton, G. R., 11
Ely, 22, 25
Eriswell, Robert, 98n
Exeter, 125
Eyer, John, 258

famine, 55, 63
Felixstowe, 91
Finberg, H.P.R., 12
Flanders, 90-91, 94-96, 109
Florence, 93
Fornham, Nicholas, 143-144
France, 3, 91, 168
Franciscans (Grey Friars), 183, 220-222, 226, 229
frankpledge, 105, 166, 169, 171
fraternities, 180-192
freeman's rolls, 9, 265
Froissel, Richard, 229

gaol, 172-180; entry fees, 175; inventory, 176; provisioning, 176-178; escapes, 178-179
gaol delivery rolls, 265
Gardner, Stephan, 153
Glastonbury Abbey, 74
Glemsford, 100, 188, 192
Goldsmith, Emma, 148-149
Goldyng, Agnes, 149
Goodhale, Edmund, 104n
Goodwin, A., 6, 168, 268
Grafton, John, 217
Greens, John and Mrs. J. R., 8

guilds, 94-116, 187, 264-265; Alderman's, 80-81, 87, 132-136, 141-143, 147-148, 165-166, 174, 181-188; apprentices, 104, 109-110; bequests to, 191-192; Clerks of Glemsford, 191-192; *Corpus Christi*, 188-189, 191-192; Dusse (St. Nicholas), 134, 141, 147-148, 190-191, 211; journeymen, 104, 109-110; Sweet Man Jesus, 189-190; weavers and linendrapers, 102-107

Haberdon, Roger, 178
Halesworth, Thomas, 233
Halesworth, 154
Hall, Oliver, 153
Hammond, James, 212
Hammond, Thomas, 143-144
Harrison, John, 211
Haverhill, 24
Hawsted, 161-162
Hedge, John, 212, 213
Henry I, 218
Henry II, 85
Henry III, 3, 221
Henry VI, 3-5, 151, 236
Henry VIII, 12, 41, 79, 142, 162, 237, 242, 261
Herdeman, Henry, 188
Hibbert, A. B., 132
Hilborough, Alice, 86
Hilton, R. H., 14, 239
Holland, 91, 103-104, 109, 114
Hollingsworth, T. H., 49
Holt, Sir John, 176, 258
Honeybourne, William, 153
Hopton, 137
Hoskins, W. G., 249
hospitals, 192-204; *Domus Dei*, 23, 81, 197-198; St. Nicholas, 23, 198-199; St. Peter's, 23, 24, 199-200, rental of, 1295, 273; St. Petranilla's, 19, 23, 198; St. Saviour's, 24, 200-203, 228, 238; St. Stephan's, 196-197
Howard, John, 228
Howard, William, 178
Humphrey, Duke of Gloucester, 200
husbandry, 78-79, 94-95, 106, 115, 169-170, 239, 243

Iberia, 92
Icklingham, 22
industrial pollution, 114
industry, 94-120
influenza, 64-65
inheritance patterns, 284-287
Ipswich, 4, 15, 22, 25, 44, 91, 100-101, 107, 116-129, 150, 186, 193, 247, 250
Ireland, 92
Italy, 89, 93, 94-96, 240-241

Jerusalem, 185
Jerveys, John, 139, 150-153, 154
Jerveys, Thomas, 151-152, 154
Jessup, A. J., 51
Jews, 31-32, 82, 149, 194, 209, 286

Kemp, John, 206
King, Richard I, 145-146
King, Richard III, 146, 187, 240
King's Lynn, 8, 15, 22, 25, 30, 90, 92, 99, 107, 116-129, 150
Kingston-upon-Hull, 48
Kyton, Thomas, 242

Lackford, Katherine, 149
Lackford, 206
Lackford Hundred, 76
Lakenheath, 171
land ownership, 284-287
Lark River, 15-18, 27, 80, 92, 105, 113-114
Lavenham, 8, 22, 72, 99-101, 106-107, 124-126, 153, 252
Leach, A. F., 208, 209, 211
Lee family, 154, 161
Leicester, 70, 120, 247, 249, 251
Leland, John, 15, 32, 247
leprosy, 185, 194-195, 198, 199
Leroy Ladurie, E., 132
libraries, 210-212
Lincoln, 9, 122
Linnet River, 5, 16-18, 24, 25, 26-27, 34, 36, 80, 92, 105, 113-114
Lobel, M. D., 5, 6, 52, 135, 148, 173-174, 176, 209, 257, 268, 274-275

London, 3, 4, 8, 9, 24n, 48, 84-86, 91, 107, 116-123, 133, 134, 135, 142, 143, 144, 153, 165, 193, 203, 206, 215-216, 227, 229-230, 238, 245, 247, 248-249, 253
Long Melford, 8, 72, 100-101
Lübeck, 93
Luton, Abbot Simon, 218, 240-241, 268
Lydgate, John, 157, 212
Lynn, John, 92

Magnus, King of Norway, 93-94
Malmsbury, 169
Mannyng, John, 184
Marham, James, 93
McClure, Peter, 68, 70
McKinley, R. A., 68
Meopham, Simon, 230
Merchant Adventurers, 97-98, 106
Merchants of the Staple, 97-99
Middleton, Geoffrey, 235
migration from towns, 94-95, 109
Mildenhall, 25, 233
military musters, 52-54, 261
Miller, Edward, 12
Morley, Sir Robert, 227-228

Needham Market, 25
Netherlands, 22, 91, 93, 104, 106, 109, 147, 150, 244, 252-253
Newcastle, 4, 9, 122, 262
Newman, 207
New Market, 21, 22, 24, 123, 234
Nicole, John, 185
Norfolk Archdeaconry, 69, 281
Northampton, 120, 247, 249, 251
Northwold, Abbot John, 133-134, 268
Norton, John, 217
Norway, 93-94, 252
Norwich, 4, 5, 8, 15, 25, 86, 90, 91, 116-129, 150, 165, 178, 193, 203, 228, 234, 247, 248, 249, 250, 264
Norwich Archdeaconry, 69, 280-281
Nottingham, John, 77, 139-141, 151
Nottingham, 4, 70
Nuremberg, 253

occupations and trades, 111-120; almoners, 23, 36, 83, 256; bailiffs, 30,

87, 90, 103, 134-135, 169, 249; bakers, 59n, 87, 111-120, 264; barbers, 87, 111-120, 205; bellfounders, 40, 111-113; blacksmiths, 26, 59n, 88, 111-113; booksellers, 212; burgesses, 86, 134, 207, 210, 215-236; butchers, 31-33, 88, 111-120, 144, 169; cellarers, 19, 23, 29, 72-82, 83, 86, 113-115, 169-170, 173, 197, 256, 265; chamberlains, 23, 28; chaplains, 19; clothiers, 34, 100, 104, 105, 110, 111-120, 144-145, 181-182, 249, 288-290; cooks, 3-5, 30, 88, 111-120; corvisers (cordwainers), 88, 107-120, 144, 264; coverletweavers, 41, 111-120; drapers, 41, 59n, 88, 111-120, 136, 138, 145, 147, 153, 156, 181-182, 248, 288-290; dyers, 94-107, 111-120, 144; fishermen, 18, 111-120; fishmongers, 88, 111-120; fullers, 26, 95-107, 111-121; gaolers, 175-180; gentlemen, 59n, 207, 210, 288-290; goldsmiths, 82, 87, 111-113, 238; grocers, 59n, 111-112, 144, 147-148, 181-182, 288-290; hostelers, 23, 83, 256; infirmarers, 23, 256; lavenders, 88; leather workers, 41, 87, 88, 111-121; linendrapers, 102-110, 111-112, 169, 264; mercers, 41, 59n, 94-121, 139-148, 181-182, 288-289; physicians, 112-113, 115, 119, 203-207, 288-290; pittancers, 19, 23, 36, 83; portreeves, 132-133; priors, 23, 86, 132, 173, 197, 256, 265; sacrists, 23, 26, 81, 83, 86, 132, 134-135, 169-171, 195-196, 209-210, 256, 259, 265; shermen, 100, 107, 111-120; skinners, 88, 111-120; subcellarers, 23, 257; surgeons, 41, 111-113, 115, 204-207; tailors, 87, 93, 105-106n, 111-120; tanners, 41, 111-120; treasurers, 83, 256; victuallers, 34; wardens, 23, 194-202, 207n, 256; weavers, 59n, 93, 94-120, 144, 169, 264; woolmen, 102, 111
Odeham, John, 149-150
Odeham, Margaret, 149-150, 177n, 184, 187
Orford, 119

Orlow, Agnes, 213
Orwell, 99
Oxford, 4, 48, 122, 212-213

Parfay, Katherine, 148, 185
Parfay, John, 44, 147-148, 187
Parker, Thomas, 180
Parliament, 162, 201, 223, 225, 262
patriciate, 12, 131-132, 136-143, 248-249; assumption of leadership, 165-166; *rentiers*, 143-144; sense of public responsibility, 142-143; statistical information for, 288-290
Philippa, Queen, 149
Phythian-Adams, Charles, 10, 249
Picardy, 91
pilgrimage, 81, 183, 185-186
Pirenne, Henri, 132
Place, William, 213
plague, 51, 63-67, 237, 246-247, 289; Black Death, 51, 63, 81, 108, 123, 124, 144, 198, 232, 237, 246-247; *pestis secunda*, 51, 63, 65; *pestis tertia*, 63
Platt, Colin, 9, 10
Poll Tax of 1377, 261
population, 46-72, 289-290. See Bury St. Edmunds
Postan, M. M., 8, 9
Pugg, William, 178
Pugh, Ralph, 173, 179

Rattlesden, 22
Reading, 125
Reading Abbey, 74
Rede, Master Doctor, 206
Redgrave Manor, 54-59, 200, 202-203, 249
Redstone, V. B., 18, 52, 190
revolts, 1264, 218-219; 1292, 220; 1327, 176, 202, 220-231; 1381, 231-236
Reynolds, Susan, 9, 10
Richard II, 98, 168, 186, 188, 232, 235
Rickinghall Manor, 200
Ridges, John, 147
Risbridge Hundred, 76
Rochester, 48
Rome, 185
Rouse, Anthony, 242

Rudde, Henry, 199, 206, 212
Rudham, Thomas, 34
Russell, J. C., 50, 51, 261
Rutland, 53
Rycher, William, 147

St. Albans, 79, 128-129, 203, 250-251
St. Albans Abbey, 74
St. Edmunds Abbey: abbots, 107-108, 167-169, 269; charity, 83; consumer of goods, 82-84; control of borough institutions, 171-214; control of courts, 168; decline, 41-43, 236-244; dilapidation of its property, 43-45; dissolution of, 77, 131, 176, 236-245; economic power of, 73-82; effects of declining population on, 71-72; financial woes, 238-243; judicial system, 170-171; landlord, 15-45, 78-80, 84, 236-240; lesser sources of income, 81-84; liberty, 75, 167-169, 259; markets, 80-81, 84-86; medical traditions, 193-196; military obligations, 168; milling rights, 79-83; money markets, 89-91; officers of, 169-172; privileges, 20, 166-172; restoration and lack thereof, 3, 43-45, 243-245; royal fees, 82-83; rebellions against, 215-236; *rentier*, 77-78; royal visits to, 3-6; shortage of monks, 51; town-abbey relations, 11-13; waterways, 79-80
Salisbury, 4, 9, 125
Samson, Abbot, 82, 85-86, 171, 200, 208-210, 216-217, 219
Schapman, John, 143-144
schools, 209-211; grammar school, 208-210; monastic school, 207, 208; song school, 92-93
Shrewsbury, 123
Sjoberg, Gideon, 132
Slack, Paul, 7
smallpox, 64-65
Smith, John (Jankyn), 77, 98, 141-142, 149-150, 153, 174, 187, 190, 240
Smith, Lawrance, 147
Smythe, Richard, 206
social mobility, 143-144, 152-153
Soham Mere, 80
Southampton, 8, 247

Southwold, 91
Spor, John, 98n
Spring family, 99, 124, 153
Stacy, Thomas, 45, 205n
Stansted, 22
Stanton, Edmund, 185
Stour Valley, 7, 94-101, 248
Stow Market, 21, 22, 25
Sudbury, 21, 22, 100, 122-123, 206
Sudbury Archdeaconry, 69, 278-279
Suffolk Archdeaconry, 69, 279-280
surnames, 68-70
Sutton, Thomas, 143
sweating sickness, 64
syphilis, 64

Tait, James, 286
Taxatio Ecclesiastica, 83
taxes, 50, 116-130, 167, 172; *hadgoval*,
    36-37, 169, 209-210, 224, 250, 255-
    257, 286; poll taxes, 45-52, 123-124;
    relevia, 29, 38, 169, 257; subsidies,
    40-43, 124-125; stallage fees, 88,
    264; wealth measured from, 116-124
Tay Fen, 16-18, 19, 25, 80, 113-114
tolls, 90-92
textile industry, 7-8, 94-107, 114, 124
    247-248; fluctuations in, 8-10; frui-
    tion of, 72-79, 247-248; growth of
    industrial centers, 23-24, 249; tech-
    nological advances, 95-96
Thedwestrey Hundred, 76
Thetford, 21, 25, 95n, 153
Thingoe Hundred, 76
Thompson, Thomas, 92-93
Thorney Manor, 59-60
Thornham, Thomas, 229-231
Thorpe Morieux, 22
Thrupp, Sylvia, 14

Thurston, 147-148, 161, 164
Timworth, Abbot John, 168, 233, 268
Tiptoft, John, 179
Trype, Richard, 101
typhus, 64-65

urban crisis, 4-10, 246-253

Valor Ecclesiasticus, 74, 198, 212, 241
de Vere family, 77, 154, 159

Wacy, John, 205
Wallerstein, Immanuel, 252
Walsingham, 186, 194
Walter, physician of St. Albans, 204
wardens of hospitals, 207n
Wareyn, Beneyt, 104n
Wastrell, John, 213
wealth, 116-130
Weber, Max, 132
Westley, 177
Westminster Abbey, 74
Whitop, John, 285
wills, 55-70, 74-90, 125-130, 259-261
women, 148-150
Woode, John, 205
Woolpit, 22
Worliche, John, 153
Wrawe, Jack, 232-235
Wryth, Richard, 205
Wyseman, Matthew, 178

Yarmouth, 8, 91, 92, 93, 99, 116-129,
    150
Yates, Richard, 6, 268
York, 4, 9, 10, 70, 86, 122, 125, 165,
    247, 249
York Abbey, 74
Ypres, 90

Library of Congress Cataloging in Publication Data

Gottfried, Robert S., 1949-
  Bury St. Edmunds and the urban crisis, 1290-1539.

  Bibliography: p.
  Includes index.
  1. Bury St. Edmunds (Suffolk)—Economic conditions.
2. Bury St. Edmunds (Suffolk)—Social conditions.
3. Bury St. Edmunds (Suffolk)—Politics and government.
I. Title.
HC258.B87G67   330.9426'44   81-11984
ISBN 0-691-05340-5   AACR2